FACTS AND IDEAS IN PSYCHOANALYSIS

Facts and Ideas in Psychoanalysis

Charles Hanly

International Psychoanalytic Books (IPBooks)
New York • http://www.IPBooks.net

Facts and Ideas in Psychoanalysis

Published by IPBooks, Queens, NY
Online at: www.IPBooks.net

Copyright © 2022 Charles Hanly

ISBN: 978-1-956864-14-4

To my wife, Margaret Ann

Contents

Preface

This collection of papers reflects my interest and training in both philosophy and psychoanalysis. To the questions I had about my own life and being and the lives and being of fellow humans which motivated my interest in philosophy, I eventually found answers of greater depth and detail in psychoanalysis and in the philosophical implications of its discoveries about human nature. My ambition in my doctoral research was to modify psychoanalysis by integrating it with existentialist ideas about freedom and consciousness based on the study of Freud in psychoanalysis, and of Sartre, and to some extent Merleau-Ponty, in philosophy. I began my doctoral research as an existential voluntarist and concluded it as a psychic determinist.

I am grateful to my philosophy colleagues, not a few of whom were unable to agree with my conclusions, and to the University of Toronto for making it possible for me to train in psychoanalysis, to teach psychoanalysis as a humanity, and to practice it clinically part time while retaining my professorship in the Department of Philosophy.

These papers were all previously published in journals or as chapters in books on psychoanalysis. I have not altered any of their ideas and arguments as published, but I have modified the articulation of some ideas and have added some sentences in order to make them clearer for the reader. In this

I have been very ably assisted by the exceptional editorial skills, knowledge, and understanding of Ian Drummond (PhD in philosophy).

I wish to dedicate the book to my wife Margaret Ann Fitzpatrick Hanly (PhD in English literature), who is also a trained and practicing psychoanalyst.

Note on citations to the works of Freud. All citations to the works of Freud are to the *Standard Edition of the Complete Psychological Works of Sigmund Freud*, edited by James Strachey with Anna Freud, Alix Strachey, and Alan Tyson, in 24 volumes (London: Hogarth Press, 1950–1974), here abbreviated as SE.

I

Issues in Psychoanalytic Epistemology

CHAPTER 1

A Problem of Theory Testing*

The consistency of a science is an essential requirement of its logical structure. A science may lack unity as a result of gaps in its theories. This type of disunity is inevitable in any evolving science; it is the result of new observations requiring the construction of theories which explain the observations but remain logically disconnected from already established theories. This situation obtained in physics prior to Einstein's discovery of relativity, which provided a theory that explained the new observations and integrated Newtonian mechanics into the new physics, from which it could be derived as a special case. The explanatory scope of Newtonian mechanics was circumscribed by relativity theory, but the old and the new physical theories form a logically consistent body of knowledge.

A science may also lack unity because one or more of its theories are inconsistent with others. This type of disunity is a serious flaw because it means that the science is failing to meet one of the basic logical criteria for counting as knowledge. The problem becomes acute when members of the same scientific community using the same methods of observation claim that contradictory theories can be empirically demonstrated. Psychoanalytic theory—described for the purposes of this paper as the body of theories about mental functioning espoused by psychoanalysts—is currently problematic

---

* Originally published in *The International Review of Psycho-Analysis* 10 (1983):393–405.

in this way at a number of points: object relations theory (Kernberg, 1975; Calef & Weinshel, 1979), metapsychology (Gill, 1976; Klein, 1976; Gedo, 1977; Brenner, 1980), instinct theory, and self psychology. The situation is rendered ambiguous by the fact that certain of the proposed theoretical revisions (e.g., Schafer, 1976, 1978) are stated in such a way as to leave it uncertain whether or not substantive changes in instinct or structural theory are actually intended, and if they are intended, precisely what those changes are and what new observations, if any, demand the revisions (Brenner, 1980). However, some of the epistemological and logical issues can be brought into focus by a consideration of certain of the problems surrounding the conflict between classical theory and self psychology.

THE LOGICAL NATURE OF THE PROBLEM

Freud's (1914, 11916–917, 1923) theory—the so-called u-tube theory—states that insofar as libido undergoes a narcissistic development, there occurs a reduction in object libido. Kohut's theory states that some libido undergoes a narcissistic development without reducing the sum of object libido, or stated differently, that there are two relatively independent lines of libidinal development. These propositions are contradictories: if either of them is true, the other must be false. It follows that there is a logical problem that has to be dealt with in any attempted integration of self psychology with classical theory. Self psychology cannot be treated as an addition to psychoanalysis without making far-reaching alterations to some of the premises of classical libido theory, and conversely.

THE OBSERVATIONAL PROBLEM

These contradictory hypotheses are inductively derived from clinical observation. The independence hypothesis is derived from the observation of narcissistic personality disorders that emerge in the transference of certain patients in the apparent absence of significant structural conflicts, and from the observation of patients who have severe disorders in their narcissistic development but who suffer no apparent impoverishment of their investment of appropriate objects with sexual libido, or to the extent that they suffer such impoverishment it is as a consequence of their narcissistic conflicts (Kohut, 1971, 1977, 1978; Goldberg, 1978). The interconnection hypothesis is derived from the observations that patients with narcissistic problems also suffer from object-libidinal conflicts intrinsically connected with them and that such patients experience a diminution of their capacity for object love that causes them guilt (Coen, 1981; Eisnitz, 1980, 1981; Hanly, 1982; Hanly & Masson, 1976; Modell, 1975; Orgel, 1977; Perman, 1979; Renik, 1978; Rothstein, 1979, 1980b; Segal, 1981; Tyson & Tyson, 1982; Wallerstein, 1981). In addition, it has long been observed that the substitution of an identification with an object for a relation with it modifies the relationship to the object by a partial decathexis of it. This process involves the conversion of object libido into narcissistic libido (Freud, 1914, 1917, 1923). The latency period with its diminished sexual libido is the product of this powerful psychological process.

Accordingly, there is an epistemological problem logically related to the theoretical problem. The contradictory hypotheses are inductively inferred from clinical observations made under the same conditions of the analytic situation and by means of the same technique, namely, free association. How can this problem be solved?

A PHILOSOPHICAL SOLUTION

Goldberg (1976) has proposed a solution to the problem based on a current philosophical epistemology. He states: "When two individuals with roughly similar neurophysiological equipment view the same thing or event and each sees it differently, it is not necessarily true that one is incompetent or even wrong; rather it may be that they each observe with a different theory." This statement implies an idealist epistemology which assigns precedence in the knowledge of objects to ideas over perception. This view is contrary to the psychoanalytic concept of reality testing, which rests upon an empiricist epistemology. Goldberg's argument draws upon one side in a current philosophical controversy. It will therefore be useful to consider the nature of this controversy in some detail.

There is an historical precedent for Goldberg's thesis. Bernfeld (1941) put forward the view that in modern science "from seeking to gain insight into Nature we have shifted the emphasis to agreeing with our fellow scientists on an intersubjective body of knowledge." This view presents some serious difficulties. Waelder (1970) has already pointed out that this viewpoint leaves the door dangerously open to the power and authority of persons as against the authority of impersonal facts. Bernfeld would not, in fact, have walked through this door. In the paper in which he states this view, Bernfeld (1941) also sets out a proposal for objectively testing psychoanalytic methods of observation in order to determine what is genuinely factual in them; in this way one could *objectively* establish the objectivity of the psychoanalytic observing instrument (i.e., free association) and thus answer one of the most persistent philosophical criticisms of it (Nagel, 1959; Popper, 1963; Wittgenstein, 1966). However, the view stated by Bernfeld suggests at least a willingness to make psychoanalysis more defensible as a science by weakening the epistemological criteria for scientific knowledge in general. It is unsatisfactory as a defense of the scientific status of psychoanalysis because it contains the hint that psychoanalysis cannot really lay claim to "having gained insight into [human] nature" as Freud (1933) thought it could, and that its failure to do so can be excused on the grounds that other sciences cannot do so either.

This view in philosophy has been advocated by Kuhn (1970) and Feyerabend (1965). Feyerabend (1965) asserts that "the meaning of observation statements is determined by the theories with which they are connected. Theories are meaningful independent of observations; observational statements are not meaningful unless they have been connected with theories" (p. 213). The essential point is that observations are not epistemologically independent of the theories held by the investigator who is making the observations to test the theory. Consequently, the truth of the theory is made to rest upon the agreement of experts working with the theory, rather than upon the agreement of the theory with fact. What psychoanalysts who draw upon this philosophical view often seem to fail to appreciate is that the view is itself philosophically controversial because it has some inherent difficulties. Reference is usually limited to the more familiar and popular statement of it by Kuhn.

The arguments of Kuhn and Feyerabend have been extensively analyzed and found wanting as a theory of knowledge in the social sciences (Cunningham, 1973). I shall limit my remarks on it to only a few points. Philosophical opinion on the subject is divided roughly equally. The objectivist thesis has been defended by Alexander (1963), Bergmann (1957), Bohm (1957), Braithwaite (1953), Butts (1966), Cunningham (1973), Gibson (1960), Hempel (1965), Kaufmann (1944), Mason (1962), Nagel (1961), Rudner (1966), Scheffer (1967), Shapere (1966), Smart (1963), and Werkmeister (1959). Anti-objectivist arguments have been advanced by Berlin (1954), Burtt (1932), Butterfield (1957), Collingwood (1946), Hanson (1958), Leach (1968), Maciver (1931), Mannheim (1936), Mises (1958), Myrdal (1958), (1969), Nadel (1951), Parsons (1949), Polanyi (1946,

7

1958), Quine (1960), Toulmin (1961), Weber (1949), and Winch (1958). It would thus be misleading for psychoanalysts to rely upon the anti-objectivist thesis of Kuhn as if it were uncontroversial in philosophy.

Although philosophical opinion on the issue remains divided, the scientists who have actually brought about revolutionary changes in knowledge have been objectivists. Copernicus, Galileo, Harvey, Newton, Darwin, Einstein, and Freud implicitly or explicitly held objectivist epistemologies. Freud (1927) thought that the human senses had become progressively adapted to reality as a consequence of environmental pressure and evolutionary selection. Indeed, if objects and natural forces were not able progressively to impose indications of their true nature upon the human mind independently of beliefs held about them, it would be difficult to account for the advance of human civilization beyond the stage of animism.

Moreover, the subjectivist thesis does not do justice to the reliability of the scientific methods of observation and thought—to the creative genius of human intelligence which submits its concepts to the demands of fact and logic. Do scientists really agree that the planets orbit the sun only because they happen to have adopted the Copernican paradigm, and hence see and interpret the organization of the solar system in this way? Is there any possible paradigm in anatomy that could lead anatomists to begin to see that the flow of blood in organisms is discontinuous after all, just as Galen had thought? There are many areas of uncertainty in science, but there are also areas of empirical certainty. A satisfactory model of scientific discovery and knowledge should be able to take both into account. In those areas where certainty prevails it is reasonable to think that science has achieved insight into nature and not merely the agreement of experts upon the use of a paradigm. In areas where uncertainty remains the achievement of insight still remains an ideal. The Kuhn-Feyerabend theory of scientific knowledge entails an unwarranted skepticism.

Finally, the subjectivist thesis is subject to a *reductio ad absurdum*. If the Kuhn-Feyerabend view of scientific knowledge is true, it must be because it fits the facts of the development of scientific knowledge. But this argument implies a covert appeal to the objectivist thesis. Otherwise, it is merely an epistemological paradigm in terms of which the facts of scientific knowledge are viewed by its exponents.

Similarly, the Kuhn-Feyerabend theory lends itself to a damagingly unscientific use by psychoanalysts and others as an intellectual defense against the task of finding a factual and/or logical basis for adjudicating the truth of competing hypotheses. This theory is invoked when a psychoanalyst who has an investment in a particular theoretical innovation is confronted with clinical observations that falsify it. The appeal to Kuhn is tantamount to asserting that the falsifying observation acquires its status as a fact because of its connection with an alternative theory; it thus does not stand on its own feet, and is disqualified as a crucial observation. Those who use Kuhn in this way often fail to realize that they are wielding a double-edged sword. The application of the same epistemological theory to the evidence for the new hypothesis similarly causes it to lose its probative force. The result is a highly unsatisfactory situation in which there ceases to be any independent observational basis for testing the merits of alternative theories. The test of truth becomes consensus; collaborative scientific work can then easily deteriorate into factional dispute.

Rothstein (1980) has examined this problem in terms of the narcissistic investment in paradigms. This argument agrees with his findings and makes the additional point that the subjectivist thesis, because of its logical and epistemological weaknesses, facilitates a narcissistic investment in theories which effectively makes them ideologies. An epistemology that assigns precedence in the definition of reality to ideas over neutral observation has already taken one step in the direction of the omnipotence of the subject. Empiricism, by contrast, which has been the traditional epistemology of

9

psychoanalysis, imposes a certain humility on the ego because it requires it to submit its beliefs to the often difficult and frustrating task of testing them against impersonal observations. The Kuhn-Feyerabend thesis in philosophy does not provide a satisfactory basis for resolving the problems of theory testing with which psychoanalysis is now confronted. It is better to be able to discover that one has been wrong than to be confronted with the prospect of never being able to know whether or not one is right.

THE REDUCTIONIST SOLUTION

Psychologists of the self have offered a second solution. If psychoanalytic theory is in a state of disunity, analysts can nevertheless find a basic unanimity in their adherence to a common method of observation and treatment. Goldberg (1978) has stated that psychoanalysis should be "defined by its methods and not by its evolving theories" (p. 453). This statement suggests that psychoanalysis does have a method of observation that can, in the long run, provide the observations required to test alternative theories. This implication is inconsistent with the Kuhn-Feyerabend thesis. But, also, it would seem to be unnecessarily regressive to define psychoanalysis as merely a method, however intrinsic to psychoanalysis its method of observation is, when there actually does exist a large body of well-established theory. In his early works, at least, Kohut (1977) did not call in question the reliability of the classical theory of hysterical and obsessional neuroses despite the hints of a tendency to treat the psychology of the self as a foundational theory from which the classical theory might be derived in some modified form. But this is not the essential point. A method of observation in science cannot be said to be reliable if from its use there can be inductively derived contradictory theories. Biologists using a technique of microscopic observation which

10

yielded contradictory descriptions of an organism would scarcely be satisfied with the experimental procedure. The appeal to a common method of observation which on the surface seems so reasonable does nothing more than add fuel to the fire of the philosophers of science (e.g., Nagel, 1959) who claim that psychoanalytic observational technique is defective in just this respect. Hence, a reductionist definition of psychoanalysis which limits it to its method does not offer a viable solution.

A TAXONOMIC SOLUTION

Kohut (1971) has proposed a classification of types of neuroses which seems to offer a way out of the difficulty of the fact that different analysts make clinical observations that lead to contradictory theoretical conclusions about the nature of libidinal development, arrestment, and conflict. Let us suppose with Kohut that there are three types of neuroses: structural neuroses (hysteria, obsessionality, and character disorders), narcissistic personality disorders, and pseudo-narcissistic personality disorders. Pseudo-narcissistic personality disorders are of special importance in the classification because in them narcissistic pathology serves as a defense against an underlying structural neurosis. Thus, when cases are reported that appear to falsify the findings of self psychology because the narcissistic conflicts have functioned as regressive defenses against object-libidinal conflicts, it can be argued on the basis of the classification that such cases are instances of pseudo-narcissistic personality disorders. Hence, the evidence that might otherwise be seen to be inconsistent with the libido theory of the psychology of the self can be explained by means of this classification as an error of classification. In general, any such evidence would have to show that the narcissistic psychopathology of a patient is regressive and defensive, and that once resolved, a classical transference neurosis will evolve in the analysis. The

11

classification can thus be used to neutralize any clinical evidence that might otherwise count against the Kohutian libido theory.

However, this feature of the classification also poses a problem. A meaningful scientific hypothesis must be falsifiable (Popper, 1959, 1963). But if any clinical evidence brought against the Kohutian theory is ruled out of court on the grounds that it is evidence of a pseudo-narcissistic personality disorder, then no evidence could possibly falsify it, and thus it ceases to qualify as an adequate scientific hypothesis. The classification of types of neurosis must itself be subject to empirical confirmation or falsification by means of clinical observation.

A THEORETICAL SOLUTION

Perhaps there is a way to bring about a theoretical resolution of the problem. Perhaps the logical analysis that reveals the contradictory nature of the two hypotheses about libidinal development and its vicissitudes is based on an excessively abstract consideration of an overly simplified formulation. Accordingly, one possibility recommends itself. Freud (1914) speaks of a certain continuity of narcissistic development, such that the ego ideal inherits the narcissism that accrues from disappointments with object relations during the early stages of instinct organization; Freud (1914, 1917, 1923) also advanced the view that there is a conversion of object libido into narcissistic libido involved in the process of identification out of which the superego is formed. To these considerations there can be added the conservative influence of the pleasure principle on instinct organization (Freud 1914, 1920). Finally, in his attempt to unify his instinct theory, Freud (1914) linked the ego instinct of self-preservation to narcissistic libido.

From this vantage point, it is necessary to qualify the statement that Freud did not recognize such a thing as healthy narcissism (Hanly &

Masson, 1976). Surely Freud found that sexual abstemiousness makes a person vulnerable to neurosis but that deferring sexual pleasure because of loyalty to one's spouse and feeling good about doing so is healthy? Is it not but a short step to Kohut's postulate of an independent line of narcissistic development with a psychopathology unique to it involving failures to develop adequate mechanisms for the regulation and maintenance of self-esteem? Is it not possible then that the increments in narcissistic libido brought about by the substitution of an identification for an object relation involved in melancholia (Freud, 1917), but more generally in the dissolution of the Oedipus complex (Freud, 1923), could involve no more than a supplement to an independent process of narcissistic development that occurs in relative independence of the vicissitudes of object libido? In theory, might it not be possible for there to occur a reasonably satisfactory resolution of the Oedipus complex accompanied by failure to integrate the accrued narcissism into adequately established structures for maintaining self-esteem in the face of the loss of instinctual gratification? The aims of phallic libido and aggression are abandoned, and after latency can be supplanted by a mature genital organization, but ego development remains impaired and fixated at an infantile narcissistic stage of development. Under such circumstances, the types of transference analyzed by self psychologists would surely appear, and the task of analysis would consist essentially of facilitating their development into mature forms.

However, some problems arise. One difficulty that stands in the way of this sort of integration is that it would result in a theory of normal development that would seem to impoverish relationships of object libido, something that is contrary to the facts of human nature and the imperatives of species survival. Given that the quantity of libido in anyone is finite, if to the sum of an intrinsically narcissistic libido which cannot change into object libido there is added the narcissistic libido deriving from the necessary processes of identification, there would appear to be little libido left over to sustain the passion of normal adolescence and adulthood.

Moreover, on the basis of the psychoanalytic theory of the neurosis, it would not be possible for a fixation of narcissistic libido to occur without its having been causally connected with object-libidinal conflicts, with respect to both its origin and its consequences in subsequent character development and symptom formation (Fenichel, 1935, 1945; Brenner, 1976). Of course, further investigation might reveal this assertion to be false. But for the present at least, there is no simple theoretical basis for resolving the contradiction we are examining.

Before leaving the question of theoretical coherence, it is of interest to note that Grunberger (1971) has proposed an understanding of narcissism that anticipates a number of the key formulations of the psychology of the self while placing them in a more integral relationship with Freud's libido and structural theories. (These ideas were published by Grunberger in a series of papers dating from 1957 to 1967, although they were not published as a collection until 1971 and did not appear in English translation until 1979.) Grunberger describes a line of narcissistic development originating in the fusional biological condition of the infant *in utero*. The vehicle of narcissistic development is the self, which for this purpose is conceived of as differentiated from the ego, id, and superego. That is to say, in Grunberger's theory the self is something more than the unity of id, ego, and superego, and has an agency of its own as a result of its narcissistic libidinal cathexis. Grunberger identifies and describes in detail three phases of its development: merging, mirroring, and idealizing, each of which may find its way into the analysis of any transference neurosis. Indeed, it is Grunberger's view that it is a narcissistic investment of the transference repeating infantile projections onto the parents that provides a necessary support for the analysis of conflicts. The confirmation of the self is conditional upon parental attitudes. (One is reminded of the Book of Genesis, where God is said to have rested from his creation of the cosmos, and having looked at it, saw that it was good.) The pleasure principle is thus thought to require a narcissistic supplement from objects. The gratifications of genital activity require the support of a narcissistic confirmation through a fusion of narcissistic libido with the genital function.

Even this abbreviated and inadequate summary of some of Grunberger's ideas indicates the extent to which they have anticipated certain of the central notions of the psychology of the self. However—and this is the point to be emphasized here—they remain Freudian insofar as the development of narcissistic libido is intrinsically connected (by complementarity) with the development of object libido. Disturbances of narcissistic development issue from narcissistic injuries bound to traumata at the oral, anal, and phallic stages. Their analytic resolution requires the simultaneous or sequential interpretation of the narcissistic disturbances and the related object-libidinal conflicts which go hand in hand with them. Thus, the thrust of Grunberger's theory is consistent with classical libido theory and inconsistent with self psychology.

Grunberger's approach suggests a view of the psychology of the self which would not remove the contradiction in libido theory, but would, as it were, suspend it pending further clinical investigations. There is an advantage to be gained from the reconsideration of established theories by examining them in the light of alternative hypotheses, for it provides an opportunity for renewed theory testing on the basis of fresh empirical evidence. From this vantage point, the psychology of the self can be seen as a group of experimental ideas which shed light upon the role of narcissism in normal and psychopathic development and upon narcissistic elements in the transference and countertransference. It is unlikely that adherents of the new psychology of narcissism would find such an approach acceptable (Rothstein, 1980), but that need not deter other analysts from using their hypotheses as an opportunity for reinvestigating the facts of libidinal organization and development upon which a reliable and comprehensive libido theory must be based.

THE ECLECTIC SOLUTION

Psychiatry is accustomed to emphasizing a variety of theoretical orientations in its treatment of mental disorders. Eclecticism is imposed upon psychiatry by the fact that it is obliged to attempt to understand and treat illnesses that are organically determined, organically and psychologically determined, and psychologically determined in the absence of a coherent and unified body of knowledge that establishes the interconnections of these different causal mechanisms (Hanly, 1970a). Efforts to construct a unified psychophysiological theory of mental functioning are still at a preliminary and pioneering stage (Hartmann, 1959). Psychiatric eclecticism is, in this respect, a logically valid approach to psychiatric diagnostic and treatment problems because the organic hypotheses are not inconsistent with psychodynamic ones.

However, eclecticism in psychoanalysis is untenable as a solution to our problem because it yokes together contradictory theories. The psychology of the self cannot be simply added to classical theory on the assumption that the psychology of the self provides a satisfactory explanation of narcissistic personality disorders while the classical theory continues to be a satisfactory explanation of the structural neuroses. The basic laws for the formation of narcissistic personality disorders cannot be inconsistent with those for the formation of structural neuroses. Human nature, however variegated and conflicted, remains a unitary entity in its organization and dynamics. Unity is demanded of the psychological science that seeks to understand by the unity of its subject. However appealing an eclectic approach may be on pragmatic grounds, it is untenable here, for it must founder and break apart when it runs up against the reef of a basic theoretical contradiction.

For the same reason, it is not possible to use the concepts of overdetermination and multifunction to solve the problem. These concepts imply the conjunction of forces. They have the logical form "both x and y," but the theoretical problem we are confronted with has the logical form "not both x and y." Once a decision is made as to the real nature of the relation between object and narcissistic libido, these concepts correctly come into play, but they cannot be used to solve the theoretical problem.

AN EMPIRICIST SOLUTION

The existence of a contradiction between two hypotheses logically implies that the facts of the phenomena that they explain cannot support both hypotheses. If they appear to do so, it is because the facts are being incorrectly (in this case, probably incompletely) observed by the adherents of one of the hypotheses in question. This much is beyond dispute, since it rests upon elementary principles of logic and epistemology.

The substantive questions are: What kind of evidence is required to test the competing hypotheses? And: How can it be established? There is a school of thought in psychoanalysis that would counsel giving up hope of ever finding evidence that could provide the basis for an empirical resolution of the problem. The theories under consideration, it is argued, are metapsychological theories of such abstraction that they do not lend themselves to either direct or indirect empirical testing. They are treated as if they were metaphysical ideas that thus fall outside the domain of verification (Hanly, 1970b). But Brenner (1980) has shown that metapsychology is not composed of a set of abstract theorems logically disconnected from the facts of clinical observations. Accordingly, the essential preliminary question is: What sort of evidence will test the theories?

Let me begin, then, with one of the most vexatious issues: the question of the value of narcissism. It has been claimed that there has been a cultural distortion of the superego which has placed a supreme value on object love. "Love thy neighbor as thyself," and, one might add, "*at least* as thyself." Self-sacrifice based on object love has long been held to be the highest moral excellence. The issue of the primacy of self-love and the love of others was extensively discussed in the early nineteenth century. In this discussion, Hazlitt (1805) affirmed the idea that one has to be able to love others in order to love oneself giving primacy to object love. However, Hazlitt's idea could be thought of as a personal declaration that expressed the superego distortion in question. Can this issue be tested psychoanalytically?

In the classical theory, it is the superego that carries out the functions of self-observation, self-approval, and disapproval, and consequently it is the source of self-confirmation and self-esteem, or of self-confirmation. Individual autonomy depends upon the formation of an independent superego which is able to carry out those same functions which were originally performed on the child's behalf by his parents. An independently functioning superego is able to sustain and confirm the individual's sense of rightness in the face of familial and societal opposition—those university students and others in Russia who are opposed to Putin's invasion of the Ukraine, for example—and to punish with guilt such thoughts and actions which society would not condemn. In the typical transference neurosis, the second condition regularly obtains. The person is obliged to suffer inhibitions of behavior (e.g., of sexual behavior in marriage) which society would not condemn. One clinical test of the spontaneous valuation placed on object love is as follows: a supreme value may be said to be placed on object love if under such circumstances patients are regularly observed to experience guilt concerning their deprivation of their partner and to experience fear of

18

his/her loss. This finding would be further substantiated if these anxieties are observed to act as motive forces for the tasks of the analytic work. A further test during the concluding phase of a successful analysis would be the observations of specific improvements in object relations accompanied by the release from guilt and depression brought about by the resolution of psychic conflict. If, on the other hand, the successful completion of this work still left the person abjectly dependent on others for his sense of self-worth, constantly seeking confirmation of his worth through attachment to idealized objects, depressed, hypochondriacal, etc., then these observations would indicate the irreducible value of narcissism independently of the sense of self-worth that derives from the realized capacity for object love. My purpose here is not to consider evidence bearing upon the question for which we would like to have an answer; rather, it is to establish the prior epistemological point that psychoanalysis has an objective method for finding such evidence.

Similarly, a reliable observational test of the contradictory libido theories can be achieved so long as two conditions are fulfilled. Analysts are accustomed to holding in suspension a number of interpretive hypotheses from which a selection is made on the basis of the patient's associations, the nature of the affects that invest them, the defenses at work, and the quality of the transference as the analytic process unfolds. For example, it is often necessary actively to consider at what level (oral, anal, or phallic) fixations of libido are at work in a patient's communications. In the same way, so long as the analyst is preserving an objective and receptive approach to the indications of the patient's problems, it is possible to entertain alternative hypotheses concerning the origins and nature of these problems as they manifest themselves in the transference so as to allow them to speak for themselves. It is only when the patient's neurosis is allowed to speak for itself in this way that reliable therapeutic work can be accomplished. By the same token, it is when theoretical judgment is suspended to this extent that theoretical formulations can be submitted to scientific evaluation. The listening to the patient by the analyst needs to be able to tolerate the falsification of the theoretical ideas that assist him in the construction of his interpretive hypothesis; otherwise the patient's psychic life may be fitted into the Procrustean bed of fixed ideas with no therapeutic or scientific benefit. The Kuhn-Feyerabend thesis presupposes that something like this always happens in science. My argument has been that the Kuhn-Feyerabend thesis describes scientific work when it has lost its moorings in objective observation but fails to describe scientific work in psychoanalysis or any other empirical science when it is functioning adequately.

The second condition for testing the alternative libido theories under consideration is that each must have determinate consequences concerning what is observed in analysis. Specific discriminate facts available to any trained observer must be derivable from the competing hypotheses; that is to say, what one will observe if the classical hypothesis is true and what one will observe if the self-psychology hypothesis is true must be capable of precise statement prior to observation, and of being tested by means of observation. Four such groups of observations are now stated without any attempt at completeness. Crucial, or theory-testing observations will be those concerning: (a) the concomitant variation in the quality and strength of the individual's sexual, aggressive, and narcissistic investment of objects, including the transference; (b) the presence or absence of dynamic connections between narcissistic transference phenomena (merging, mirroring, idealizing) and structural conflicts; (c) the presence or absence of dynamic connections between structural conflicts and problems of self-esteem; and (d) the occurrence of regression to narcissism as a defense against sexual conflicts.

Without drawing directly on clinical material, these groups of observations can be stated in a more particularized clinical form (again, only by way of illustration). The interdependence or not of object and

20

narcissistic libido could be crucially tested by the regular observation of an impoverishment of sexual affective relations in patients suffering from narcissistic psychopathology, or conversely, the regular observation of patients with narcissistic psychopathology along with robust and unconflicted heterosexual relations. For example, a patient who is suffering from hypochondriasis, depression, and diffuse anxiety about his capacity to work develops a mirror transference and also is able to carry on a satisfying sexual relationship with appropriate intimacy and care, and manifests no oedipal ambivalence of feeling towards his father nor castration anxiety during a successful treatment.

The presence or absence of dynamic connections between narcissistic transference phenomena and object-libidinal conflicts could be tested by observing whether these transferences regularly terminated in and were resolved by the associative uncovering of memories of narcissistic impoverishment at the appropriate narcissistic developmental stage, or, on the contrary, of oral, anal, or phallic conflicts and trauma. The analysis of a patient who develops a transference need to merge with the analyst would confirm the hypothesis of self psychology if reconstructions of experiences of early maternal unavailability as a shelter for a fragile infantile ego were sufficient to bring about therapeutic progress in the absence of any other factors. The analysis would count against the self psychology hypothesis and in favor of the classical hypothesis if the patient's associations also brought to light sexualized fantasies of passively dissolving into the mother, defending against the sadistic impulses and anxiety provoked by primal scene experiences.

The theory of self psychology concerning the regulation of self-esteem would be confirmed by a patient whose depressing need to find a sustaining acceptance and approval in an idealized other resolved into an integral and autonomous self-confidence without the analysis having to uncover and work through infantile memories of feeling humiliated because of genital inadequacy or oedipal guilt. The routine observation of just this sort of connection between problems with self-esteem and childhood sexual memories would, on the other hand, confirm the classical hypothesis and falsify self psychology.

The defensive function of the narcissistic organization of libido as implied by the classical theory would be evidenced by the observation of patients who substituted narcissistic object relations or intrapsychic organizations for conflicted sexual investments. A patient who sought closeness to others but remained introspectively aloof from real engagements with others because of anxiety about exhibitionistic and voyeuristic impulses would provide evidence for the intrinsic defensiveness of narcissistic configurations and against the hypothesis of their autonomy. On the other hand, a patient who had successfully resolved object-libidinal conflicts and was deeply and happily engaged in object relations but continued to experience fusional experiences of a religious nature, would offer evidence of the autonomy of narcissistic needs.

These examples are obviously incomplete and simplified. But even so, they point to facts of causality that the conscientious psychoanalyst is able to observe so long as his interest in the reality of his patients is greater than his interest in demonstrating the truth of a personally favored theory. In order to understand a patient and to offer him therapeutic interpretations, it is necessary to let his neurosis speak for itself. The psychoanalyst cannot proceed in the grand manner of Kantian epistemology as "an appointed judge who compels the witnesses to answer questions" (Kant, 1781) when the "answers" of our "witnesses" are unknown to them. Effective healing and objective theory testing are united in a respect for the patient and what his life has to reveal, a respect that refuses any attempt to confine his person or the facts of his life in the straitjacket of preconceived ideas. When psychoanalysts are divided as to where the truth lies, it is better to suffer the discomfort of the division than to paper it over with a denying epistemology, methodological reductionism, a fact-neutralizing set of diagnostic categories, or an appeal to eclecticism. When contradictory hypotheses are advocated by psychoanalysts, it follows logically that someone is mistaken because both cannot be true. Scientific as well as therapeutic progress in psychoanalysis will be best served by grasping the nettle and patiently setting about solving the problem empirically. In any case, the only sting the nettle has is the blow to the narcissism of those of us who turn out to have been in error, and for such a blow a better-secured relation to reality and truth is ample compensation.

SUMMARY

It is argued that the problem of testing inconsistent hypotheses in psychoanalysis cannot be satisfactorily solved by appeal to an epistemology of theoretical relativism. Science and a substantial body of philosophical thought are based upon an objectivist epistemology. Consequently, psychoanalysts who appeal to the authority of philosophers such as Kuhn and Feyerabend in order to protect their hypotheses from falsification are employing the material fallacy of *argumentum ad verecundiam* in the absence of evidence that psychoanalysis has a crippling epistemological defect not characteristic of other sciences in that its theories are not subject to verification but must rely upon the point of view and basic assumptions of groups of analysts.

It is then argued that psychoanalysis is able to test empirically hypotheses which are currently under dispute. The logical and observational requirements for testing conflicting hypotheses concerning the value of object-libidinal as opposed to narcissistic investments, the u-tube as opposed to the two-streams theories of libido, competing hypotheses concerning the regulation of self-esteem, and the defensive and compensatory nature (or not) of narcissistic configurations are set out.

In conclusion, it is argued that it is in the best interests of clinical work in psychoanalysis and the further development of psychoanalytic knowledge to resolve theoretical agreements by an appeal to observations that are compelling because they are objective and clinically helpful.

REFERENCES

Alexander, P. (1963). *Sensationalism and Scientific Explanation.* New York: Humanities Press.

Bergmann, G. (1957). Imperfect knowledge. In M. Brodbeck (Ed.), *Readings in the Philosophy of the Social Sciences* (pp. 415–435). New York: Macmillan, 1968.

Berlin, I. (1954). *Historical Inevitability.* London: Oxford University Press.

Bernfeld, S. (1941). The facts of observation in psychoanalysis. *Journal of Psychology* 12:289–305.

Bohm, D. (1957). *Causality and Chance in Modern Physics.* New York: Harper, 1961.

Braithwaite, R.B. (1953). *Scientific Explanation.* Cambridge: Cambridge University Press, 1964.

Brenner, C. (1976). *Psychoanalytic Technique and Psychic Conflict.* New York: International Universities Press.

——— (1980). Metapsychology and psychoanalytic theory. *Psychoanalytic Quarterly* 49:189–214.

Burtt, E.A. (1932). *The Metaphysical Foundations of Modern Physical Science.* London: Routledge & Kegan Paul, 1949.

Butterfield, N. (1957). *The Origins of Modern Science, 1300–1800.* New York: The Free Press, 1968.

Butts, R.E. (1966). Feyerabend and the pragmatic theory of observation. *Philosophy of Science* 33:382–394.

Calef, V., & Weinshel, E.M. (1979). The new psychoanalysis and psychoanalytic revisionism. *Psychoanalytic Quarterly* 48:470–491.

Coen, S.J. (1981). Notes on the concepts of self-object and preoedipal object. *Journal of the American Psychoanalytic Association* 29:95–411.

Collingwood, R.G. (1946). *The Idea of History.* New York: Oxford University Press, 1956.

Cunningham, F. (1973). *Objectivity in the Social Sciences.* Toronto: University of Toronto Press.

Eisnitz, A.J. (1980). The organization of the self-representation and its influence on pathology. *Psychoanalytic Quarterly* 49:361–392.

——— (1981). The perspective of the self-representation: Some clinical implications. *Journal of the American Psychoanalytic Association* 29:309–336.

Fenichel, O. (1935). A contribution to the psychology of jealousy. In *The Collected Papers of Otto Fenichel, First Series.* New York: Norton, 1953.

——— (1945). *The Psychoanalytic Theory of the Neurosis.* New York: Norton.

Feyerabend, P.K. (1965). Problems of empiricism. In R.G. Colodny (Ed.), *Beyond the Edge of Certainty: Essays in Contemporary Science and Philosophy* (pp. 145–260). Englewood Cliffs, NJ: Prentice-Hall.

Freud, S. (1914). On narcissism: An introduction. SE 14:72–102.

——— (1917). *Introductory Lectures on Psycho-Analysis.* SE 15–16.

——— (1917). Mourning and melancholia. SE 14:243–258.

——— (1923). The ego and the id. SE 19:1–66.

——— (1927). The future of an illusion. SE 21:1–273.

——— (1933). The question of *Weltanschauung.* SE 22:158–182.

Gedo, J. (1977). Review of M.M. Gill & P.S. Holzman (Eds.), *Psychology versus Metapsychology: Psychoanalytic Essays in Memory of George S. Klein. Psychoanalytic Quarterly* 46:319–325.

————(1980). Reflections on some current controversies in psychoanalysis. *Journal of the American Psychoanalytic Association* 28:363–383.

Gibson, Q. (1960). *The Logic of Social Inquiry.* London: Routledge & Kegan Paul.

Gill, M.M. (1976). Metapsychology is not psychology. In M.M. Gill & P.S. Holzman (Eds.), *Psychology versus Metapsychology: Psychoanalytic Essays in Memory of George S. Klein* (pp. 71–105). New York: International Universities Press.

Goldberg, A.G. (1976). A discussion of the paper by C. Hanly and J. Masson on "A critical examination of the new narcissism." *International Journal of Psychoanalysis* 57:67–70.

———— (1978) *The Psychology of the Self.* New York: International Universities Press.

Grunberger, B. (1971). *Narcissism.* New York: International Universities Press, 1971.

Hanly, C. (1970a). *Mental Health in Ontario: A Study for the Committee on the Healing Arts.* Toronto: The Queen's Printer.

———— (1970b). On being and dreaming. In C. Hanly & M. Lazerowitz (Eds.), *Psychoanalysis and Philosophy* (pp. 155–187). New York: International Universities Press.

———— (1977). An unconscious irony in Plato's *Republic. Psychoanalytic Quarterly* 46:116–147.

————. (1982) Narcissism: Defense and the positive transference. *International Journal of Psychoanalysis* 63:427–444.

Hanly, C., & Masson, J. (1976). A critical examination of the new narcissism. *International Journal of Psychoanalysis* 57:49–66.

Hanson, N.R. (1958). *Patterns of Discovery.* London: Cambridge University Press.

Hartmann, H. (1959). Psychoanalysis as a scientific theory. In S. Hook (Ed.), *Psychoanalysis, Scientific Method and Philosophy* (pp. 3–37). New York: Grove Press, 1960.

Hazlitt, W. (1805). *Essay on the Principles of Human Action.* London: J. Johnson.

Hempel, C.G. (1965). *Aspects of Scientific Explanation.* New York: Free Press.

Kaufmann, F. (1944). *Methodology of the Social Sciences.* New York: Humanities Press, 1958.

Kernberg, O. (1975). *Borderline Conditions and Pathological Narcissism.* New York: Jason Aronson.

Klein, G.S. (1978). Freud's two theories of sexuality. In M.M. Gill & P.S. Holzman (Eds.), *Psychology versus Metapsychology: Psychoanalytic Essays in Memory of George S. Klein* (pp. 14–70). New York: International Universities Press.

Kohut, H. (1971). *The Analysis of the Self.* New York: International Universities Press.

——— (1977). *The Restoration of the Self.* New York: International Universities Press.

——— (1978). *The Search for the Self.* 2 vols. New York: International Universities Press.

Kuhn, T.S. (1970). *The Structure of Scientific Revolutions* (2nd ed.). Chicago: University of Chicago Press.

Leach, J. (1968). Explanation and value neutrality. *British Journal for the Philosophy of Science* 19:93–108.

Maciver, R.M. (1931). *Society.* New York: Holt, Rinehart & Winston, 1949.

Mannheim, K. (1936). *Ideology and Utopia.* New York: Harcourt, Brace & World.

Mason, S.F. (1962). *A History of the Sciences.* New York: Collier Books.

Mises, L. von (1958). *Theory and History.* London: J. Cape.

Modell, A.H. (1975). A narcissistic defense against affects and the illusion of self-sufficiency. *International Journal of Psychoanalysis* 56:275–282.

Myrdal, G. (1958). *Value in Social Theory* (Ed. P. Streeten). New York: Harper.

——— (1969). *Objectivity in Social Research.* New York: Pantheon Books.

Nadel, S.F. (1951). *The Foundations of Social Anthropology.* Glencoe, IL: Free Press.

Nagel, E. (1959). Methodological issues in psychoanalytic theory. In S. Hook (Ed.), *Psychoanalysis, Scientific Method, and Philosophy* (pp. 38–56). New York: Grove Press, 1960.

——— (1961). *The Structure of Science.* New York: Harcourt, Brace & World.

Orgel, S. (1977 A form of acting out in the narcissistic transference. *Psychoanalytic Quarterly* 47:684–685.

Parsons, T. (1949). *The Structure of Social Action.* Glencoe, IL: Free Press.

Perman, J.A. (1979). The search for the mother: Narcissistic regression to a pathway of mourning in childhood. *Psychoanalytic Quarterly* 48:448–464.

Polanyi, M. (1946). *Science, Faith and Society.* Chicago: University of Chicago Press, 1964.

——— (1958). *Personal Knowledge.* Chicago: University of Chicago Press.

——— (1959). *The Logic of Scientific Discovery.* New York: Harper & Row, 1965.

Popper, K.R. (1963). *Conjectures and Refutations: The Growth of Scientific Knowledge.* London: Routledge & Kegan Paul.

Quine, W.V.O. (1960). *Word and Object.* Cambridge, MA.: Technology Press of the Massachusetts Institute of Technology.

Renik, O. (1978). Neurotic and narcissistic transferences in Freud's relationship with Josef Popper. *Psychoanalytic Quarterly* 47:398–418.

Rothstein, A. (1979). Oedipal conflicts in narcissistic personality disorders. *International Journal of Psychoanalysis* 60:189–199.

——— (1980a). Psychoanalytic paradigms and their narcissistic investment. *Journal of the American Psychoanalytic Association* 28:385–395.

———— (1980b). Toward a critique of the psychology of the self. *Psychoanalytic Quarterly* 49:423–455.

Rudner, R. (1966). *Philosophy of Social Sciences*. Englewood Cliffs, NJ: Prentice-Hall.

Ryle, G. (1949). *The Concept of Mind*. London: Hutchinson's University Library.

Schafer, R. (1976). *A New Language for Psychoanalysis*. New Haven: Yale University Press.

———— (1978). *Language and Insight*. New Haven: Yale University Press.

Scheffler, I. (1967). *Science and Subjectivity*. Indianapolis: Bobbs-Merrill.

Segel, N.P. (1981). Narcissism and adaptation to indignity. *International Journal of Psychoanalysis* 62:465–476.

Shapere, D. (1966). Meaning and scientific change. In R.G. Colodny (Ed.), *Mind and Cosmos* (pp. 41–85). Pittsburgh: University of Pittsburgh Press.

Smart, J.J.C. (1963). *Philosophy and Scientific Realism*. London: Routledge & Kegan Paul.

Toulmin, S. (1961). *Foresight and Understanding*. Bloomington: Indiana University Press.

Tyson, R.L., & Tyson, P. (1982). A case of "pseudo-narcissistic" psychopathology: A re-examination of the developmental role of the superego. *International Journal of Psychoanalysis* 63:283–293.

Waelder, R. (1970). Observation, historical reconstruction, and experiment. In C. Hanly & M. Lazerowitz (Eds.), *Psychoanalysis and Philosophy* (pp. 280–326). New York: International Universities Press.

Wallerstein, R.S. (1981). The bipolar self: Discussion of alternative perspectives. *Journal of the American Psychoanalytic Association* 29:377–394.

Weber, M. (1949). *The Methodology of the Social Sciences* (Trans. E. Shils and H. Finch). New York: Free Press.

Werkmeister, W.N. (1959). Theory construction and the problem of objectivity. In L. Gross (Ed.), *Symposium on Sociological Theory* (pp. 483–508). Evanston, IL: Row, Peterson.

Winch, P. (1959). *The Idea of a Social Science.* London: Routledge & Kegan Paul.

Wittgenstein, L. (1966). *Lectures & Conversations on Aesthetics, Psychology, and Religious Belief* (Ed. C. Barrett). Oxford: Blackwell.

CHAPTER 2

Inductive Reasoning in Clinical Psychoanalysis*

Presented at the 37th Congress of the International Psychoanalytical Association, Buenos Aires, July–August 1991. I am grateful to my colleagues at the Austen Riggs Center for the opportunity provided to me to research and write this paper during my tenure as the Erik H. Erikson Scholar.

The debate concerning the nature of psychoanalytic knowledge continues among psychoanalysts and philosophers. It raises some basic questions: Is psychoanalysis an empirical science or is it a hermeneutic psychology? If it claims to be an empirical science, is this claim justified? If psychoanalytic knowledge is hermeneutic, the usual standards of objectivity and inductive proof are no longer required, but how can psychoanalysis defend itself against the charge that its results are based on nothing more than persuasion, suggestion, and conversion to a point of view? Psychoanalysis would be left having to rely upon the analyst's untested intuition.

I shall argue that clinical and theoretical hypotheses can be tested by clinical observations and that psychoanalysis is therefore an empirical, observational science. This is a crucial question although it is only one of a number of questions that have to be answered, if psychoanalysis's claim to be a science

---

* Originally published in *The International Review of Psycho-Analysis* 73 (1992):293–301.

is to be vindicated. Grunbaum's recent (1984) criticisms of psychoanalysis on this score are especially threatening, because they call into question the probative value of clinical observations in psychoanalysis. Psychoanalysis is a clinical discipline, not an experimental one; all the knowledge we have comes from clinical observation. If our clinical observations cannot be used inductively to test, correct, and validate our theories, these theories can be no more than a personal credo based on personal experience, except—and this exception offers only cold comfort to the clinician—insofar as they can be established by extra-clinical observations. The argument that follows is not so much a critique of Grunbaum (whose ideas concerning the nature of scientific knowledge I share, as did Freud), as an exploration of some ways in which clinical observation and reasoning in psychoanalysis meet these criteria for empirical knowledge.

Grunbaum's arguments, if their premises are correct, imply that clinical observations have no probative value for psychoanalytic theory. At best, clinical observations can suggest hypotheses for extra-clinical testing. But there is a further, no less important implication for the therapeutic action of psychoanalysis. Grunbaum's analysis attacks the keystone that enables psychoanalysis as science and therapy to form an arch that can support the superstructure of theory. This keystone idea is that the essential agent of the therapy, however necessary other factors such as acceptance, sympathy, reliability, etc. may be, is the truth of the interpretations made by the analyst to the patient, or by the patient to himself. If this idea is unsound and without a basis in fact, the fundamental link between therapy and science that is peculiar to psychoanalysis is broken.

It is for these reasons that, although I consider work such as that of Glassman (1987) to be very important in itself, it does not tackle the central problem, nor does it claim to. Glassman's work shows that competing theories (e.g., Kernberg's and Kohut's models of narcissism) can be empirically tested. His test shows that "Kohut's self psychology is more parsimoniously explained as a special case of Kernberg's ego psychology-object relations theory" (p. 597). But the data on which this finding is based is extra-clinical. Similarly, Mackay (1989) has given us a definitive study of the scientific structure of psychoanalytic knowledge by exhibiting the logical relations between clinical observables and the causal hypotheses of psychoanalytic theory.

But this analysis, correct and valuable as it is, and though it shows that psychoanalytic knowledge has the logical structure of an empirical science, leaves unanswered the question of whether or not psychoanalysts have been able to use that structure to generate reliable empirical knowledge. What psychoanalysis needs at the present time is an understanding of the conditions under which clinical observation can be used to do the required theory testing. This paper is only a first attempt at explicating the inductive use of clinical observations for testing psychoanalytic theories. Its purpose is to show that psychoanalytic theories can be tested clinically, rather than to publish the results of such testing. It is an exploration of some aspects of causal and inductive thinking and observation in clinical work.

The following argument first approaches the problem indirectly by considering the question: Can clinical observations be used to test competing theories in psychoanalysis by employing the usual methods of inductive reasoning? Let us consider two such competing theories in self psychology and classical psychoanalysis. Self psychology, after an initial hesitation (Kohut, 1971), now asserts that drive conflicts are secondary to narcissistic deficits (Kohut, 1977, 1978; Goldberg, 1988) in the causation of neurosis. The classical theory affirms, on the contrary, that drive-determined conflicts are primary. Brenner (1982) does not include narcissistic privations among the calamities of childhood that are sufficient causes of neurosis. Which theory is true? Can clinical observation decide this issue? What part does inductive reasoning play in such testing?

Each of these theories specifies certain conditions for the occurrence of neurotic symptoms and malfunctions. Self psychology claims that one or more developmental failures in the self-object relations of merging, mirroring, or idealizing cause neurosis. Self psychology does not disregard sexual, aggressive factors, but it considers them secondary to the narcissistic ones. (Self psychology has its own version of the Oedipus complex which explains, on the assumptions of self psychology, the derivative and secondary nature of the Oedipus complex as described in psychoanalysis; see Kohut, 1984, pp. 14–16.) Psychoanalysis, for its part, does not disregard narcissistic factors but it considers drive-related conflicts to be primary determinants of neurosis.

Together, these two theories provide a list of possible conditions for neurosis. The rules of inductive reasoning first formalized by Mill (1843) and recently revised by Von Wright (1957) provide a logical means of determining which possible conditions for some occurrence, such as a neurosis, are necessary conditions and which are sufficient. (A necessary condition for an event cannot be absent if the event occurs; a sufficient condition for an event cannot be present when the event does not occur.) Inductive reasoning can be used to test competing psychoanalytic hypotheses. How would this work? Let us consider some clinical data.

Ann was a highly intelligent and accomplished woman in her early thirties. She had sought out analysis because of a sleep disturbance and because of her inability to maintain an intimate relation with a man. She assured me that the problem had to do with her personal life. Her professional career, at which she was highly accomplished and successful, was fulfilling; her personal life was not. But the early stages of her analysis revealed something else. Ann felt devalued and pushed aside in her work by her male colleagues. Her seniors overvalued her male peers and undervalued her. After an initial denying enthusiasm about her appointment, she now, it emerged, felt herself to have been assigned the role of the token woman in the firm by her male colleagues. She had felt similarly unappreciated by her father. The father had been a reliable provider, but had become passive, silent, and withdrawn from my patient and her two younger sisters in their early childhood and from the mother who had disparaged him. He had taken no interest in Ann's childhood learning, her adolescent intellectual development, or her adult academic and professional achievements.

Although I was aware, in the transference, of a certain emptiness caused by her withheld feelings of anger, which affected her experience of me, I had no reason to doubt that there was a substantial measure of truth in what Ann communicated about her experience, first with her father and now with her male colleagues. Whether or not it was the whole truth, the analysis would have to decide. She was unconsciously enacting her identification with the first man she had loved and causing me to experience what she had suffered in that relationship (Porder, 1987). There was also an unreality in her depressed conviction that she could never find recognition in her field—that she had to either tolerate her current position or change careers.

As she became aware of her depression and anger, of her longing for a helpful father whom she could respect, or if that could not be, for a retreat into a maternal alliance that would repeat her sublimated homosexual relationship with her mother, Ann was able to begin looking for a new position in her chosen field.

This picture accords well with self psychology. It is a picture of a little girl whose father provided her with neither mirroring of her childish femininity nor a suitable object for idealization and identification. These would seem to be among the conditions for Ann's neurosis. If these conditions were sufficient to account for her symptoms, then we would expect that an alteration in them would result in a symptom change. If a theory postulates that an improvement in self-object relations, self-cohesion, and self-esteem is a sufficient condition for symptom reduction, and such improvements occur in the absence of symptom reduction, then the postulated connection would not hold.

Ann found an excellent new position. She was surprised to discover that she was treated on an equal footing with her male peers by her senior male colleagues. Her knowledge and talents were recognized and rewarded. She was happy to find herself not only fairly treated but liked and respected by senior male colleagues, whom she liked and respected. Those aspects of the relationship to a father, in which she had been failed by her own father, were now available to her in surrogate relations with professional colleagues. She had been able to use her relation to her analyst to take the necessary risks of failure and humiliation. Evidently, the analyst had functioned as an adequate self object. Ann was happy about these changes in her life.

But she was no less disappointed that no improvement was taking place in her sleep symptom or sexual conflict. I might add that her analyst shared this disappointment. She continued to have difficulty in falling asleep at night, and regularly awoke at three or four in the morning unable to return to sleep.

As the beneficial changes were taking place in her career, Ann had fallen in love with a suitable man and had then, after a few months, broken off the relationship in a repetitive way. After an initial enthusiasm sufficient to make her think of giving up her career for marriage and family (these ideas also partly expressed her fear that she might not be able to pursue her career successfully), she had begun to feel trapped and enslaved. She began to feel a panicky need to break off the relationship with this man, who at first seemed strong but now seemed tyrannical and weak. Ann had ceased to be angry and depressed as far as her work was concerned and felt confirmed in her self-respect, but her neurosis remained essentially intact.

These observations count as inductive evidence against the central role assigned by self psychology to narcissism in the aetiology of neurosis. The theory of self psychology predicts that the patient's problem with self-esteem should have been ameliorated, and her sexual problems should have improved as a consequence of this development. These things did not occur. A complete account of the analysis, which space does not permit and the purpose of this paper does not require, would show that drive conflicts were probably the sufficient causes of Ann's neurosis. Here is a brief summary of the factors, the analytic resolution of which did result in the amelioration of her symptoms.

Ann's work threw her into competitive, even combative relations with men. She could not really accept or genuinely integrate the respect that she had won for herself in her new position at work until she had resolved her unconscious wish to triumph over men. The unconscious fantasy that informed her sexual identity and her attitude to it, was of a person with a defective and ugly genital. Allied with this fantasy was an erotic cannibalistic wish that made itself known in dreams during the analysis, in memories from childhood of experiences of excited disgust when sharing meals with her father, of being unable to tell a school nurse what she had eaten for breakfast and, latterly, in her panicky flight from men whose "Achilles' heel" she had found.

This wish had its masochistic complement in a fantasy of being subjected to a violent sexual assault dating back to her fifth year. This fantasy was the major factor in her sleep symptom. In childhood, she would try to stay up with her parents while they watched TV, even though she wanted to go to bed. She did this because she feared that if she went to bed she would have pleasant sexual thoughts, which would turn into the fear that a thief would enter the house, walk past her parents, come up the stairs, and, seeing her in the shaft of light cast into her room from the hall, would murder her by stabbing her over and over again with a knife. When she left home for university, this fantasy returned in a conscious form. It obliged her to work at her studies until the early hours of the morning when, with the promise of daylight, she finally dared fall asleep.

These drive demands motivated in turn Ann's identification with a mother, who in Ann's fantasy had castrated her father and had subjected Ann to maternal injunctions never to depend upon a man, always to keep the upper hand with men, and never to make a fool of herself by yielding to a man without being in control of him. Whenever Ann contemplated a relationship with a man, she was inwardly lacerated by fears that she might transgress these maternal cautions. It was only with the greatest difficulty that she could dare even to explore the potentials of relationships offered to her. Although she developed an intense positive transference, it was unconsciously maternal and homosexual. It was dominated by a repetition of the oath to herself that she had made as a teenager never to have a sexual relationship—indeed, any romantic relationship—with a man so long as she lived under her mother's roof, or now, until after she had completed her analysis—which, of course, this transference, had it remained intact, would not have allowed.

In my view, the evidence of this case is inconsistent with the aetiological theory of self psychology. (But there is not room here for a sufficiently detailed account of the analysis to authenticate the data reported, and the data of the analysis also needs to be evaluated and tested by others, including analysts committed to self psychology.) It may turn out that the factors identified by self psychology contribute to the causation of neurosis in conjunction with other object-relational and drive factors but that they do not have the primacy attributed to them by the theory.

In any case, as I have indicated above, my purpose in presenting these clinical observations is not to try to refute the theoretical claims of self psychology, but to point out that clinical psychoanalysis can do much more than merely illustrate theories. It can also test them. If psychoanalysts use clinical observations as illustrations of theory (and they usually do), it is because of stylistic convenience, a need to avoid scientific controversy, or a failure to utilize the logical potential of the analytic situation, but not because of any intrinsic failure of a properly conducted analysis to meet the logical requirements of inductive reasoning. Inductive reasoning does not require evidence based upon experimentation; observation is sufficient (Skyrms, 1986; Brenner, 1970).

Let us now consider a second theoretical dispute in psychoanalysis. Bowlby (1973) hypothesized that pathological anxiety (phobia) owes its origin to two factors. (1) An individual is subjected to some or all of the following anxiety-causing stimuli to which he/she has a genetically inherited susceptibility: being alone, being in the dark, being in a strange place, hearing noises, something suddenly approaching. (2) The individual does not have available to him/her an adequate attachment object who is able to facilitate containment of the anxiety.

In certain respects, this hypothesis is in agreement with the psychoanalytic model, which also identifies the importance of the anaclitic bond as the child's "first protection against danger" (Freud, 1927, p. 24). Moreover, although Freud's theory does not identify genetically inherited reactions of anxiety to the stimuli that signal danger in the environment of evolutionary adaptedness as Bowlby does, his theory leaves the door open to such biological factors. Anxiety is a signal of danger whether the danger is external or internal. Where the theories differ substantially is in the exclusion from Bowlby's theory of drive factors (wishes) and defenses against them, and their inclusion in Freud's.

This theoretical difference can be tested by child observation. A child of three suddenly becomes afraid of going to bed. She cannot tolerate being left alone in her room illuminated by a small night light. Her mother is not so available to her as she had been earlier in the child's life, on account of the birth of a baby sister. On the face of it, this evidence seems to confirms Bowlby's theory. Two of his listed necessary conditions for pathological anxiety are present—being alone, being in relative dark, shadows and unlit places under the bed and in the closet—as is his sufficient condition—the reduced availability of the mother. However, the development of the anxiety occurred some nine months after the birth of the sibling. The mother had been less available to the older child during those first weeks and months than she was at the time of the development of the anxiety. Thus, if Bowlby's theory were correct, the outbreak of anxiety should have occurred much earlier than it did. If the unavailability of the mother as an attachment object were a sufficient condition for the pathological anxiety, then it could not occur in the absence of the symptom. But the symptom had been absent until something else happened.

Further investigation revealed that the anxiety had actually occurred earlier, but that it had been successfully deferred by a defense: the child had taken possession of all the toys that the baby had been given and had played with them, apparently happily. In this way she had preserved her own identity as the baby, had denied the reality of her rival, and hence had kept in abeyance the death wish that her sibling's arrival had aroused in her, along with her fear of the loss of the mother and the mother's love. The child's current symptom had been precipitated by a parental decision to oblige her to allow the baby to have her own toys.

The causation of pathological anxiety appears to be more complex than Bowlby's theory allows. The evidence indicates that an infant, at an early stage of development, is able autonomously to defend against anxiety to some extent, even if the defenses are untenable for long-run healthy development and viable object relations. Even in the earlier stage of anaclitic love, a child is not so object-bound and dependent as Bowlby's theory suggests. Or perhaps more precisely, children are already able to substitute fantasies of objects for the real objects to a greater extent than Bowlby's theory allows. A child is able to tolerate sharing the love of the mother so long as she finds her share to be sufficient. Anxiety will occur, but it will not become pathological.

If she finds her portion of love to be insufficient, as happened with the child described above, she will become pathologically anxious when, as a result of this threat to her anaclitic needs, she develops a death wish toward her sibling in order to try to restore the earlier state of affairs. Drive and defense appear to play an essential part in the pathological outcome. This evidence suggests that Bowlby's hypothesized inherited susceptibilities to anxiety-causing stimuli may contribute to phobia by acting as possible partial causes, but they are probably not necessary causes.

Being alone and in the near-dark were present in the case of the little girl described. But normal illumination, which the parents had tried, had not reduced the child's anxiety. There had always been dark places, though these had not frightened her before. They seem to have been not so much frightening in themselves as having been made frightening by the meaning they acquired as a consequence of the child's death wish. Being alone is a complex factor. As far as the child was concerned, during the period of her anxiety, being left alone at bedtime by mother or father was tantamount to them being inadequate attachment objects, although this had not been so before, during the period when the child was still herself the baby in her fantasy. If the demand that the older child allow her younger sibling to have her own toys, since she had plenty of her own, causes a parent to be an inadequate attachment object, then what parents could be adequate attachment objects? The younger child needed to be able to possess her own things.

However, Bowlby's hypothesis might be preserved. The child did not manifest the symptom at the time of her sister's birth when the mother was most occupied with the new infant. If the father had been an adequate substitute attachment object for the child during that period and then ceased being so at the time the symptom appeared some nine months later, then this loss could have precipitated the child's anxiety. But there was no evidence that this had happened. Moreover, it would not account for the part that the loss of the toys had played. The child could go to sleep after the usual tucking-in activities by either father or mother up to the time when they insisted that each child have her own toys. This was the precipitating event. The demand placed on her by her parents destroyed the fragile defense the child had erected against the anxiety aroused in her by her hostility toward her sister.

This evidence does suggest that Bowlby's theory is incomplete. Since the factors postulated by this theory were present when the phobia they are supposed to cause was absent, these factors cannot be on their own sufficient causes of phobia. They could be partial causes, however; in particular, the unavailability of an adequate attachment object, or in classical terminology, a suitable object for anaclitic bonding, may be jointly a sufficient cause along with a conflict-causing drive demand such as a sibling death wish.

If so, the drive factor acquires a primacy, insofar as, from the point of view of the child—and that is the point of view that matters—it was the failure of the parents to understand her hostility to her sister and to help her with it that made her experience them as inadequate and unavailable. And insofar as this is true, the child's perception was correct. The consultation with the parents was a success. Over several weeks, as they enabled their daughter to talk about her feelings about her sister, she came to feel restored to them, her hostility to her sister abated, and her symptom gradually subsided.

Let me reiterate once more that my purpose is not to defend Freud's theory of anxiety or to refute Bowlby's, but to argue that these theories are inductively testable—that is, that psychoanalytic clinical and child observation provides data that allow for reality-bound progress in psychoanalytic knowledge. I have to admit that I have been able only to illustrate my thesis by means of incomplete examples rather than prove it, although I have published elsewhere observations and their inductive analysis that bear upon the testing of both self psychology (e.g., Hanly, 1982) and Bowlby's object-relations theory (see Hanly, 1978). The empirical testing of this thesis requires the collaboration of many analysts working under the constraints of three requirements: the logical analysis of theories so as to define the observations that will test them; making and reporting the critical observations so that they can be checked by others against their clinical observations of similar psychological processes; and inductive causal analysis of these results.

But here we come upon another problem, with which I shall conclude. Philosophers of science—Grunbaum (1984), Nagel (1959), and others yet earlier—have claimed that psychoanalytic clinical observation is rendered unreliable because the influence of suggestion upon what is observed cannot be ruled out. As evidence for the correctness of this criticism, Nagel (1959) repeated Stekel's admission that "patients dream in the dialect of whatever physician happens to be treating them.... Sadger's patients dream about urinary eroticism; mine perhaps of the symbolism of death and religion; Adler's of 'topdogs' and 'underdogs' and of the masculine protest" (pp. 49–50). If patients dream so compliantly, they will also associate while awake no less compliantly. The observations made by analysts will cease to have probative value. The rules of inductive reasoning produce reliable results only when they are applied to objective data which are independent of the observer and his preferred ideas. Grunbaum (1984) also fastens upon Freud's "avowed brain washing" (p. 151). Perhaps it would be worth looking again at Freud's reply to Stekel's claim.

Freud (1916–1917) acknowledged that the dreams of patients are influenced by ideas imparted by the analyst. But he also pointed out that this influence is upon the manifest content of the dream. The latent dream, in which its meaning is to be found, is not dominated either by the patient's ego, or by his beliefs about the analyst's beliefs, or by his relation to the analyst; it is determined by the wishes that originate from the fixated or regressed drive organizations and the repressed memories that give them content and meaning. The disguise can be influenced by suggestion, or at the very least by the transference, but the unconscious wish cannot.

The instinctual life of the individual and the memories that are bound up with its developmental vicissitudes constitute an autonomous core of psychic activity that is not subject to alteration by suggestion (see also Freud, 1894, p. 295; 1923, pp. 113ff.). This core and its derivatives form an essential part of the object of psychoanalytic observation. Grunbaum (1984) oversimplifies and restricts Freud's approach to the problem of suggestion in psychoanalysis when he limits it to the tally argument.

The conclusion of Freud's argument based upon the structure of dreams can be inductively tested. Consider the following simple example. A five-year-old girl became obsessed with the mechanism of toilets. Every evening she demanded of the parent who helped her with her bath and preparations for bed that the cover of the toilet be removed and the mechanism be demonstrated to her. On the first occurrence the proud parent took the child's curiosity to be a sign of a childish scientific interest in how things work. She was a bright and curious child who asked many similar sorts of questions, but on other occasions she would easily become satisfied with explanations and demonstrations appropriate to her learning capacity. But this time her curiosity was insatiable; she also became worried that the toilet would overflow.

Her curiosity and anxiety were not abated by various parental strategies aimed at extinguishing it by reassurances or diversions. These actions and communications were so many suggestions to the child based upon parental authority about what she should believe and feel. This is a powerful form of suggestion in the life of a small child, however kindly intended and conveyed. Then it dawned on one of the parents that the child had recently wet her bed after a long period of sleeping dry and that her anxiety was not about the toilet but about herself.

The next evening when the child expressed her wish to examine the plumbing of the toilet, the parent kindly said to her, "Jannie, you are worried about wetting the bed." To this she responded with a flush of shame and described being teased at school when she had confided the episode of her bed-wetting to a companion, who had turned out to be untrustworthy. Her excessive curiosity and anxiety about the toilet ceased and did not recur, although it was probably incompletely interpreted. In this simple example from ordinary life, we find that suggestion (as well as empathy, non-punitive acceptance, etc.) was not sufficient to extinguish the symptom, whereas communication with the child about the true nature of her anxiety was sufficient.

Clinical practice continually confronts the analyst with this phenomenon. For example, an accountant patient, who was on the verge of abandoning his professional practice, suffered from no lack of suggestions concerning his competence and reliability from his clients, his colleagues, and his family, and by real success in his practice. He seized upon these suggestions from outside himself to try to shore up his faltering sense of self-worth. But it did not work. His confidence in himself was constantly eroded, and his enthusiasm for and interest in his work were constantly enervated by the guilty expectation that he would commit some terrible blunder that would be financially ruinous for someone. The loyalty and confidence of his clients, the respect of his colleagues, the encouragement of his wife and family, and the facts of his practice over fifteen years could not diminish his obsessional fear.

The analysis uncovered through the transference and eventually in recovered memories the damaging consequences of an oedipal triumph. His father had fallen seriously ill during the patient's fifth year, requiring prolonged hospitalization. When the father returned home, the mother, ostensibly for fear of infection, permanently consigned the father to the guest bedroom, which, along with other similar domestic arrangements resulted in an intensified and unresolved Oedipus complex in the patient. One significant transference occurrence involved a psychological error. My patient's secretary had received a request from a woman caller for an appointment concerning her husband's affairs. Although the name did not really much resemble mine, when his secretary spoke to him about it, he took the caller to be my wife and formed the fantasy, which preoccupied him during the day, that I had been involved in some shady business dealings (this fantasy denied his wish to deprive me of his fee) for which I would no doubt be imprisoned. He would be called upon to manage my wife's affairs and save her from disaster.

Is it likely that persuading him to believe that his obsessional guilt was caused by an oedipal triumph that had occurred in his fifth year, when nothing of the kind had happened, would have had any beneficial effect? How could such a tale be persuasive, if it were in fact only a tale? How could a false and fantastic history be used by the patient to overcome his obsessional fear when his knowing that the fear had been contradicted by reality for years had failed to do so? Similarly, supposing the recalled childhood events had actually occurred, how could persuading the patient by suggestion that these events were causes of his obsessional anxiety bring about the resolution of the anxiety if in fact they had nothing to do with it?

The problem of suggestion and the reliability of psychoanalytic observations generally is not theoretical or logical. It cannot be settled by the success or failure of the tally argument. It is essentially a methodological or technical problem. Arlow (1959) has given a definitive characterization of the means by which the analytic situation seeks to provide a "field of observation in which the data are supplied by the subject exclusively" (p. 202). Analysts are taught to recognize the defensive aspects of compliance. The analytic work itself instructs analyst and patient alike in the therapeutic futility of compliance.

For example, a patient began his analysis with tearful confessions of childhood sexual episodes. While doing so, he also revealed that he experienced himself entirely as a victim and that he expected his analyst to be his champion, who would vindicate him and provide restitution. Here is a positive transference of sorts. The patient is revealing shameful episodes from his past which he correctly believes the analyst wants to hear about. And in due course, they will play an important part in his analysis.

But before that can happen, his attitude to these events as revealed in his transference has to be identified for him and recognized by him, and its sources in these or other happenings in his life explored. His attitude toward his own life and his analyst has to undergo a modification. This modification can be brought about by its interpretation. Thus, the work proceeds, and as it does, the patient is able to tolerate and communicate more of himself as he is and remember more of his past as it was.

The abatement of symptoms is one indicator of such an advance. Another is the correction or elaboration of memories as they recur in the analytic process. For example, in the case of compliance alluded to above, during an early confessional stage of the analysis the patient reported an episode in which, during latency, he was forced to masturbate a priest. At a later point, this memory returned with further details. He had not been alone. Other boys were present. He had been fascinated by the priest's erect penis and had willingly responded to the priest's request to be masturbated. He had not been intimidated or threatened. He could have run away. In this edition of the memory, although a victim, he had not been helpless. He had been seducible because of feelings of his own about which he was then able to question himself in the analysis.

But the analyst does not at this point close the enquiry. More details may yet emerge. Questions persist: for example, is the second version of the memory a more subtle form of masochistic submission? These questions can be answered by changes in the transference, further analysis of the patient's masochism and also of his homosexual aggression if further indications of it emerge, as one would predict from the shift in the content of the memory, etc. This prediction can also be tested. Thus, changes in the content, the affects, and the transferences that make up the analytic process provide opportunities for observations that test the probative value of the data. The probative value of clinical data is clinically testable.

Psychoanalysis is an inductively testable body of knowledge. The psychoanalytic clinical method, correctly and completely applied, provides us with crucial observations which can be used inductively to falsify and verify psychoanalytic hypotheses. If there is a lack, it is the lack of a will among analysts to use these resources scientifically.

SUMMARY

It is argued that clinical observations can be used to test psychoanalytic theories. Psychoanalysis cannot use controlled experiments, but it can use the standard canons of inductive reasoning to test the reliability of conflicting theories. Conflicting hypotheses concerning narcissism and object relations are analyzed to identify crucial observations that can be used for testing. If these experiments in theory testing are reliable, they show that psychoanalysis is not merely a hermeneutic discipline but has legitimate claims to being a natural science.

REFERENCES

Arlow, J. (1959). Psychoanalysis as scientific method. In S. Hook (Ed.), *Psychoanalysis, Scientific Method and Philosophy* (pp. 201–211). New York: Grove Press.

Bowlby, J. (1973). *Attachment and Loss*. Vol. 2: *Separation, Anxiety and Anger*. New York: Basic Books.

Brenner, C. (1970). Psychoanalysis, philosophy or science. In C. Hanly & M. Lazerowitz (Eds.), *Psychoanalysis and Philosophy* (pp. 33–45). New York: International Universities Press.

—— (1982). *The Mind in Conflict*. New York: International Universities Press.

Freud, S. (1894). Psychotherapy of hysteria. SE 2:253–305.

—— (1916–1917). *Introductory Lectures on Psycho-Analysis*. SE 15–16.

—— (1923). Remarks on the theory and practice of dream-interpretation. SE 19:109–121.

—— (1927). The future of an illusion. SE 21:4–56.

Glassman, M. (1988). Kernberg and Kohut: A list of competing psychoanalytic models of narcissism. *Journal of the American Psychoanalytic Association* 36:597–625.

Goldberg, A., ed. (1988). *Learning from Kohut*. Vol. 4: *Progress in Self Psychology*. Hillsdale, NJ: Analytic Press.

Grunbaum, A. (1984). *The Foundations of Psychoanalysis*. Berkeley: University of California Press.

Hanly, C. (1978). A critical consideration of Bowlby's ethological theory of anxiety. *Psychoanalytic Quarterly* 47:364–380.

—— (1982). Narcissism, defence and the positive transference. *International Journal of Psychoanalysis* 63:427–442.

Kohut, H. (1971). *The Analysis of the Self*. New York: International Universities Press.

—— (1977). *The Restoration of the Self*. New York: International Universities Press.

—— (1978). *The Search for the Self* (Ed. P. Ornstein). New York: International Universities Press.

————— (1984). *How Does Analysis Cure?* Chicago: University of Chicago Press.

Mackay, N. (1989). *Motivation and Explanation: An Essay on Freud's Philosophy of Science.* Madison, CT: International Universities Press.

Mill, J.S. (1843). *A System of Logic, Ratiocinative and Inductive.* Collected Works 7–8. Toronto: University of Toronto Press, 1973.

Nagel, E. (1959). Methodological issues in psychoanalytic theory. In S. Hook (Ed.), *Psychoanalysis, Scientific Method and Philosophy* (pp. 38–56). New York: Grove Press.

Porder, M. (1987). Projective identification: An alternative hypothesis. *Psychoanalytic Quarterly* 54:431–451.

Skyrms, B. (1986). *Choice and Chance.* Belmont, CA: Wadsworth.

Von Wright, G.H. (1957). *The Logical Problem of Induction.* Oxford: Blackwell.

CHAPTER 3

Clinical Advantages and Disadvantages of Multiple Models*

This paper was written during my tenure as Erik H. Erikson Scholar at the Austen Riggs Center in Stockbridge, MA. I am indebted to the Center for the opportunity and to its staff for their collegiality.

I shall argue that multiple models, in Pine's (1990) sense, are essential to clinical psychoanalysis but that the classical model provides the basis for their integration. It is not just that the classical model provides the conceptual tools necessary for integrating the observational findings and technical recommendations of object relations theory and self psychology. If true, that would be theoretically and logically interesting, but not clinically important in itself. The classical model provides an approach to the understanding of the interconnections among drives, ego, object relations, and narcissism. Herein lies its clinical usefulness and its peculiar strength as a guide to the understanding of psychopathology.

The classical model, let it be clear, does not place a greater weight on drives than on object relations as aetiological factors in neuroses. Freud no more abandoned the pathogenic importance of object relations than he

* Originally published in *The International Review of Psycho-Analysis* 14 no. 2 (1994):164–184.

abandoned the pathogenic influence of sexual seduction in childhood. You will recall what Freud (1916–1917) had to say on this subject:

Are neuroses *exogenous* or *endogenous* illnesses? Are they the inevitable result of a particular constitution or the product of certain detrimental (traumatic) experiences in life? More particularly, are they brought about by fixation of the libido (and the other features of the sexual constitution) or by the pressure of frustration? This dilemma seems to me no more sensible on the whole than another that I might put to you: does a baby come about through being begotten by the father or conceived by the mother? (p. 346; see also Freud, 1906, p. 279; 1937, p. 220)

The classical model envisages a continuum from neuroses that are primarily constitutionally (drive) determined to those that are primarily determined by calamities with objects. This hypothesis implies a clinical recommendation: Always help patients explore both what they did and wanted to do, and what they suffered at the hands of others.

Let us consider a clinical example, that of phobias. In what follows, I draw upon and supplement clinical material from a detailed examination of Bowlby's object-relational theory of phobias, which includes a more comprehensive analysis of the theoretical issues (Hanly, 1978). Bowlby (1969–1973), as an object relations theorist, postulates an attachment to objects that is independent of and prior to libidinal drives. Attachment to the mother provides a homeostatic regulation of anxiety in the face of naturally occurring anxiety-arousing stimuli. Pathogenic anxiety occurs as a result of the unavailability of the attachment figure, and not, as Freud (1905) claimed, because of unconscious sexual wishes that can also cause pathogenic anxiety. In Freud's view, pathogenic anxiety can be object-relational or instinctual (constitutional) but is most frequently both, whereas Bowlby proposes that pathogenic anxiety is always primarily object-relational.

Ms. J, a librarian in her mid-twenties, developed an intense fear of dark places at a certain point in her analysis. One such place was the lower floors of the library stacks, which were poorly illuminated; another was a dark lane in which she parked her car behind the apartment where she lived with her boyfriend, Stewart. The fear attacks occurred when she found herself alone in these places and heard footsteps or other noises. She was worried that the anxiety would become so severe that she would be unable to go to work. Here we find three of Bowlby's natural clues to danger: being alone, being in the dark, and hearing noises.

Ms. J also had fears of abandonment. She badly wanted a proposal of marriage from Stewart, but he was refusing to make one. She also asked him to demand that the landlord install a light at the back of the apartment to illuminate the parking area; he refused on the grounds that the landlord might increase the rent. He also failed to keep the car in good running order or to make repairs about the apartment. Ms. J often gave voice to her sense of neglect.

The evidence suggests that what required interpretation was the patient's masochistic involvement in a relationship in which her need for a suitable attachment object would be frustrated, thus exposing her to pathogenic levels of anxiety. The solution to her problem would be to find an adequate attachment object. Since Ms. J had a long history of highly unsuitable sexual object choices, one could see this history and her current circumstances as a repetition of an original failed internalized maternal or paternal object relation. Interpretations based on these perceptions had already been made and had been useful.

Freud's theory of anxiety which, like Bowlby's, acknowledges the centrality of anaclitic ties in the lives of children, shows how essential this line of interpretation can be. Freud (1926, pp. 1136–1138) clearly takes into account both the anxiety caused by "a growing tension due to need" and the anxiety caused by being separated from the mother who has satisfied these needs, as well as—and this addition is important—the connection between the two. The object relations model would invite us to close the book on this chapter of the analysis at this point. But if we did, we would miss an essential part of the chapter and much of the rest of the book as well.

The content of Ms. J's fear was of being attacked by a sadistic man— perhaps sexually attacked, but it was not clear. But Ms. J's associations to her image of the sadistic attacker did shed some light on the nature of the assault and its perpetrator. To this image, she associated her own version of a movie, in which a psychiatrist treating a young female patient turned out to be a madman who was planning violent surgery on her to gain possession of her brain. Further associations made it clear to Ms. J that she had cast her analyst in the role of her feared assailant.

A second symptom had developed along with the phobic symptom. Ms. J had long enjoyed eating meat. To her consternation, she now found the thought of eating meat disgusting. Her boyfriend was an intellectually gifted law student whom Ms. J admired and envied: he could spend evenings watching basketball on television until just prior to major examinations, when a couple of evenings of study enabled him to achieve excellent results, and she had often marveled at this capacity of his. Even before she knew Stewart, Ms. J had complained of having a congenitally defective brain, although in reality she was an intellectually gifted person. But there was another important facet to Ms. J's feelings. She also admired the amenable ways in which her boyfriend used his intellectual talents. He was tolerant of the shortcomings of others and fended off aggression from others in an easygoing way, if perhaps with some excess of passivity. Although Ms. J was uneasy about this streak of passivity, she found that her own sadistic tendencies to seek out opportunities to cleverly ridicule others, and to mercilessly assault with her cutting wit and tongue anyone who crossed her, reflected back to her unfavorably in Stewart's amiable character. And although Ms. J's complaints about her lover's neglect had recently intensified, there were also other ways in which she valued him.

The transference provided a focus for the conjunction of the phobia and the inhibition. Just before the emergence of the phobia, Ms. J had talked of wanting a holiday in Europe, which she felt her analyst should prescribe as a necessary break from her exhausting treatment. She wished to finance the holiday by not having to pay fees during her absence. Subsequently, in association to the sadistic psychiatrist fantasy as it emerged in the analysis, Ms. J rather teasingly announced that she had learned that I had a nickname among my academic colleagues—Chuck—and that she had been using it to refer to me in her own mind for some time. She then toyed with the name. Her playful repetitions hinted at various things, but predominantly ridicule, before they shifted through appreciation to disgust as she said, "Chuck, chuck steak, beef, hamburger, ground up," and then laughed, "That's something to be eaten." I broke the silence that ensued by saying, "You have been having trouble eating meat lately, which you used to enjoy. And you have become afraid that a maniac psychiatrist covets your brain so much that he wants to attack you to get it." As the process unfolded, opportunities for other interpretations presented themselves. "What if I am the maniac psychiatrist?" "Do you suppose that you are angry at me for frustrating your wish to have me care for you and not be neglectful by helping you have a vacation?" "I think you wanted a vacation because you have been working hard, but also you wanted a break from your analysis. Something is coming up in your love for Stewart that is frightening you—your envy of his brain." "Your guilt about your wish to devour and get for yourself something belonging to Stewart made you afraid that a man—that I— coveted your brain so much that I wanted to rip it from you." "In the fantasy, you are the one with the coveted brain, so that made you feel better, but you became afraid in the dark, unable to eat meat, and angry and accusing toward Stewart, when you actually love him despite his sometimes being somewhat neglectful." As these and further interpretations were made in the analytic work, the phobia and the eating inhibition disappeared. My interpretations did not explicitly refer to penis envy, although I left the door open to this interpretation at a later time by substituting for "Stewart's brain," or "my brain" in some of my interpretations, "something belonging to." I left it to the patient's neurosis to decide, when she was ready, what the brain symbolized. That it was symbolic was clear from the disparity between the evident worth of her own brain and her estimation of it.

The classical model integrates object-relational and drive considerations. In this integration is to be found its utility. An analyst following an object relations model, premised on an independence of drive and object-relational factors, could have been led into a countertransferential exaggerated sympathy for Ms. J's feelings of abandonment. These feelings had a certain legitimacy, but to consider them the whole story of this important phase of the analysis would have seriously interfered with the identification and interpretation of their defensiveness against penis envy and could have led the analyst to make interpretations that would reinforce the defenses.

It would be a mistake to either exaggerate or underestimate the consequence of a failure to interpret drives and the unconscious fantasies they produce. Ms. J was an intelligent young woman who was genuinely engaged in the struggle to overcome severe neurotic conflicts, and any neurosis has a life of its own, and given half a chance, will find a way to assert itself sufficiently to educate the reluctant analyst in its ways and means. Ms. J would not have left Stewart, whom she genuinely loved and eventually married, but no matter what interpretations of her attachment needs had been made, the failure to interpret the drive conflicts at work would have resulted in a missed opportunity. It would have deepened the patient's feelings of guilt about her envy, it would have intensified her anxiety, and worst of all, it would have encouraged her aggressive narcissistic belief in her ability to manipulate men (in this case her analyst), which would have left her injured self-esteem unrepaired (to be discussed later). In this respect, multiple models are no better than partial theories based on *pars pro toto* thinking, since having broken the organic unity of the classical model, they can only juxtapose theories, which then have at best a mechanical unity.

A further comment on Ms. J will serve as a transition to my next topic, narcissism. If Ms. J envied her lover's brain, it was because she devalued her own. She was a very gifted person whose work and wit were appreciated by friends and associates, but she did not have a just sense of her own worth. She covered over disparaging feelings about herself with a technicolor display of cleverness that could be derogating of others but that was often engaging, charming, and funny. Ms. J found it painfully difficult to tolerate sharing a friend with anything, let alone anyone, else. She had become depressed and angry toward an earlier boyfriend who had dared to spend time tinkering with his prized sports car on a weekend excursion. She loved being loved. The narcissism of children, which adults often find charming, she found repugnant: children demand things and do not have anything to offer.

These feelings of inadequacy had an origin in her relations with her father, at whose hands she had received a severe blow to her self-esteem. Throughout her childhood her adoring father had been her playmate and knight errant. She had been an only child. She had been utterly unprepared when she went to school for sharing the interest of the teacher with many new and utterly strange siblings. She had had playmates, but they had come to *her* well-supplied backyard and recreation room where *she* ruled. When, on the first day of school, another little girl had injured herself and was being comforted on the teacher's knee, Ms. J rushed up and tried to push her off and claim the injured child's place for herself. When the father received the first report from the teacher of a series of such incidents, he became enraged at her, denounced her, accused her of being spoiled, and ordered her to behave like the other children. At school she conformed as best she could. She gave up demanding the teacher's attention in the old way. She substituted for it an exhibitionistic, clever naughtiness that made her the leader of any rebellious forces in the classroom and kept the teacher's attention as captive as possible by means of any behavior that would not lead to punishment. At home, she withdrew from her father into an alliance with her mother. Together they forged an attitude of superiority toward the father that enabled the child to deny the terrible damage to her self-esteem but not to repair it. The mother saw herself as a cultivated woman—a university graduate who kept up her interests in literature, theater, and the arts. The father was a salesman whose career had never managed to take off, a man who liked to pretend that his Chevrolet was a Corvette. He came, progressively, to be regarded by his daughter as an overweight, vulgar, stupid boor. She could get things from him when she wanted to, but she did not have to take him seriously. As an adult, she liked to manipulate men, to play with them sexually in polymorphously perverse ways, to be cuddled, pampered, and adored by them. But her choice of men was still governed by a wish to humiliate her father as she had once felt humiliated by him. Her father was, in her opinion, a redneck fundamentalist "racist." One of the symptoms that caused her to seek psychoanalysis was recurrent hysterical pregnancies, the analysis of which revealed the fantasy that she was pregnant with a black baby out of wedlock. The analysis helped her to discover, in addition to her angry, guilty vengefulness, her debilitating anxiety, her failure to find reliable adult sexual pleasures, and her forlorn sadness and emptiness.

In this there is evidence of the narcissistic trauma Ms. J suffered at the hands of her father. He had played with her, had entered into her childhood magical world to the extent of submitting gladly to the laws of the world of the dollhouse he had made for her, in which she had ruled supreme. He had not helped her through the stage-appropriate phases of omnipotence toward a greater acceptance of reality articulated by Ferenczi (1913). Her father had been too blinded by his own narcissistic overvaluation of her. She had shattered this illusion and had precipitated a narcissistic rage in him by causing him to be ashamed of her. One might speculate that had he loved her more as a child and less as an instrument of his own narcissism, he would not only have become less disappointed in her but may have seen better what the world would expect of her and been better able to prepare her for it.

The classical model places no obstacle in the way of considering the narcissistic relation with the father and its rupture as a pathogenic childhood catastrophe. Its characterological derivatives are evident. But neither does it trace the patient's mute feelings of emptiness, forlornness, and sadness to this experience and its subsequent repetitions alone; nor does it have to trace her feelings of envy and inadequacy (castration anxiety) to a fragmented oedipal self caused by the empathic inadequacy of her father as a self-object for her (Kohut, 1984, pp. 14–16). The classical model asks rather that through the tactful interpretation of resistances and defenses in a reliable relationship of acceptance, the inner dynamic of the neurosis and its genetic roots be permitted to evolve.

Her father's narcissistic outrage at her social immaturity at school combined with Ms. J's rage at the insult it inflicted on her still-intact infantile grandiosity and narcissistic neediness, was peculiarly malignant because it destroyed any ability he might otherwise have had to help her with her difficulty. His attitude motivated in the child a reaction formation against any wish to seek help from him. Moreover, she could no longer allow him to be an oedipal object for the sexual feelings that could have facilitated her separation from her mother and could have stimulated her social maturation. Here we reach a crucial point in the clinical consideration of the multiple causalities at work, and hence of the model or models required for their comprehension, interpretation, and explanation.

Although Kohut (1984) made an ingenious attempt to "save the appearances" and incorporate the Oedipus complex into his theory, his self psychology erroneously derogates incest wishes and ambivalence by treating them as breakdown products of a disintegrated self caused by the failure of parents to react with "a glow of empathic joy and pride" to the oedipal child's expanding capacity for affection and assertiveness (p. 14). Incest wishes and castration anxiety in the boy and fear of the mother in the girl are created when affection and assertiveness are degraded into "lust" and "hostility" by parental failure to receive the originally innocent oedipal affects joyously. Marx said of Hegel's philosophy of history that Hegel had history marching on its head. Marx claimed to have put it back on its feet by replacing Hegel's preoccupation with "the march of Absolute Spirit through time" with his own study of the ownership of the means of producing the goods and services needed for survival. The reverse has happened with psychoanalysis: Freud had human nature walking on its feet, and Kohut has tried to make it walk on its head. Kohut has the Oedipus complex beginning with an expansion of affection and assertiveness, that is, with aim-inhibited libido and aggression, which may degrade into incest wishes and hostility as a result of a lack of parental appreciation. This hypothesis turns upside down the classical view.

Here we come upon a logical limit to the clinical use of multiple models. Some of the available models are logically inconsistent with others. Specifically, the drive hypotheses of the classical model are logically denied, perhaps also psychologically denied, by self psychology, by object relations theory as stated by Fairbairn (1941, 1952) and Guntrip (1968), by analytic psychology, and by existential and phenomenological psychology (Hanly, 1979, 1985). If the use of multiple models by one analyst is to work, it cannot be on the basis of an eclecticism that arbitrarily pastes together logically inconsistent ideas. The clinician who escapes from the battles of the schools in psychoanalysis into an eclecticism guided by the clinical maxim that one should use whatever theory fits the patient, has only adopted without knowing it the improbable theory that there are as many human species as there are theories of neurosis (Hanly, 1983).

Pine's (1990) multiple-model view does not contain this error. Instead it rejects those elements of object relations theory and self psychology that are inconsistent with the classical drive theory. To put it somewhat differently, Pine's multiple-model view is not a form of eclecticism, but an integration based on the requirement of logical consistency, which, is after all one of the logical criteria of the reality principle. But now a question occurs. Is there a way to get beyond the necessary but limited criteria of coherence to a theory that dynamically interconnects the causalities identified by the multiple models? My argument is that there is such a way. It is offered by the classical model.

It is perfectly possible to accept, as the classical model does, that the relations parents have with their child can exert a powerful influence on the outcome of the child's Oedipus complex without asserting with self psychology that the pathogenic potential of the Oedipus complex derives only from bad parenting at one stage or another. The meeting of the drives with the object, both the fantasy object and the real object, along with the history of preoedipal conflicts, the state of psychic structure, and ego endowment will determine the complications of the plot and the outcome of the conflict in each new oedipal drama.

The narcissistic insult Ms. J received from her father drove her into a negative oedipal alliance with her mother. But this alliance retained its usual defensive character as a means of separating the parents and warding off the mother's anger. The difference caused by the narcissistic insult was that the alliance also became an instrument of the child's rage against her father. Fortunately, there was another element beneath the narcissistic rage—a rage which by itself could have omnipotently and magically annihilated the father by withdrawal of affect (Sharpe, 1930; Hanly, 1982), and could have dangerously ruptured the object tie with him that was so crucial to her further development. This other element, which was never withdrawn from him, and which he had to suffer, no doubt deservedly for many years, was her oedipal rage at being jilted. Her sexual love-wishes remained covertly invested in him; this state of affairs was evident in her hysterical pregnancies in which she "bore" babies that would simultaneously punish her father by being illegitimate and black, and punish her by being defective. Similarly, her feelings of forlornness, emptiness, and sadness, which had a narcissistic determinant, also expressed her mute awareness, in her inner moods, of the impasse in her sexual life that threatened the possibility of her ever having a good pregnancy with a good man.

Because of the fundamental place in development—and hence in psychopathology—that the classical theory assigns to the Oedipus complex, adherence to it as a clinical model may place the analyst at risk of always "finding" it and interpreting it. Surely a multiple-model approach has the advantage of the greater balance it offers to the clinician at work in the consideration of logically consistent possible interpretations. Such a balance is indispensable to interpretation, whether it be of a dream, a poem, a novel, a philosophical idea, or a historical event. It is the capacity to wait patiently, to expose oneself to the indications of the text or the associations, to hold possible interpretations in suspension until the integrating details of the object make the selection. Does not, then, a multiple-model approach provide a better basis for the willing suspension of belief about how things should be, and thus enhance the clinician's ability to understand how things are (Hanly, 1990)?

With this question we come upon the epistemological core of the problem. Does not the place assigned by the classical model oblige the analyst who employs the model to "find" the Oedipus complex in the associations of the patient and to treat its resolution as the bedrock of the therapeutic work? Despite the integrative advantages of the classical model, does this disadvantage not outweigh them? Is not a multiple-model approach such as Pine's (1990), which leaves the variables disconnected in "four psychologies," to be preferred? Does it not give credence to the self psychologist's criticism of the classical model for an empathic cognitive failure in its clinical stance? Is the classical analyst impervious to phenomena that would prove the self psychologist's claim that castration anxiety does not occur "as a feature of the oedipal phase of the healthy child of healthy parents" (Kohut, 1984, p. 14)?

These doubts may well apply to clinicians who have had a "failed" training analysis, who have rote-learned the classical theory, who have substituted an identification with their Freudian analysts for a working-through of their own unconscious conflicts, and who have consequently never fully developed the capacity for objectivity and independence of thought and observation. The same is true of clinicians who have in this way become adherents of any school of thought in psychoanalysis. And it remains true of clinicians who have tried to resolve this dilemma by jumping from one school to another. Their adherence to one or several models continues to be based on substituting an identification with their training analyst for the work involved in viewing the world objectively on their own.

This substitution of identification for investigation is not a requirement of the classical model. It results from a failure to grasp and use its theoretical and technical resources correctly. The description of the multiple-model approach as having a special advantage in clinical work by holding as many interpretations as possible, is only a different way of stating in the language of scholarship what Freud (1912, 1923) called "evenly suspended attention." Freud (1912) characterized its epistemic value as follows:

As soon as anyone deliberately concentrates his attention to a certain degree, he begins to select from the material before him; one point will be fixed in his mind with particular clearness and some other will be correspondingly disregarded, and in making this selection he will be following his expectations or inclinations. This, however, is precisely what must not be done. In making the selection, if he follows his expectations, he is in danger of never finding anything but what he already knows; and if he follows his inclinations, he will certainly falsify what he may perceive. (p. 112)

This familiar technical recommendation is worth repeating because it contains a radical methodological implication. A correctly conducted analysis is always one that can falsify the model in terms of which it is being conducted. "Evenly suspended attention" implies an even-handed treatment of the interpretive possibilities of available models until the no less even-handed observations of the associations and the transference of the analysand have determined the choice. In this respect, the technique of the classical model involves a multiple-model approach. The technical recommendations of classical analysis are very different from those of self psychology, which demands of the analyst a commitment to self psychology as a theory as the only means of testing its applicability (Goldberg, 1988).

The primacy of technique in the classical model can be illustrated by some further material from the analysis of Ms. J. During the first part of her analysis, well before the phobic transference symptom, Ms. J reported a dream in which she was reclining on a couch in a handsomely appointed room. A man was seated before her engaged in an animated conversation. Then they were interrupted. A woman with a noisy vacuum cleaner began to clean the room, but the intruder was coldly dismissed by the man. Ms. J's first associations to the dream were to the analytic situation (lying on a couch) in an opulent room (the opposite of my somewhat sparse academic office, which she had often ridiculed) talking to a man whom she could see (what she was denied, and at first often demanded). It was not a great step to identify the man in the dream as the analyst. The cleaning woman called forth speculative thoughts about my wife. Thus, given that the dream, as a whole, features the dreamer in the position of the little princess, the object of the male analyst's, therefore father's, adoring attention, preferred by him to the derogated cleaning woman, or mother, a Freudian analyst would be expected to pursue the trial of an oedipal dream and proceed to so interpret. But this would be to forget the technical rule of evenly suspended attention, that the meaning of a dream is not to be found in its manifest, but in its latent content, which can only be reached by associations, and that this particular well-read and intelligent patient already had developed a defense within the transference of telling witty and clever vignettes to enthrall the analyst, as a substitute for associating freely. Could the manifest content be a clever oedipal vignette to put the Freudian analyst off the track? As the associations proceeded, Ms. J eventually came to connect her reclining on the couch to a painting by Goya which presented a beautiful naked woman gazing at herself in a mirror held by a female servant. At this point I said to her, "You want all of my adoring attention." The interpretation led to memories of her alliance with her mother against the outcast, derogated "castrated" father. The manifest dream had disguised the underlying narcissistic wish by reversing sexual identities, that is, by casting the male figure as the mother and the cleaning woman as the analyst-father. The dream was instigated by an anal-narcissistic wish rather than an oedipal one (Hanly, 1982; Shengold, 1988).

Let us pause in the study of Ms. J to consider a parallel instance of pseudo-oedipal material—a transference fantasy—of a patient, Mrs. M, whose analysis has been much more extensively elaborated elsewhere (Hanly, 1982). Mrs. M had had a series of dreams in which she found herself in such situations as standing alone in front of a large house in the country with a mountain behind her, or on the seashore with a high promontory overlooking the beach. The affect in the dream was pleasurable, although her associations distressed her because they recurrently ended in thoughts of having to leave her husband and live alone. One could surmise that these were transference dreams; but what conflicted wish instigated the dreams, and from what developmental phase? Interpretations to the effect that the dream seemed to be arousing guilty feelings of leaving her husband, that she did not seem to be alone in the dream, and that the house, the mountain, and the promontory had some meaning not yet apparent to her led to the unfolding of a transference fantasy. I saw her in an office at the university, but my home address was on my bills. She had contrived a Sunday drive with her husband so that he would drive her past my house. In the fantasy I was an old man, living alone in the house. She imagined visiting me, bringing wood for the fire (she had noticed the chimneys of the house), and food. She imagined sitting quietly for hours before a fireplace with her head resting against my knees without speaking, basking in the warmth of the fire and my undivided, caring attention. The dreams had occurred during a period of long analytic silences. It was this unconscious fantasy that had instigated the dreams and had informed the transference silences. Evidently, the dream derived from a narcissistic wish for mirroring from an idealized object. Although the subsequent evolution of Mrs. M's analysis made it clear that a sexual conflict was latent in the fantasy, it would have been inappropriate at the time of its emergence to interpret to her that her image of me as a helpless old man who needed her to look after him defended against sexual wishes. The mutative interpretations were that she needed reassurances that her gifts could be good, that her father had taken pride in her despite the years of silence. (The parents had divorced when Mrs. M was eleven, and, although she knew where the father was, she had seen him only once in his office very briefly at her own instigation when she was eighteen. She had written to him and had invited him to graduations and to her wedding, but he never replied.)

Mrs. M told of a photo of herself being held by her mother, who was standing beside her father on the day of her baptism. Her father appeared to be looking down at her, although his officer's cap cast a shadow over his eyes. She said that she saw herself as a scrawny, ugly baby dressed up in baptismal finery. To my interpretation, "You want so badly to believe that your father was gazing proudly down on you," Mrs. M sat up on the couch with her head tucked against her knees and wept ruefully. The mourning that resulted was a crucial phase of Mrs. M's analysis.

One can be an adherent of the classical model and also make use of clinical knowledge derived from other models. Originality in the description of narcissistic and object-relational trauma and in the articulation of their mutative interpretation can be acknowledged and put to work without having to accept the metapsychological innovations that some psychoanalysts wish to derive from them. The classical concepts of narcissism and object relations do not prohibit the interpretation of trauma, and its technical precepts not only license but require such interpretations.

I employ the classical model clinically because of what happened next in Mrs. M's analysis, which I have found again and again not to be in the least unrepresentative of the evolution of analyses in which narcissistic conflicts have played a significant role. The period of mourning that was ushered in by these developments gave way to impressive oedipal conflicts in Mrs. M, the analysis of which led to a sexual flowering that brought to an end many years of hysterical frigidity that had been her major presenting symptom. This finding points to interconnections among ego functions, object and narcissistic libido, and object relations such that only a model that integrates them by specifying their causal links and the complex defensive connections that may occur among them can best serve as a guide for clinical work.

Ms. J's pseudo-oedipal dream led her from the memories of her alliance with her mother against her father to the narcissistic trauma that she suffered at his hands, and hence to her rage, shame, and grief, against which her negative Oedipus complex had been enlisted as a defense. But the trauma was not by any means purely narcissistic, as the course of her analysis revealed. Her shyly burgeoning sexual feeling for her father caused his anger to be experienced as an insult to her love as well. No less significant were preoedipal fixations to anal sadism in the derogation of the father (as in the dream) and to oral sadism in the wished-for phallic incorporation (as in the phobia and the eating inhibition). Each illustrates the intrinsically sexual and object relational aspects of Ms. J's neurosis. They were interconnected by her libidinal development and the effects of preoedipal trauma on it. These preoedipal traumata, inflicted by her mother, played their part in the intensity of her early relation to her father insofar as they had contributed to a precocious turning away from the mother—yet another aspect of the patient's forlornness and sadness. We find the results of these traumata brought together in the trends at work in the child's latency relationship with her mother. This relation was defensive against her repressed and arrested sexual feelings for her father. It had a negative oedipal organization. It was narcissistic. In self-psychological terms, the mother had become an idealized, mirroring self object. Also, the girl identified with the mother; the mother became her ego ideal. This ego ideal was also prohibiting and punitive. It formed the major organizing identification of the child's conscience, enhanced no doubt by the memories of the oral and anal pain and privation the child had suffered at her mother's hands. It was a source of aim-inhibited sexual pleasure. The relationship involved a masochistic surrender.

This list is incomplete, and it inadequately details the causal interconnections among the factors that are listed. Nevertheless, it suggests that the interconnection of narcissistic and sexual libido, aggression, object relations, and ego strengths in the lives of people are such that only a theory that *recognizes and articulates* these interconnections can be adequate to its object. It is for this reason that the classical model remains the best guide for clinical work in psychoanalysis: it coherently integrates drive and object-relational considerations, while allowing for variable weightings and continuous clinical testing of the full range of the causalities that other models either reduce, omit, or disconnect.

Any multiple model that fails to achieve logical coherence has only disadvantages for clinical work. A multiple model that combines different explanatory models that are consistent with each other—and only insofar as they are consistent with each other—has two significant clinical advantages: it promotes an attitude in the clinician that is open to the full range of interpretive and explanatory possibilities of any given analytic situation; and it allows the choice of interpretation to be made by the associations and transference manifestations of the analysand. The disadvantage of a multiple model is that, while it acknowledges the integrity of the causalities at work in the individual life, it does not give a dynamic account of their interconnections and hence of their acknowledged integrity. Thus, it fails to provide the interpretive and explanatory possibilities needed to clinically articulate the continuing connections among the causalities postulated by the different models or psychologies of the multiple model. Because the classical theory has the clinical advantages of multiple models and avoids their disadvantages because of its greater unity, it remains, in my view, the best resource we have for clinical work.

In emphasizing the primacy of observational knowledge in psychoanalysis as the source and the test of theory, I am only following Freud's repeated dictum on this subject. But this emphasis does not diminish the importance of theory. It is from theory that one draws the explanatory ideas that one suspends in a state of epistemic possibility in even attention. Preliminary ideas are essential in the search for a correct understanding of the motivations at work in the patient. From the dilemma generated by the opposition between the methods of reasoning advocated by Bacon on the one hand and Descartes on the other, there is an escape. The search for significant observations needs to be guided by the best available preliminary ideas; otherwise, it will be only random. In this respect, Bacon exaggerated the primacy of observation. But these preliminary ideas are not innate to the mind; they arise out of experience. In this respect, Descartes exaggerated the primacy of preliminary ideas. The epistemology that guided Freud's work was based on this more sophisticated empiricist position (Hanly, 1990). It remains (or at least should remain) the basis of contemporary classical analysis both in clinical practice and in theorizing.

The integration of the classical theory is not merely methodological, but also conceptual and logical. Its theoretical unity is not merely an illusion generated by its familiarity. Nor are the integrative hypotheses of the classical theory so unspecific as to fit any observation and thus become unfalsifiable. Nagel's (1959) detailed formulation of this critique of classical theory has already been answered (Hanly, 1979). Popper's (1963) claim that Freud's theory fails to meet the test of falsifiability has been shown to be false by Grunbaum (1984).

The theoretical unity of the four-psychologies model, insofar as it can be said to have this property, depends on an implicit reliance on the classical theory both logically and conceptually. To the logical dependency I have already alluded: the model does not provide for an integration of self psychology and object relations theory with id psychology and ego psychology. All the premises of self psychology and object relations theory that are inconsistent with the classical model are rejected. Conceptually, the model employs Wälder's (1930) notion of multiple function to interconnect the four psychologies. But the idea of multiple function originates in and is most cogently defined in terms of the classical structural theory. There appears to be an implicit reliance on the classical model to conceptually integrate the four psychologies. Yet at the same time the four psychologies disintegrate the classical model by postulating one psychology of the id and another of the ego, both of which are abstractions torn from the unity in which they are held within the classical model.

I now conclude by briefly describing some aspects of the nature and efficacy of the way in which the classical model integrates the major variables of drives, narcissism, object relations, and ego as guiding hypotheses for clinical work. The structural model, as already noted, provides the theoretical basis for the principle of multiple function, and hence for a crucial aspect of the clinical hypothesis of psychic overdetermination. It is also the explanatory foundation of psychic conflict, compromise formation, and conflict resolution—all concepts that are essential guides to clinical work. As such, it provides both a historical and a dynamic account of the *interaction* of drives, object relations, ego functions, and narcissism. Thus, spontaneous (genetically programmed) drive development ushers in the oedipal phase that invests primary object relations with phallic heterosexual and aggressive wishes. These wishes excite the ego with the greatest promises of pleasure and the most threatening expectation of calamity. The sense of danger is partly caused by past and present real experiences of the parents, fantasies of them, and the degree of narcissistic phallic investment. The continuous interrelation of these factors in ego functioning needs to be continually taken into account clinically.

The superego, which functions as part of a major compromise formation as a consequence of the resolution of the oedipal conflict, is made possible by the capacity of the ego to substitute identifications for object relations. These identifications entail a composition of forces (motives) involving (1) historical experiences of and with the parents, in part reality-bound and in part fantasy-determined, and (2) idealizing (narcissistically invested) fantasies of them proportional to the threat investing the repressed memories and fantasies of them, fantasies that may open up a more reality-bound perception of the parents insofar as they actually possess the idealized qualities, and may disturb the perception of reality and arouse new anxieties

71

insofar as they do not possess them. Further, the feelings of self-mastery, autonomy, self-worth, and self-righteousness that compensate the ego for the loss of sensual excitation and pleasure are narcissistic ego states generated by the exercise of superego functions that cannot be comprehended apart from the drive demands against which they are reaction formations. Moreover, the healthy maturation of these narcissistic affects and the ego functions that give rise to them depends on the extent to which they only defer the gratification of these drive demands until they have themselves achieved genital maturity. An adequate clinical orientation is one that is simultaneously and continuously open to the varying balances in the play of these forces in the lives of patients. It is detrimental to clinical thinking to isolate them theoretically in four psychologies.

I have focused these concluding reflections concerning the explanatory integrity of classical psychoanalysis on the oedipal phase because of its intrinsic importance. But the same results would follow from a consideration of, for example, anality and orality and perversions, or the development of object relations, including narcissistic object relations, the idea of which was made explicit in "On narcissism: An introduction" (Freud, 1914). Pine's four-psychologies model breaks apart the historical and dynamic explanatory integrity of the classical model by postulating a drive psychology, an object relations psychology, an ego psychology, and a narcissistic psychology. These psychologies are historical and scientific artifacts of the four-psychologies model. Having isolated these psychologies, the model makes connections among them methodologically on the basis of the principle of multiple function (which presupposes the structural model) to avoid a facile eclecticism and the unfalsifiability that goes with it.

However, Pine does provide an empirical, as well as a theoretical, justification for his four-psychologies model in terms of two basic propositions: (1) the hypotheses of the four psychologies provide a complete enumeration of the psychic determinants of mental functioning, and (2) their relative dominance varies according to phases of development. It is this variance that justifies the separation of the four psychologies. But it is not possible to determine whether or not these basic principles of the four psychologies are inconsistent with the classical theory, since the details of the shifts in dominance from drives to narcissism, to ego, and to object relations in discrete developmental phases are not sufficiently spelled out. After all, the classical theory is also premised on the recognition of phase-specific variations in the relative weight, primacy, and character of these factors in the life history of an individual. If there are significant differences between the four-psychologies model and the classical theory—if, for example, the four-psychologies model predicts that narcissism or object relations is the dominant factor in a developmental phase for which the classical theory predicts that anal eroticism is primary—then the four-psychologies model will have a theoretical significance of its own, one that does not depend on an implicit reference to and reliance on the classical theory. If the four-psychologies model can generate no such empirically testable predictions that differentiate it from classical theory, either its use of the thesis of phase-specific variations in developmental causalities is merely rhetorical, or it covertly depends for its empirical relevance on classical theory.

These reflections give rise to a conclusion in the form of a question: Does the four-psychologies model enhance clinical psychoanalysis in any way that could not be better achieved by the further amendment, precision, and enrichment of classical theory?

REFERENCES

Bowlby, J. (1969–1973). *Attachment and Loss.* 2 vols. New York: Basic Books.

Fairbairn, W.R.D. (1941). A revised psychopathology of the psychoses and psychoneuroses. *International Journal of Psychoanalysis* 22:50–279.

———— (1952). *An Object-Relations Theory of Personality.* New York: Basic Books.

Ferenczi, S. (1913). Stages in the development of the sense of reality. In *First Contributions to Psycho-Analysis* (pp. 213–239). London: Hogarth Press, 1952.

Freud, S. (1905). Three essays on the theory of sexuality. SE 7:125–243.

———— (1906). My views on the part played by sexuality in the aetiology of the neuroses. SE 7:271–279.

———— (1912). Recommendations to physicians practising psycho-analysis. SE 12:111–120.

———— (1914). On narcissism: An introduction. SE 14:73–102.

———— (1916–1917). *Introductory Lectures on Psycho-Analysis.* SE 15–16.

———— (1923). Two encyclopaedia articles. SE 18:233–260.

———— (1926). Inhibitions, symptoms and anxiety. SE 20:78–172.

———— (1937). Analysis terminable and interminable. SE 23:209–254.

Goldberg, A. (1988). *A Fresh Look at Psychoanalysis.* Hillsdale, NJ: Analytic Press.

Grunbaum, A. (1984). *The Foundations of Psychoanalysis.* Berkeley: University of California Press.

Guntrip, H. (1968). *Schizoid Phenomena, Object Relations and the Self.* New York: International Universities Press.

Hanly, C. (1978). A critical consideration of Bowlby's ethological theory of anxiety. *Psychoanalytic Quarterly* 47:364–380.

———— (1979). *Existentialism and Psychoanalysis.* New York: International Universities Press.

—— (1982). Narcissism, defence and the positive transference. *International Journal of Psychoanalysis* 63:427–444.

—— (1983). A problem of theory testing. *International Review of Psycho-Analysis* 10:393–405. [Chapter 1 in this volume]

—— (1985). Logical and conceptual problems of existential psychiatry. *Journal of Nervous Mental Disease* 173:263–281. [Chapter 18 in this volume]

—— (1990). The concept of truth in psychoanalysis. *International Journal of Psychoanalysis* 71:375–383. [Chapter 10 in this volume]

Kohut, H. (1984). *The Restoration of the Self.* Chicago: University of Chicago Press.

Nagel, E. (1959). Methodological issues in psychoanalytic theory. In S. Hook (Ed.), *Psychoanalysis, Scientific Method and Philosophy* (pp. 38–56). New York: Grove Press, 1960.

Pine, F. (1990). *Drive, Ego, Object, and Self: A Synthesis for Clinical Work.* New York: Basic Books.

Popper, K.R. (1963). *Conjectures and Refutations.* London: Routledge & Kegan Paul.

Sharpe, E.F. (1930). Survey of defense-mechanisms in general character traits and in conduct. In *Collected Papers on Psycho-Analysis* (pp. 38–52). London: Hogarth Press, 1968.

Shengold, L. (1988). *Halo in the Sky.* New York: Guilford.

Wälder, R. (1930). The principle of multiple function. In S. Guttman (Ed.), *Psychoanalysis: Observation, Theory, Application* (pp. 68–83). New York: International Universities Press, 1976.

CHAPTER 4

On Facts and Ideas in Psychoanalysis*

This paper was presented at the 75th Anniversary Conference of the International Journal of Psychoanalysis *in São Paulo in April 1995.*

An important controversy has been developing in psychoanalysis. Although this controversy is essentially psychoanalytical, it has philosophical premises, for it concerns the question of an epistemology for psychoanalysis. I propose to clarify this controversy and certain of its implications, both philosophical and psychoanalytical, by constructing an analytic overview of the important series of conferences in each of the three IPA regions sponsored by the *International Journal of Psychoanalysis* to celebrate its seventy-fifth anniversary. The unifying theme of my analysis and commentary is the use of ideas in observation.

It might be thought that an enquiry into the nature of fact in psychoanalysis is an escape from the controversies about some of the basic facts of psychoanalysis that have dogged psychoanalysis. Is the Oedipus complex an inevitable development of the drives, the resolution of which stabilizes the foundations of mature psychic structure, or is it the avoidable result of empathic failures by parents? Is human aggression primarily

---

* Originally published in *The International Journal of Psychoanalysis* 76 (1995):901–908.

masochistic or primarily sadistic? Is human aggression a death instinct, and does it spontaneously bring about a paranoid-schizoid position in infants at the breast? It scarcely needs to be said that the answers to these questions have far-reaching consequences for psychoanalytic theory and technique. Have psychoanalysts, wearied by these chronic disputes about the first-order facts of psychoanalysis, retreated to second-order questions about the nature of fact and the relation of theory to fact in psychoanalysis? Perhaps, but it is also possible that an enquiry into these epistemological questions can facilitate a new and more decisive enquiry into the first-order facts. It can be useful to disengage from controversy and step back to a position from which one can survey the fundamental relations between theory and observation that must obtain in any school of thought in psychoanalysis.

It will be my thesis that, unfortunately, the philosophical second-order perspectives upon psychoanalytic knowledge are no less controversial than the first-order facts of psychoanalysis. There appears to be no reprieve from controversy in this direction either. Nevertheless, to undertake such an enquiry takes a certain amount of courage because the enquiry is located at the confluence of psychoanalysis and philosophy, and hence runs the risk of a flight into abstraction. But the contributors to these conferences have taken up the challenge and have largely avoided this risk by grounding their explorations of the nature of psychoanalytic knowledge in clinical psychoanalysis, that is, in psychoanalytic *praxis*. And it is always possible that psychoanalysis will itself have something to contribute to the resolution of this epistemological controversy, just as it has contributed to the free will–determinism debate and various other controversies in philosophy (Hanly, 1992).

However, it would be an equal and opposite error to adopt a naive view of the self-evidence of experience. The concept of "experience-near," which has become fashionable in psychoanalysis, is philosophically and psychoanalytically untenable when it is used, as it too often is, to claim self-evidence for ideas merely on the grounds that they are experience-near and because theoretical and inferential thinking are not required in order to reach them. Ptolemaic astronomy is much more experience-near than Copernican astronomy, and shall forever remain so, but it has turned out to be false. Ideas that are remote from experience may open up new ways of thinking that reveal unexpected aspects of reality. Euclidean geometry is experience-near and Reimannian geometry is not, yet Reimannian geometry enabled Einstein to provide physics with a much closer approximation to the behavior of matter in space than Euclidean geometry could.

We need ideas in order to take notice, to become aware, to observe, to comprehend. A patient's account of what is happening in his life may be very experience-near for him and for us, but it may be a poor approximation to the motives that are causing his difficulties. The idea of an erotized transference may make the analyst alert to motivational possibilities that are often experience-far from the patient and are evident to the analyst only from inferences based on subtle and oblique indications or on theoretical considerations. Grounding our thinking about psychoanalytic knowledge in clinical psychoanalysis does not require us to adopt a naive view of experience.

There was a dialogue running through these conferences, sometimes explicitly but more often implicitly, concerning an epistemology for psychoanalysis. From this dialogue, one can analyze the basic elements of two opposing epistemologies, each with its own internal coherence and relevance to the five topics of the conferences. These epistemologies have been subjected to much philosophical analysis and debate for centuries. They assume diverse detailed definitions and justifications in the thought of different philosophers. I shall refer to them as *critical idealism* and *critical realism*.

One's view of the conceptualization of clinical facts has a logical bearing on one's view of the nature of clinical facts. Turning first to critical idealism, if one holds that theoretical investments determine what can count as a fact, then clinical facts are the artifacts of clinical theories. If one believes that, in psychoanalysis, the patient's associations are invariably the outcome of an interaction between the analyst's countertransference and the patient's transference, then clinical facts are artifacts of that interaction, which creates their meaning. Interpretations are the analyst's contributions to the narrative of the patient's life emerging from the clinical process. The validation of an interpretation is reached when a consensus is reached between analysand and analyst. The factual foundation of a clinical report will consist of the theory-laden descriptions of the consensual situations that arise in the clinical process. The description of clinical fact takes the form of a narrative that tells the story of the patient's life from the vantage point of the interaction that took place between the analysand and the analyst in the course of the analysis. There may be several true psychoanalytic narratives of a person's life among which there is no factual or theoretical basis for a final choice.

I call this epistemological position critical idealism. In philosophy, an epistemology is idealistic if it postulates that the ground of knowledge is located in the mind. The epistemology that I have just outlined postulates that the meaning of clinical facts in psychoanalysis is grounded in the theoretical ideas to which the analyst adheres because clinical observations are unavoidably theory-saturated. Psychoanalysis has no access to theory-independent facts against which theory-bound interpretations can be tested. Epistemologically, conceptualization precedes observation. Analysts who propose idealism as an epistemology for psychoanalysis place themselves philosophically in the tradition of Plato, Descartes, Kant, Hegel, and in modern times Husserl, Merleau-Ponty, Sartre, Feyerabend, and the later Putnam.

I have added the important adjective "critical" because this epistemological view in psychoanalysis is based, in at least some writers, on a skepticism about the claims of psychoanalytic observation to objectivity. This skepticism is sometimes based on quite general philosophical propositions about the nature of knowledge as such, but more often it is based on the technical psychoanalytic view that the analyst's countertransference is ubiquitous and influences observation in ways that do not permit of correction. In either case, we can further characterize this epistemology as *subjectivist*.

Alternatively, from the point of view of critical realism, we may make the epistemological assumption that a clinical fact is a reality, a datum of experience that exists independently of how we perceive it or conceive of it. A clinical fact is intersubjective in the philosophical meaning of the term, that is, it is basically the same for any competent observer. (The philosophical use of the term "intersubjective" is consistent with usage in ordinary language, common sense, and science. In some current psychoanalytic theorizing, however, the term has precisely the opposite meaning; the psychoanalytic "intersubjectivists" deny that there are any intersubjective clinical facts. Psychoanalytic intersubjectivism is thus a form of epistemological idealism.) When one makes the assumption that there are intersubjective clinical facts, the task of knowledge in psychoanalysis is to cultivate methods of perception, thought, and interpretation that will make them adequate to the reality of the lives of our patients, while acknowledging that this goal may be very difficult or beyond our means to realize in a given set of circumstances. We are, as it were, under an epistemological obligation to "get out of ourselves" in order to form trial identifications with our patients, neither as we want or think them to be nor as they want us to think them to be, but, to the best of our ability, as they are. For critical realists, conceptualization must be guided by and based on the clinical facts. While conceptualization may precede observation psychologically and temporally, observation has epistemological priority over conceptualization. Observation is the touchstone of truth.

Interpretations need to approximate what has actually happened and is being repeated in the life of the patient. Interpretations should have a beneficial impact on the functioning of the patient. Interpretations should reveal: they should facilitate free associations from which the history of the patient in its material and psychic reality can be known through recovered memories or reconstructed by inference with reasonable probability.

In the view of the critical realist, the dreams, symptoms, and associations of the patient have a life of their own that is sufficiently independent of the analyst and his interpretations so that the associations of the patient can function as a test of the correctness of an interpretation. Of particular importance for validation are the associations and shifts in the transference that follow upon interpretations. For these reasons, psychoanalytic case histories have, in principle, the methodological and epistemological resources to test psychoanalytic theories, techniques, and causal explanations.

Psychoanalysts who adopt a critical realist epistemology locate themselves in the tradition of Aristotle, Epicurus, Hobbes, Locke, Mill, Ryle, Feigl, and Grünbaum in philosophy. It is also the epistemology of natural science and of Freud. For critical realism, the ground of knowledge is in the object, and for this reason it can be said to be *objectivist*.

I have tried to show that critical idealism and critical realism are coherent epistemologies in psychoanalysis that have equivalent explanatory power insofar as they each provide a consistent account of the five issues raised by these celebratory conferences. These epistemologies are no less controversial in philosophy than in psychoanalysis; consequently, one cannot settle a dispute in the epistemology of psychoanalysis by an appeal to philosophy. The controversy between idealism and realism in psychoanalysis will no doubt continue. The challenge for psychoanalysts is to formulate a genuinely psychoanalytic epistemology for psychoanalysis, and in so doing to explore what psychoanalysis can contribute to the clarification of the nature of human self-knowledge and hence to the central Socratic question of philosophy.

In the pursuit of answers to this question, it is important to avoid simplistic dichotomies and affinities. It would be easy, for example, to identify philosophical hermeneutics with critical idealism and natural science with critical realism. But the crucial distinction between interpretive human sciences and causally explanatory natural sciences in Habermas can be recognized within a realist epistemology no less than within an idealist epistemology, although the meaning of the distinction will be very different in each. Generally, it would be easy, though erroneous, to think of critical idealism as being more congenial to a humanistic point of view in psychoanalysis, while thinking of critical realism as tying psychoanalysis, restrictively, to a natural science perspective.

I have employed the term "critical realism," rather than the more common "scientific realism," in order to do justice to the psychoanalytic critique of a naive experience of self and others, but also to include humanistic thought and imagination within realism, where, in my view, they genuinely belong. Moreover, we should be willing to consider at least the possibility of an epistemology for psychoanalysis that integrates subjectivity and objectivity. Is the philosophical differentiation of epistemology into these two schools of thought itself unnecessarily dichotomizing? Is there a way to integrate the contributions of subjectivity and objectivity to psychoanalytic knowledge? Perhaps Nosek (personal communication) was pointing in this direction when he advanced the concept of "fantastic realism," which we might take as the equivalent in epistemology of magic realism in art.

One thing is clear: these epistemological questions cannot be settled by the facile claim, made by some contributors to these discussions, that we live in a post-positivist age. This claim is made for the purpose of shoring up an idealist critique of epistemological realism (Spence, 1994; A. Ornstein &

P. Ornstein, 1994; A.-M. Sandler & J. Sandler, 1994). Etchegoyen (1994), Israel (1994), and Steiner (Britton & Steiner, 1994) set out positions that are grounded in critical realism and hence are implicitly opposed to the idea that psychoanalysis must be brought into conformity with the allegedly dominant post-positivist trend in modern thought.

But the idea of a "post-positivist era" is ambiguous and misleading. If what is meant by post-positivism is that the grand system of Comte, the verification theory of meaning, and the epistemology of logical positivism (the Vienna Circle), in particular the sense datum theory (Ayer, 1953), are largely of only historical interest to philosophers, then it is true that philosophy at least is in a post-positivist era. However, although the verification theory is not an adequate theory of meaning as such (Hanly, 1970), it is still considered a useful criterion for meaningful scientific hypotheses, including psychoanalytic hypotheses. It is an instance of positivism in contemporary philosophy. Moreover, the fundamental tenet of Comte, of Mill, of the Vienna Circle, and of Freud that we cannot expect to get by other means the knowledge that we cannot gain from science and the humanities, is more widely accepted today by philosophers, writers, and intellectuals than it was in the late nineteenth century.

If what is meant by a "post-positivist era" is that the novels of Turgenev, Balzac, and George Eliot are no longer of interest, that Mill's logic no longer formulates the logic of inductive reasoning in science and everyday thought, or that the epistemological and ontological premises of Freud's work, which are shared by natural science, have now been relegated to the history of ideas, the assertion that ours is a post-positivist era is simply false. Moreover, even if it could be shown that positivism plays no part in contemporary culture, it does not follow that psychoanalysis should give up its search for objective knowledge. For several decades some European countries were in a post-democratic era, but it would not follow from this state of affairs that democratic rights and institutions would not have made for a better life for the citizens of those countries. Even if x is so, it does not follow either that x must be so or that x should be so. Facile, highly dubious generalizations are no substitute for rational analysis and argument.

The post-positivist thesis is not infrequently supported by the argument that quantum physics has proven that the observer always influences the observed and that therefore quantum mechanics justifies the complacent view that the analyst's subjectivity cannot be subtracted from the patient's associations. But in order to make the argument sound, it is necessary to demonstrate the factual basis of the implied analogy between the conditions of observation of subatomic particles in physics and the conditions of observation in clinical psychoanalysis. Quantum mechanical laws apply to subatomic particles the velocity and position of which can only be characterized statistically with inverse exactitude. Physicists are uncertain about how to interpret this fact ontologically. Some physicists suppose that the uncertainty principle describes the inherent nature of the behavior of protons and neutrons; others suppose that the phenomenon is a consequence of the fact that in order to observe the position and velocity of subatomic particles it is necessary to have them interact with light, and no method can be devised to observe this interaction in the absence of the particles reacting to light. It cannot be taken for granted that either of these interpretations can be used as premises for a correct understanding of the cognitive and observational activities involved in clinical psychoanalysis.

Nevertheless, on the basis of this dubious analogy some analysts can abandon Freud's epistemology, which warranted his quest for objectivity, as a naive and antiquated adherence to a nineteenth-century Newtonian point of view. However, they do not pause to consider that all of us live our lives in a reality governed by the laws of Newtonian mechanics (which of course can be derived mathematically as a special case of relativity theory), or that all the sciences that study phenomena of greater magnitude than atoms and lesser magnitude than the solar system employ, for the most part, explanatory laws of the same basic conceptual form as nineteenth-century physics, chemistry, and biology. From the indeterminacy of subatomic particles one cannot derive the unknowability of human subjectivity and behavior at the level of our experience, or even at the level of the neurological processes that sustain their existence.

We have something to learn from Proust about the way in which an idea, even one that is subjective in origin, can open our eyes to reality. In *The Cities of the Plain* (1921), Proust describes a scene at a party in which a man is becoming increasingly irritated with a certain lassitude, a mild absence in the withdrawn inner contemplation of a lady he had previously been able to charm and fascinate with his talk and with whom he is now trying to strike up a conversation. He is about to ask the woman rather rudely what is the matter with her when a friend whispers in his ear, "The lady is pregnant." Suddenly he is able to see what he has for some time been looking at—the indicative thickening about the waist, revealed even by her attempt to hide it by her choice of attire.

Proust proceeds to describe the Narrator's discovery of the homosexuality of the Baron, M. de Charlus. The Narrator has been aware of a puzzlement at inconsistencies and contradictions in the Baron's attitude to him, sometimes friendly and helpful far beyond the demands of courtesy or kindness, only to suddenly become peremptory and haughtily dismissive for no apparent reason. The Baron's excessively macho conduct at the Jockey Club and his socially engaged yet distant relations with women have posed a mute question to the Narrator. Now, by chance, he has an opportunity to observe undetected a meeting between the Baron and Jupien. For the first time, he is able to entertain the idea that M. de Charlus is homosexual. Then, before his eyes, he can see unfolding a ritualized sexual dance, a foreplay, in which, with even a certain beauty, the question of dominance and submission is settled between the Baron and Jupien.

It is this idea that enables the Narrator to see what, at a blow, removes the contradictions from the Baron's behavior and renders intelligible his motives, character, and conduct. In this sense, the ground of the Narrator's ability to see is the idea, a ground which assigns a role to subjectivity in the knowledge of others. But the idea does not alter the reality. Whether the Narrator sees the Baron's homosexuality with desire, with disgust, or with indifference, the observation discovers the homosexual desire that the Baron must hide from his familial and social world, but does not create it. In this sense, the meaning of the Baron's behavior is inherent in his life and character, which are the ground of the knowledge that the idea enables us to gain. Perhaps there is a way between subjectivity and objectivity that is also a way forward.

We are reminded of the need for a ground for knowledge that is independent of subjectivity by the consideration that while we must depend on ideas to know, they may obscure or even distort, as well as illuminate and clarify. Prejudicial ideas do not appear prejudicial to those who hold them, and they blind their adherents to the observations that could correct them. The devout do not experience their cherished beliefs as wishful thinking. Subjectivity, even of the most refined form, has turned out not to be a safe domicile for truth. Descartes's subjective intellectual criteria of clarity and distinctness of ideas no more allows for the possibility of non-Euclidean geometry than does Kant's transcendental derivation of space as a pure form of perception. The Euclidean axiom of parallels satisfies Descartes's criteria of ideational clarity and distinctness as its Reimannian denial does not, and the axiom appears to naive common sense to be a condition for the perception of objects, as Kant claimed it to be. But Euclid's axiom of parallels is not universally and necessarily true as the Cartesian and Kantian epistemologies imply, nor does it apply to the behavior of objects in spaces larger than small portions of the earth's surface and its atmospheric environment, any more than our perception of the setting sun reveals to us its motion. Einstein was led by these considerations to criticize idealist epistemologies which, he believed, "have had a harmful effect upon the progress of scientific thinking in removing certain fundamental concepts from the domain of empiricism where they are under our control to the intangible heights of the *a priori*" (1922, p. xvi). What is even more essential than having ideas "under our control" is to allow our ideas, especially those that we find most luminous and most self-evident, to be tested by the objects to which they refer.

Does subjectivism in psychoanalysis have the effect of removing certain of our concepts "to the intangible heights of the *a priori*"? The Narrator's idea of homosexuality, in the example that I have drawn from Proust above, appears from the context to have a subjective source, although it is by no means *a priori* in Descartes's or Kant's sense of the term. The Narrator is described by Proust as behaving like a voyeur and eavesdropper; there is nothing here of the detached and impersonal thinker or observer. Nevertheless, we are convinced by the Narrator when he says, "Until then, because I had not understood, I had not seen" (p. 635). Saturated with subjectivity as the idea may be in its origin, however surreptitiously and clandestinely and with whatever accompanying phantasies the observations of M. de Charlus were made, the use to which the Narrator puts the idea opens up and renders intelligible what he is now able to see, by means of it, in the Baron's behavior. The idea is "rescued" from its subjectivity by being grounded in and tested by the object. Whatever idea of homosexuality the Narrator may have had before, it is now enriched and potentially corrected by a mass of impressions specific to the Baron's homosexuality, which the idea made visible to him.

If objective knowledge is available under the circumstances and with the motives for knowing described by Proust in the Narrator, is it not unnecessarily modest, or even defeatist, on the part of certain analysts to insist that the best psychoanalysis can manage is a portrait of the patient that is an inextricable composite of the patient and the analyst? Would not such an inextricability of the observer with the observed be inconsistent with the elementary capacity for subject-object differentiation that we must all develop in order to survive? Is not this capacity for subject-object differentiation further refined in analysts by their personal analysis and analytic training? Is not this differentiation facilitated by the analytic set-up? Subjectivism in psychoanalysis may not remove ideas to the Olympian heights of the *a priori*, but does it not shelter theoretical ideas from being tested? Does it not discourage as Sisyphean the analyst's ceaseless efforts to reach beyond himself to an understanding of the patient as he is in himself? Does not epistemological subjectivism, consequently, through its denial of any experiential and inferential access to the life and experience of another, implicitly allow the analyst to lay claim to an adjudicative interpretive authority no less apodictic than Kant's transcendental unity of apperception, which, he believed, imposes (projects) categories of understanding (causality and substance) and the pure forms of sense experience (space and time) on the world?

Any affirmative answers to these questions must take into account certain strengths of idealist psychoanalytic epistemology. First, as heuristic thought, subjectivism underscores and focuses all of the difficulties that lie like a many-headed hydra in the way of an objective psychoanalytic understanding of persons and their histories. Secondly, it opposes the complacency of a facile objectivism that leads directly to the stultifying self-assurance of dogmatism and orthodoxy in theory and a highly subjective imposition of the analyst's own ideas on the patient in therapy. Thirdly, it seeks to do justice to the extent to which psychoanalytic ideas, even if they have an objective source, must make a passage through the analyst's subjectivity in order to acquire an authentic clinical use. To understand that another is motivated unconsciously, one must be in touch with one's own unconscious motivation; to recognize and understand the homosexuality of another one must be able to know one's own homosexuality either as memory or as phantasy and impulse. It is by finding their subjective roots that ideas in psychoanalysis can be used objectively.

It is in the direction indicated by this Socratic injunction that we will find the convergence, if not the integration, of an authentic subjectivity and objectivity in psychoanalytic epistemology.

REFERENCES

Ayer, A.J. (1953). *The Foundations of Empirical Knowledge*. London: Macmillan.

Britton, R., & Steiner, J. (1994). Interpretation: Selected fact or overvalued idea? *International Journal of Psychoanalysis* 75:1069–1078.

Einstein, A. (1922). *The Meaning of Relativity: Four Lectures Delivered at Princeton University, May, 1921* (Trans. P. Adams). London: Methuen.

Etchegoyen, H. (1994). Validation in the clinical process. *International Journal of Psychoanalysis* 75:83–92.

Hanly, C. (1970). On being and dreaming. In C. Hanly & M. Lazerowitz (Eds.), *Psychoanalysis and Philosophy* (pp. 155–187). New York: International Universities Press.

——— (1992). *The Problem of Truth in Applied Psychoanalysis*. New York: Guilford Press.

Israel, P. (1994). On formulations to patients. *International Journal of Psychoanalysis* 75:1051–1068.

Ornstein, A., & Ornstein, P. (1994). On the conceptualisation of clinical facts in psychoanalysis. *International Journal of Psychoanalysis* 75:977–994.

Proust, M. (1921). *Remembrance of Things Past.* Vol. 4: *The Cities of the Plain* (Trans. C.K. Moncrieff & T. Kilmartin). Harmondsworth: Penguin, 1954.

Sandler, A.-M., & Sandler, J. (1994). Comments on the conceptualisation of clinical facts in psychoanalysis. *International Journal of Psychoanalysis* 75:995–1010.

Spence, D. (1994). The special nature of psychoanalytic facts. *International Journal of Psychoanalysis* 75:915–926.

CHAPTER 5

Some Case Material Bearing on the Question of a Unitary Psychoanalytic Theory*

I shall present elements from the analysis of a highly intelligent, gifted, good-looking, tall, slender woman who was thirty years old when she began her analysis. The parts of the analysis are selected for their relevance to the question: Is psychoanalysis a consistent and integrated theory, or is it a collection of disconnected and even, in some cases, contradictory theories? I do not agree with those who take theories to be metaphors that entitle us to exercise personal preference in choosing them. Theories describe or fail to describe what is real, and about what is real we have no right of choice: the real is given. Consequently, I also hold that clinical observations can and must decide which, if any, of the current psychoanalytic theories describe psychic reality and which fail to describe it. To *describe*, as I am using the word here, also includes to *explain* and to *understand*.

I have selected the analysis of Ms. B for presentation because I have already published this part of it (Hanly, 1992) in sufficient detail that I can offer a summary here and turn to some of its other aspects. The argument of that paper, as well as the argument of a second paper (Hanly, 1994), is germane to the present discussion. In it I argued that conflicting psychoanalytic theories can be clinically tested using the usual standards of

---

* Originally published in *The Journal of Clinical Psychoanalysis* 6, no. 4 (1997):501–515.

inductive reasoning. Psychoanalysis can be an integrated, composite theory as envisaged by Rangell only if it has adequate rational means of testing its theories against the facts of observation. Otherwise, it will continue to be fractured into many theories, each with its partisan adherents.

Ms. B was a litigation lawyer, a profession for which she had outstanding intellectual and verbal gifts that she carried with a graceful unpretentiousness. She was the eldest of three daughters of postwar European immigrants to Canada. Her father was a taciturn steel worker of minimal education, a reliable but detached and remote breadwinner for his family. The mother was a woman with social ambitions from a prosperous family that had suffered during the war and its aftermath. Her much loved and idealized elder brother, an accomplished athlete and university-educated budding political leader, had died in a German concentration camp because of his opposition to the Nazis. The rather severe and demanding mother let her eldest daughter know that she, the mother, had married beneath herself and that she considered her husband to be her inferior, and she told the child stories of her heroic brother.

During the late stage of the mother's third pregnancy, when Ms. B was four, a quarrel arose between mother and father late at night. Ms. B remembers being awakened and taken with her sister to spend the night with neighbors by a mother who was afraid her father might do some violence to them. Ms. B recalls walking through the kitchen to the back door and seeing what seemed to her to be the gleam of a knife reflecting light from a streetlight shining into the darkened house. Her father seemed to be standing in the shadows holding the knife. She recalls being more excited than afraid. The next day they returned home. Neither parent spoke to her about the quarrel then or subsequently. There were no recurrences of such quarrels between the parents. The father began to spend more and more of his time at home alone in a workshop that he had fashioned in the basement. The parents continued to sleep together. When Ms. B was at university, the parents divorced. Ms. B was surprised that her father soon remarried a woman who respected and even seemed to admire and enjoy his workman's ways, while her attractive, romantic mother remained single, dating inappropriately young men, and involved in her new career.

When Ms. B first came to see me, she had had a series of failed relationships with men. She was depressed and afraid that she might never be able to establish a durable, gratifying relationship with a man, to marry, and have children. In her analysis, she sadly reported how her GP, a woman, would remind her during her annual physical examination of what a fine pelvis she had for childbearing. Ms. B suffered from early wakening. She would wake at three or four every morning, even on weekends, with the result that she spent her days oppressed by fatigue. She could not avoid her symptom by going to bed earlier because she could not fall asleep before midnight or later. She felt trapped, tormented, and depleted. One area of her life about which she spoke only positively was her career as a litigation lawyer in a large law firm. She had been a gifted student of literature, but had abandoned her graduate studies when she saw that there were few opportunities for an academic career for the foreseeable future, and having turned to law she found that she greatly enjoyed the challenges of litigation. As it turned out, this rosy picture of her career was true so far as it went, but it denied the extent to which she was struggling with depression and loss of self-esteem in her work. The first task she posed for her analysis turned out to be focused on her employment.

Ms. B's first mutative self-realization was that the enthusiasm she had for her career was carried entirely by her real enjoyment of the practice of law. But she had to exaggerate this satisfaction in order to deny her angry resentment at her treatment by male colleagues in the firm. Male peers whom she considered, no doubt correctly, to be at best her equals in service to the firm, were preferred over her by senior colleagues in assignment of cases, promotion, and salary. She realized how depressed she was and the extent to which her self-esteem had been eroded. She believed that no law firm would treat her differently, since they were all dominated by men. And although she wanted to do courtroom law out of a law office, she felt that her only alternative was to seek salaried employment in government or business.

During this first period of her analysis, Ms. B's associations also provided a sporadic narrative elaboration of her early life based on accessible memories, among them the memory of the parental quarrel described above. I use the term "narrative elaboration" because Ms. B was "filling me in" or "putting me in the picture" of her life as she remembered and knew it. She informed me about her failed love relationships with men. In her adolescence she had been attracted only to the leather jacket–wearing, drop-out motorcycle boys, although she was very shy and did not go out on dates. One of these boys once came by on his motorcycle, but she remained hidden in her room while, to her surprise and consternation, her mother entertained him in the kitchen. She had friendships with boys in her high school class who were excellent students and good athletes, but she was not sexually attracted to them. She had vowed to herself that she would not have sex until she left home. Her first sexual relationship was with a fellow student with whom she lived for a year while at university. The relationship did not work out. She gradually found him to be oppressively demanding. She felt restricted and cooped up in the relationship, and finding herself unable to break it off, she found ways to get him to do it. This pattern repeated itself several times, the last of which occurred during this phase of her analysis. She had met a young research scientist at the wedding of a friend. At first, she was enthralled. Her romance with him eased the jealous feelings aroused by the marriage of her friend, and she thought seriously about abandoning her law career, moving to the United States, and having a family. However, she began to find flaws in him; his ways became irritating to her, and her sexual interest flagged. Moreover, our work was beginning to bear first fruit, as we shall see in a moment. As a result, the two extraneous motives for her attachment to this man vanished at a time when the intrinsic motives became unbearably conflicted.

In her search for childhood memories, Ms. B had an isolated memory of an accident before her second sister was born, when she would have been in her second year. She was carrying a cup of tea to her father in the garden when she tripped and cut herself on the cup, which had broken in her fall. She remembered crying, more in disappointment than hurt, and a lot of blood, although she could not see how she could have been cut that badly. The incident was inadvertently portentous of the pain in her future relation to her father. She divided her history into a vaguely golden age before her father's withdrawal from her and the family, at approximately the time of the parental quarrel, and the "fallen" time that followed, when the father was there without being with her. He had taken no interest in her early schooling or in her academic successes at high school and university. The same was true of other aspects of her development and life. After his divorce and remarriage, he continued to live in the same city near Toronto where she lived. Each year she arranged a dinner for him with her sisters to celebrate his birthday and visited him at Christmas, but he never asked her about what she was doing and scarcely ever made any effort to keep in touch with her.

Ms. B's father had failed to provide her with mirroring of her childhood femininity or her intellectual talents. He had failed to serve her as a suitable object for idealization. The failure of male superiors in the law office to acknowledge her ability and contributions reverberated with her father's years of indifference. I was made aware of the affective meaning of this indifference through a projective identification, in Porder's (1987) sense, caused by Ms. B's transference. She withheld affect in such a way as to leave me always uncertain of where I stood with her. She was punctual, paid her bills, and followed the basic rules, but preserved herself as an affectively absent presence. Her identification with her father made me experience part of what it had been like to be his daughter.

It was difficult to assess at this stage what in her difficulties with men at home and at work was the result of narcissistic injury at the hands of her father, what was the result of unresolved libidinal and aggressive conflicts, and what was owing to the men with whom she worked and made love. Since her career problem was at center stage in her analysis, I was guided in my interpretive efforts by an acceptance that she *was* being shabbily treated in her current employment, while I took her belief that no male litigation lawyers would ever treat her differently to be a symptom of depression and a flawed self-esteem having its roots in her relationship with an inadequate father. As these issues were worked through in the analysis, Ms. B sought and found a suitable position in another firm, where to her great surprise and happiness she found herself to be genuinely appreciated and fairly treated. At this time she was still involved with her scientist boyfriend. She became aware that she was no longer prepared to marry him if it meant abandoning a career in law that she greatly enjoyed. As it happened, at this time he found himself without prospect of work in the United States and began looking for a university position in his field in Toronto and its environs.

However, while there was this one distinct improvement in Ms. B's life, her other symptoms continued without significant amelioration. Her sleep was no less problematic. The more evident it became to her that her scientist boyfriend was making great efforts to adapt himself to her career interests, the more she began to have an almost panicky need to find fault with him. She maneuvered him into breaking off the relationship. She now told me about another symptom connected with her practice of law that had persisted. In the conduct of discovery, she would often enough find that her opposites were more senior male lawyers who would treat her in a rather condescending avuncular way that they seemed to take as a kindness to her. (She would have preferred them to treat her with the expected professional competitiveness.) By the end of the day, they would have found how knowledgeable in the law and calmly expert in her presentation of it in her arguments about its application to the case at issue, and they would be angry at her for her lack of gratitude and for being willing to take advantage of some sloppiness in the conduct of their side caused by their complacent derogation, and underestimation of her. By the time she returned from the court to her office, her exhilaration in her victory and her satisfaction in having served her client well would have given way to a numbing, uncomprehending guilt that she could not understand, but that would reduce her to wretched tearfulness in the privacy of her office. Her self-derogating hostility to men had been, at best, only partly resolved by her greatly improved professional circumstances.

In the earlier paper (Hanly, 1992), I argued that the narcissistic determinants in Ms. B's relation to her father, however important they were in themselves, were not the decisive factor in her major symptoms. Ms. B was in analysis with an analyst she appeared to find suitable as a paternal selfobject in the transference. She had father surrogates available to her at work who appreciated her abilities and her work, and freely expressed their appreciation verbally and in the tangible form of challenging files, remuneration, and promotion. This finding would tend to invalidate self psychology as a comprehensive theory of neurosis on the grounds of its being based on the fallacy of *pars pro toto* resulting in an overvaluation of narcissistic libido as compared with sexual libido.

However, the narcissistic factors in object relations that self psychology has focused on, and with which I worked in this analysis, can readily be included within Rangell's idea of a composite theory through a self-psychological supplement to the theories of narcissistic object relations developed by Freud (1914) and others (Ferenczi, 1913). Only those hypotheses of self psychology that are inconsistent with well-established hypotheses of the composite or mainstream theory have to be excluded (Hanly, 1983; Pine, 1990).

From early in her analysis Ms. B would at intervals recall an episode when she was in Grade 1 at school. A nurse had visited her class to interview the students about their health. When Ms. B's turn came, the nurse asked her what she had eaten for breakfast that morning. She remembered that mother had served her French toast, but she could not tell this to the nurse. She broke into tears, could say nothing, and became increasingly agitated as the nurse tried to oblige her to speak until the mother had to be called to the school to calm her. The memory remained isolated. Ms. B could not associate to it. That it was significant was evident from the frequency of its recurrence, but what its significance might be was unclear. I occasionally ventured the interpretation that she must have been feeling very troubled about something. I speculated that it must have had to do with eating, but I wanted to let her find her own way to its explanation. At these times, she would reflect on the memory, expressing her incredulity that she could have been afraid of reporting a breakfast of French toast even to a rather authoritarian, insistent stranger.

In the third year of her analysis, during a period when we were exploring her preoccupations with men who she was convinced had an interest in her but who never made any real advances, Ms. B had a dream that became important for her analysis and that shed light on the memory. She was in the basement of her childhood home, where a table was set out for dinner just outside her father's workshop. On the table there was a large cauldron filled with stew that had odd, disgusting-looking things in it. She now remembered the French toast incident, and in its train came memories of a dietary phobia she had had at that time about eating, particularly eggs and meat that were not thoroughly well-cooked. She also remembered that her inability to take this sort of food into her mouth was much greater when her father was at the table. Why, she wondered, was the dinner in the basement? Her father was present in the dream, in his workshop out of sight. Her thoughts then turned to the dish and its contents. How strange and disgusting they seemed! She then became painfully aware that the contents were human body parts. She thought of her baby sisters and of her father. Her father was in his workshop in the dream, but part of him also seemed to her to be in the disturbing stew.

This dream now entered into the work, replacing the school memory and branching out into associations about her sisters, her father, her mother, and herself. Her anxious early waking began to somewhat ameliorate. She dreamed that a chef with black hair and mustache was showing her around the kitchen of a restaurant. He apologized for having only a dry bar and no wet bar. She recalled that her father had been dark-haired, had worn a mustache when he was young, and had ridden a motorcycle. Her father had invited her and her sisters to a brunch with him on the weekend. The sisters were late, and she had found it very uncomfortable being alone with her father. She managed to seat herself as far away from him as possible, leaving closeness to the father to her sisters by taking a seat opposite him, although by thus yielding to her sisters she had taken the place at the table her divorced mother would have occupied. Her father asked her if she would like something to drink. She would have liked a drink, but she refused his offers. In her discomfort, she tried to start a conversation by asking him an ordinary question, which he answered in a way that made her feel even more distressed because he seemed to long for further questions from her and did not reciprocate with any of his own. She was relieved by the arrival of her sisters.

I thought that the kitchen in the dream with its deficient bar may have resulted from a displacement of Ms. B's cannibalistic wish from food to drink, causing her to want to accept but to have to refuse her father's offer to buy her a drink. I surmised that her distress had to do with an unconscious phantasy of his depletion and ruin by castration. (I have been impressed

101

by Freud's archeological metaphor for the analytic process. As soon as the archeologist suspects the presence of an artifact in the clay and debris of the excavation, he proceeds all the more cautiously and patiently. The analyst too must exercise caution so as not to disturb, but rather to facilitate the patient's process of uncovering.)

Ms. B was intellectually brilliant, but she also had a prosaic view of life that made her vulnerable to isolation of affect and intellectualization. My interpretation was that she seemed to fear accepting a drink from her father as she had feared eating runny eggs as a child, and that despite her refusal her father seemed weak and needy, wanting her attention and interest as he might from a mother or wife but unable to offer her any of his own.

Freud (1907) noted how important it is in treating a delusion to let it be for a time and to enter into it in order to point the way beyond it. Ms. B had neurotic delusions (Freud, 1924; Shengold, 1995) about men's interest in her and about her mother. She was astonished to realize that her plan to take her mother on a skiing trip was a phantasy. She was herself an expert skier and believed that her mother, who was in her late fifties and had not skied since her childhood, would have no trouble keeping up with her on the most difficult slopes. In the delusion, she was taking the place of her mother's much admired and loved elder brother, who, in her mother's memory at least, had been a masterful skier and had taught her how to ski some fifty years before. Ms. B believed, probably rightly, that it was the mother's undying love for her dead brother that caused her mother to hold her father in such low esteem. Her negative oedipal, homosexual wish to take the place of the father with the mother was partly motivated by a wish to make the mother happy by being like her dead uncle (the mother's brother), with whom she identified (the uncle had studied law).

The day after the restaurant dream, Ms. B had a somewhat different version of a recurrent dream, in which she was alone in her family home with a man attempting to force an entry. This time he is at the screened back door wanting to kiss her, but she is able to keep him out. Then the door changes and he gets in and kisses her. She associated the man in the dream to a young lawyer of Eastern European origin who was taciturn like her father. She had the feeling of disgust in the dream that she had had at the restaurant when her father offered to buy her a drink, and expressed her amazement that such a slight incident could have had so great an effect on her. I interpreted that the man in the dream seemed to represent her father and that perhaps some distressing sexual phantasy about her father had been awakened in her. I linked the feeling of disgust to the disgust she used to feel when eating supper with him. Ms. B then reported more of the dream. In it the man became passive and weak, and swooned; he was like Rodin's sculpture of a dreaming woman. I interpreted that she had made him into a woman with her kiss and that this was why she was so afraid of his sexual aggression. Her associations turned to her first lover and how disturbing sex had become for her toward the end of their relationship and how desperate she had been to get rid of him. She now recognized that he had not been demeaning to her or unduly demanding of her; on the contrary, he had shopped and prepared dinner when she was late getting home because she liked to linger after seminars talking with her fellow students. I interpreted that she believed that she had done to him what her mother had done to her father. In the fight between father and mother, mother had gained possession of the knife. Ms. B's dilemma was that her identification with her mother, which provided her with a path to mature feminine sexuality, was compromised by a mother who had, in her daughter's unconscious phantasy, castrated her father because, in reality, she had diminished him. Ms. B's sexual attachment to her father ceased to be primarily a means of separating her from her mother through object love, and became instead a means of taking the father's place with the mother by identification in unconscious phantasy.

This negative oedipal aspect of Ms. B's conflicts was also evident in recovered memories. She remembered that in the summer of her fifth year she had broken her leg and had to wear a cast. She recalled sitting opposite a neighbor boy with whom she sometimes played, and being able to look up the legs of his shorts with curiosity and pleasure to see his penis. She wanted him to have the same feelings about her genitals, but although she was not wearing panties because of the cast, she was too frightened to allow it because she felt that her genitals were ugly. She could not bear the shame of seeing the expression of disgust that she believed would disfigure his face if she indulged her own wish to show him her genitals. During her latency, when she had grown tall, strong, and athletic, she developed an intense dislike for a slightly older homosexual boy in the neighborhood. He had a penis but he behaved like a girl, and this disturbed her. One day he came by her house. She picked a quarrel with him, knocked him to the ground, and became frightened by the rage she felt and the ferocity of the kicks and blows she gave him as he lay writhing on the lawn. She felt that he did not deserve a penis because he did not know how to use it, whereas if she had one she would know. In another gender identity episode during her early teens, she had looked forward with great excitement to getting her driver's license. She wanted to drive her mother on shopping trips so that mother would no longer have to depend on father to drive her. She was puzzled and disappointed that even after she was licensed and drove well, her mother still preferred to be taken shopping by father despite all her complaints about his many shortcomings. I hypothesized that the memory of falling and cutting herself while taking a cup of tea to her father was the first in this series of memories, which early in the analysis had served as a screen for these later memories. This memory indicated a time when she had loved her father dearly. We imagine a small girl with a sense of the importance of the occasion proudly, if precariously, carrying the cup to her father. In her adult delusion of taking her mother skiing, which was a new expression of her wish to provide for her mother as her father had not, we wonder about a retribution against the mother for disappointing her possessive homosexual wish, as well as an ambivalence caused by her love for her father.

Woven through this homosexual material there were indications of Ms. B's positive oedipal attachment to her father. Ms. B's sleep symptoms turned out to owe much to these wishes and feelings. These symptoms consisted primarily of anxious early wakening at three to four in the morning, difficulty in falling to sleep being secondary. In train with Ms. B's expanding and deepening memories of the roots of her homosexual attachment to her mother, there came memories of the evolution of her oedipal love for her father that established its connection with her sleep symptoms. It began with a startled recollection that at university she had habitually worked at her studies until the sky began to lighten. She had rationalized this sleep pattern as a requirement of her student bohemianism, although it was the only manifestation of bohemianism in her otherwise bourgeois life.

She now realized that she was too afraid to go to sleep during the night. Her awareness of this connection had been clouded by the shift in the symptom from going to sleep to remaining asleep. She recalled the frightening phantasy of a man coming into her apartment to rob and kill her. The phantasy was occasioned by a newspaper report of a somewhat similar crime. One can observe how closely intertwined were the unconscious homosexual and heterosexual phantasies: the fear of being robbed came primarily from the former and the violent assault came primarily from the latter. Memories returned of the phantasy's childhood original. She would beg to be allowed to stay up to watch television with her parents in order to avoid going to bed, even when the program did not at all interest her. In bed she would experience sexual feelings, and then the phantasy of a man coming into the house, slipping past the room where her parents were watching television, to climb the stairs, and guided by the hall light that shone through the door onto her as she lay in bed, he would attack her with a knife. Her childhood choice of her father as a sexual object is evident in her choice of boys during her adolescence. The risk of father's violence that had left her impressed as a three-year-old, now invested the excitement and fear aroused by the nocturnal phantom intruder who came to do violence to her.

The violence of the intruder had a number of determinants. It expressed her exciting, dangerous image of the primal-scene father. It provided an image for the deferred anxiety from the night of the parental quarrel. (Ms. B was never sure whether or not she had actually seen her father with the knife that night; however, she did associate the knife of the intruder with the knife that she had seen or hallucinated.) It was an image that mirrored and punished, according to the talion law, her unconscious castration wish. It was a punishment for her wish to take her father from her mother. She envied her mother and entertained dark suspicions about her for sleeping with her father and for watching TV with him at night.

It should be noted incidentally that although father's self-exile to his basement workshop and his withdrawal from the family was real enough, it apparently was also exaggerated by Ms. B. This exaggeration satisfied her conflicted wishes to have him for herself (the father had rejected the mother for her) and her wish to have the mother for herself (mother had rejected father). Ms. B also envied her mother for insinuating through her heightened excitement when the motorcycle youth came visiting that unlike her timorous daughter, she knew how to entertain a man with a motorcycle. Ms. B feared her mother and her criticisms enough to keep a vow to herself that she would never have sex with a man so long as she lived under her mother's roof. It turned out that an important resistance and a motive for having phantasy romances with men was a maternal transference to me as a jealous mother who expected her to be good and not have sex until her analysis was completed. As the associative process uncovered these conflicts and began working through them, there was a steady amelioration of Ms.

B's early waking, she gave up her delusional romances with unpromising, if eligible, men, and she became capable of real heterosexual passion.

McDougall (1995) has described the fundamental developmental task that Ms. B faced:

> [F]or the little girl will not become a man, will never possess her mother sexually, will never make babies with her, and will never receive a baby from her father.... Because this phantasmic form of possession, common to all children, implies the destruction of the "other," it brings in its wake confused feelings of guilt and depression.... [E]ventually, all children must accept the fact that they will never possess both genders and will forever be only half of the sexual constellation. This scandalous affront to infantile megalomania is further complicated by the need to come to terms with the oedipal crisis in both its homosexual and heterosexual dimensions, and with the impossibility of sexually possessing either parent. (p. xiv)

But if all girls and boys must succeed in this struggle in order to mature well, what brought it about that Ms. B did not mature well despite her exceptional gifts and intelligence? Ms. B did not have a father who was a good enough object for her oedipal feelings. He abandoned her to her phantasies. A father can fail because he is seductive and provocative; a father can also fail because he cannot be, or allow himself to be, an object for the romantic, sexual, and competitive strivings of his daughter by respecting and acknowledging with pleasure these feelings in her without exploiting them.

It may be supposed that this understanding of Ms. B is not a classical one because it places such a strong emphasis on the quality of object relations available to a child. It does not assign a transcendent etiological value to drives and defenses against them. But such has always been the classical position. Freud (1916–1917) stated his position clearly enough that it should not be misunderstood as often as it is:

Are neuroses *exogenous* or *endogenous* illnesses? Are they the inevitable result of a particular constitution or the product of certain detrimental (traumatic) experiences in life? More particularly, are they brought about by fixation of the libido (and the other features of the sexual constitution) or by the pressure of frustration? This dilemma seems to me no more sensible on the whole than another that I might put to you: does a baby come about through being begotten by its father or conceived by its mother? Both determinants are equally indispensable. (pp. 346–347)

This general etiological formulation can be derived from Freud's concept of an instinct or drive as a need for satisfaction that is object-seeking. A drive is a demand for work upon psychic functioning that motivates a search for an object. The unavailability or inadequacy of the object results in a failure to achieve maturity. I take these inseparable concepts of drives and object relations along with Freud's idea of a complemental series of causal factors to be foundational for a unitary psychoanalytic theory, just as I have tried to show in the case of Ms. B that they provide the clinical analyst with an indispensable orientation.

Much ink has recently been spilled by psychoanalysts about the way in which the theories held by the analyst influence the analysis. Not a little of this has been on behalf of the subjectivist view that the theories of the analyst, aided and abetted by transferences and countertransferences, bring it about that, as the late Merton Gill (1994) paradoxically stated during the plenary session at the West Point Scientific International Journal scientific meeting, "it is a fact that there are no clinical facts in psychoanalysis." This view has some rather momentous implications for the possibility of a unitary psychoanalytic theory. If there are no clinical facts, theory testing is impossible in psychoanalysis. And if this is so, a composite psychoanalytic theory is not worth the name because it could only be at best an arbitrarily pasted together collection of theories without logical unity, integrity, or correspondence with reality.

But subjectivism does not do justice to the variety of influences that theories can have on observation. Ideas can enable us to see and hear what is there to be seen, or in the case of psychoanalysis, what is struggling in our patients, despite disguises and resistances, to be heard and put into words. Subjectivism, starting from the difficulties in the way of objectivity, ends in a solipsistic denial of the possibility of objectivity. Naive realism, starting from the self-evidence of some of our knowledge, ends in an authoritarian absolutism. What is required for a unified psychoanalytic theory is that interpretations, and hence the theories that prompt them, be testable. For this testing we have the analysand's associative responses to interpretations, shifts in the transference, and the liberation of functions and activities that we can observe with a fallible but sufficient measure of objectivity. It is in this spirit that I offer these portions of the analysis of Ms. B for the purpose of testing Rangell's idea of a unified psychoanalytic theory.

REFERENCES

Ferenczi, S. (1913). Stages in the development of the sense of reality. In *First Contributions to Psycho-Analysis* (pp. 213–239). New York: Brunner/ Mazel, 1980.

Freud, S. (1907). Delusions and dreams in Jensen's *Gradiva*. SE 9:1–93.

——— (1914). On narcissism: An introduction. SE 14:67–102.

——— (1916–1917). *Introductory Lectures on Psycho-Analysis*. SE 15–16.

——— (1924). The loss of reality in neurosis and psychosis. SE 19:181–187.

Gill, M. (1994). Contribution to the concluding discussion. *International Journal of Psychoanalysis* Seventy-Fifth Anniversary Celebration Conference, West Point, April 8–10.

Hanly, C. (1983). A problem of theory testing. *International Review of Psycho-Analysis* 10:393–405. [Chapter 1 in this volume]

——— (1992). Inductive reasoning in clinical psychoanalysis. *International Journal of Psychoanalysis* 73:293–301. [Chapter 2 in this volume]

——— (1994). Reflections on the place of the therapeutic alliance in psychoanalysis. *International Journal of Psychoanalysis* 75:457–467.

McDougall, J. (1995). *The Many Faces of Eros.* New York: Norton.

Pine, F. (1990). *Drive, Ego, Object, and Self: A Synthesis for Clinical Work.* New York: Basic Books.

Porder, M. (1987). Projective identification: An alternative hypothesis. *Psychoanalytic Quarterly* 54:431–451.

Shengold, L. (1995). *Delusions of Everyday Life.* New Haven: Yale University Press.

CHAPTER 6

Commentary on Unitary Theory*

Rangell's central proposal is that psychoanalysis as a body of knowledge is, in itself, an evolving, unitary, coherent, and composite theory, whereas contemporary psychoanalytic culture makes it out to be a collection of alternative and inconsistent, but equally viable theories. I am in basic agreement with his view. We already have his clear historical and discursive elucidation of the issues. I propose to focus more closely on a few of them.

Theoretical plurality is based, as Rangell says, on political and administrative convenience and not on established scientific validity. But what are the sources of this political administrative convenience? Here are some possibilities: egalitarianism, peace at any price, a disillusionment about the clinical testability of psychoanalytic theories.

Egalitarianism is a principle of democratic social organizations from professional societies to nation states where fundamental rights are recognized including opportunity. But genes do not distribute endowments according to a principle of equality and very short men do not have the same opportunity to become professional basketball players as very tall men. Egalitarian principles do not apply to the choice of theories in science any more than they apply to the choice of basketball players. The theory that will

---

* Originally published in *The Journal of Clinical Psychoanalysis* 6, no. 4 (1997):485–493.

carry the day is the one which is observationally or experimentally verified; its competitors will be discarded.

But the situation is not so simple. The history of psychoanalytic theory is not akin to that of the theory of evolution, for example, in which Darwin's observations validated natural selection and rendered its Lamarckian competitor *de trop*, but left the theory incomplete until Mendel discovered genetic mutations. The history of psychoanalytic theory is more akin to that of twentieth-century philosophy with its proliferation of schools of thought: logical positivism, ordinary language philosophy, existentialism, phenomenology, conceptual analysis, etc. Although innovative psychoanalytic theories have tended to originate in fallacies of *pars pro toto*, as Rangell (1997) has pointed out, they have been developed into comprehensive theories, from Jung to Kohut, which aim to replace Freud's theory. Psychoanalysis has not had an orderly development of the kind that has characterized physics, for example, in which Newton's theory of gravity can be derived from Einstein's relativity theory, which replaced it. Why not a permissive peace at any price, if theoretical conflict has become chronic?

But why is theoretical conflict in psychoanalysis chronic? The comparison with philosophy may help to clarify. Philosophy was once largely speculative, but it is now largely a second-order discipline that analyzes arguments and ideas. Philosophy has no agreed-upon method of observation and no body of data of its own for theory testing. Why then is psychoanalytic theorizing so similar to philosophical speculation when psychoanalysis has data provided by its own method of observation? Is the method a failure? Does it only provide the data required by the analyst's theory? Do the free associations of a patient never cast doubt upon an interpretation? Does an analysis never falsify a theory in psychoanalysis? These questions are posed by Rangell's (1997) description of changes of theoretical affiliation in Los Angeles: "Any claim that theory follows a period of observations could be seen to have evaporated after each rapid conversion to explanatory systems of such different etiologic bases" (p. 475). I have observed the same phenomenon in my own city. Why is psychoanalysis so vulnerable to charisma and group identifications? Psychoanalysts, rather like philosophers, seem to adopt theoretical positions for reasons other than the strictly rational ones of fact, logic, and explanation. Unlike philosophers, however, psychoanalysts are analyzed. Analysis should strengthen reality testing. Is there a compromise of reality testing in the personal analysis of too many analysts? Is a compromise of reality testing a consequence of a failure by training analysts to analyze the idealizing and aggrandizing transference of the candidate analyst to the training analyst, so that candidate analysts are at risk of basing their theoretical views on an unanalyzed personal affiliation to their training analyst rather than on their own clinical observation of themselves, their patients, and the clinical literature?

I sometimes wonder if the current eclecticism among psychoanalysts does not also owe something to the philosophy of science critique by Grünbaum (1984), which followed on earlier attacks by Popper (1963) and Nagel (1959). In any case, psychoanalytic hermeneutics, and the various forms of subjectivism that have acquired a current popularity, provide a logical defense of psychoanalysis against their critiques by denying that psychoanalysis is a science. But this defense is a double-edged sword, for it also denies that there is any reliable method for deciding between alternative psychoanalytic theories. It thus rationalizes a chronic eclecticism.

As Rangell makes clear in his account, psychoanalysis was not constructed in this way. Freud abandoned his belief that the seduction theory was a complete theory of neurosis when he discovered that the therapeutic results predicted by the theory were not forthcoming. One cannot but compare Freud's psychoanalytic and scientific attitude unfavorably with that of a contemporary analyst who has advanced beyond Freud and who can consider successful his "analysis" of a thirty-five-year-old patient who suffered from a depressing inability to form a durable relationship with a man. This "success" followed an analysis of five years duration, five times a week. It was considered successful by the analyst because the patient was prepared to write an ambiguous testimonial about how meaningful it had been, despite the fact that her sexual love disability had not been in the least improved. The lack of improvement was due to the fact that the analyst had such respect for the patient that he had not made any effort to analyze her sexuality or her resistance to such discussion, because she had required him to agree at the beginning not to bring up anything to do with sex.

Psychoanalytic theory so far as Freud was able to develop it was built upon the clinical testing of theory. This testing motivated the major changes in Freud's theory: infantile sexuality, the dual-instinct theory, the structural theory, the gender differentiation of the Oedipus complex and the theory of anxiety. It does not follow, of course, that Freud's theory was or has been empirically established. For example, I do not think that the evidence for a death instinct is convincing, or that there is evidence for Freud's assumption of a phallic preference in libido or for his idea that male conscience is morally superior to female conscience. But these are questions that have to be decided by the clinical evidence of well-conducted analyses, and not by unconsciously determined, idealizing identifications with Freud or anyone else.

Rangell has correctly pointed out that I take Freud's theory to be the core of a unitary psychoanalytic theory, as he does. I want to make it clear that, in doing so, I continue to consider Freud's durable theories to be the best empirical hypotheses available for this purpose, and I therefore consider them to be subject, like any empirical hypotheses, to continuing clinical testing and logical evaluation. The formulation of new explanatory hypotheses in the form of alternative theories is an essential part of this endeavor to improve and develop psychoanalysis. It is the preference for the easy, exhilarating transformation of new and old theories into charismatic ideologies that causes a failure or a refusal to engage in this difficult, painstaking work.

I agree with Rangell that the enterprise of building an empirically based, unitary theory has been damaged by a facile eclecticism rationalized by Wallerstein (1988) on the basis of a mistaken philosophy of science (see also Hanly, 1983). Wallerstein argued that psychoanalytic theory need not be unified because different theories are only different metaphors that happen to be personally satisfying to those who espouse them. Clinical practice is what counts; differences at the metaphorical and abstract theoretical level wash out at the clinical level. But this view will not stand up to examination. Scientific theories are not metaphors: they are hypotheses that describe causal forces at work in nature, as does, for example, the theory of natural selection in biology. Different theories specify different forces, and thus provide different explanations and different predictions about what will be observed. The same is true of theories in psychoanalysis. Classical theory hypothesizes that sexuality has its onset at birth infancy, proceeding through stages to the Oedipus complex and latency. Self psychology hypothesizes that the Oedipus complex is caused by parental empathic failures, whereas the classical drive explanation postulates that even the children of very good and highly empathic parents will develop an Oedipus complex. The difference does not lie merely in the choice of metaphors for imagining an identical state of affairs. The theories attribute different courses of events to individual development and history, such that both theories cannot be true, although both could be false.

No less damaging to an empirically based unitary theory were some of the contributions to the recent seventy-fifth *International Journal of Psychoanalysis* (*IJP*) Anniversary Conferences by those contributors who advanced post-Freudian, post-positivist, postmodern ideas, first advocated by fifth-century BC sophists in ancient Athens, and by others who were not so much relying on post-this and post-that thinking as expressing a radical skepticism based on a subjectivism typical of ancient sophists such as Protagoras and Gorgias (Owens, 1959). Although these ideas did not predominate, they were prominent. But subjectivism is incompatible with a composite, unified psychoanalytic theory. If, in psychoanalysis, "man is the measure of all things" as the ancient sophist Protagoras claimed, eclecticism and pluralism are radicalized, because every analyst will have his own irreducibly subjective observations that confine him solipsistically within his own theory.

I was also struck by the fact that although the theme of the conference was explicitly philosophical, no philosophers were invited to participate. Of course, as I have explained, philosophy is an eclectic discipline (although it is one in which amateurs can lose their way), so one can always find philosophers who espouse subjectivism, such as David Bloor (1996) or Bruno Latour (1979), who are social constructivists. However, the dominant epistemology, in English-speaking philosophy at any rate, is realist, as represented by Richard Boyd (1991), Michael Devitt (1938), and W.H. Newton-Smith (1981). This includes the evolutionary epistemology of Clifford Hooker (1978), and it is evolutionary epistemology that Freud espoused, though without explicitly formulating it.

Here are some examples of subjectivist psychoanalytic theorizing drawn from the *IJPA* conferences. Jordan-Moore (1994) claims that in science there are no facts independent of theory. This statement is highly ambiguous. The statement can mean any of three quite different things. It could mean (1) that the domain of fact relevant for the testing of a theoretical hypothesis is determined by the hypothesis to be tested. Or it could mean (2) that the investigator depends cognitively upon the hypothesis for identifying and seeking out the facts that will test the theory. For example, Harvey had to seriously entertain the idea of the circulation of the blood in order to be able to design the experiments that proved it (see also Hanly, 1995, for an analysis of Proust's imaginative description of the contribution of ideas to the perception of fact). Or it could mean (3) that the observation of the facts is irreducibly subjective because the observations are influenced by the theory in such a way as to deprive them of objectivity: the world seen through the lens of a particular theory is different from the world seen through the lens of a different theory. This bit of philosophical conceptual analysis draws out the possible implications of Jordan-Moore's assertion. The first two implications are tenets of a critical realism that repudiates the third implication. The third implication defines a form of subjectivism. The generalization about scientific knowledge is hopelessly ambiguous until the meaning of the crucial term "not independent of theory" is defined. Once it is defined, it can be seen that the generalization is false, if it is intended to include the third implication. In science, facts are epistemologically independent of theories. The question is whether or not psychoanalysis qualifies as a science.

It has been argued that Freud moved beyond the validation of constructions by establishing their correspondence with historical reality, while modern analysts now hold that a construction or interpretation is validated if it adds to the further course of the analysis (Michels, 1994). This notion of clinical validation, it is argued, is based on a pragmatic concept of truth. An interpretation is theoretically valuable if it works clinically. A distinction is being drawn between pragmatic truth and truth by correspondence, or descriptive truth. But a psychoanalyst-philosopher would want to ask how a false or irrelevant interpretation can be useful clinically. How could such interpretations be useful for resolving a neurosis when the patient himself can and does invent lots of false and irrelevant rationalizing explanations of his own predicaments to no effect at all? Philosophers would also be skeptical about a concept of pragmatic truth that has been cut loose from correspondence. First among these philosophers would have been William James, who unequivocally rejected the notion that a distinction can be made between correspondence and pragmatic truth when he affirmed in "Pragmatism's Conception of Truth" (1907) that to say that an idea is true because it is useful and to say that an idea is useful because it is true are identical statements. When truth has ceased to find a domicile in the clinic, psychoanalysis has begun a descent into being satisfied with making the patient feel better, when its primary aim should be to enable the patient to *function* better.

We are informed by Widlocher (1994) that "a clinical vignette... is... not designed to prove a theory... but to illustrate a particular clinical view" (p. 1233; in the context, "clinical vignette" can be taken to mean "case material"). If this statement is true, psychoanalysts cannot function as a scientific community and so cannot work toward a comprehensive and unified theory. A philosopher would ask whether this statement is intended to be a description or a statement of epistemological and psychological principle. If it is descriptive, it implies that psychoanalysts are unable to achieve enough detachment from their own preferred ideas to provide a record of their observations by which they could be tested. It implies that psychoanalytic case reporting is a form of rhetoric because analysts are unable to be factual. Apparently, psychoanalysts are no longer able to look for negative instances, although Freud did. It is interesting that analysts espousing diverse theories have reached a consensus that Freud's (1905) fragment of his analysis of Dora does indeed involve some crucial failures, including the one Freud himself pointed out concerning Dora's libidinal tie to Frau K. Evidently, Freud wrote up case material in such a way as to enable him and subsequent analysts to question his view of the analysis at the time he carried it out. Even Grünbaum (1984), Freud's most severe contemporary philosophical critic, gives him full credit for actively seeking out facts that would disprove his theories, and for abandoning theories because of "negative instances" (i.e., contrary evidence).

As a description, then, Widlocher's statement presents problems. If what is being asserted is that it is impossible in principle to do anything better in psychoanalysis than to use clinical observations to illustrate theories, then psychoanalysis cannot ever be a reliable body of knowledge of any kind because its hypotheses can never be clinically tested. There cannot be any intersubjective (in the philosophical sense of the term) facts against which to test psychoanalytic ideas. Widlocher (1994) suggests that those who think that analysts can publish observations that meet scientific criteria suffer from a "scientistic utopianism"; on the contrary, however, "the objective of psychoanalytic publication is to deepen knowledge relating to and resulting from psychoanalytic practice" (p. 1234). But how is a case report that merely illustrates a view but fails to report clinical facts that confirm, disconfirm, or modify our understanding of some aspect of psychic functioning going to deepen our knowledge? Scientific criteria are not utopian in themselves. They have made it possible for humans to visit the moon, to cure diseases, to enhance communication. Does therapeutic efficacy in psychoanalysis have nothing to do with scientific criteria?

Are there reasons for optimism? Let us briefly return to the putative parallel between psychoanalysis and philosophy. Philosophical schools come and go. Logical positivism, existentialism, and Oxford philosophy have each had their day. I would predict that interest in subjectivist epistemology will soon wain because it is inconsistent with the epistemologies of science and common sense. Perhaps interest in the clinical testing of psychoanalytic theories will revive.

Despite the fact that philosophy does not have its own method of observation, one can detect in its history some progress toward more realistic thinking. The verification theory of meaning that logical positivism used to attack systematic metaphysics such as the Hegelian, Marxist, Kantian, or Cartesian systems, has been shown to be inadequate in itself. Nevertheless, it is unlikely that any philosopher will ever again attract a following by embarking upon the grandiose enterprise of metaphysical system building. And philosophy has progressively come to depend on science, logic, and the humanities to provide it with the concepts and facts needed for cogent philosophical analysis and argument.

119

Perhaps this feature of the history of philosophy has its counterpart in psychoanalysis. European Freudians, Kleinians, and ego psychologists are still predominant in psychoanalysis. They share a critical realist, scientific epistemology; they have also moved closer together on the theory of the primal scene. Kleinians in Latin America are returning to the study of Freud; those in Europe seem to be moving in the general direction of a theoretical rapprochement with European Freudians. If these movements continue, and if they are guided theoretically and clinically by a humanistic scientific spirit, it is possible that an observation-driven and observation-guided unification of psychoanalytic theory will take place. If philosophical thinking can achieve a greater approximation to reality over time, I do not see why psychoanalytic thinking cannot.

REFERENCES

Bloor, D. (1996). *Scientific Knowledge: A Sociological Analysis*. Chicago: University of Chicago Press.

Boyd, R. (1991). *Philosophy of Science*. Cambridge, MA: MIT Press.

Devitt, M. (1938). *Realism and Truth*. Princeton: Princeton University Press.

Freud, S. (1905). A fragment of an analysis of a case of hysteria. SE 7:1–122.

Grünbaum, A. (1984). *The Foundations of Psychoanalysis*. Berkeley: University of California Press.

Hanly, C. (1983). A problem of theory testing. *International Review of Psycho-Analysis* 10:393–405. [Chapter 1 in this volume]

——— (1995). On facts and ideas in psychoanalysis. *International Journal of Psychoanalysis* 76:901–908. [Chapter 4 in this volume]

Hooker, C. (1978). *Foundations and Applications of Decision Theory*. Boston: D. Reidel.

James, W. (1907). Pragmatism's conception of truth. In *A New Name for an Old Way of Thinking* (pp. 159–176). New York: Hafner Library Classics, 1948.

Jordan-Moore, J. (1994). Intimacy and science: The publication of clinical facts in psychoanalysis. *International Journal of Psychoanalysis* 75:1251–1266.

Latour, B. (1979). *Laboratory Life: The Social Construction of Scientific Facts.* Beverley Hills: Sage.

Michels, R. (1994). Validation in the clinical process. *International Journal of Psychoanalysis* 75:1133–1140.

Nagel, E. (1959). Methodological issues in psychoanalytic theory. In S. Hook (Ed.), *Psychoanalysis, Scientific Method and Philosophy* (pp. 38–56). New York: Grove Press.

Newton-Smith, W.H. (1981). *The Rationality of Science.* Boston: Routledge & Kegan Paul.

Owens, J. (1959). *A History of Ancient Western Philosophy.* New York: Appleton Century Crofts.

Popper, K.R. (1963). *Conjectures and Refutations: The Growth of Scientific Knowledge.* London: Routledge & Kegan Paul.

Rangell, L. (1997). Commentary on unitary theory. *Journal of Clinical Psychoanalysis* 6: 465-484.

Wallerstein, R. (1988). One psychoanalysis or many? *International Journal of Psychoanalysis* 69:5–21.

Widlocher, D. (1994). A case is not a fact. *International Journal of Psychoanalysis* 75:1233–1244.

CHAPTER 7

The Third: A Brief Historical Analysis of an Idea*

In what follows, I try to clarify historically the idea of "the third" in philosophy and in psychoanalysis. My account takes its own point of view, the evidential justification of which is, of necessity, only scantily presented. My commentary suggests an agreement and differences among various definitions of philosophical thirds and psychoanalytic thirds found in this issue of the *Psychoanalytic Quarterly* that are representative of variations in the literature. Even the agreement that emerges is at present controversial. I make no claim that this commentary on the topic and its underlying arguments escape the influence of the current controversy. My purpose is to provide background and to raise questions.

THE THIRD IN PHILOSOPHY: PEIRCE

It was Charles Sanders Peirce (1903) who introduced the term "the third" into philosophy. As a philosophical concept and as Peirce used it, the third has nothing to do directly with any psychoanalytic notions of thirds, of triadic relations, or of triangular "space." In Peirce, the third is simply the

---

* Originally published in *Psychoanalytic Quarterly* 73, no. 1 (2004):267–290.

meaning captured by general concepts, a means of describing the epistemic nature of general concepts and their crucial place in knowledge. Peirce's third can seem like a new idea about meaning because he thought that clarity in our thinking about objects could be achieved by considering the practical effects of the objects whose nature is being contemplated. It was for this reason that James considered Peirce to be the first pragmatist. However, Peirce was also an epistemological realist in the tradition of the medieval scholastic philosopher Duns Scotus (c. 1266–1308). Scotus was a "moderate," or Aristotelian near-empiricist realist, as opposed to a Platonic idealistic realist. For whatever reason, Peirce either was unaware of or failed to appreciate the devastating criticism that the empiricists (Bacon, 1620; Hobbes, 1651; Locke, 1690) and the rationalists (Descartes, 1641; Spinoza, 1673) had made of Aristotelian scholastic epistemology. Consequently, Peirce's notion of thirdness is epistemologically naive, insofar as he—like Scotus, and before him Aristotle—believed that the concepts by which we *know*, and the objects *that* we know, are connatural (i.e., of the same substance). This view is a form of rational animism because it assumes that material objects do not differ in their basic nature from the ideas we construct in our efforts to know them.

Perhaps Peirce was influenced by the spirituality of New England transcendentalism. What is clear is that he could not entertain the possibility, for which there is plentiful pragmatic evidence (e.g., the effects on mental functioning of a blockage in the carotid artery), that psychic life depends for its existence on the living matter of the brain and central nervous system. Instead, he believed that the universe is the sign of a self-developing God whose habitual thoughts are the laws of nature. Hence, Peirce could view ideas and things as fundamentally the same in their fundamental nature. However, he stopped well short of a co-creation of nature by God and man. Nevertheless, as in Aristotle, Peirce's third, that is, the general concept, simply abstracts what is taken to be the essence of the object of which it is a concept. Connaturality applies to ideas about our own psyche—its organization, activities, and contents. For example, the *idea* of the instinctual unconscious is connatural with its object, the instinctual unconscious. But the *idea* of any inanimate, material object is not connatural with the object that the idea of its atomic constituents and their dynamics enables us to comprehend. In this respect, Peirce's idea of the third is fundamentally mistaken and unsuitable for use in psychoanalytic theorizing.

Concepts are general, but by means of them, we seek knowledge of particular objects. Concepts are true when the properties, structures, dynamics, and relations they articulate are actually to be found in the objects to which they refer; when they are not, the concepts are artificial and false. The proposition that "man is mortal" is true, even though each person dies his or her own death in an individual way.

Peirce postulated a triumvirate of categories of concepts. *Firsts* are potential, uninterpreted, sensible qualities. *Firstness* is exemplified by a possible impression of a person's mood, facial expression, hesitation, discomfort, anxiety, or physical gait, or the way a patient takes his or her place on the couch. *Secondness* is an actually existing object made up of qualities that engender a percept in the mind, such as a patient's entering briskly and cheerfully into a clinician's office. A percept is a sense image or sensory representation (as in Locke, 1690) of an object ripe with the possibility of being known by means of concepts. Peirce, like his scholastic predecessors and unlike Locke, uses the term "percept" to refer both to the sense impression of an object and the object sensed. This usage leaves the door open for an idealist type of metaphysics (one in which all things are *mind)*. Peirce's concept of percept differs from Locke's concept of representation, although Peirce sometimes uses the latter term.

Thirdness is the concept by which we grasp what is *general* in a class of objects. The concept is real (and true as well) because it gains access to the reality of the object revealed by the percept. The concept, if correctly abstracted from the particularities of the object, can achieve generality on the basis of the observation of one individual—an Aristotelian notion. The concept is imbued with its reality and truth from the object via the percept of the object. A concept that is true of an individual will be true of the natural class of things of which the individual is a member.

Peirce proceeded to formulate a pragmatic criterion of meaning, truth, and reality. For Peirce, the third is an *intellectual conception*; a third is an affirmation or denial about the nature of an object. The meaning of any concept is to be ascertained by considering "what practical consequences might conceivably result by necessity from the truth of that conception; the sum of these consequences will constitute the entire meaning of the conception" (1905, p. 6, para. 9). This crucial definition implies that concepts are real *when* and *because* they have a real external counterpart, some basic aspect of which is articulated by the concept. For example, the latent content of the dream is, in Peirce's definition, the referent in the object (the dreamer) of the topographical theory of dreams. If the observations specified by the theory are forthcoming (e.g., wish-laden memories and fantasies in the analysand's associations), the latent dream is a real property of the dreamer, according to Peirce's definition of pragmatism.

Thus, Peirce's pragmatism requires epistemological realism: "The real is that which is not whatever we happen to think it is, but is unaffected by what we may think of it" (1871, p. 15, para. 12). Objects are not altered by being observed; they are not co-created. For Peirce, an object is real if and only if its nature is independent of how any individual happens to think it to be; otherwise, an object is an artifact of experience, a phantasm of our subjectivity. Competent observers (those who have made themselves competent by divesting themselves of such personal idiosyncrasies as could only produce subjective impressions that reflect themselves and their individual beliefs) who perform similar experiments, or who make observations under similar conditions of a real object, will come up with similar results.

This concept of the competent observer can itself be evaluated pragmatically. Peirce's concept of intersubjectivity is that of science and common sense; it is diametrically opposed to the meaning of the term as used by psychoanalytic intersubjectivists. Observers who have been unable to divest themselves of idiosyncratic ways of experiencing objects, Peirce would say, will form subjective impressions that fail to correspond to the object as it is. It cannot be fairly said, however, that Peirce was a naive realist, despite his Aristotelianism; his pragmatism implies fallibility. But neither was he a naive subjectivist who believed that his perceptual field was only an expression of himself, leaving him unable to make experiential contact with independently existing real objects, despite his idealist metaphysics. On the basis of Peirce's epistemological third, if psychoanalysts were irreducibly subjective, their knowledge claims would have to be considered meaningless.

Peirce's concept of thirdness is of interest to psychoanalysis because it is itself a third in a rather different sense, a sense that is found in other philosophies: it is an *epistemological* third. An idea, or at least a good idea, offers a perch, a prospect, a position from which we are able to better observe, become acquainted with, and hence better grasp or comprehend someone or something. Elsewhere (Hanly, 1995), I have noted this function of ideas, drawing on Proust. It is something that abounds in Freud's thinking. For example: "We can say that the patient's resistance arises from his ego, and we then at once perceive that the compulsion to repeat must be ascribed to the unconscious repressed" (Freud, 1920, p. 20). Peirce's idea of thirdness is itself, implicitly, an epistemological third.

DESCARTES

This more specific, epistemological idea of the third is implicit in diverse philosophical ideas and arguments. The cornerstone of René Descartes's (1641) systematic doubt is the idea of an all-powerful Evil Deceiver. This idea permitted Descartes to take up a reflective third position, which in turn enabled him to conceive of the possibility that his experience was irreducibly subjective—that he was alone with and encased in his sense experience, memories, feelings, and thoughts. Descartes's *cogito* and his idea of God are rationalist, epistemological thirds that release him from his irreducible subjectivity.

LOCKE

John Locke (1690) used the idea of representation as a third. This offered him an ideational perspective from which to examine the nature of the relation between the perceiving subject and the object perceived. Locke accepted the testimony of our sense experience as reflected in common sense, natural science, and almost all philosophies (Peirce's among them), specifying that the people and things that make up the world have a nature and existence independently of our experience of them or our ideas about them. Even George Berkeley (1710), who believed that *to be* is *to perceive* or *to be perceived*, never seriously entertained the idea that there is no reality independent of our experience of it.

The answer to the old chestnut about the falling tree, mentioned by Gerson's (2004) patient (p. 67), is that in Berkeley's theory, when a tree falls, a sound occurs in the Divine Sensorium, whether or not an animal with auditory sensory apparatus is about. For Locke, for whom the universe is made up of physical bodies and forces, the fall of the tree causes sound

128

waves that then cause the sound of the fall to be heard. The experience of the sound of the fall will occur, and thus actually occur, if and only if there is an animal sensory apparatus in the vicinity to respond to the sound waves; otherwise, the sound waves will occur without the sound. Peirce would have said the same thing as did Locke, in different words; sound waves for him would be a potential sound. In either case, any curious animal in the vicinity could check out what caused the sound, if it were not already obvious from its pattern and volume (the swish of the branches descending, the crackles and snaps of branches breaking, and the thump of the trunk), by moving in the direction from which the sound came, and could see if a tree had actually fallen, without having to have it confirmed or disconfirmed by someone else.

From the vantage point of the third, however conceived, was Gerson's patient making a "philosophical" point about the relational unconscious and the cultural relativity of meaning, or was he expressing an infantile transferential dependency on the analyst, in order to reduce his anxiety about trusting the evidence of his own senses or his ability to make his own decisions? No doubt the patient received the benefit of analytic interpretations of his dependency on his analyst and its history at the appropriate time. Might one not wonder whether the patient reaped this benefit despite the hypothesis of a relational unconscious, rather than because of it?

Locke, who used the idea of perceptual representation as a third, differentiated the primary qualities of objects from their secondary qualities. The primary qualities of shape, mass, solidity, number, location, motion, and rest are intrinsic properties of physical objects. The secondary qualities of color, sound, smell, taste, and so on are subjective. The colors we see and the sounds we hear are intrinsic to our sensory experience of objects and guide us in our relations with them, but they are not inherent in the objects themselves. Intrinsic to objects is the power to cause, by means of their reflection or absorption of uncolored light waves that impinge on our eyes, to generate the colors we see in them, and by soundless sound waves that impinge on our ears to generate the sounds they emit. These "sensible qualities," which Locke called secondary qualities, are therefore irreducibly subjective, though also for the most part passively received, unavoidable, and, in their own way, normative. Primary qualities, which can be quantified and described geometrically and mathematically, are objective. Locke was able to use the idea of representation to understand how our experience of primary qualities can be mistaken even though they are real properties of material objects. Motion and rest are primary qualities of objects. Yet we experience the sun to be in motion relative to the earth and the earth to be at rest. We experience the sun as being larger at the horizons than at its zenith. The idea of representation enabled Locke to incorporate into epistemology the implications of the new discoveries of Copernicus and Galileo in astronomy and of Descartes and Newton in optics.

Like Descartes (1641) and other rationalists such as Baruch Spinoza (1673), Locke (1690) considered self-awareness to be essential to the use of ideas as epistemological thirds. Consciousness is reflexive in the sense that when we perceive objects, imagine them, have feelings about them, or think about them, we are aware that we are perceiving, imagining, feeling, and thinking. Self-awareness, for Locke and for Descartes, was not an automatic and necessary concomitant of consciousness, for we can and do "lose ourselves" in thought, imagination, observation, feeling, or action. However, we also "come back" to ourselves from reveries, even in instances when we cannot recall what had so occupied our thoughts. Psychoanalysis can help people—albeit with great difficulty—to get back from being lost in severely dissociated states. For Locke and Descartes, self-awareness was of fundamental importance to cognitive activities because of its attesting and correcting functions. Although Locke repudiated Descartes's theory of innate ideas their epistemologies rejected Aristotelian epistemology because it limited knowledge to the classification of things to the exclusion of the more significant knowledge of their mainly physical and mechanical explanation. And self-awareness was assigned a yet more fundamental importance in German idealism.

KANT

In Immanuel Kant's (1781) epistemology, the "synthetic unity of apperception" (pp. 155–157) becomes the ultimate ground of knowledge and objectivity. "I think" (pp. 152–153) must accompany every sort of propositional thought and representation. The reflexive nature of consciousness lays down certain conditions that any thought must satisfy in order to be a thought about objects. The "I think" imposes its own subjective categorical conditions of thought on our knowledge of objects. For example, we cannot think about an object unless we think about it in terms of substance and attribute and causality. These are subjective conditions that the mind imposes on knowing anything.

As a result, Kant drew the skeptical conclusion that we can only know objects as they appear, but not as they are in themselves —hence, his distinction between phenomena and noumena. The Kantian third— the *idealist third*—is made up of the reflexivity of consciousness and the categorical conditions it imposes on knowledge. Whereas Descartes (1641) and Locke relied upon the attesting, cognitive function of self-awareness, Kant assigned to it a legislative function in knowledge.

HEGEL

G.W.F. Hegel (1807) went much further: "The individual is the immediate certainty of himself and ... he is therefore unconditioned being" (p. 40).

131

Psychoanalysis has taught us that self-knowledge comes only with labor, and is seldom, if ever, certain. Perhaps Hegel is referring to a consciousness without content. But how could consciousness confer "unconditioned being," if there is such a thing, on anything, including itself? In Hegel, we find the third of *absolute idealism.*

Even this highly selective, abbreviated, and truncated account of the epistemological third in philosophy presents a complicated picture. Self-awareness is of crucial importance for each of the philosophers considered here, except Peirce. Peirce's pragmatic fallibility logically requires a philosophical third that includes self-awareness armed with the capacity to sustain self-criticism, self-approval, and self-doubt. Yet Peirce denied individual identity. He thought of a person, and even of God, as a "bundle of habits," far removed from Kant's synthetic unity of apperception, Descartes's (1641) *cogito,* or Hegel's (1807) grandiose notion of unconditional being. Peirce considered personal identity to be a "vulgar delusion."

Psychoanalysts who espouse theories in which relations are prioritized over individuals, and who claim that the failure to give primacy to relations results in an untenable one-person psychology, can find some support for their views in Peirce. However, Peirce cut the psychological ground from under his pragmatism when he eliminated the possibility of critical self-awareness of believing, which many feel accompanies belief. Self-awareness must be capable of distancing itself from a belief, in order to critically consider that belief or to adopt an attitude of skepticism toward it, or to treat it with impartiality and neutralize one's adherence to it as conditional upon being able to submit that belief to the pragmatic test. Peirce's concept of thirdness is not consistent with the ideas of co-created relational thirds of the sort proposed by Ogden (2004) and Benjamin (2004) in this issue, or by other psychoanalytic intersubjectivists.

From a philosophical perspective, a third requires an idea. Otherwise, the functioning of self-awareness is limited to self-experience. An idea such as Descartes's Evil Deceiver or Locke's representation is required to, as it were, "lift" self-awareness to a position from which the cognitive activities of the self can be scrutinized, analyzed, and evaluated. The third can be the idea of a thing existing independently of the experience of it by human observers (Cavell, 1998). Such a third is to be found in philosophers who are otherwise as much at odds as Descartes and Locke.

Benjamin (2004), Gerson (2004), Minolli and Tricoli (2004), and Ogden (2004) tend to be critical of the idea that a third requires an idea (theory), let alone that a third requires an object independent of it (Descartes, Locke, Peirce). These analysts are concerned that a third in the form of an idea (knowledge, theory) at work in the analyst will have a detrimental effect on interaction within the analytic dyad by subordinating, derogating, or isolating the analysand in a variety of ways.

Britton (2004), Green (2004), Widlöcher (2004), and Zwiebel (2004) recognize the importance of ideas in the work of a third. Philosophically, there can be no third without an idea. Since Peirce "eliminated" self and self-awareness, for him a third is only an idea. However, other philosophers have recognized the need for both in the formation of an epistemological third. Wittgenstein (1921) treated philosophy itself as a self-eliminating third, a third that self-destructs as soon as it has achieved its purpose, namely, a rational relation to reality. Philosophy does not itself provide us with a knowledge of reality; rather, it helps us to realize that gaining knowledge of reality requires science. "He [the philosopher] must, so to speak, throw away the ladder [philosophy] after he has climbed up on it" (p. 151).

Embedded in or logically connected with the epistemological third is some idea of truth and verification. For Descartes, clear and distinct ideas warrant certainty no less in anatomy than in mathematics. For Locke, the truth of an idea depends on its empirical verification with the fallibility that attends it. For Peirce, ideas, however clear and distinct, require pragmatic

133

testing of their consequences. Russell (1946) pointed out some of the difficulties with pragmatism as a criterion of truth.

We can say of the philosophical third that it is typically (Peirce's views excepted) a function of self-awareness informed by an idea, though the exact nature of this idea differs in different philosophies.

THE THIRD IN PSYCHOANALYSIS

An idea of the third is also implicitly at work in psychoanalysis. In deriving and formulating this implicit idea and thus making it explicit, it is necessary to differentiate threesomes, triangular relations, and the use of the metaphor of "triangular space" or "triangulated space" from the third as such, although important linkages with them may be found; for example, Freud's (1905) explanation of smutty humor requires a threesome, but it does not involve a third. Nevertheless, the third is at work and is an object of implicit inquiry from the beginning of Freud's work.

Freud ([1895]1950) plausibly described the psychological genesis of the third, as Peirce understood it, with the beginning of instinctual object seeking, reality testing, and subject-object differentiation. This genesis takes place in earliest infancy with the differentiation between the image of the satisfying object that does not satisfy and the real object that does satisfy. At the heart of this experience is the first rudimentary awareness that images represent but do not duplicate, that they point beyond themselves to the needed, real satisfying object. The primitive rudiments of Locke's empiricist third are present in the structure, dynamics, and content of the primary infantile experience of need satisfaction, as Freud ([1895]1950) described it.

The Kleinian depressive position (Klein, 1935) is also a third. The depressive position is made possible by the infant's capacity to see the mother as a whole person who is both satisfying and frustrating, both good and bad, and to compare this real mother with the projections of the paranoid-schizoid positions. The third is an awareness of the difference between the largely subjective experience of an idealized and denigrated object and the more reliable experience of the object as it actually is.

There are innumerable dyadic parent-child situations in which a child becomes aware, while retaining self-awareness, that he or she is an object for another. An opportunity is provided for the child to gain a sense of how another sees him or her. These opportunities are building blocks for the child's evolving ability to objectify the self. However, seeing oneself with the eyes of another may either benefit or harm this inner capacity to be educated to reality. There are situations in which anxiety can cause a loss of self-awareness as a consequence of becoming an object for another. In these instances, the child feels overwhelmed, invaded, and taken over—consumed, as it were, by an object for whom the child has become nothing but an instrumentality. The result is a dyadic unity based on domination by the sadistic parent or surrogate, and diminution of the self-awareness and identity of the masochistically surrendering child.

Britton (1987) and Feldman (1997), among others, have explored these sorts of factors in the transference and the role of the analytic third in the countertransference. Benjamin (2004) describes situations of this sort in psychoanalysis. The differences observed between the point of view expressed by Britton (2004) on the one hand, and that of Benjamin and others of the relational school on the other, pose the question of whether clinical experience supports Kleinian/Freudian realism or relational, intersubjective idealism. Put differently: Which notion of the psychoanalytic third best helps the analyst to recognize, understand, and remedy these pathological situations and the analyst's involvement in them? It is my opinion that the radical revisions involved in the idea of Gerson's (2004) relational unconscious are not required to understand Jacobs's (2001) description of his becoming aware of a therapeutically disadvantageous countertransference.

The same is true, I think, of what Arlow (1979), Loewald (1979), Bird (1972), and Boesky (1990) have to say along the same lines.

The preoedipal child has a benign, anaclitic reliance on both parents, especially on the parent of the same sex, as surrogate egos to test reality and to identify danger—a dependency that allows the child full enjoyment of his or her fantasy life. In this relation, the child becomes aware of the difference between the way in which a parent experiences an object and the way the child experiences the same object. The recognition of this difference invites the child to sufficiently detach from the narcissistically naive self-evidence of his or her own experience to be able to question it and to treat it as, in Locke's terminology, a perceptual representation that may not be true of the object in some respects. In these ways and others, an education to reality takes place by pragmatic increments, made possible by a developing capacity for sensory and affective discrimination. The template provided by these early relations forms some of the psychological background for Cavell's (1998) argument concerning triangulation and objectivity. Fundamental to this process is primary identification.

Freud's increasing understanding of identification enabled him to clarify the psychological foundations of thirdness, that is, the preparation of the mental capacity for objectivity, and to advance his thinking on the role of identification in character formation and relations (Freud, 1917, 1921). He described how the strengthening of the child's identification with the parent of the same sex in the resolution of the Oedipus complex enables the child to internalize the position of the rivaled parent in relation to herself or himself, and thereby the parental prohibitions (Freud, 1923).

This identification internalizes a crucial aspect of an indispensable object relation, and in so doing, deeply modifies both the child's relation to the parents and to the child's own ego. In this way, the child consolidates an improved capacity for critical self-awareness, for self-approval or self-condemnation, and for a new measure of objectivity about self and primary objects (although at this point, the child cannot be expected to have an adequate measure of his or her parents). Whereas earlier, the child found her or his sense of worth primarily in the parent's love or withdrawal of it, sanctioned inwardly by shame, the child is now able to perform this function independently, sanctioned inwardly by guilt. The child has acquired a measure of moral autonomy and responsibility. The reflexivity of consciousness has been informed by a deontological morality.

But more than moral conscience is involved in this transformation as it proceeds. In the end, these developments provide for a fallible but reliable, self-critical, epistemic self-awareness, enabling us to objectify ourselves sufficiently to some genuine extent (some more than others), in order to test our experience for its objectivity, to adopt measures to reduce its subjectivity, and to test evidentially the beliefs to which our experience gives rise. We feel a diminution of our self-esteem when we are caught by ourselves or by others being logically inconsistent. In this way, psychoanalysis provides a psychological explanation of the origin and nature of the philosophical idea of a third position. This explanation is inconsistent with the Cartesian, Kantian, and Hegelian thirds, but consistent with the non-Aristotelian core of Peirce's third (see also Green, 2004) and with the empiricist third.

Freud's (1923) focus was on the moral, behavioral, and relational consequences of oedipal identification. Early on, Wälder (1934) noted the further implications of Freud's hypothesis: "What is common to these modes of super-ego attitudes [moral, humorous, cognitive] is self-observation, objectification of oneself, the attainment of a position above one's ego" (p. 104). This position "above one's ego" is a third in the philosophical sense. In addition, psychoanalysis provides Peirce with psychological grounds for classifying logic, along with morals, as a normative science, by setting out rules for valid reasoning and methods for empirical falsification and verification.

Rickman (1950, 1951) first introduced the idea of numbered psychologies (Hanly & Nichols, 2001). Having introduced the term "two-person psychology," based on Freud's uncovering of transference and countertransference, Rickman detailed what he considered to be the limitations of a two-person psychology, among them that it is confined to the here and now and to the immediate interactions between analysand and analyst. A perspective upon the past in the present, essential to the genetic orientation of psychoanalysis, is lacking. The transference, after all, is only a sign, to use Peirce's semiotic definition (as distinct from Saussure's signifier) of the analysand's past. The same is true of the analyst's countertransference. The transferential and countertransferential interactions of the dyad are but signs of these signs, which can only be read aright from a perspective that includes the past.

But analysis must seek out the past by means of free association. The horizon that opens a way to the past in the present requires the analyst to become aware of the analyst-analysand relation itself, by gaining a perspective or a position from which the relation can be objectified—that is, viewed for what it was and what it now is. This position is made possible by the third person, either real or imaginary, of the oedipal triangle. Rickman does not adequately formulate this notion because of his failure to grasp the importance and effect of oedipal identifications and their profound influence on self-awareness (the reflexivity of consciousness, as philosophers would say).

Nevertheless, Rickman goes to the heart of the matter. According to Rickman (1950, 1951), psychoanalysis, as Freud formulated it, is neither a one-person nor a two-person psychology. It is a three-person psychology that requires the analyst to be able to observe the dyadic analytic relation from the position of a third person—or more important, from the position of an observer who is sufficiently impersonal and unbiased to not be caught up in and confined by dyadic interaction. Freud set out how the analyst can function as the third in the analytic situation, as can the analysand. But given that the patient is debilitated by neurotic conflicts, and given the analytic contract, it is incumbent on the analyst to be able and prepared to facilitate the restoration or development of the function of the third in the analysand. The question arises as to whether or not and how, in this circumstance, a co-created third could serve this function.

This objectivity—in the sense of getting "outside" or "above" one's own subjectivity, in whatever form of complacency, partiality, dogmatism, preoccupation with self, or squeamishness it may take, in order to become aware of it, think about it, and disengage it (even partially) from the analysis—is psychologically grounded in the self-awareness made possible by oedipal identification. This identification internalizes the observing function of the parent as auxiliary ego during the earlier, more anaclitic stages of development. The subsequent development of this function is in the direction of greater impersonality and impartiality—doing what is right rather than what one has been told to do; crediting one's senses rather than received opinion and belief; and submitting one's observations, imaginings, and thoughts to the demands of reality, logic, and empirical testing.

This position "outside" the dyadic relation also opens the way to thinking about how the analysand experiences the analyst and his or her interpretations, as well as how the analyst experiences the analysand and his or her reactions to interpretations. There is nothing special about this analytic third; it belongs to common sense, science, art, and literature, as well as to everyday life. It is certainly not infallible, though experience, knowledge, and practice can improve it; in this respect, the analytic third, thus conceived, stands in opposition to the idealization of self-awareness found in the Cartesian, Kantian, and Hegelian thirds. Nor is this analytic third immune to psychopathology.

Britton (1987, 1998) traces the origins of the third position to the oedipal triangle, which provides for being seen in a relation with another and seeing a relation between two others. This experience lays down a template for a "capacity for seeing ourselves in interaction with others and for

139

entertaining another point of view whilst retaining our own, for reflecting on ourselves whilst being ourselves" (1987, p. 87). What is crucial about the oedipal identification is that it internalizes these templates, drawing them from triangular relations. Nowhere else in these discussions of the psychoanalytic third is there an explicit recognition of the contribution made by the resolution of the Oedipus complex to the cognitive use of thirdness. However, Green's (2004), Widlöcher's (2004), and Zwiebel's (2004) contributions appear to me to be compatible with Britton's insight and its relation to the philosophical, empiricist third.

Benjamin explicitly questions the oedipal contribution to the psychoanalytic third when she takes Britton (1998) and Feldman (1997) to task for running the risk of "privileging… the analyst's relation to the third as theory… as well as… an overemphasis on the oedipal content of the third" (Benjamin, 2004, p. 12). Gerson (2004) also criticizes Britton's (1998) idea of the third for being insufficiently intersubjective. Minolli and Tricoli (2004), as well as Ogden (2004) adumbrate psychological theories in which the Oedipus complex and its resolution appear to have little part to play, if any.

A DIALECTICAL DISCUSSION

Some papers in these explorations of the analytic third use the term "dialectical" without defining it. There are at least five different, serious uses of the term in philosophy: two from Plato and one each from Kant, Hegel, and Marx.

One of the best-known uses of the term "dialectic" is with reference to the Socratic dialectic of the Platonic dialogues. Often, the dialogues are searches for definitions of moral virtues, justice, love, the soul, etc. The search is conducted dramatically by means of arguments in favor of some definition—for example, that justice is the interest of the stronger, or a compromise between what we most and least want—advanced by a character in the dialogue. Socrates then points out weaknesses in the definitions and eventually advances one favored by Plato. Dialectic is the cut and thrust of intellectual arguments. Plato in the *Republic* also used the term to refer to some undefined process of reasoning that was supposed to lead from the contemplation of the forms of natural kinds—artifacts, arithmetical and geometric ideas, virtues, etc.—to the form of all forms, the Form of the Good.

Plato's notion of dialectic as intellectual debate is scarcely of use in psychoanalytic clinical thinking because, although some analysands want us to engage in such disputatious exchanges with them, their treatments are not served by our going along with the wish to engage in intellectual combat. Psychoanalysis teaches us the futility of trying to reason a patient out of a neurotically caused belief.

Kant (1781) used the term "dialectic" to refer to the futility of trying to prove the immortality of the soul, the infinity of the universe, and the existence of God (favorite undertakings of metaphysics) because as Kant believed, the soul, the universe, and God are not objects of possible experience. This exercise of pure reason (i.e., the use of concepts without content), Kant tried to show, results in arguments with contradictory conclusions. He called this exercise the *dialectic of pure reason.*

Hegel (1816) sought to go beyond Kant with a dialectical logic in which contradictions generate higher truths in which the contradictions are overcome. Hegel believed that dialectical logic is at work in thought, in history, in the organization of society, and in the cosmic evolution of nature. For Hegel, dialectic is the logic of an ultimately unifying, self-actualizing, spiritual force, which he called *Absolute Spirit.*

Marx (1873) invented the fifth meaning of "dialectic" by substituting materialism for Hegel's idealism. Marx asserted that Hegel had dialectic

141

standing on its head; Marx turned it right side up by hypothesizing that economic forces are the fundamental causes of historical change. Marx thus took over Hegel's dialectical logic, leaving it otherwise unchanged.

Psychoanalysts who use the word "dialectic" should clarify and carefully define the meaning of their use of the term. They should consider whether it has a specific psychoanalytic meaning that refers to something more than, or other than, psychic conflict (e.g., ambivalence, struggles between narcissistic libido and object libido, etc.). This semantic task is not trivial, as I shall now try to show.

SOME FURTHER PHILOSOPHICAL-PSYCHOANALYTIC REFLECTIONS AND QUESTIONS

Hegelian ideas make their appearance in several of these papers on the psychoanalytic third. Minolli and Tricoli (2004) make the most extensive use of Hegelian ideas, drawn from a sound translation into English by Baillie of Hegel's *Phenomenology of Mind* (1807). Suffice it to consider just one problem that cannot be avoided in formulating psychoanalytic findings in Hegelian terms. For Hegel, everything in a developmental process is animated by conflict. Hence, on the surface, his idea of dialectics might seem to agree with the centrality of conflict discovered by psychoanalysis in individual psychic development. Unfortunately, it does not. According to Hegel, any and every process is dialectically conflicted; an initial state generates its opposite. This opposing second state stands in contradiction to the first. The conflict then produces a resolution in a higher synthesis that overcomes the contradiction. These processes are teleological, irreversible, and progressive. Marx (1873), despite his materialist repudiation of Hegelian spirituality, nevertheless derived his utopianism directly from Hegel's logic. According to Hegel's logic, two fundamental vicissitudes that psychic processes undergo cannot occur: interruption of development by fixations, and the reversal of development in regressions. Moreover, needs and wishes cause individual and collective life to have purposes, but psychoanalysis does not view human life as the fulfillment of some cosmic teleology, such as the self-realization of Absolute Spirit in Hegel or the inevitable advance to a utopia in Marx.

To make Hegelian dialectic suitable for psychoanalytic theorizing, one would have to strip it of the logic peculiar to it or deny that there are fixations and regressions of needs, desires, and wishes. Why translate valuable psychoanalytic observations into a system of thought that runs counter to common sense? Marx's (1873) materialistic correction of Hegel's spirituality has not increased the credibility of dialectical logic. Any Hegelian definition of dialectic is incompatible with basic facts of human psychic life.

Ogden (2004) implicitly raises a fundamental issue. In understanding the analyst-analysand relationship, he states:

> The task is not to tease apart the elements constituting the relationship in an effort to determine which qualities belong to whom; rather, from the point of view of the interdependence of subject and object, the analytic task involves an attempt to describe the specific nature of the experience of the unconscious interplay of individual subjectivity and intersubjectivity. (p. 168)

This recommendation is based on the assumption that, in addition to the two persons who make up the analytic dyad and their interactions, there is a third, more fundamental, relational reality —their intersubjectivity—which is an amalgam of the two persons. This amalgam is a "subjectivity that seems to take on a life of its own" (p. 169). According to what one might call the Freudian/Kleinian third or the oedipal third, when such a predominantly preoedipal transference and countertransference develops, it falls to the analyst to sustain the analytic third in himself/herself, so that the analyst may continue to observe the self, the analysand, and the interplay between them in the sessions in order to enable the analyst to assess the therapeutic efficacy of their relationship.

Such conflicting assumptions currently divide psychoanalysis. There does not appear to be any way to reconcile them. The otherwise very different philosophical positions considered earlier agree that individual self-awareness is essential to thirdness (except Peirce's). To be sure, self-awareness is not sufficient in and by itself; an idea is needed to inform it and give it direction, but there are no philosophical precedents for intersubjective relational thirds, apart from individual consciousness—which is, of course, a consciousness of both self and others.

In the philosophical third, in one way or another (depending on the philosopher), the function of the third is to organize and direct the mind to take cognizance of itself in order to be better prepared to observe and understand both the self and the world. It is readily apparent how closely psychoanalysis agrees with—and enriches and improves the prospects of success in—this broad philosophical project, which Bacon (1620) traced back to the ancient Greeks. Perhaps Hegel could be made out to be an exception, despite the primacy he gives to individual self-awareness, but any attempt to use Hegelian ideas runs into the problem of the dialectical logic by means of which he derives the other from the subject.

Of course, conscious and unconscious relations of fundamental importance to the analysis are established between analyst and analysand. The analyst, by means of empathic trial identifications, needs to be able to feel, imagine, and think something (hopefully to a sufficient degree) of what it is like to be the analysand. But the analyst may feel himself or herself drawn into a fusion with the patient, in which the analysand comes to feel disorganized and enmeshed with the analyst. The same experiences may occur in the analyst. An analysand, for example, may feel drawn into

144

a fusional bond with the analyst that is focused on the soothing, to him or her, sound of the analyst's voice. But does the revival of such infantile experiences, and others like them, warrant the inference of a third entity that exists independently of the different transferential, countertransferential, and reality-bound relations formed by one member of the analytic dyad with the other?

If we follow Peirce back to medieval philosophy, we find William of Ockham, of the school of Scotus—who, with his now-famous razor, declared that entities should not be unnecessarily multiplied. Perhaps, upon further reflection by analysts, such entities as intersubjective thirds, the relational unconscious, and others will, like Platonic forms, fall under the cutting edge of Ockham's razor—or perhaps not. Yet in science, as in philosophy, the simplest theory to comprehend the phenomena will be most serviceable for the advancement of knowledge and more likely to turn out to be true.

Philosophy, as indicated by the foregoing all too brief survey, is almost universally committed to epistemological realism. Even philosophers like Peirce and Hegel, who were metaphysical idealists, were epistemological realists, as were Plato and Aristotle. Epistemological subjectivism is an unusual doctrine—espoused perhaps by Protagoras, but by few others. Some intersubjectivists, at least, adhere to the idea of irreducible subjectivity, a highly ambiguous notion (C. Hanly & M.A.F. Hanly, 2001). If its meaning is psychological, it signifies only that each person's feelings, motives, experiences, thinking, etc., are his or her own and no one else's. Objects can be shared and experiences can be verbally shared, but my experience of the object is mine, and yours is yours. They are psychologically irreducibly subjective because each individual is the owner of her/his own sensory apparatus.

This statement says nothing about our capacity to have the same experiences, however, or to know that we have different experiences of one and the same object; nor does it say anything about our ability, by means of

145

sense perception, to become aware of the existence and nature of objects that exist apart from and independently of our own subjectivity—as Peirce and Locke, but also Descartes and Berkeley philosophically affirmed. But if the meaning of irreducible subjectivity is cognitive, and hence epistemological, it means that our perceptions, thoughts, etc. must inevitably fail in making us aware of the existence and nature of objects that exist apart from and independently of our own minds. No method of investigation, no correction of perceptual illusion, will serve. Our minds are inevitably locked within their own subjectivity.

Thus, if the notion of irreducible subjectivity is implied by intersubjectivity, and if the notion of irreducible subjectivity is taken as an epistemological one, rather than merely as the assertion of an elementary psychological and neurological fact, we are each located in our own worlds, as contrived by Descartes's Evil Deceiver. Most authors, in fact, treat irreducible subjectivity as a cautionary notion—not an epistemological premise, but a warning against naive realism. These warnings are obviously helpful; however, the concept as often used carries the implicit, false implication that all realists are naive realists. This is perhaps true of Aristotle and Plato, but not of Locke or Peirce, or of Galileo, Harvey, Newton, Einstein, Darwin, or Freud.

That psychoanalysis is a process, who could doubt? That it is greater than the conscious volition or detailed comprehension of analyst or analysand need not be in doubt either. But these facts do not require a special ontology of the primacy of relations. What *can* be doubted is that there is a third participant making up the process, a co-created subjectivity of some sort, with some kind of life of its own. Aristotle's classic third-man critique of Plato's forms would appear to apply here. It is an infinite-regress argument. Since the analyst and analysand co-create a first relational third, the analyst will have to form some kind of relation with this third. But this relation will co-create a *second* relational third, and so on ad infinitum. The same will apply to the analysand.

I can understand that psychoanalysts might not be as impressed as philosophers by the problem posed for theories by infinite-regress arguments. Such arguments do indicate serious logical and conceptual flaws in theories when they apply. In any case, would it not be adequate, as well as simpler, to assume that the analytic dyad is made up of two persons with separate identities, needs, characters, and motives, who relate to each other according to their respective needs, characters, and motives, one of whom is in need of help and one of whom is there trained to help? The work of the analyst's analytic third in differentiating what is subjective and what is objective in the patient and in the analyst and in their relationship is essential to the help that analysts seek to provide.

REFERENCES

Arlow, J. (1979). The genesis of interpretation. *Journal of the American Psychoanalytic Association* 27:193–206.

Bacon, F. (1620). *Novum Organum*. New York: Willey Book Co., 1944.

Benjamin, J. (2004). Beyond doer and done to: An intersubjective view of thirdness. *Psychoanalytic Quarterly* 73:5–46.

Berkeley, G. (1710). *The Principles of Human Knowledge*. In M.W. Calkins (Ed.), *Berkeley* (pp. 99–216). New York: Scribner's, 1929.

Bird, B. (1972). Notes on transference: Universal phenomenon and hardest part of analysis. *Journal of the American Psychoanalytic Association* 20:267–302.

Boesky, D. (1990). The psychoanalytic process and its components. *Psychoanalytic Quarterly* 59:550–584.

Britton, R. (1987). The missing link: Parental sexuality in the Oedipus complex. In J. Steiner (Ed.), *The Oedipus Complex Today* (pp. 83–101). London: Karnac.

———— (1998). Subjectivity, objectivity and potential space. In *Belief and Imagination: Explorations in Psychoanalysis* (pp. 41–58). London: Routledge. [Reprinted 2004. *Psychoanalytic Quarterly* 73: 47–62]

Cavell, M. (1998). Triangulation, one's own mind and objectivity. *International Journal of Psychoanalysis* 79:449–467.

Descartes, R. (1641). *Meditations on First Philosophy* (Trans. E.S. Haldane & G.R.T. Ross). In *The Philosophical Works of Descartes*, vol. 1 (pp. 144–199). New York: Dover, 1955.

Feldman, M. (1997). The dynamics of reassurance. In R. Schafer (Ed.), *The Contemporary Kleinians of London* (pp. 321–344). Madison, CT: International Universities Press.

Freud, S. ([1895]1950). Project for a scientific psychology. SE 1:281–391.

———— (1905). *Jokes and Their Relation to the Unconscious*. SE 8.

———— (1917). Mourning and melancholia. SE 14:237–258.

———— (1920). Beyond the pleasure principle. SE 18:1–64.

———— (1921). Group psychology and the analysis of the ego. SE 18:65–144.

———— (1923). The ego and the id. SE 19:1–66.

Gerson, S. (2004). The relational unconscious: A core element of inter-subjectivity, thirdness, and clinical process. *Psychoanalytic Quarterly* 73:63–98.

Green, A. (2004). Thirdness and psychoanalytic concepts. *Psychoanalytic Quarterly* 73:99–136.

Hanly, C. (1995). On facts and ideas in psychoanalysis. *International Journal of Psychoanalysis* 76:901–908. [Chapter 4 in this volume]

Hanly, C., & Hanly, M.A.F. (2001). Critical realism: Distinguishing the psychological subjectivity of the analyst from epistemological subjectivism. *Journal of the American Psychoanalytic Association* 27:193–206.

Hanly, C., & Nichols, C. (2001). A disturbance of psychoanalytic memory: The case of John Rickman's three-person psychology. *Philosophy of the Social Sciences* 31:279–301.

Hegel, G.W.F. (1807). *The Phenomenology of Mind* (Trans. J.B. Baillie). London: George Allen & Unwin; New York: Humanities Press, 1971.

———— (1816). *The Science of Logic* (Trans. A.V. Miller). London: George Allen & Unwin, 1969.

Hobbes, T. (1651). *Leviathan*. Harmondsworth: Penguin, 1974.

Jacobs, T.J. (2001). On unconscious communications and covert enactments: Some reflections on their role in the analytic situation. *Psychoanalytic Inquiry* 21:4–23.

Kant, I. (1781). *Critique of Pure Reason* (Trans. N.K. Smith). London: Macmillan, 1950.

Klein, M. (1935). A contribution to the psychogenesis of manic-depressive states. In *The Writings of Melanie Klein* (pp. 262–289). London: Hogarth Press, 1975.

Locke, J. (1690). *An Essay concerning Human Understanding*. In J.A. St. John (Ed.), *The Philosophical Works of John Locke*, vol. 1. London: George Bell & Sons, 1898.

Loewald, H. (1979). Reflections on the psychoanalytic process. In *Papers on Psychoanalysis* (pp. 372–383). New Haven: Yale University Press, 1980.

Marx, K. (1873). *Capital*, 2nd ed. (Ed. F. Engels; Trans. S. Moore & E. Aveling). London: William Glaisher, 1909.

Minolli, M., & Tricoli, M. (2004). Solving the problem of duality: The third and self-consciousness. *Psychoanalytic Quarterly* 73:137–166.

Ogden, T. (2004). The analytic third: Reflections about the internal analytic working process. *Psychoanalytic Quarterly* 73:167–195.

Peirce, C. (1871). Fraser's edition of *The Works of George Berkeley*. In A. Burks (Ed.), *Collected Papers of Charles Sanders Peirce*, vol. 8 (pp. 9–38). Cambridge, MA: Harvard University Press, 1966.

———— (1903). *Pragmatism as a Principle and Method of Right Thinking: The 1903 Harvard Lectures on Pragmatism* by Charles Sanders Peirce (Ed. P.A. Turrisi). Albany: State University of New York Press, 1997.

———— (1905). Preface [excerpted from "Pragmatism"]. In C. Hartshorne & P. Weiss (Eds.), *Collected Papers of Charles Sanders Peirce*, vol. 5 (pp. 1–9). Cambridge, MA: Harvard University Press, 1966.

Plato. *The Republic* (Trans. B. Jowett). Cleveland: World Publishing, 1946.

Rickman, J. (1950). The factor of number in individual- and-group dynamics. *Journal of Mental Science* 96:770–773.

———— (1951). Number and the human sciences. In *Selected Contributions to Psychoanalysis* (pp. 224–283). London: Hogarth Press, 1957.

Russell, B. (1946). *History of Western Philosophy*. New York: Routledge, 1996.

Spinoza, B. (1673). *Ethics*. In J. Wild (Ed.), *Spinoza: Selections* (pp. 94–400). New York: Charles Scribner's Sons, 1930.

Wälder, R. (1934). The problem of freedom in psychoanalysis and the problem of reality testing. In *Psychoanalysis: Observation, Theory, Application* (pp. 101–120). New York: International Universities Press, 1976.

Widlöcher, D. (2004). The third in mind. *Psychoanalytic Quarterly* 73:197–214.

Wittgenstein, L. (1921). *Tractatus Logico-Philosophicus* (Trans. D.F. Pears & B.F. McGuinness). London: Routledge & Kegan Paul, 1961.

Zwiebel, R. (2004). The third position: Reflections about the internal working process. *Psychoanalytic Quarterly* 73:215–265.

CHAPTER 8

The Interplay of Deductive and Inductive Reasoning in Psychoanalytic Theorizing*

A version of this paper was presented as the 2005 Freud Anniversary Lecture at the New York Psychoanalytic Institute.

Deductive and inductive reasoning both played an essential part in Freud's construction of psychoanalysis. Inductive reasoning derives general truths from particular truths of observation and confirms (or falsifies) predictions and causal explanations. Deductive reasoning derives particular truths from general truths and the observational consequences of theoretical explanatory assumptions or causal laws. In addition, deductive reasoning allows us to draw out the implications for psychoanalysis of the findings in adjacent sciences, as Freud (1920) attempted in drawing upon cellular biology to shore up his postulate of a death instinct, and as analysts now seek to do using recent findings in brain sciences. These abstract definitions (of deductive and inductive reasoning) will be contextually illustrated, elaborated upon, and given further connotative and denotative definition as we proceed. In scientific thinking, these two forms of reasoning go hand in hand. We shall see why (and how) it is that inductive reasoning is fundamental.

---

* Originally published in *Psychoanalytic Quarterly* 83, no. 4 (2014):897–915.

Historically, the necessity of this alliance between inductive and deductive reasoning was not always fully understood. Bacon (1620), the father of inductive reasoning, did not appreciate the need for ideas and the inferences drawn from them in the formation of scientific hypotheses that can be inductively tested. Descartes (1641) appreciated the role of ideas, but then exaggerated that role by assuming that all knowledge can be deductively derived from ideas that are clear and distinct, which are ideas he took to be self-evidently true. As a result, although Bacon made many observations, he did not advance scientific knowledge as did, for example, the ingenious William Harvey (1578–1657) in the field of anatomy. And despite having invented analytic geometry and having made original contributions to optics, Descartes was able to persuade himself that Harvey's demonstration of the circulation of the blood was grounded in a clear and distinct idea innate to the mind. Furthermore, despite his radical philosophical skepticism, Descartes failed to consider the possibility that physical space may not be rectilinear, as Euclid's synthetic geometry and his own analytic geometry assumed.

This dichotomy between empiricism and rationalism is bridged in scientific thinking and observation. Freud's (1915) working awareness of this integrated epistemological position is apparent in the following statement:

We have often heard it maintained that sciences should be built up on clear and sharply defined basic concepts. In actual fact no science, not even the most exact, begins with such definitions. The true beginning of scientific activity consists rather in describing phenomena and then proceeding to group, classify and correlate them. Even at this stage of description it is not possible to avoid applying certain abstract ideas to the material in hand, ideas derived from somewhere or other but certainly not from the new observations alone. Such ideas—which will later become the basic concepts of the science—are still more indispensable as the material is further worked over.... We come to an understanding about their meaning by making repeated references to the material of observation from which they appear to have been derived, but upon which, in fact, they have been imposed. Thus, strictly speaking they are in the nature of conventions—although everything depends on their not being arbitrarily chosen but determined by their having significant relations to the empirical material. (p. 117)

Freud's statement agrees with a similar epistemological position set out by Einstein (1922) on the basis of his experience of having constructed relativity theory and seen it validated by predicted observations:

The only justification for our concepts and system of concepts is that they serve to represent the complex of our experiences; beyond this they have no legitimacy. I am convinced that the philosophers have had a harmful effect upon the progress of scientific thinking in removing certain fundamental concepts from the domain of empiricism, where they are under our control, to the intangible heights of the *a priori*. (p. xvi)

I propose to explore this happy marriage of empiricism and rationalism in Freud's use of deductive reasoning in the construction of psychoanalytic theory. To do this, I will consider three major amendments Freud made to his theory: (i) infant and childhood sexuality, (ii) the structural theory, and (iii) the theory of signal anxiety. But before doing so, let me first clarify the epistemological position that I call *critical realism* (and which I share with Freud and Einstein) by way of a brief examination of the inferential reasoning used by Harvey in his discovery of the circulation of the blood.

Harvey's demonstration, contrary to Baconian inductive expectations, did not involve any direct observations of circulating blood in humans or other animals (Singer, 1957). However, the truth of his deduction depended on a crucial observation of the amount of blood pumped from the heart of a sheep. The truth of the hypothesis about human anatomy (i.e., that the blood circulates) was deductively derived from observations of a naturally occurring simulation of the action of the human heart.

Originally, Harvey believed (with Galen, a Greek physician who lived in the second century AD) that blood was brought to the heart from the lungs and stomach by veins and distributed to the extremities by the pumping action of the heart. Existing anatomical ideas, based on Galen's work, held that the pumping action of the heart supplied energy and heat to the body, which, once it had used up its supply, was smoothly resupplied by new blood from the stomach and lungs with each succeeding pulse. Harvey's ingenuity consisted, first, of daring to question the long-established authority of Galen by considering the contrary and alternative hypothesis that a stable supply of blood is pumped from the heart into the body and is drawn back to the heart, enriched by nourishment and air from the stomach and lungs while providing warmth and energy to the body. Second, Harvey correctly hypothesized, through deductive inference from Galen's explanation, that if the amount of blood pumped into the body by the heart was used up, the body would have to replace it by consuming and ingesting an amount of nourishment and air every twenty-four hours that would be equal to the mass of blood distributed by each pulse multiplied by the number of pulses in a day. This inference from Galen's theory was crucial because it linked the theory to observable reality in a way that made it empirically testable. It is upon inferences of this kind that the advancement of knowledge depends.

Since Harvey could not legally (or morally) measure the amount of blood pumped into the body by a human heart, he had to turn to a non-human animal with a heart and body of comparable size to the human heart and body, namely, a sheep. Having captured and weighed the blood from a single pulse of a sheep heart, Harvey made the calculation based on Galen's model, and found that it would be impossible for any sheep to ingest the gargantuan amounts of air, solids, and liquids required in a twenty-four-hour period. Therefore, he concluded, the circulatory systems in mammals must be continuous.

This fundamental fact of human anatomy was derived deductively by Harvey without any direct observation of blood coursing through the human body, that is, of the object that the circulatory theory accurately describes. But neither was it deductively derived from a Cartesian clear and distinct idea. Rather, it was derived from a combined use of deductive inference and observation that exploited the fact that there are only two alternatives: the anatomical system is either linear or circular (and not both).

The observation of the mass of blood pumped in one beat of a sheep's heart is the crucial fact, which enables an inductive inference to the circulatory systems of other mammals, on which the truth of the deductive derivation depends. From this, Harvey was able to infer as well, without further observation, that arterial blood nourishes tissue from where the blood is taken up by veins and resupplied with the required nutriments when it is returned to the heart. Anatomical observation confirmed Harvey's inferences. One is reminded of Freud's ([1895]1950) deductive discovery of neuronal synapses.

The bare bones of the deductive inference involved in Harvey's anatomical proof can be rendered in two syllogisms (a deductive form of argumentation). The first is an alternative syllogism:

1. Either the blood system of mammals is discontinuous or it is circulatory.
2. It cannot be discontinuous.
3. Therefore, it must be circulatory.

The second is a categorical syllogism:

1. The blood systems of mammals are circulatory (the conclusion above).
2. Human beings are mammals.
3. Therefore, the circulatory system of human beings is circulatory.

These deductive inferences can be shown to be formally valid. However, there is an inductive generalization upon which the whole depends: the generalization from sheep to the whole class of mammals. The deductive argument is valid, but it is sound only in the important sense of deriving a conclusion that is true if the premises are true. Here the fundamental role of observation and inductive reasoning in science is clear.

Yet there is also a further factual consideration that bears upon the probability of the truth of this generalization. Could the environment sustain any mammal omnivorous enough to supply a discontinuous blood system? The answer would seem to be a resounding "not at all likely." From these considerations, we can draw three epistemologically significant inferences: (1) deductive reasoning can provide only formal certainty (i.e., certainty subject to the condition that the premises it employs are true); therefore, (2) since knowledge depends upon observation, inductive reasoning is primary and sets limits to the certainty of knowledge; but (3) Harvey's theory of the circulation of the blood in mammals qualifies for the highest level of probability because there is no reason to think that it could ever be vulnerable to negative instances.

As Einstein (1922) pointed out, systems of geometry are only formally certain until the axioms on which they are based are observationally tested, and then the best they can achieve are levels of empirical probability. By this measure, Freud's theory of unconscious psychic processes is much more probable than Euclid's axiom of parallels, even though Descartes believed the axiom to be self-evidently clear and distinct, because Euclid's rectilinear geometry of space does encounter fundamental negative instances in relativity physics. If we now consider the impact of Harvey's deductive reasoning on his observations, we can see that he was decisively influenced in his search for telling observations by the idea that he should consider the amount of nourishment needed to supply a discontinuous blood system. The idea told him what he should look at. But the epistemological influence of the idea does not extend so far as to influence the observation he made, namely, the mass of the blood or his method of measurement. His guiding idea, which determined the measurement he needed to make, did not alter the weight of the blood pumped into the body by one pulse. This value was not epistemologically compromised by Harvey's guiding idea. Harvey's anatomical finding refutes all those who would claim that science in general is, in principle, unable to ground its knowledge in reliably objective observations that are not compromised by the observer or by his methods of observation.

However, what if clinical observation in psychoanalysis, unlike observation in other sciences, is unavoidably subjectively compromised— "irreducibly subjective," as it has been characterized (Renik, 1993)—and thus compromised in principle or a priori? What if psychoanalysis is fated never to be able to meet Einstein's standard of scientific knowledge? Certainly, clinical psychoanalysis is dependent upon the observation of the qualities of the psychic lives of persons rather than upon the quantification of any of their physical properties. Morality prohibits clinical experimentation on patients. No other animals are equipped, so far as we know, with psyches that could be used to simulate the human psyche—that is, there is no equivalent to Harvey's sheep's heart. It would be reasonable to assume that psychic reality is more difficult to observe than physical reality.

Moreover, contemporary psychoanalysts of the subjectivist school will assert, contrary to critical realism, that objective observation is an authoritarian myth and that thinking is irremediably *a priori*, since the mind has no alternative but to impose, in some Kantian-like fashion, the stamp of itself in the construction of everything it perceives or contemplates. Critical realism, on the other hand, is the epistemological idea that there is a real world that exists independently of our senses, and which we can know, to some extent, by the use of appropriate methods of observation in science and through unaided observation that allows us to acquire common-sense knowledge of other persons and other things.

Freud (1927) advanced a group of arguments against the subjectivist position in epistemology, of which I will mention three:

1. The human mind has "developed precisely in the attempt to explore the external world, and it must therefore have realized in its structure some degree of expediency" (p. 55) in testing reality—an evolutionary argument.
2. The human psyche is part of nature and is as knowable as any natural object—an ontological argument.
3. The human mind is not only determined by its own organization, but also by the objects that affect it—a psychological argument.

To these I would add a historical/developmental argument. The animistic cultures of ancient times owed their psychological origins to ancient men and women projecting their own psychic nature onto objects (Hanly, 1988a). As these projections gradually diminished (a process that Epicurus tried to hasten with his philosophy of material naturalism), the material nature of physical objects became more apparent to the senses and more conceivable by the intellect. It was, in part, the deanimation of their experience of nature that allowed Copernicus, Galileo, and others to develop the basic concepts and methods of natural science. The human mind was becoming more affected by the nature of inanimate objects than by itself, and thus was undergoing what Freud (1927) called an "education to reality" (p. 49), which generated a reduction in the self-glorification of cognitive subjectivity, an increase in the capacity for realism, and the satisfaction of curiosity for its own sake that is needed for scientific work.

This profound transformation in the human experience of nature has been the major paradigm shift in civilized life. Nor was it limited to the experience of the physical world, for it equally transformed self-experience and the way we experience other persons (Hanly, 1988b). The same educational-cultural transition takes place in the development of the individual from early childhood to latency in modern human beings. Ego regression involves the loss of objectivity when projections, denials, and splitting dominate perception and thought. Hence, although objectivity is an achievement rather than a given, cognitive subjectivity can be reduced, and when it is, objectivity becomes proportionately more attainable. An early psychoanalytic account of the psychology of this process of education to reality during infancy and childhood was insightfully sketched out by Ferenczi (1913).

Concerns about the reliability of psychoanalytic clinical observation will continue, as they should. There is no end to the need to critically observe and correct our clinical observing, just as there is no end to the need to test our clinical responsiveness, countertransferences, and our interpretations against changes in the patient's transferences, associations, and functioning inside and outside the analytic situation. Analysts who have espoused a subjectivist epistemology have contributed usefully to the inventory of the ways in which analysts fail to allow the patient to be and to be understood.

The problem is not with the criticism—namely, that some clinical observations of analysts are subjective—but with the assertion that *all* clinical observations are necessarily subjective. Without ideas there can be no observation, and without observation we cannot know what ideas we should be entertaining and whether or not they are reliable. I endorse the critical realist assumption that, while many difficulties stand in the way of our understanding human psychic reality, with psychoanalytic insight into these difficulties they can be overcome sufficiently to bring therapeutic benefits to our patients and to build a body of scientific knowledge.

I now turn to an exploration of the interplay of deductive and inductive reasoning in Freud's construction of psychoanalysis with a consideration of (1) infant and childhood sexuality, (2) the structural theory, and (3) the theory of signal anxiety.

CHILDHOOD SEXUALITY

Freud's first attempt at an explanation of neurosis was his seduction theory, which focused on sexual seduction in childhood. The memories of these experiences, when they are revived and their meaning apprehended with the onset of sexuality (at this time, Freud assumed that sexuality originates with the physical and mental changes experienced at puberty), cause psychological symptoms when, on account of moral or aesthetic anxiety, they are subjected to repression in adolescence.

The theory's clinical and therapeutic corollary was the cathartic theory. Freud introduced the required supplementary hypothesis of *deferred action* to account for the delay of the symptomatic appearance of the trauma from childhood to puberty. These and other hypotheses making up the total theory were coherent, that is, they were logically consistent with each other.

Freud's proud enthusiasm for his theory, for which he was prepared to risk his friendship with Breuer and his reputation, was short-lived (Freud, 1897). The theory predicted symptom remission and functional improvements when the childhood scenes of seduction were recalled and their affects were abreacted, but these remissions were not regularly occurring and were too often temporary when they did (Freud, 1897, 1925,

1933). Here we come upon an example of Freud's deductive thinking (the Cartesian element) at work in his drawing out, in the form of a hypothetical syllogism, the observable clinical outcomes predicted by his theory.

We also come upon a crucial aspect of Freud's inductive thinking (the Baconian element): his search for negative instances, that is, for clinical observations that would falsify his theories. Freud's thinking willingly paid homage to the codependency of inductive and deductive thinking in scientific work and tolerated the misery of a negative outcome: "I am tormented by grave doubts about my theory of the neurosis" (Freud, 1897, p. 259). Freud submitted to the impersonality and the sublime indifference of logic and fact to our wishes.

For the purposes of this exposition, I will disregard the other cogent reasons that Freud (1897) had for doubting his *neurotica* (except for the second argument, which is built into the discussion below), in order to proceed at once to the reasoning that opened the way forward to Freud. His starting point was his observation of affect-laden scenes of seduction occurring in his patients' free associations. One of the tasks of scientific thought in the Renaissance was to *save the appearances*. For example, one of the important appearances that theory in astronomy had to save in order to provide the grounds of a scientific astronomy was the apparent diurnal rotation of the sun around the earth, plain for every observer to see. Both objectives were accomplished by Copernicus's theologically unwelcome hypothesis of the diurnal rotation of the earth on its axis, which explained the apparent motions of the sun and other heavenly bodies to be an unavoidable visual illusion caused by the diurnal rotation of human observers.

This great discovery in astronomy reveals the shortcomings of naive or simplistic realism linked to inductive reasoning. Ordinary perceptual experience teaches us much about nature. But it also keeps some of the most fundamental facts of nature secret. It was reason (rather than experience) that led Copernicus to the hypothesis that would reveal the astronomical

161

secret of the earth's rotation. The task posed for Freud was to save the scenes of sexual seduction disclosed by his clinical observations, scenes that his seduction theory took to be memories of real historical events, as did his patients.

There were three possibilities: the seductions were either inflicted, imagined, or suggested. The logical alternation in this enumeration of possibilities is not exclusive as it was with Harvey's alternatives. In Freud's case, the disjunctive alternatives are mutually compatible, and all three could be true. A patient could have imagined being seduced, as well as having suffered seduction at the hands of another, and the patient's awareness of these events could be the result of a resistive, intellectual compliance with the importuning of an overzealous, dogmatic, and naive therapist, rather than an authentic recovery of remembered events or wishful fantasies.

Freud realized that, although childhood seduction when combined with a "failure of repression" could be a sufficient cause of neurosis in adults, it is not a necessary cause. It is implausible to suppose that seductions could account for the number of neuroses that occur because it would require a yet greater number of perverse parents (especially fathers, including his own). This argument is based on impressions and estimations rather than observations. However, Freud (1897) did have a reason for thinking that the incidents of seduction would have to be greater than the incidents of neurosis. Conditions in addition to a history of childhood seduction— specifically, "a failure of repression"—would also have to have occurred. What the argument needed were occurrences of neuroses despite the absence of seduction.

During this period of searching for a better theory, Freud's self-analysis provided him with such a case. At first, he traced his hysteria and travel phobia to a memory of having been seduced by his father. But in the next months, Freud recaptured more early childhood memories, including a memory of his nurse. These memories, corroborated in some important details by his mother, provided him with two important pieces of evidential data: first, the part his own childhood sexuality played in his predisposition to hysteria, and second, the realization that a memory of seduction by his father had been a disguising fantasy.

Here we come upon the crucial inferential step that revolutionized Freud's thinking. The basic ideas of infantile sexuality and the substitution of a fantasy for reality came from Freud's self-analysis and his clinical experience. He was able to stumble on them because of the defeat of his efforts to clinically confirm the seduction theory. What could "save the appearance" of memories of sexual seduction that arose in the free associations of patients in analysis? They could be explained if fantasies, strongly invested with the patient's sexual wishes, had been subjected to repression, only to reappear later as memories of childhood sexual seductions associated with neurotic symptoms.

This hypothesis had a number of crucial implications. First, the underlying psychic processes involved in symptom formation do not differentiate fantasy from reality. This implication agreed with Freud's clinical observations, in particular with his growing realization that dreams are disguised wish fulfillments of hallucinatory intensity. The hypothesis became a cornerstone of the topographical model, as the primary differentiation between unconscious and conscious thought activity, by defining the cognitive and volitional (motivational) liability of the pleasure principle. This implication would help account for the appearance in consciousness of fantasies as memories of actual happenings.

Second, psychic development can be as influenced by such fantasies as by real experiences. If so, this causal efficacy is a constitutional factor that partially defines psychic reality. Narcissism would also have to play a part by affirming the reality of a desired experience that had not occurred, but had suffered frustration. This influence of narcissism is also found in the treatment of ego ideals that ought to be followed even when they are not. Third, sexuality has its onset with birth and not with puberty, which is when it makes the final transition to its adult genital organization. This last implication, combined with the second, has the further implication that human sexuality enters into the fabric of human experience and development prior to genital sexuality and serves functions other than reproduction—specifically, a series of intensely pleasurable sensations. This inherited organizing, constituting, and motivating function of sexuality in psychic development led Freud to introduce the term *libido* in place of *sexuality* to signal these far-reaching conceptual differences .

These ideas owe their origin to experience, even though the processes and experiences to which they refer are partly caused by genetic inheritance. They are Baconian empirical concepts consistent with Locke's (1690) idea of the mind as a tabula rasa. They are very far from Cartesian innate ideas, even though they owe their origin to innately caused self-experience (Hanly, 1988b). However, their place in psychoanalytic theory, their interconnections, and their implications were worked out deductively. At this stage, Freud was not primarily seeking clinical confirmation of causal hypotheses or descriptive generalizations, although he clearly had this possibility in mind; rather, he was considering the question: What could account for the prevalence of scenes of sexual seduction appearing as memories of real experiences in the associations of neurotic patients?

The ideas elaborated above form a group of hypothetical ideas that, if true, would account for the occurrence of these scenes and their pathogenic consequences, despite the absence of a history of sexual seduction. They form a logically connected group of hypothetical ideas from which explanations can be constructed and predictive inferences drawn, which can then be inductively tested by clinical observation. By treating libido as an instinct and by postulating further that fixation and regression are the two major vicissitudes of instinct, Freud was able to account for the predisposition to neuroses, the psychic processes at work in dreams, parapraxes, and symptoms, as well as significant elements of character formation. Freud's reasoning generated explanations for previously incomprehensible aspects of human psychic activity.

THE STRUCTURAL THEORY

The topographical model contained a serious flaw. Moral and aesthetic imperatives and ideals that oppose certain libidinal demands were located topographically along with perception, thought, and behavior within consciousness. From this locus, these imperatives could successfully oppose libidinal demands for satisfaction. Since ego functions are subject to the overarching reality principle, it follows that the imperatives and ideals of moral and aesthetic conscience have been subjected to reality testing, which has established their benefit to the individual, to the family, and to collectivities. Thus, although conscience contributes to psychopathology by opposing the satisfaction of fixated or regressed libidinal wants, conscience is not itself subject to psychopathology. Included in the task of psychoanalytic treatment is the maturation of libidinal wants so that they will no longer be in conflict with conscience. What is repressed is unconscious, but what does the repressing is conscious, or at most, preconscious.

The reasoning that contradicted this implication of the topographical model can be summarized as follows:

1. If the unconscious is the repressed, then what does the repressing is conscious.
2. But what does the repressing is unconscious.
3. Therefore, the unconscious cannot be equated with the repressed.

This reasoning has the form of a modus ponens, hypothetical syllogism, that is, an argument in which the consequence of a hypothetical proposition (first premise) is false (second premise), from which it validly follows that the antecedent of the first premise is false. Freud (1923) stated this conclusion of his reasoning as follows: "We recognize that the Ucs. [the Unconscious] does not coincide with the repressed; it is true that all that is repressed is Ucs., but not all that is Ucs. is repressed" (p. 18). Here Freud is correctly relying on the fact that the subject (but not the predicate) of universal affirmative categorical propositions is distributed. This means that, unlike universal negative categorical propositions, in which both subject and predicate are distributed, they cannot be converted.

Again, we notice the interdependence of inductive and deductive reasoning in scientific thinking. The first premise is a deductive inference from the topographical model, the truth of which is being evaluated. The truth of the crucial second premise (i.e., that which does the repressing is unconscious) is inductively established by clinical experience. The evidence for the truth of the second premise, cited by Freud (1923), is that the motives of repression are "also unconscious and ... require special work before ... [they] can be made conscious" (p. 17).

Further specific clinical evidence for its truth is the *negative therapeutic reaction* (Freud 1923). The conclusion is the cornerstone of the structural theory. Once laid down, this cornerstone opened the way for Freud's (1923) account of the crucial contribution of the resolution of the Oedipus complex to the formation of conscience and its vulnerability to psychopathology when this resolution is imperfectly accomplished.

THE THEORY OF ANXIETY: FROM CONVERSION TO SIGNAL

Freud's first theory of anxiety was the conversion theory. But despite phenomena that appear to corroborate it, Freud (1926) found it necessary to fundamentally revise it. The conversion theory of anxiety had a fatal flaw, which is that it treats anxiety as a byproduct of repression: when a libidinal demand undergoes repression, the pleasure that would otherwise have attended its fulfillment is converted into unpleasure in the form of anxiety. This account of the genesis of anxiety appears to be confirmed by, for example, the patient who, while driving to pick up his mother at the airport shortly after the death of his father, is overtaken by the anxiety that he is having a heart attack similar to the one to which his father had recently succumbed. An old incestuous, possessive wish, revived by his father's death, has been further stimulated by his mother's arrival for a visit after the funeral, and has undergone repression. The conscious product of this repression is the experience of being overwhelmed with anxiety about suffering his father's fate, to such an extent that he has to pull off the road and be taken to an emergency ward by a concerned fellow motorist. At the hospital he is assured, but not convinced, that his heart is perfectly healthy. It is not difficult to notice the same sequence—forbidden libidinal impulse, repression, anxiety—in cases other than conversion hysteria as well, such as in obsessional rituals (Freud, 1916–1917) and phobias (Freud, 1909, 1918). Baconian (and even Humean) empiricism would justify Freud's inductive inference that anxiety is caused by the conversion of libido into anxiety by repression of the libido.

Indeed, Freud (1916–1917) generalized from libidinal impulses to any affect or impulse, including aggression: "Anxiety is therefore the universally current coinage for which *any* affective impulse is or can be exchanged if the ideational content attached to it is subjected to repression" (pp. 403–404, italics in original). More specifically, neurotic anxiety is the discharge of libido, "which is subjected to repression" (p. 410). Hence, neurotic anxiety is a vicissitude of libido and has its origin in the instinctual unconscious, whereas realistic anxiety is a similar vicissitude of ego libido or narcissism.

However, despite the ease and frequency with which this sequence is observed, the conversion theory cannot be true, that is, it cannot offer a consistent explanation of the genesis of anxiety. Repression is a psychic process, and all psychic processes are motivated; hence, repression too is motivated. Repression and other defensive processes do not occur randomly or arbitrarily. What else but anxiety, then, we must ask, could motivate defensive processes—not in the sense of guiding or directing them, but in the sense of activating and setting them in motion? There has to be a source of anxiety that precedes any anxiety resulting from the conversion of libido by repression. Anxiety must have a genesis that is independent of and precedes the repression of libido.

Freud's theory of *signal anxiety* resolves the explanatory dilemma of his conversion theory. His new theory of anxiety allowed him to abandon the dubious thesis that anxiety, including even realistic anxiety, is inexpedient and that only realistic action taken to avoid danger is expedient. Instead, Freud was able to assume that the capacity to be mobilized by anxiety could well be the result of the evolutionary expediency of this capacity. It allowed him to postulate that it is from the ego that anxiety proceeds as a result of the stimulation of a memory of painful helplessness. He could hypothesize that in any individual life history, the original experience of helplessness could be birth. The theory allowed Freud to connect anxiety with libido (and aggression) by tracing the progressive enrichment and modification of the anxiety template consequent upon its links to the stages of psychosexual and ego development: fear of loss of the object, fear of the loss of the love of the object (shame), fear of parental revenge, fear of self-imposed retribution (guilt).

Moreover, two of the principal advantages of the conversion theory are preserved in the theory of signal anxiety. A libidinal or aggressive demand is still the precursor of the anxiety, and the strength of the anxiety is still proportional to the strength of the unconscious demand for satisfaction. However, the change in the sequence of events is the exchange of places whereby anxiety intervenes and a defensive process is mobilized. Consequently, it still follows that sexually inhibited persons are not sexually inhibited merely because they are anxious persons in the sexual sphere (as well as others). They are sexually inhibited because unresolved unconscious sexual wishes have made even conscious sexual feelings anxiety-provoking.

Here there is no claim that Freud actually followed this course of deductive reasoning. In fact, he states just the opposite: "It is not so much a question of taking back our earlier findings as of bringing them into line with more recent discoveries" (1926, p. 141). Freud goes on to reaffirm that "anxiety arises directly out of libido" (p. 141) in "actual" neuroses, as a discharge of the "surplus of unutilized libido" (p. 141). It was not until later that Freud (1933) published his abandonment altogether of this last vestige of his hypothesis of a direct conversion of libido into anxiety.

My assumption is that the discoveries to which Freud is referring are observational rather than conceptual. My point is that the hypotheses of Freud's theory are sufficiently rich, reality-bound, and inferentially interrelated that theoretical reasoning, even without observation, can identify explanatory problems and indicate the direction in which a solution may be found. This is true even in the face of the apparent observational confirmation of the conversion theory, which can be deductively shown to be theoretically unviable. This truth about psychoanalytic theory does not depend upon its having been recognized by its creator. However, everything happens as though Freud knew that his conversion theory of anxiety was, at best, so incomplete that its generalization produced a contradiction; it presupposes anxiety of a different nature from another source to motivate the repression required by the conversion theory.

Thus, even though he did not finally surrender his attachment to the phenomenological and observational grounds for conversion anxiety until more than a decade later (Freud, 1933), this assumption would account for the fact that all the elements of the signal theory of anxiety are already present in Freud's (1916–1917) most complete statement of the conversion theory. Some explicit Cartesian deductive logical analysis of the theoretical implications of the conversion theory could have hastened Freud's reformulation.

This speculative reconstruction calls our attention to certain logical and rational functions of the economic unconscious. We habitually evaluate our own reasoning and the reasoning of others without being aware of doing so, even without rendering our thoughts in logical form as I have done above. This evaluation is carried out by a savoir-faire about valid reasoning exercised by a reflexive critical function that is not already outfitted with the formal means of evaluating validity. Unless one has studied formal logic, one would make the judgment that the syllogisms I have constructed are valid on the basis of this preconscious critical function, which appears to be the byproduct of the acquisition of language and those experiences of practical successes and failures in reasoning that tutor us in the structure of reality. Boolean class logic, the algebraic expression of the structures of propositions, Venn diagrams, systematic symbolic logic, and Wittgenstein's truth tables are not Cartesian innate ideas that could provide a foundation and guide for the infallible exercise of this critical function. This imperfect, usually inarticulate but reasonably functional, sense of logical validity and invalidity is an essential component of reality testing.

It is remarkable that this logical, evaluative function is as reliable as it is, but it is by no means infallible. We are quite able to overlook inconsistencies, contradictions, and explanatory inadequacies in our thinking—not only on account of unconscious conflicts or narcissism, but also on account of apparent but superficial or erroneous observational confirmation. Our ordinary experience of the apparent motion of celestial bodies offers no observational clue that the earth is rotating daily on its axis; the perceptual illusion is complete. Only reason employing abstract thought can find the way to correct our understanding, and the correction of our understanding alters nothing in our perceptual experience; it alters only our understanding of our perceptions by teaching us to compensate for the motion of the platform from which we perceive. Further, we can use our perceptions to successfully satisfy purposes even while naively trusting false beliefs about what we see. We can go on believing that the sun revolves around the earth while successfully using its locations during the day to orient ourselves in space and time. Here we come upon the limits of pragmatism rather than the relativity of truth.

Nevertheless, without subscribing to Kant's (1781) *a priori* (a way of gaining knowledge without appealing to any particular experience), we can agree with him that concepts without perception are empty, while perceptions without concepts are blind. This formulation agrees with the epistemological insight shared by Freud (1915) and Einstein (1922). Although abstract concepts need not be directly derived from observations, their usefulness for building knowledge depends upon their being confirmed by observations. Consequently, the basic epistemological issue for psychoanalysis is whether or not the analytic situation and the individual psychic life we seek to know can yield observations that are reliable enough to confirm (or disconfirm) the ideas upon which we have to rely to make them.

REFERENCES

Bacon, F. (1620). *Novum Organum*. In E.A. Burtt (Ed.), *The English Philosophers from Bacon to Mill* (pp. 5–123). New York: Modern Library, 1939.

Descartes, R. (1641). *Meditations on First Philosophy* (Trans. E.S. Haldane & C.R.T. Ross). In *Philosophical Works of Descartes* (vol. 1, pp. 133–199). New York: Dover, 1955.

Einstein, A. (1922). *The Meaning of Relativity: Four Lectures Delivered at Princeton University, May 1921* (Trans. P. Adams). London: Methuen.

Ferenczi, S. (1913). Stages in the development of the sense of reality. In *First Contributions to Psycho-Analysis* (pp. 213–239). London: Hogarth Press, 1952.

Freud, S. ([1895]1950). Project for a scientific psychology. SE 1:281–391.

——— (1897). Letter 69. SE 1:259–260.

——— (1909). Analysis of a phobia in a five-year-old boy ("Little Hans"). SE 10:1–150.

——— (1915). Instincts and their vicissitudes. SE 14:109–140.

——— (1916–1917). *Introductory Lectures on Psycho-Analysis*. SE 15–16.

——— (1918). From the history of an infantile neurosis (the "Wolf-Man"). SE 171–124.

——— (1920). Beyond the pleasure principle. SE 18:1–64.

——— (1923). The ego and the id. SE 19:1–66.

——— (1925). An autobiographical study. SE 20:1–74.

——— (1926). Inhibitions, symptoms and anxiety. SE 20:75–176.

——— (1927). The future of an illusion. SE 21:1–56.

——— (1933). New introductory lectures on psycho-analysis. SE 22.

Hanly, C. (1988a). From animism to rationalism. In *The Problem of Truth in Applied Psychoanalysis* (pp. 155–168). New York: Guilford, 1992.

———— (1988b). Metaphysics and innateness: A psychoanalytic perspective. *International Journal of Psychoanalysis* 89:389–399.

Kant, I. (1781). *Critique of Pure Reason* (Trans. N.K. Smith). New York: St. Martin's Press, 1965.

Locke, J. (1690). *An Essay concerning Human Understanding.* In E.A. Burtt (Ed.), *The English Philosophers from Bacon to Mill* (pp. 238–402). New York: Modern Library, 1939.

Renik, O. (1993). Analytic interaction: Conceptualizing technique in light of the analyst's irreducible subjectivity. *Psychoanalytic Quarterly* 62:553–561.

Singer, C. (1957). *A Short History of Anatomy and Physiology from the Greeks to Harvey.* New York: Dover.

CHAPTER 9

Skeptical Reflection on Subjectivist Epistemologies*

I am pleased to respond to the comments of Druck (2014) and Reis (2014) on my paper, "The Interplay of Deductive and Inductive Reasoning in Psychoanalytic Theorizing" (C. Hanly, 2014), of which the primary focus is an exploration of deductive reasoning in psychoanalytic theory. It is a companion piece to an earlier paper (C. Hanly, 1992) in which I affirm the fundamental place of observation and inductive reasoning—facts of observation and inferences from those facts—in psychoanalytic knowledge, without which theory remains too conjectural and speculative.

Epistemology is a theory of knowledge. It includes questions of the reliability and generalizability of clinical observations in psychoanalysis, such as the question at the extreme end of the spectrum of whether or not there is such a thing as a clinical fact to observe. However, the importance of epistemology as a philosophical discipline can be exaggerated, insofar as clinicians may work as critical realists while espousing some form of subjectivist epistemology.

I shall argue in what follows that at least some psychoanalytic epistemologists are inconsistent subjectivists or inconsistent objectivists. An analyst who is working for the most part by relying rigidly on received,

---

* Originally published in *Psychoanalytic Quarterly* 83, no. 4 (2014):949–968.

preferred ideas—rather than being receptive enough to the patient to test his preferred ideas against the actual experience, memories, fantasies, conflicts, and motivation of the patient that are repeatedly available in observation of associations and transferences—may think that he is a realist because of his own unconscious and unresolved veneration of the source (e.g., an analytic school, a personal analyst, or a supervisor) of his preferred ideas. Such an analyst would qualify as an inconsistent objectivist—one who is philosophically committed to realism but is practicing subjectivism.

I agree with the arguments of Druck and Reis that such an analyst is in need of what I would call *trial alternative perspectives.* Whether or not an analyst is able to be objectively understanding of his patients is not determined by the epistemology that he explicitly espouses (Canestri, 2006); it is determined rather by his receptivity, sympathy (empathy), knowledge, experience, countertransferences, and the like. Adopting an empiricist (objectivist) epistemology no more guarantees the analyst's objectivity than does the knowledge that the earth's diurnal rotation on its axis causes a person to no longer see the sun moving from east to west. We need ideas in order to observe our patients and the meaning of their words and behavior, but we also need to be sufficiently receptive to patients to be able to allow what we observe to correct our ideas about them (C. Hanly, 1995).

In discussing these epistemological questions, it is useful to pay attention to the meaning of the key words "subjective," "subjectivity," and "subjectivism," and to their opposites, "objective," "objectivity," and "objectivism." I have used the definitions found in the *International Webster New Encyclopedic Dictionary* (1975) and the *Shorter Oxford English Dictionary* (1952). In particular, we should not be confused by the fact that there is a dictionary definition in which subjectivity is a universal characteristic of human psychic life. Our psychic lives are largely hidden in our heads because that is where our brains are; apart from an individually variable but rather rich array of behavioral and expressive communication of beliefs in action, emotions, attitudes, likes, dislikes, attractions, and aversions, we remain highly dependent on language to let others know what we believe, feel, think, imagine, dream, etc.

I wonder if it is not sometimes this natural, inevitable subjectivity in the sense of the interiority of the mind—which has been called *psychological* or *ontological subjectivity* (C. Hanly & M.A.F. Hanly, 2001), in order to differentiate it from *epistemological subjectivity*—that some analysts have in mind when they speak about the subjectivity of the analyst. In this psychic meaning of subjectivity, all mental processes are subjective, including the clinical use of ideas that guide our interpretations but that we keep to ourselves in clinical work. However, from the fact that mental states, processes, and contents are irreducibly subjective in the sense that one's experience of oneself, of others, and of the world are always one's own psychologically and ontologically, it does not follow that they are irreducibly subjective *epistemologically*. Confusion of the two distinct meanings can make epistemological subjectivism seem more convincing than it is and can result in a disregard of its philosophical and theoretical problems.

Druck (2014) attributes this semantic confusion to me when he asserts that I imply that "there is inevitable subjectivity, but this can be 'overcome sufficiently' to allow the analyst to make relatively objective observations that he can use to modify his theory" (p. 921). I do think that psychological (ontological) subjectivity is inevitable, but I also think that it cannot be overcome: it remains even as we communicate our feelings gesturally, behaviorally, and verbally to others. It is *epistemological* subjectivity that can be sufficiently overcome for us to be able to observe others without altering them in making the observation—by seeing and interpreting them to be more as we think ourselves to be than others actually are. This distinction was clarified in an earlier paper (C. Hanly & M.A.F. Hanly, 2001).

This semantic confusion is also evident in Druck's previous paragraph: "Hanly believes that, of course, we need to continually test our observations against our countertransferences (thus acknowledging the pull of inevitable subjectivity)" (pp. 920–921). Inevitable psychological subjectivity is ongoing; it is not "correctable," but this fact has no bearing on *epistemological* subjectivity. Unconscious countertransferences have a potential for causing epistemological subjectivity in the analyst, but this effect is not inevitable, for their influence can be modified and they may become useful aids to understanding the patient—especially when the wants bound to the fantasies have ceased to clamor for satisfaction in the analyst. An unconscious countertransference, once caught sight of, can bring with it the cognitive benefits of recovered memories of traumatic experiences, which can facilitate the formation in the analyst of broader empathic horizons and receptive sympathy for the patient's suffering, as well as indicating directions for speculation about its causes.

This confusion concerning my use of *subjectivity* appears to be at the root of Reis's (2014) claim that I have made subjectivism into "a huge container for all Kantian and post-Kantian approaches" (p. 941). Reis writes:

Into this category goes every post-Freudian psychoanalytic theory: all are "subjectivist" and therefore compromised when compared with the approach of critical realism. One need only reflect on who would be grouped together in this way (e.g., Klein; Bion; Lacan; all object relations, self-psychological, and contemporary Freudian theorists, including Schafer and Loewald; interpersonalists, relationalists, and intersubjectivists as diverse as Renik and Ogden; as well as others) to understand some of the difficulties involved in Hanly's juxtaposing his view against those of nearly every other psychoanalyst who is not a critical realist. (pp. 941–942)

If "post-Kantian approaches" refers to philosophy generally, Reis would be claiming incorrectly that I think empiricist philosophers such as Mill, as well as Oxford ordinary-language philosophers, advocate subjectivist epistemologies. I shall therefore assume that Reis is referring to the post-Kantian German idealism of Fichte, Schelling, Hegel, and Schopenhauer. But whereas Kant (1781) rejected any dialectic of pure reason, Hegel (1816) reaffirmed the power of pure reason to know Reality and espoused dialectical logic in order to grasp the structure and dynamic of Absolute Spirit (Hegel's name for a spiritual ultimate Reality).

In opposition to Kant's critique of pure reason, Hegel's metaphysics and epistemology were a form of Platonic realism. That is to say, Hegel, like Plato, thought that pure reasoning could gain access to a realm of spiritual reality. Kant's categories of the understanding and the pure forms of intuition (i.e., space and time) are subjective in the sense that they are *a priori* (imposed by the mind on all sense experience and thought) and not derived *a posteriori* from experience (the reason for Einstein's criticism of a priori philosophical thought).

There is a sense in which Kant might have called himself a partial empiricist. Kant expressed his gratitude to the British empiricist philosopher Hume for awakening him from his Wolffian dogmatic slumber, but he was not fully roused. The crucial fact is that post-Kantian empiricism, both philosophical and scientific, postulates—for good reasons—that space and time, as well as the categories of understanding, such as causality and substances and their attributes, are based on properties of things and processes that we derive from sense experience. Any classification of philosophical theories that I would subscribe to would have to take these real differences into account.

The assumption that I classify almost all psychoanalysts as subjectivists is also incorrect. I do not think that Klein and the Kleinians are subjectivists, nor that most North American and European Freudians are. British object relations theorists are realists for the most part; Kohut and the Kohutians are realists, in my opinion, though with some qualifications. Although I might

179

be in error in thinking that probably most analysts are realists, such is my conviction based on reading of the clinical material of epistemologically diverse analysts.

Moreover, I would not classify either Renik or Schafer simply as subjectivists, but rather as *inconsistent* subjectivists. They are subjectivists in their explicit epistemologies but critical realists when they write up case histories. This point has been made concerning Schafer's concept of narratology (M.A.F. Hanly, 1996). Similarly, Goldberg (1976) has used subjectivist epistemological ideas to explain why Freudians see evidence in patients that an Oedipus complex is caused by drive development, whereas self psychologists see evidence that it is caused by parental narcissistic failure. However, Goldberg's analytic work, as gauged by his case descriptions and explanations, suggests (at least to me) that he is seeking to give an objective account of the lives, neuroses, and analyses of his patients.

Let us briefly test Druck's (2014) claim that a belief in Arlow's (1979) subjectivist thesis enables the analyst to be more objective:

I think that an analyst who is consciously and unconsciously trying to "overcome" his countertransference (which, by traditional definition, is inevitably unconscious and cannot be readily known) is *less* capable of "objectivity" than one who tolerates and holds his subjective reactions and uses them as data. The latter analyst, less defensive, is more capable of objectivity. (pp. 924–925, italics in original)

First, using subjective reactions as data to explore the interaction between analyst and patient is critical realism. However, if the underlying premise is that all perception and thought is always sufficiently influenced by unconscious fantasy to render them so cognitively subjective that they no longer represent the object well enough to make a telling interpretation, then it could be said that Arlow is an epistemological subjectivist. If the premise is that this happens sometimes, and that when it does, it renders observation deceptively convincing that it is objective when it is actually subjectively distorted, then certain indications may show a requirement for self-analysis, a return to analysis, or the prospect of a limited or damaged analysis.

I suppose that some analysts who remain too given to self-righteousness may defensively deny indications of shortcomings by protesting their realism, and fail to seek to remedy whatever their limitations might be. Such analysts would fall into the category of the inconsistent objectivist (see the foregoing) in relation to such indications of analytic inadequacy. However, the comparison should also be made with those who go beyond tolerating their shortcomings as analysts and take constructive steps to improve. Self-toleration may be better than denial, so long as it is not complacent but is only the first step in the direction of remedy by means of self-analysis or further analysis.

In psychoanalytic case studies, most interfering countertransferences are seen to involve prolonged and intense affective responses to the patient. The crucial point is that there is in principle a remedy available to the analyst. The first interpretation of Arlow's epistemological premise (that unconscious fantasies always render clinical observation subjective) rules out the possibilty of any remedy. The first premise generates the problems of a subjectivist epistemology, while the second does not. The second interpretation, with the crucial modification of replacing "always" with "sometimes," is critical realism. There are no disagreements, or if there are any, they are technical issues concerning the waxing and waning of unconscious fantasies and the defenses deployed against them, and how and to what extent unconscious fantasies inhibit understanding of self and other. The same analysis applies to the epistemological implications of Gabbard's (1997) compromise thesis. The underlying issue is the question of *all* or *some, always* or *sometimes, must* or *can,* and other similar oppositions.

Druck (2014) quotes Loewald's (1960) observation that an adult son does not see his father as he did when he was a child. One could cite several such shifts as a child's observational and reality-testing capacities strengthen, the animism of childhood thinking recedes, and the need for the use of adults as auxiliary egos declines. Who would disagree? These are reliable facts about individual psychic development. We are aware of these changes in ego functioning in ourselves, and we can observe them in others. Who would doubt that changes of this sort help analysts to be more discerning clinicians (i.e., epistemological realists), not just in theory (philosophy) but in clinical practice?

But the inference to epistemological subjectivism does not hold. These developments in psychic functioning enable individuals to strengthen their capacities for subject-object differentiation, which is the platform on which reality testing is built. These developmental changes certainly take place in the subjective life of the individual, facilitated by good parenting and education, and they are subjective in the sense of being *psychologically* subjective (C. Hanly & M.A.F. Hanly, 2001); but there are no grounds for inferring that these developments could leave individuals trapped in their own minds—that is, limited cognitively to *always* modeling others and the world on themselves. On the contrary, they enable individuals to become aware of differences among people and between themselves and others.

Let us take into account that Loewald (1979) also affirmed the continued activity of the Oedipus complex throughout life: "In adolescence the Oedipus complex rears its head again, and so it does during later periods in life, in normal people as well as in neurotics" (p. 753). Loewald was making a generalization about people's lives. Druck quotes Loewald's (1960) distinction between "new discovery of objects" and "discovery of new objects" (p. 18), which formulates a critical-realist idea. Loewald's (1979) generalization is not about a new object created by analyst-analysand interaction; it is about the renewed discovery of unexpected old objects, the oedipal parents, during the stages of adolescent and adult life. According to Loewald's (1979) clinical evidence, the Oedipus complex has an extended waning that was not fully appreciated by Freud. His "new discovery" about the waning of the Oedipus complex is presented explicitly as a correction of certain statements by Freud about the dissolution of the Oedipus complex because it more adequately corresponds to the psychic lives of people.

Druck draws a clinching quote from Loewald (1960): "The analyst may become a scientific observer to the extent to which he is able to observe objectively the patient and himself in interaction. The interaction itself, however, cannot be adequately represented by the model of scientific neutrality" (pp. 18–19). It would indeed be an error to suppose that the analyst's personal responses to patients and their transferences are scientifically neutral in the sense of being indifferent and without affect. Evolutionary biologists are not subject to negative transferences from the fossils they are studying; but surely it would be unjustified to say that an analyst who picks up on a patient's sadness, even when disguised by her being superficially upbeat, needs to be free of any sympathetic appreciation of the patient's sadness in order to be a reliable (scientific) and clinically neutral observer. It would be unjustified to claim that such a sympathetic reaction would disable the analyst's ability to confirm or disconfirm the authenticity of the patient's affect and the reliability of his own interpretive surmises by attending carefully to the patient's responses to interpretations.

Critical realism does not require affectlessness on the part of the analyst as a prerequisite for objectivity in sensing a patient's affective state. The crucial questions are: What is the dominant affect of the patient? Is the analyst's affective response appropriate? And what use does the analyst make of it? I agree with Druck and Loewald that this "monitoring-third" activity of the analyst can be reliably carried out. I would only add that affective responsiveness to the patient, while in need of critical assessment by the analyst like anything else, does not in principle render clinical observation subjective. On the contrary, the analyst's affective responses to the patient often contribute to objective knowledge of the patient that is essential to therapeutic work, no less than does the analyst's observation of the interaction.

Loewald (1960) accurately articulated the position of critical realism when he affirmed the analyst's ability to "observe objectively the patient and himself in interaction" (p. 18; see also C. Hanly, 2004; Hanly & Nichols, 2001). It seems to me that the meanings of "objective" and "subjective" that Loewald was using are similar to those that I have used, whereby "objective" means *belonging to the object of thought,* and "subjective" means *belonging to the thinking subject.*

In the clinical instance we have been considering, a latent sadness is thought by the analyst to belong to the object, namely, the patient; sympathy for the sadness and the idea that it is left unattended by the patient's exaggerated and effortful enthusiasm belong to the thinking and feeling subject, namely, the analyst. (The patient discovered her sadness through grief and mourning and their relation to a despairing anger that caused her to be unable to go onto the balcony of her high-rise apartment, and by becoming aware of the depth of her fatigue.) These are examples of meanings that are rooted in the psychic lives of patients and analysts and reflected in ordinary language, and are used in philosophy and science and recorded in dictionaries (e.g., *International Webster New Encyclopedic Dictionary,* 1975, s.v. "subjective": "belonging to the thinking subject rather than to the object of thought: opposed to *objective"*).

Critical realism does not require that the relationship of the analyst to the patient be scientifically neutral in the sense of unfeeling, but only that, despite its not being scientifically neutral, the analyst is able, often and well enough, to function as a third (C. Hanly, 2004). As Loewald (1960) put it, the analyst "may become a scientific observer to the extent to which he is able to observe objectively the patient and himself in interaction" (p. 18, as quoted by Druck, 2014). I state the conclusion of this discussion hypothetically: if Loewald were an epistemological subjectivist, then my conclusion would be that his position is one of inconsistent subjectivism; otherwise, I would suppose him to be a critical realist with a penchant for dramatic, insightful articulations of obstacles in the path of good psychoanalytic work.

I have mentioned Renik (1993) because of his clear and detailed—although mistaken, I think—arguments based on his conclusion of the *irreducible subjectivity* of clinical psychoanalysis. If "subjectivity" in the expression "irreducible subjectivity" refers to *psychological* or *ontological* subjectivity, then it is tautologically true, for we are subjects who are psychological; but if it is an affirmation of the irreducible *epistemic* subjectivity of clinical observations in psychoanalysis, then it is the statement of a basic premise of philosophical subjectivism (see C. Hanly, 1999; C. Hanly & M.A.F. Hanly, 2001). Druck is mistaken in his assertion that I have "confounded" the question of biased observation with the ontological question of existence. Neither Renik nor I, despite differences concerning psychoanalytic epistemology, has ever doubted that other persons, the solar system, and the universe exist, or that natural science has gained knowledge of them by means of observation. No such idea can be inferred from the claim that the analyst's clinical experience is irreducibly subjective. Renik's *epistemological* idea of irreducible subjectivity is not compatible with scientific realism, as far as clinical psychoanalysis is concerned, but it does not follow from the epistemological thesis that the existence of clinical patients is in doubt; the subjectivist thesis denies only that they can be known as they are in and for themselves.

"Irremediably" in the expression "irremediably subjective" means "incapable of being remedied or repaired" (*International Webster New Encyclopedic Dictionary*, 1975, s.v. "irremediable"), "does not admit of remedy, cure, or correction" (*Shorter Oxford English Dictionary*, 1952, s.v. "irremediable"). Given this meaning, repairing irremediable subjectivity in psychoanalysis would seem to be akin to Sisyphus finally succeeding in rolling the stone to the top of the hill. However, Renik (1998) offered an interesting remedy for "irremediable" epistemological subjectivity. The remedy is the use of predictions of the effects of interpretations on the functioning of patients. For example, predicting that the interpretation of sibling rivalry in a patient would reduce their apparently vicarious aggressiveness with people at work. This method was used by Freud to test the seduction theory— the first psychoanalytic outcome study.

However, predictions are of avail for this purpose only if the observations that are made to test them are not influenced by the predictions or the point of view on which the interpretations were based. Making predictions does not magically remedy the irremediable. The repair does not work unless it repairs the factors causing the irremediable subjectivity. How would making predictions, for example, enable the observer to be equally accepting of confirming and disconfirming observations? And if clinicians can make observations that are objective when they are looking for evidence for or against predictions validly inferred from interpretations, then these observations contradict the epistemological premise that all clinical observations are irremediably subjective. Clinical observations that confirm or falsify predictions are objective. I agree with Renik (1998) that psychoanalysis can predict as well as retrodict; but realistically, I would rather say that it *can be objective*, for there is an ever-present danger of looking only for what would confirm a prediction, and of avoiding what would falsify it and hence would also falsify both the interpretation and the theory implied by the interpretation.

However, if the prediction argument is sound and valid, then logic requires the epistemological theory to be modified from the statement that "all clinical observations in psychoanalysis are irremediably subjective," to "some clinical observations may be subjective and some may be objective." But this is a statement of critical realism!

Similar reasoning applies to the subjectivism of Schafer (1981). Schafer correctly points out that a patient's story can be influenced in the telling by what the patient thinks the analyst wants to hear or by the fear of what the analyst will hear and might think; thus, involuntarily and without design, the analyst exerts an influence on what the patient tells. But Schafer makes this routine clinical factor, which is usually corrigible, into an epistemological theory by generalizing it to all clinical processes with his assertion that "reality is always mediated by narration.... Far from being innocently encountered or discovered, it is created in a regulated fashion" (p. 45).

We can agree that reality is not "innocently encountered" in the search for knowledge (C. Hanly, 1999, p. 439). However, the "always" in "always mediated by narration" is Schafer's generalization (not mine), one which leads the way to the subjectivist epistemological statement that follows. If Schafer's narratological point is treated as a heuristic caution, then it suggests only that by being mindful of the influence of the listener on the narrator, the analyst *may* be able to better understand and interpret resistances in the patient's transference that arise from the patient's need to please and the fear of what he may have to say.

It is important to recognize that psychoanalysis is different from other observational sciences, because the observing analyst is also the instrument by which the observation is made. But the purpose of the "critical" in the term "critical realism" is to acknowledge that difference. And as Loewald (1960) notes, the analyst's use of his reflexive capacity as a third to observe the interaction between analyst and patient enables the analyst to be a scientific observer. Perhaps the gulf between Harvey's anatomical observations (Hanly, 2014, pp. 900–901) and clinical observations in psychoanalysis is not as wide as Reis and Druck seem, at least in some respects, to want to have it.

I would add only that the analyst's reflexive awareness enables him, well enough and often enough, to differentiate what in the interaction is owing to the analyst and what to the patient—a differentiation that is fundamental to objectivity (Cavell, 1998; Hanly & Nichols, 2001). The issue of the logical distribution (*some* or *all*, *sometimes* or *always*, etc.) of the fundamental epistemological principle that *clinical observations are subjective* is the basic difference between epistemological subjectivism and critical realism. It is the claim of universality by the subjectivists is that generates the dichotomy between a subjectivist epistemology and critical realism, because critical realism accepts that clinical observations can be subjective, but when subjectivism is universalized it denies that there are any objective clinical observations.

In the philosophy of science, a distinction is made between methods of discovery and methods of proof. Methods of discovery can include anything that enables the theorist to formulate an adequate hypothesis. A philosophy colleague joked that being inspired to form an idea by reading *Alice in Wonderland* is acceptable so long as the idea is verifiable—that is, so long as there is a method for finding evidence that would show whether the idea is true or false (Freud, 1915). It is the verifiability of a hypothesis that is essential to its scientific or scholarly worth (C. Hanly, 1970). I believe that psychoanalytic interpretations are, for the most part, descriptive or explanatory hypotheses even when not grammatically expressed as such, a view I share with Renik (1998). It seems to me that Reis and Druck are critical of my paper because, given its subject, it does not take up the topic of the analyst as a source of interpretations. On this point, I am in agreement with them: the analyst's subjectivity, as distinct from his externally acquired knowledge, can be a fertile source of ideas for testable interpretations, made according to the method of discovery. But in our daily work, we do not and should not exempt these interpretations from the requirement of evidence. We must be attentive to what follows in the patient's associations and transference and to changes in functioning within and outside the analysis. The method of proof requires that these interpretations, like any others, be tested against the effects that they have on the functioning of the patient.

This observational activity of the analyst searches for evidence of the soundness (or not) of an interpretation, and hence of its objectivity—its being about the patient and not the analyst. The problem I have with the claim that analysis is a co-creation, for example, is that the work of analysis is thought to consist in an analyst and patient developing a coherent and mutually agreed-upon co-creation of the meaning of the patient's life, which leaves out of the picture the critical matter of the correspondence of the co-created history with the patient's real life (Eagle, Wolitzky, & Wakefield, 2001; C. Hanly, 1999; C. Hanly & M.A.F. Hanly, 2001). The meaning of a life invests the life of the person living it. I agree that co-creation occurs; but when it is asserted on principle that it must always occur, the possibility of carrying out the requirements of the psychoanalytic method are negated.

Much of what Reis and Druck have written on behalf of subjectivism falls within the method of *discovery* as distinct from the method of *proof*. The door against which they have enthusiastically but rather recklessly thrown themselves, without first looking at it, was never closed. I recently made the following statement:

To know the atomic structure of a molecule does not depend upon self-knowledge; to know a patient does. In order to know our patients with realism and compassion, analysts need to be able to recall their own memories and phantasies that parallel the memories and phantasies of our patients, and which are causing their painful inhibitions, symptoms, neurotic anxiety, and depression. (C. Hanly, 2013)

The associations, transferences, and behaviors of patients have to make a passage through the analyst's psyche via affects and aroused memories and fantasies, from the senses to thoughts and interpretations aimed at improving the patient's self-understanding and psychic functioning.

However, the objectivity of the analyst's interpretations—the extent to which they tally with what is going on in the patient—is unavoidably grounded in the object (the patient), not merely in the subject (the analyst). What the analyst communicates of his own affective responses in the interpretation when it is appropriate to the patient's affective state is likely to enhance the therapeutic efficacy of the interpretation, and when not, then not (C. Hanly, 1994). The subjectivity of the analyst—his character, personality, moods, attitudes, and life experience—is always at work, for better or worse. (It is my impression, incidentally, that substituting "subjectivity of the analyst" in these discussions for the more specific "character, personality, moods, attitudes, etc., of the analyst" can cause confusion because of the former expression's vague generality and ambiguity. More discriminating descriptions of what makes for subjective thinking are needed.)

Both Reis and Druck assert that I have contradicted my own argument concerning Freud's replacement of the conversion theory with the signal anxiety theory. I included this discussion in my paper—despite the fact that Freud (1926) refers only to new "discoveries," which leaves ambiguous whether they were observational or conceptual discoveries—because I wanted to make a point not about Freud's genius, but about the theory that he had by then constructed. The title of my paper refers to psychoanalytic theory; in fact, Druck quotes the sentence in my paper that makes that clear. The argument is not about Freud's use of deductive reasoning, but about the inferential deductive richness of the psychoanalytic theory that Freud constructed—a composite theory that is sufficiently rich, reality-bound, and inferentially interrelated that theoretical reasoning by Freud or any other adequately knowledgeable person could identify theoretical explanatory problems when they occur—which is a sign of a mature theory.

Reis puts to the realist a dilemma: either the realist must assert that there is no subject, or he must admit that the dichotomy between critical-realist and subjectivist positions is actually a far more complex relation than one of opposing epistemologies. The first alternative is untenable, for it would be quixotic to eliminate subjects (conscious persons) in order to, allegedly, do away with the idea of subjectivity altogether: psychological subjectivity is natural to the human mind. The distinction between what is owing to the person (the subject) and what is owing to the object is in things and events themselves, and we require a verbal means of identifying the difference when it occurs. The second alternative is also untenable. Complexity cannot reduce the dichotomy between what is subjective and what is objective in our experience of self and objects. As Cavell (1998) points out, psychological subjectivity must "normally include an ability to differentiate between subject and object in order to identify within evolving experience and to conceptualize the difference between how things seem and how they are" (p. 458). The opposition between these epistemological positions is tautological, as is evident from their dictionary definitions. It is not something that can be altered by any amount of "complexity" without making recourse to merely verbal solutions. Obviously, both objective and subjective elements may be at work in experience. The question is, can we meaningfully differentiate them?

Reis's conjecture about my understanding of the paradigm shift from animistic to scientific thinking is mistaken. Aristotle formulated the rules of syllogistic validity and an early form of inductive reasoning in the fourth century BC. The problem was that his cosmological thinking, while perfectly logical, nevertheless relied upon basic animistic ideas: matter as pure potentiality actualized by psychic, substantial essences (Platonic forms relocated in species), primarily by teleological causality in a Ptolemaic cosmos. It was the replacement of these ideas by philosophers and scientists, with the realization that material things are organized chemical substances subject to efficient physical causality in a Copernican universe, that was at the heart of the Renaissance and Enlightenment paradigm shift from animism to science. It was the telescopic observations of Galileo, Descartes's studies of the behavior of light passing through media, Harvey's anatomical work, etc.—all substantive discoveries—that brought about this paradigm shift (Weinberg, 1998). Moreover, logical validity and truth are independent: the conclusion of a valid argument is necessarily true only if its premises are true. Psychotic cosmological thought, even while being tragically detached from reality, is remarkable for its logical coherence. Logic alone could not be the driver of paradigm shifts.

I can agree that Reis's (2014, pp. 944–945) "conjectured" (a rather indoctrinating thought experiment?) "Kleinian training" and "successful practice," in which the idea of unconscious fantasy is employed, does not prove the existence of unconscious fantasy at work in the patient's psychic life—nor does it permit any other conclusion, for that matter. Implied by the conjecture is the relativistic notion that the consistent application of any theory and its specific technical rules can result in therapeutic success. This statement implies a malleability of individual psychic reality that makes it unsuitable for realistic observation. Is this lack of an organized psychic nature true only of patients, or does it apply equally to analysts, who also can have an at best slippery awareness of who they are, leaving them with only a makeshift ability to differentiate themselves from their patient's transferences without encasing themselves in an unquestionable theory? A philosopher cannot but sense, in this conjecture, a slide toward Sartrean nothingness (C. Hanly, 1979; Sartre, 1943), precariously arrested by recourse to coherent authoritarianism and bad faith.

I notice that Reis's conjectural conclusion concerning the dubious existence of unconscious fantasies is inconsistent with Druck's account of Arlow's subjectivism (based on the pervasive influence of unconscious fantasies on perception, I might add). Druck asserts that new perspectives can enable the discovery of new facts, and I agree. But Druck then cites self psychology as evidence, and here there is a problem. The perspective of self psychology that focuses our attention on narcissism has produced results that contradict classical drive theory. In particular, self psychology finds that the Oedipus complex is caused by narcissistic failures in the parents' responses to the intrinsically innocent burgeoning of sexual and aggressive feelings in the phallic/clitoral stage, whereas Freudian analysts find that incestuous wishes and ambivalence are caused by drive development and will occur without parental failures. These observations are inconsistent, and it is just this inconsistency that Goldberg (1976) was addressing, as discussed earlier. The philosophical and logical problem is that if two propositions are in contradiction and one of them is true, the other must be false.

The movement from perspective to perspective in psychoanalysis is useful and necessary for the clinical exploration of different basic assumptions, but when this exploration results in contradictory results, it is not just a matter of a plurality of compatible theories. A possible case of perspectival compatibilities is the Kleinian perspective on very early development based on Freud's death instinct theory, but this perspective led to an incompatibility concerning the nature of aggression between Freudians who accept the death instinct theory and those who reject it. Moreover, there is a problematic difference between the Kleinian and the Freudian death instinct theories. The meaning of a theory is in part determined by it implications or consequences. Klein attributed the paranoid-schizoid position in infancy to the death instinct and Freud did not. Confronted with these complexities in the evolution of psychoanalytic theory, one can sympathize with those who adopt pluralism as a way out, combined with subjectivist epistemologies of theory-bound (or otherwise bound) clinical observation. This is essentially the path suggested by Goldberg (1976).

If clinical observation and logical theorizing cannot resolve these problems, psychoanalysis will remain an unintegrated and inconsistent body of knowledge—a plurality of theories, some of which are compatible while others are not. The academic enemies of psychoanalysis will happily take this situation to be the result of the fact that psychoanalysis was and remains, as Wittgenstein (1966) claimed, a method of persuading someone to believe a mythology (C. Hanly, 1971), or as Grunbaum (1984) claimed, the predictable result of different analysts practicing a suggestive therapy and thus making different suggestions to patients.

Logic is an asset in the work of checking alternative theories precisely because it is impersonal and can do its work independently of the bias of investments in theory. However, one can appreciate the value of abstract reasoning without derogating or disregarding the place of personality, attitude, and feelings in the search for knowledge of human nature in oneself and in others. Consider the valid Epicurean syllogisms beautifully cloaked in the passionate and seductive language in Shakespeare's sonnets or in Andrew Marvell's "To His Coy Mistress" (Person, 1986), with their *carpe diem* conclusions. While knowledge and theoretical thinking are essential to good clinical work (Britton, 2004; Britton & Steiner, 1994), therapeutic interpretations are poetic in their synthesis of insight and the appreciation of affect.

Neither Reis nor Druck appears to share my interest in the fact that one need not be able to state the rules of valid reasoning, or be familiar with tests for validity, in order to reason validly. I find this to be an interesting fact of our intellectual life, and in my paper, I offer a topographical account of it that enables us to understand, for example, how psychotic cosmological thinking can be amazingly coherent despite its delusional premises. My point here is that the poetic and personal aspects of the analyst's interpretations need not be at odds with objectivity (despite the risk that they *may* be), to the extent to which the relevant aspects of the analyst's personality remain dynamically unconscious.

I have previously dealt more extensively with the issue of clinical factuality and the matter of personality, idea, and fact (C. Hanly, 1995) in an effort to explore whether there is "a way between subjectivity and objectivity that is also a way forward" (p. 906). I have explored the way in which an idea (question) that may at first be considered only subjective, and may have a subjective source, can enable what is objective to be seen. I have continued this exploration with a coauthor in a later publication (C. Hanly & M.A.F. Hanly, 2001): "Clearly, the analyst's personality and subjectivity exercise their influence on the patient and on the process" (p. 526).

By way of a philosophical and theoretical conclusion, I will make the following points. A difficulty of subjectivist epistemologies for psychoanalysis is that they imply concurrence with some of the most telling philosophical (although, I think, ultimately mistaken) attacks on psychoanalysis. Philosophically and theoretically, however, I find subjectivist epistemologies to be intrinsically problematic, since in order to function as epistemologies they require a universal statement of principle in the place of a specific useful account of a heuristic difficulty, and such universal statements give rise to inconsistencies and contradictions. In summary form, I would argue (deductively) that any observation that supposedly proves the truth of a subjectivist epistemology falsifies it because it is claimed to be an objective truth about knowledge. It is this logical flaw in subjectivist epistemological theories that is alluded to in the jokes made by philosophers about solipsism. At least some of the subjectivist arguments cease to have this problem when they are treated as heuristic insights.

The cognitive risks of strongly invested unconscious fantasies are of great importance to the clinical analyst even without their epistemological elevation to a decisive influence upon all observations. This is also why, since the time of Plato and Aristotle, philosophers have espoused realism, even when their ontologies are idealistic and when sense experience is disparaged, as it was by Plato. But Plato was also the first philosopher to construct an argument against relativistic perspectivism as first elaborated by Protagoras (Owens, 1959). For whatever reason, Plato, in Book 10 of the *Republic* in a reply to Protagoras, was thinking of a bed and considered whether the bed, which appears to be different when seen from different angles, is actually different. Plato's answer to Protagoras was that the bed *appears* different but *is* the same.

I hope that readers will find this discussion of some interest and usefulness. I am grateful to the editor of *The Psychoanalytic Quarterly* for the opportunity to reply to my critics.

REFERENCES

Arlow, J.A. (1979). The genesis of interpretation. *Psychoanalytic Quarterly* 38:1–27.

Britton, R. (2004). Subjectivity, objectivity, and triangular space. *Psychoanalytic Quarterly* 73:47–61.

Britton, R., & Steiner, J. (1994). Interpretation: Selected fact or overvalued idea? *International Journal of Psychoanalysis* 75:1069–1078.

Canestri, J. (2006). *Psychoanalysis: From Practice to Theory*. London: Karnac.

Cavell, M. (1998). Triangulation, one's own mind, and objectivity. *International Journal of Psychoanalysis* 79:449–467.

Druck, A. (2014). Objectivity and subjectivity in the evolution of psycho-analytic theories. *Psychoanalytic Quarterly* 83:917–937.

Eagle, M., Wolitzky, D.L., & Wakefield, J.C. (2001). The analyst's knowledge and authority: A critique of the "new view" in psychoanalysis. *Journal of the American Psychoanalytic Association* 49:457–488.

Freud, S. (1915). Instincts and their vicissitudes. SE 14:109–140.

——— (1926). Inhibitions, symptoms and anxiety. SE 20:75–176.

Gabbard, G.O. (1997). A reconsideration of objectivity in the analyst. *International Journal of Psychoanalysis* 78:15–26.

Goldberg, A. (1976). A discussion of the paper by C. Hanly and J. Mason. *International Journal of Psychoanalysis* 57:67–70.

Grunbaum, A. (1984). *The Foundations of Psychoanalysis: A Philosophical Critique*. Berkeley: University of California Press.

Hanly, C. (1970). On being and dreaming. In C. Hanly & M. Lazerowitz (Eds.), *Psychoanalysis and Philosophy* (pp. 155–187). New York: International Universities Press.

——— (1971). Wittgenstein on psychoanalysis. In A. Ambrose & M. Lazerowitz (Eds.), *Ludwig Wittgenstein: Philosophy and Language* (pp. 73–94). London: George Allen & Unwin.

——— (1979). *Existentialism and Psychoanalysis*. New York: International Universities Press.

——— (1992). Inductive reasoning in clinical psychoanalysis. *International Journal of Psychoanalysis* 73:293–301. [Chapter 2 in this volume]

——— (1994). Reflections on the place of the therapeutic alliance in psychoanalysis. *International Journal of Psychoanalysis* 75:457–467.

——— (1995). On facts and ideas in psychoanalysis. *International Journal of Psychoanalysis*. 76:901–908. [Chapter 4 in this volume]

——— (1999). Subjectivity and objectivity in psychoanalysis. *Journal of the American Psychoanalytic Association* 47:427–444.

——— (2004). The third: A brief historical analysis of an idea. *Psychoanalytic Quarterly* 73:267–290. [Chapter 7 in this volume]

——— (2013). Opening ceremony address. Paper presented at the International Psychoanalytical Association Congress, Prague.

——— (2014). The interplay of deductive and inductive reasoning in psychoanalytic theorizing. *Psychoanalytic Quarterly* 83:897–915. [Chapter 8 in this volume]

Hanly, C., & Hanly, M.A.F. (2001). Critical realism: Distinguishing the psychological subjectivity of the analyst from epistemological subjectivism. *Journal of the American Psychoanalytic Association* 49:315–333.

Hanly, C., & Nichols, C. (2001). A disturbance of psychoanalytic memory: The case of John Rickman's three-person psychology. *Philosophy of the Social Sciences* 31:279–301.

Hanly, M.A.F. (1996). "Narrative," now and then: A critical realist approach. *International Journal of Psychoanalysis* 77:445–457.

Hegel, G.W.F. (1816). *Science of Logic* (Trans. A.V. Miller). London: Allen & Unwin, 1969.

The International Webster New Encyclopedic Dictionary of the English Language and Library of Useful Knowledge (1975). Chicago: English Language Institute of America.

Kant, I. (1781). *Critique of Pure Reason* (Trans. N.K. Smith). London: Macmillan, 1952.

Loewald, H.W. (1960). On the therapeutic action of psycho-analysis. *International Journal of Psychoanalysis* 41:16–33.

——— (1979). The waning of the Oedipus complex. *Journal of the American Psychoanalytic Association* 27:751–775.

Owens, J. (1959). *A History of Western Philosophy*. New York: Appleton-Century-Crofts.

Person, J.E. (1986). Andrew Marvell (1621–1678). In *Literature Criticism from 1400 to 1800* (pp. 391–451). Detroit: Gale Research.

Plato. *The Republic* (Trans. B. Jowett). New York: Liberal Arts Press, 1948.

Reis, B. (2014). Some questions regarding reality, subjectivity, and psychoanalytic theory construction. *Psychoanalytic Quarterly* 83:939–948.

Renik, O. (1993). Analytic interaction: Conceptualizing technique in light of the analyst's irreducible subjectivity. *Psychoanalytic Quarterly* 62:553–571.

——— (1998). The analyst's subjectivity and the analyst's objectivity. *International Journal of Psychoanalysis* 79:487–497.

Sartre, J.-P. (1943). *Being and Nothingness* (Trans. H.E. Barnes). New York: Philosophical Library, 1956.

Schafer, R. (1981). Narration in psychoanalytic dialogue. In W.J.T. Mitchell (Ed.), *On Narrative* (pp. 25–49). Chicago: University of Chicago Press.

Shorter Oxford English Dictionary (1952). Ed. C.T. Onions. Oxford: Clarendon Press.

Weinberg, S. (1998). The revolution that didn't happen. *New York Review of Books*, October 8, pp. 48–52.

Wittgenstein, L. (1966). *Lectures and Conversations on Aesthetics, Psychology, and Religious Belief* (Ed. C. Barrett). Oxford: Blackwell.

II
On Truth

CHAPTER 10

The Concept of Truth in Psychoanalysis*

Presented at the 36th International Psychoanalytic Congress, Rome, July 1989.

Psychoanalysis is passing through a difficult period in its history (Wallerstein, 1988). It is still unclear whether there will emerge further splintering, further dilution, or a gradual reunification and reintegration (Rangell, 1988). This paper seeks to explore a core issue in our current differences: the concept of truth in psychoanalysis.

Philosophers have advocated two different theories of truth: the correspondence theory and the coherence theory. I take up the pragmatic theory in the two papers that follow (Hanly, 2002, 2009). It is not taken up here, in order to focus on the terms of the current discussion in philosophy and psychoanalysis. This procedure is philosophically justified by James (1907), who considered the pragmatic theory to be a specific form of the correspondence theory. The correspondence theory states that truth consists of the degree of correspondence between an object and its description. It assumes that under normal conditions the human mind is able to gain knowledge of objects by means of observation and its instrumental and experimental refinement. This observational knowledge can then be used

---

* Originally published in *The International Review of Psycho-Analysis* 71 (1990):375–383.

to test beliefs and theories. The correspondence theory is implied with oblique eloquence in Galileo's "eppur si muove" (see Drake, 1978, pp. 356–357). Neither his official recantation of his astronomical discoveries, nor the majestic coherence of Ptolemaic astronomy, nor its obvious agreement with experience, nor the consensus of generations of scholars, could alter the fact that Galileo's observations of the moon, the planets, and the sun had enabled him to describe much more accurately what was actually happening in nature. This same view of truth and science has been held by the great seminal scientists Harvey, Newton, Darwin, Einstein, and Freud, and by scientists generally. The school of thought in philosophy with which the correspondence concept of truth is associated is realism; critics of correspondence would call it naive realism; advocates would say critical realism.

The coherence theory of truth adopts the following view:

What objects does the world consist of? only makes sense *within* a theory or description.... Truth... is some sort of (idealized) rational acceptability—some sort of ideal coherence of beliefs with each other and with our experiences *as those experiences are themselves represented in our belief system* —and not correspondence with mind-independent or discourse-independent "states of affairs" (Putnam, 1981, pp. 47–49)

Thus, on the coherence theory there may be more than one true description of the world, whereas, the correspondence theory allows for only one. In effect the coherence theory abandons *objects as they actually are* as the ground of truths about objects, and replaces them with *objects as they are constructed or constituted* by the belief and theory investments that govern how they are observed and how they are experienced by observers. According to the coherence theory, the mind must, as a matter of psychological and epistemological inevitability, subject the objects which it seeks to know to the conditions under which it is able to know them. The original form of this idea is traceable to Kant (1781), though he was a scientific realist. Among its modern adherents have been Bradley (1897), Merleau-Ponty (1945), Sartre (1943), Ricoeur (1970), Habermas (1971), and the philosophers of science Kuhn (1970), Feyerabend (1965), and Putnam (1981). The philosophical school of thought to which the coherence theory belongs is idealism.

Two further ideas tend to accompany the correspondence idea of truth, one epistemological, the other ontological. The epistemological premise is that objects are able to cause our senses to form more or less correct observations of them as they actually are. These observations can be, or can be made to be, sufficiently independent of theories held by observers concerning their objects that theories can be objectively tested. The ontological premise is that anyone's thoughts, and actions of any kind, are caused. Minds are part of nature.

Similarly, two further ideas tend to be associated with the coherence idea of truth. Epistemologically, it is assumed that our ways of thinking and perceiving unavoidably condition what we observe. Objects are unable to exert an independent influence upon our senses such as would enable and oblige us to correct our theory-laden ideas of them. Facts are theory-bound, never theory-independent. Objects are amorphous and unintelligible in themselves, and have no means by which to define themselves. They must wait upon the definitions inherent in the theories that we invent to try to understand them. The ontological idea is that human beings are unique in nature on account of a consciousness which supports the capacity for voluntary actions of a special kind—actions which are motivated by reasons rather than by causes. Minds constitute nature.

The idea of truth as coherence, of the intrinsic indefiniteness of persons as objects of knowledge and of volition are logically interconnected in the following way: if a person's actions are motivated by reasons which are neither causes nor caused, if a person freely chooses his motives, then his actions become at once immunized against the influence of his past and are unpredictable. Voluntarism is a source of an intrinsic indefiniteness of the human mind which allows it always to slip away from any description that would seek to correspond to some fixed and determinate nature. The link between voluntarism and the indeterminacy of psychic life has been nicely stated by May (1958):

> It has often been said that one's past determines one's present and future. Let it be underlined that one's present and future—how he commits himself to existence at the moment—also determines his past. (p. 88)

Present choice determines the meaning of the past and the motives of actions. Psychic life ceases to be sufficiently determinate to be a suitable object for descriptions whose truth resides in their correspondence with an objective state of affairs.

Bound to this view is the hermeneutic, phenomenological, existentialist, and idealist idea that self-consciousness involves the capacity for self-transcendence. Self-transcendence allows for the abrogation of causality, the transformation of motives as causes into *sui generis* reasons at the disposal of consciousness. Thus, Habermas (1971) claims that when a neurotic conflict is resolved, self-reflection has actually "dissolved" or "overcome" the causal connection between the symptom or inhibition and the repressed drive demands. Where psychic determinism was, the uncaused choice shall be.

This constellation of ideas has found its way into contemporary psychoanalytic theorizing, where it has been pressed into service in a number of ways. Sometimes there is an appeal to the coherence theory of truth as a means of defending a theory against criticism. Goldberg (1976, 1988) has used the coherence theory to defend self psychology against its critics. The philosophical idea that observations are theory-bound is used to explain differences in clinical observation: "When two individuals with roughly similar neurophysiological equipment view the same thing or event and each see it differently, it is not necessarily true that one is incompetent or even wrong; rather it may be that they each observe with a different theory" (Goldberg, 1976, p. 67). This idea also agrees with Putnam (1981) that there may be more than one true theory about the same thing because the observations that confirm theories are contaminated by the very theoretical concepts they confirm. As Putnam puts it, "the very (experiential) inputs upon which our knowledge is based are conceptually contaminated." (p. 54).

However, three difficulties arise when the coherence theory is used in this way. First, it is a double-edged sword. The observations of classical analysts cannot falsify self psychology, but neither can the observations of self psychology falsify classical (or any other) theory (Hanly, 1983). Second, one and the same patient can have a neurosis caused by a failure to resolve oedipal conflicts when he is treated by a classical analyst, and a failure to find a suitable object for idealization when he is treated by a self psychologist (Kohut, 1971). The Oedipus complex thus both is a cause, and is not a cause but only a symptom. This consequence defies an elementary principle of logic, the principle of identity: nothing can be both p and not-p. And third, a scientific theory must be falsifiable in principle. Goldberg's use of coherence implies that neither self psychology nor classical theory is scientific, since neither has a domain of observations that could ever falsify it. This use of the coherence theory results in theoretical solipsism and truth by conversion.

Goldberg (1988) has implicitly addressed these difficulties by considering the conditions for theory testing in psychoanalysis. He suggests a pragmatic test, although unlike scientific pragmatic testing, this form of testing requires "commitment" over time to the theory being tested (p. 27). However, this requirement opens the door to the claim by adherents of a theory that falsifying observations are a result of the lack of such commitment. It is of interest for our argument, however, that in the end Goldberg indirectly appeals to correspondence. If, for example, we are to be able to carry out the injunction to "remain alert to the effects of our observations" (p. 110) we must be able to make observations of objects that are not subject to these effects. This crucial issue will be further considered below.

Spence (1982a, 1982b), despite some ambiguity, comes down in favor of coherence as the criterion of truth in psychoanalysis when he claims that "the analyst functions more as a pattern-maker than a pattern-finder," and goes on to refer to analyses as "artistic masterpieces." This account agrees with the notion that a present intention or perception interprets the past—that there is no specific, particular past which continues to be what it was; there are only the diverse perspectives on the past brought about by the intentions inherent in current projects, moods, affects, attitudes, and thoughts. The idea that the meaning of a person's past, as well as its influence upon his current life, is determined by present choices is very different from the idea that contemporary affective experiences activate chains of associated memories leading back to childhood precursors. The latter idea assumes that memories thus reactivated have inherent meaning that remains the same even if its conscious recall does not; the former idea assumes that memories are a kind of opaque mass that can be redesigned and informed with meaning by present intentions and investments—that is, by volitions conceived as uncaused causes. These ideas belong with those of Habermas (1971) and Ricoeur (1974, 1981). Habermas (1971) advanced the view that psychoanalytic "self-reflection" is able to suspend or transcend psychic causality.

Although some self psychologists may not agree with his position, Kohut (1959) rested his theorizing on the coherence theory premises of indeterminacy. What we experience as freedom of choice, decision, and the like, is an expression of the fact that the I-experience and a core of activities emanating from it cannot at present be divided into further components.

They are therefore beyond the law of motivation, that is, the law of psychic determinism (p. 232).

Psychic causation becomes a product of self-disintegration along with the Oedipus complex. The cohesive self rises above the bounds of causality. Kohut (1977), in explicit agreement with Habermas (1971), introduced the idea of the mutuality of observer and observed in order to claim on behalf of self psychology a more fundamental knowledge of human nature than that of psychoanalysis. Kohut's concept of empathy disallows the degree of epistemic independence of subject and object required by correspondence. Goldberg (1988) has extensively elaborated the epistemological implications of the self-psychological version of empathy. Ricoeur (1974) asserted, in line with Habermas, that "there are no 'facts' nor any observation of 'facts' in psychoanalysis but rather the interpretation of a narrated history" (p. 186). And although Ricoeur (1981) intended to abandon his earlier (1970) view that reasons and motives are *sui generis*, he failed to do so insofar as he continued to conceive of the relation between unconscious wishes and dreams, neurotic symptoms, and parapraxes as one of referring, denoting, or signifying—that is, as a non-causal semantic relation. Ricoeur (1981) appealed to coherence in a particularly naive and unsatisfactory form: "A good psychoanalytic explanation must be coherent with the theory or, if one prefers, it must conform to Freud's psychoanalytic system" (p. 271). Such a dictum makes nonsense of the clinical testing of psychoanalytic theories which Freud advocated.

The relationship of the concept of causality to the problem of truth in psychoanalysis is also raised by Schafer (1976, 1978) and Klein (1976). Schafer (1978) asserts that "thinking historically, we do not say an agent is causally motivated to perform some action,… we say that *this* agent did *that* and perhaps gave or could have given *these* reasons for doing so" (p. 56). Like Klein, Schafer wants to deny that reasons, intentions, purposes, wishes, motives in general, are causes. Schafer and Klein erroneously identify causality with fatalism, as did Sartre (1943). They are also committed to a coherence theory of truth. There are more ways than one to understand reality (Schafer, 1976); reality is not, as Freud usually assumed, a definite thing to be arrived at or a fixed and known criterion of objectivity (Schafer, 1978, p. 66).

Once motives become reasons rather than causes, they acquire a wonderfully amorphous, open-textured nature which allows them to be "correctly" construed in a variety of ways. Interpretation is an expansion and complication of the context of an action. Different theories expand and complicate the context differently. Narrative coherence becomes the operative criterion of truth. There are as many true understandings as there are coherent, comprehensive, and unified narratives about the motivating reasons.

Schafer (1978) states the ontological basis for this relativism: "The concept of action requires us to regard each action as inherently spontaneous, as starting from itself" (pp. 48–49). This astonishing assertion certainly provides the basis for a "free" construal of the reasons for an action. But if actions are not the outcome of past and present events but really are free creations, as Kant (1785) believed of morally willed actions—actions which have consequences but no antecedents—then they do not have a history at all. Schafer's position is the same as the existentialist view of Sartre (1943) despite Schafer's (1976) disavowal, and it is fundamentally at odds with the view of Ryle (1949), upon whose ideas Schafer otherwise has relied for his attack on Freud's metapsychology. Schafer's concept of action provides no justification for widening the context of an action to earlier events and actions (conscious or unconscious); it provides a justification for a life history that is no more than a phenomenological chronology. Anything more—if indeed every action, as Schafer claims, spontaneously starts from itself— would be sheer invention: an invention for which the only possible criterion of truth would be coherence. This idea provides unlimited opportunity for Spence's pattern making.

A number of considerations lend credence to the coherence criterion of truth for psychoanalysis. First, Freud appears to have espoused coherence. Freud often (e.g., 1895, pp. 194–195; 1909, pp. 165–169) testified to his awareness of the complex, seemingly arbitrary, fragmentary, subtle, and evasive nature of the mass of material produced by associations. Is not this material typically so ambiguous, so rife with uncertainties, that the best we can achieve is a coherent account with the possibility of other, no less coherent accounts being constructed? In apparent support of Goldberg, Freud (1915) pointed out that even at the earliest stages of description a new science already applies concepts that are not drawn altogether from the field of observation to which the descriptions apply (p. 117). Freud (1927) remarked that "a number of very remarkable, disconnected facts are brought together... into a consistent whole" (p. 23) by his totem and taboo hypothesis of the killing of the primal horde father by his sons. Given the multiple variables at work in the clinical situation, which in this regard only reflects the human situation; given the complex, shifting nature of transference; and given the difficulty of sorting out what the patient has innocently suffered at the hands of others, what he has provoked, what he has only fantasized, and with what he has been complicit, is it not heuristically judicious to adopt a concept of truth that refuses to lay claim to an objectivity that is not attainable?

Moreover, does not an analysis bring about changes in the meaning that events in the patients' pasts have for them in the present and future?— for example, a woman who was unable adequately to enter into, let alone resolve, the conflicts of the oedipal stage, but who manages to do so in the transference, comes in the course of this experience to remember her father as a sexually exciting object, though during childhood she had experienced him only as an indifferent, zombie-like figure who was silent and remote. Is not this routine clinical experience evidence for Spence's "pattern-making," for Ricoeur's "narrated history," for Habermas's "self-reflection," for the determination of the past by investments in the present and the concept of truth in psychoanalysis as coherent narration?

Moreover, the current state of psychoanalytic theory lends plausibility to the idea of coherence. There is no unified theory: there are only divergent, often mutually inconsistent theories supported by clinical observations. Does not this state of affairs cohere rather well with the coherence theory? Perhaps there are as many true-life histories as there are theories that can give a consistent account of them.

Attractive as these possibilities are in certain respects, to these questions I believe the answer is No. The description above of the uncertainty of associations is tendentious and incomplete. Even when a patient is filling the hour with reports of manifest dream contents to the exclusion of associations, the details of the material are clear and determinate. There is nothing indefinite or elusive about it. Of course, it is unintelligible and uninterpretable in the absence of associations, but this fact has itself an obvious interpretation: the patient is anxiously clinging to the manifest dream content. This interpretation, properly timed and expressed and linked to the transference, will begin a process of change that will enable the patient to begin associating to his dreams, and these associations will then also be determinate and discrete. If they are incomplete, as they are likely to be, that will be because further resistances are at work. If they become vague and uncertain it is for the same reason. Vagueness and uncertainty are themselves determinate states of affairs that have an explanation; they are not characteristic qualities of mental contents and states as such.

The same is true of fantasies, memories, character traits, etc. Pattern making by the analyst is not required so long as resistances and defenses are interpreted in such a way as to allow the intrinsic forces at work in the psychic life of the patient to make themselves known. These forces will determine the pattern as they will determine the transference. The forces in question are the drives, their vicissitudes and their derivatives.

The ideas of pattern making, of theory-bound observation, and the like are rationalizations for countertransferential resistance to the threats posed by the drives, that is, by the instinctual unconscious. It is for this reason that psychoanalytic adherents of coherence have to find some way to banish them conceptually. Psychoanalytic theories that repudiate the drives are also likely to employ coherence as a concept of truth. Freud (1900, 1923) was certainly aware of the complexity of dreams and the extent to which they are representative of all mental phenomena; however, Freud (1905) also believed that the obscurities of a dream can be cleared up, that each manifest element can be traced along the paths of displacement and condensation from whence it came and that the meaning of the dream is to be found in the unconscious wishes of the dreamer. We are not always able to find the meaning, but it is there to be found, independently of any pattern-making activity on the part of the analyst. The task of interpretation as Freud conceived it is to make the interpretation correspond with the operative unconscious wishes of the dreamer—wishes that have a definite nature of their own. (For an opposing view see Viderman, 1970, 1972).

It is also true that Freud appreciated the extent to which any inquiry has to be guided by preliminary ideas. In this respect Freud's grasp of epistemology was more realistic and empirical than that of Bacon (1620), the great founder of modern empiricism. But Freud also thought that these preliminary ideas can and must be continually criticized and made to reflect the facts of observation more accurately. From the need to have a theory that will enable us to make predictions about what we will observe in order to make systematic observations, it does not follow that these predictions must govern what we will find. Harvey's (1618–1619) preliminary idea about the circulation of the blood did not add or subtract anything from his crucial measurement of the amount of blood ejected by the heart in a single pulse, the results of which Harvey (1628) published ten years later (Singer, 1957). Hawking's (1988) mathematical derivation which proves, on current thermodynamic and quantum assumptions, that black holes emit particles does not affect the observations that will now have to be made on cosmic radiation to test the empirical truth of this derivation. Freud's prediction of the incidence of infantile seduction required by his seduction theory did not in some subtle way influence the number of such occurrences or Freud's ability to estimate them. Adequately formulated scientific theories or common-sense beliefs yield predictions and give rise to expectations that can be tested by observing what actually happens. These observations have meaning in their own right, independently of the theories or beliefs we have about their objects.

Freud (1927) defended science against those philosophers who assert that all knowledge claims, whether religious or scientific, are ultimately equal because they are equally subjective. Our observations, it was argued then as now, are inevitably conditioned by what we believe and how we observe. As we have shown above, various psychoanalysts are now advocates of variants of this idea of truth. Freud offered three arguments—biological, methodological, and epistemological—on behalf of scientific realism. Mental activities have developed in order to explore the world; it is likely that they have acquired a structure that facilitates that exploration (the biological argument). These mental activities are a part of the world; they can, themselves, be investigated in order to discover their degree of facility, its causes, and methods of improvement (the methodological argument). Scientific knowledge, because of its methods, is determined not only by our mental activities and their structures, but primarily by the objects observed (the epistemological argument). I have elsewhere (Hanly, 1983, 1988) set out supporting evidence from cultural history for Freud's biological argument. His methodological and epistemological arguments are supported by evidence from the history of science. Science has been able to identify and to take into account the influence of our sensory apparatus upon our experience of nature. Copernicus and Galileo discovered the influence of the earth's daily rotation upon our observation of stars and planets, and by correcting for it they were able to construct a genuinely more objective description of the solar system. Einstein's invention of relativity theory enabled the human mind to realize that the self-evident rectilinearity of space is only a consequence of the organization of our sensory apparatus. Psychoanalysis has made its own contribution to this process of observational "correction" for the field of human phenomena. These examples indicate that the expediency of the adaptation of the human sensory apparatus and thought activity to reality brought about by environmental pressure has been sufficient to allow it to proceed beyond the requirements of survival.

Freud employed a coherence criterion within the framework of his realist epistemology. Nowhere is the use of coherence more evident than in his effort to prove the objective reality of the Wolf Man's primal scene (Freud, 1918). But even though his interpretation makes coherent sense of the details of the Wolf Man's infantile history and its connection with both his infantile and adult neuroses, Freud does not claim that he has succeeded in proving that the primal scene was an occurrence rather than a fantasy. A crucial fact concerning the Gruska scene (the boy's urination) could only be established inferentially. Similarly, Freud only claimed that his hypothesis in *Totem and Taboo* (1912–1913) was more plausible than existing theories and that it probably contained some measure of truth; he did not claim either that its coherence made it true or that such coherence constituted a limit beyond which knowledge could not reach. Freud used coherence as a necessary but not a sufficient criterion of truth. He took correspondence to be necessary and sufficient. Freud used coherence as a formal, logical criterion, and correspondence as a material, epistemological criterion. Correspondence is built into the foundations of psychoanalysis. It is part of the meaning of the reality principle.

Yet Freud may have been in error. And, in any case, it would be to argue fallaciously from authority to treat as evidence what Freud believed rather than to weigh the force of the arguments on which his view was based. Here are two additional arguments, one drawn from mathematics and physical science and one drawn from psychoanalysis.

Euclidean geometry is a mathematical system which is complete and coherent. For this reason it escapes Gödel's theorem. Yet it turns out that it does not describe the space of the universe; physics has been able to identify facts which show this to be the case. The axioms of Euclidean geometry were believed to be self-evidently true; Plato, Descartes, and Leibniz considered them to be innate to the mind, and Kant considered them to be *a priori* conditions of experience. Yet despite this self-evidence and coherence, and despite the fact that we actually do observe the world in a Euclidean fashion, these axioms have been shown by relativity physics to be approximations suitable only to regions of space much smaller than the solar system.

Psychoanalysis is familiar, in the psychoses, with systems of belief, observation, and behavior that are remarkable both for their coherence and for their detachment from reality. The following bit of case history is representative. A psychotic student in a university seminar experienced growing agitation when certain topics were under discussion while the sounds of shuffling feet were accompanied by the sounds of a streetcar passing under the windows. This agitation cohered perfectly with his belief that such conjunctions of sounds signaled the approach of evil forces at work in his Manichean cosmos. Coherent as well with his beliefs were the ritual precautions he undertook to oppose the advance of those forces. Nowhere are the shortcomings of coherence as a criterion of truth more forcefully demonstrated than in our own field. Just as an argument may be valid and yet have a false conclusion, so a system of beliefs or a narrative may be coherent but false. The concept of coherence is not sufficient to bridge the gap between ideas and objects.

Moreover, psychoanalytic findings offer a defense against one of the philosophical criticisms of the correspondence theory. Putnam (1981) has argued that realism requires, in addition to the observer and the observed, a third party to whom reference can be made in order to compare the observer's perception with the object independently of the observer. How else could we form a judgment about its correspondence? Since the human observer is not in a position to form this judgment, realism is flawed with the hidden theological assumption of a God whose perception of objects is the ideal against which human perceptions can be measured.

But psychoanalysis has shown that this third-party observer is none other than the human observer himself. During the period of the preoedipal anaclitic bond, children, while having their own perceptions of things, use their idealized parents to carry out the very function assigned to God by Putnam's argument. Parental perceptions are taken to be authoritative—the standard against which children are able to measure their own experience. Certain ego-regressed patients continue to have to establish a relation with an idealized figure because they cannot trust the evidence of their own senses unless vouched for and authenticated by an authority. Even Harvey had to attribute his discovery of the truth about the circulatory system to Galen, in whose works no such idea is to be found. Psychoanalysis has shown that the identifications involved in the resolution of the Oedipus complex normally bring into play a capacity for critical self-awareness that includes the perception of objects (Freud, 1923; Wälder, 1934; Hanly, 1979). An individual acquires the ability sufficiently to objectify his own perceptions and beliefs to enable him to consider to what extent they correspond with and are adequate to the object, and to what extent they are not. This capacity forms the psychological ground for critical common sense and for scientific realism. The reality principle requires neither the alleged Olympianism of correspondence nor the Demiurge of coherence.

In psychoanalysis, through sympathetic identification clarified by countertransference awareness, this same self-critical capacity can facilitate our search after an understanding of our patients in their terms rather than our own. The complement of this self-critical receptive observation on the part of the analyst is the struggle for self-honesty in the analysand. The view that an analysis consists of a mutual construction by analyst and analysand of the analysand's life fails to do justice to this struggle. There are analysands who have been able to use the analytic process to discover more about themselves, to recover more of their past, and to find ways to reconcile themselves with it, than their analysts could comprehend. Fortunately for our profession and for our patients, the process that the analyst facilitates can yield for the analysand a degree of resolving self-knowledge and improved functioning that exceeds that of his analyst. There is a common human nature—though to be sure not in the form of an Aristotelian essence that exists in nature—that awaits our better understanding. It is embodied in the lives lived by individuals. These individual lives are part of nature; they are there to be known, however difficult that may be. The self-honesty of an analysand in his realization that he feared his father because he wanted to murder him, or of an analysand in her realization that her frigidity and the pleasure she took in rape fantasies was caused by her wish to use intercourse to castrate men, implies that these realizations correspond with real wishes that continue to influence the individual's life. Neither the pain of those realizations nor their beneficial effects can be accounted for by any other assumption. In the end, each person has only his own life to live, however much it is shared with others. At the core of the being of each person there is a solitude in which he is related to himself. Truth resides in this solitude to the extent that one can remember one's own past as it actually was. The ground of genuine analytic work in the analyst is his attitude of respect for this solitude.

SUMMARY

A philosophical controversy concerning the nature of truth has begun to play an important part in psychoanalytic theorizing. The two major philosophical notions, the coherence and the correspondence theories, and their use in psychoanalytic theory making, are examined. It is argued that although coherence is one of the criteria of truth, correspondence is the more essential and fundamental criterion. It was in this way that Freud used these concepts in creating psychoanalysis. Psychoanalytic discoveries concerning the psychogenesis of objectivity in perception and thought support the correspondence theory of truth, and provide in addition an answer to the third-party critique of correspondence. The correspondence theory as a basic attitude of mind is a necessary element in the respect for the patient upon which psychoanalytic therapy depends.

REFERENCES

Bacon, F. (1620). *Novum organum.* In E.A. Burtt (Ed.), *The English Philosophers from Bacon to Mill* (pp. 5–123). New York: Modern Library, 1939.

Bradley, F.H. (1897). *Appearance and Reality.* London: Swan & Sonnenschein.

Drake, S. (1978). *Galileo at Work: His Scientific Biography.* Chicago: University of Chicago Press.

Feyerabend, P. (1965). Problems of empiricism. In R.G. Colodny (Ed.), *Beyond the Edge of Certainty: Essays in Contemporary Science and Philosophy* (pp. 145–260). Englewood Cliffs, NJ: Prentice Hall.

Freud, S. (1895). *Studies on Hysteria.* SE 2.

——— (1900). *The Interpretation of Dreams.* SE 4–5.

——— (1905). Fragment of an analysis of a case of hysteria. SE 7:1–122.

—— (1909). Notes upon a case of obsessional neurosis. SE 10:151–318.

—— (1912–1913). Totem and taboo. SE 13:1–162.

—— (1915). Instincts and their vicissitudes. SE 14:109–140.

—— (1918). From the history of an infantile neurosis. SE 17:1–124.

—— (1923). Remarks on the theory and practice of dream-interpretation. SE 19:107–122.

—— (1927). The future of an illusion. SE 21:1–56.

Goldberg, A. (1976). A discussion of the paper by C. Hanly and J. Masson, "A critical examination of the new narcissism." *International Journal of Psychoanalysis* 57:67–70.

—— (1988). *A Fresh Look at Psychoanalysis: The View from Self-Psychology.* Hillsdale, NJ: The Analytic Press.

Habermas, J. (1971). *Knowledge and Human Interests* (Trans. J.J. Shapiro). Boston: Beacon Press.

Hanly, C. (1979). *Existentialism and Psychoanalysis.* New York: International Universities Press.

—— (1983). A problem of theory testing. *International Review of Psycho-Analysis* 10:393–405. [Chapter 1 in this volume]

—— (1985). Logical and conceptual problems of existential psychiatry. *Journal of Nervous & Mental Disease* 173:263–281. [Chapter 18 in this volume]

—— (1986). Review of *The Assault on Truth: Freud's Suppression of the Seduction Theory*, by Jeffrey Mossaieff Masson, and *In the Freud Archives*, by Janet Malcolm. *International Journal of Psychoanalysis* 67:517–519.

—— (1988). From animism to rationalism. In S. Hook, W.L. O'Neill & R. O'Toole (Eds.), *Philosophy, History and Social Action: Essays in Honour of Lewis Feuer* (pp. 221–234). Dordrecht: Kluwer.

Hawking, S. (1988). *A Brief History of Time.* New York: Bantam.

Kant, I. (1781). *Critique of Pure Reason* (Trans. N.K. Smith). London: Macmillan, 1950.

———— (1785). *Groundwork of the Metaphysics of Morals* (Trans. H.J. Paton). London: Hutchinson, 1947.

Klein, G.S. (1976). *Psychoanalytic Theory.* New York: International Universities Press.

Kohut, H. (1959). Introspection, empathy, and psychoanalysis: An examination of the relationship between mode of observation and theory. In P.H. Orstein (Ed.), *The Search for the Self,* vol. 1 (pp. 205–232). New York: International Universities Press, 1978.

———— (1971). *The Analysis of the Self.* New York: International Universities Press.

———— (1977). *The Restoration of the Self.* New York: International Universities Press.

Kuhn, T.S. (1970). *The Structure of Scientific Revolutions* (2nd ed.). Chicago: University of Chicago Press.

May, R. (1958). Contributions of existential psychotherapy. In R. May, E. Angel & H.F. Ellenberger (Eds.), *Existence: A New Dimension in Psychiatry and Psychology* (pp. 37–91). New York: Simon & Schuster, 1967.

Merleau-Ponty, M. (1945). *Phenomenology of Perception* (Trans. C. Smith). London: Routledge & Kegan Paul, 1962.

Putnam, H. (1981). *Reason, Truth and History.* Cambridge: Cambridge University Press.

Rangell, L. (1988). The future of psychoanalysis: The scientific crossroads. *Psychoanalytic Quarterly* 57:313–340.

Ricoeur, P. (1970). *Freud and Philosophy.* New Haven: Yale University Press.

———— (1974). *The Conflict of Interpretations: Essays in Hermeneutics* (Ed. D. Ihde). Evanston: Northwestern University Press.

———— (1981). *Hermeneutics and the Human Sciences* (Trans. J.B. Thompson). New York: Cambridge University Press.

Ryle, G. (1949). *The Concept of Mind*. London: Hutchinson's University Library.

Sartre, J.-P. (1943). *Being and Nothingness* (Trans. H.E. Barnes). New York: Philosophical Library, 1956.

Schafer, R. (1976). *A New Language for Psychoanalysis*. New Haven: Yale University Press.

———— (1978). *Language and Insight*. New Haven: Yale University Press.

Singer, C. (1957). *A Short History of Anatomy and Physiology from the Greeks to Harvey*. New York: Dover.

Spence, D. (1982a). *Narrative Truth and Historical Truth: Meaning and Interpretation in Psychoanalysis*. New York: Norton.

———— (1982b). Narrative truth and theoretical truth. *Psychoanalytic Quarterly* 51:43–69.

Viderman, S. (1970). *La construction de l'espace analytique*. Paris: Denoel.

———— (1972). Comme en un miroir, obscurément... *Nouvelle Revue de Psychanalyse* 5:131–152.

Wälder, R. (1934). The problem of freedom in psychoanalysis and the problem of reality testing. *In Psychoanalysis: Observation, Theory, Application* (pp. 101–120). New York: International Universities Press, 1976.

Wallerstein, R. S. (1988). One psychoanalysis or many? *International Journal of Psychoanalysis* 69:5–21.

CHAPTER 11

Pragmatism, Tradition, and Truth in Psychoanalysis*

It is argued that neither tradition nor its opposite, novelty, provides us with any reliable assurance as to where the truth lies in psychoanalysis or in any other body of knowledge. Both traditional ideas and new ideas may be true, but not *because* they are traditional or novel. It is because they can be shown to be true or false either deductively by reason alone (i.e., by inference from an idea known to be true), or inductively by reason and observation. Of these two methods, the second is more fundamental. In a variety of ways, in the arguments I shall advance here I seek to place psychoanalysis in the context of the history of ideas and science.

Tradition implies age and the suggestion of reliability because of the durability of an idea, if not venerability and trustworthiness on account of the weight of trial by human experience over a long time. If an idea has survived many generations of experience, must it not be true? Freud (1937) drew on this association between venerability and truth when he cited Empedocles' idea of love (creation) and strife (destruction) as cosmic forces as a precursor to his final dual instinct theory. Freud consoled himself for the lack of support for his theory when he came upon its cosmic equivalent in the fragments of the pre-Socratic philosopher: "I am well aware that this

---

* Originally published in *American Imago* 63, no. 3 (2006):261–282.

dualistic theory... has found little sympathy... even among psychoanalysts. This made me all the more pleased when not long ago I came upon this theory of mine in the writings of one of the great thinkers of ancient Greece" (pp. 244–245). Evidently, even as Freud was advancing his thinking about psychoanalytic therapy, he was reading ancient Greek texts for ideas. Novelty, by contrast, implies something contemporary or, at least, recent, with the suggestion of freshness, liveliness, invention, discovery, and often enough advancement or improvement. Certain new or revived ideas, which possess an interest because they are new and different, can sometimes appear to plumb hitherto uncharted depths with penetrating insights and acquire a plausibility, especially if they justify the rejection of ideas received from the previous generation.

Considerations of tradition and novelty often enough find their way into the evaluation of observations and ideas. Imagine a bright, rebellious group of psychiatric residents in an introductory seminar on psychoanalysis. They have been given a reading list in which the papers are two or more decades old. Their complaint takes the form of a dilemma: either they are being asked to read clinical literature that has a merely antiquarian interest when they expected the latest on theory and technique, or psychoanalysis is so fossilized and moribund that no new observations or ideas are available. These bright young minds enamored of the idea that the latest is best would scarcely be persuaded by the argument that the study of Plato's *Symposium* and *Republic* can still be rewarding for the student of the human psyche. In either case, Freud and Klein are of insufficient interest to merit careful study and reflection. Nor is it likely that this conviction would be shaken by their being told that the subjectivism of much current relational psychoanalysis is a revival by postmodernity of a theory of knowledge first formulated by Protagoras in the fifth century BC.

Nevertheless, in my opinion, there is some truth in the claim that psychoanalysis is not progressing as it did earlier in its history. But the problem is not a lack of theoretical ideas and novel points of view; psychoanalysis is not in the least moribund in this respect. What is missing are the reliable, relevant observations needed to test its theories and the points of view. This failure is not infrequently rationalized on the grounds that observations in psychoanalysis can be tested only within a theory or point of view because the theory one holds or the point of view one has adopted predetermines the observations that one will make. On the basis of this epistemological assumption, subjectivity in psychoanalysis is unavoidable, and therefore theory-neutral clinical observations are not available to test conflicting psychoanalytic theories. This epistemological position intrinsically promotes an endless proliferation of fundamentally untestable theories and points of view. Psychoanalytic theories, on this view, are brilliant superstructures floating in mid-air without foundations in repeatable observations.

However, most sciences do make relatively stable progress. Consequently, the confidence of our hypothetical residents that later is better in science is not altogether mistaken. Einstein's relativity theory incorporates Newtonian physics as a special case with limited application. For some time during the last century, the cosmological theories of constant creation and the big bang were in contention, but developments in mathematics and observations of background noise in physics have brought the controversy to an end in favor of the big bang theory. Darwin's theory of evolution lacked a vital component until Mendel's genetic theory completed the explanation of the evolution of species. Even closer to psychoanalysis in time and subject matter is the steady progress—despite conflicting ideas, vigorous controversies, and uncertainties—that has taken place and continues in neurobiology (Kandel, 2006). When all this is considered, the history of psychoanalytic thought appears to have more in common with the history of philosophy than with the history of science. Theories go out of style following shifts in intellectual, scientific, or humanistic culture, or they are abandoned out of exhaustion or in the pursuit of novelty and ambition, rather than on account of new and better observations and concepts. However, none of these factors and their like (e.g., the need to reconcile psychoanalysis with religious belief or with a non-scientific humanism) provide rational grounds for abandoning one theory in psychoanalysis for another.

Whatever the motive or the inspiration, there are only two rational grounds for altering a theory. The first is observations that are inconsistent with the theory in its present form. Einstein's relativity theory replaced Newtonian mechanics not because of some change in the zeitgeist but because the paths of light rays moving through the sun's gravitational field were more accurately predicted by Einstein's theory than by Newton's. A second ground is the impact of discoveries and well-established theories in adjacent fields. Psychoanalysis has abandoned Freud's hypothesis of an archaic heritage because it implied the inheritance of acquired characteristics, which, biochemistry has shown, cannot occur. Evolutionary theory does not disprove the Oedipus complex, but it does require abandoning the explanation of its origin by the inheritance of the acquired memories of our earliest human ancestors. Consequently, the psychiatric residents touched on a problem in psychoanalytic theorizing, but their confidence that what is newer is better is not so much altogether wrong as woefully superficial and misguided. An idea is not true because it is up to date; it is true or false either because there is good observational evidence for or against it or because its truth (or falsity, as in our illustration above) can be logically inferred from other ideas known to be true because of observational evidence. New ideas can be exciting and promising, but their novelty and the affects novelty arouses have nothing to do with their truth.

Moreover, have not my hypothetical residents completely overlooked something important—the extent to which truth takes up its residence in tradition? After all, if an idea has survived for a long time, is not its longevity some indication of its utility, and in that pragmatic sense, of its truth? One of the most magnificent traditions of mathematical thought in the history of ideas is Euclid's geometry. From a small number of self-evident definitions and axioms, Euclid was able to derive a complete system of theorems about rectilinear space. Descartes, who rendered Euclidean geometry into algebra (analytic geometry), considered its axioms and definitions to be perfect exemplars of indubitable truths. Newton's laws of motion and his mechanics assumed Euclidean rectilinear space. Kant considered Euclid's geometry to be a universal *a priori* form of sense experience without which rational observation of nature, and hence science, would not be possible. What could be more traditional and self-evidently veritable than Euclidean geometry?

Yet we now know that, as a guide to the nature of real space, this tradition was almost as misleading as Ptolemaic astronomy. The traditional belief in the truth of Euclidean geometry was all the more difficult to correct because of its magnificent *coherence*, its *nearness to experience*, and its *utility* in surveying, construction, etc. Unfortunately, these factors helped to disguise its failure to tally with reality. It was not until the nineteenth century that Reimann invented a geometry of curved space by denying Euclid's axiom of parallels; it was not until the twentieth century that Einstein used a geometry of curved space in his construction of relativity theory. The observational proof that the real space of the universe is curved was finally established by the observation of the bending of light rays passing through the sun's gravitational field made possible by an eclipse. Newtonian mechanics based on the Euclidean assumption that space is rectilinear yielded a different prediction of the bending from that generated by Einstein's theory based on the assumption that the curvature of space is relative to mass. Einstein's prediction closely approximated reality; the Newtonian prediction much less so. Other observations—for example, the location of the planets in the solar system over time—confirmed relativity theory, which implied that real space is not rectilinear, despite a traditional belief that had not only seemed self-evident but had also been confirmed by experience and had proven to be useful. It appears that, in this case, novelty wins out over tradition, even the most venerable and apparently reliable of traditions. Do our rebellious residents have it right after all?

It cannot be said of contemporary psychoanalysis that it overvalues tradition. Such an attitude is incompatible with the restless seeking after new ideas and approaches that has produced the remarkable proliferation of theories characteristic of the contemporary psychoanalytic scene. For example, Kohut began by making useful contributions to the psychoanalytic theory of narcissism and its clinical application by expanding and further elaborating Freud's theory of narcissistic object relations. He ended by constructing a new theory that reduced the drives to narcissistic libido, and rendered the functions of ego, superego, and id in the structural model subordinate to a self animated by narcissism. It would appear that, after briefly waxing, self psychology is now waning as a comprehensive alternative theory in psychoanalysis. A similar pattern can be observed unfolding in the efforts to gain a better understanding of the work and place of object relations in psychopathology, which have given rise to contemporary relational psychoanalysis.

Not a little of this theorizing involves the material fallacies of *pars pro toto* and *accent*. The *pars pro toto* fallacy consists of taking a part of a complex structure, process, or relationship and treating it as the whole—for example, giving drives such primacy that they replace object relations, or conversely, giving object relations such primacy that they replace drives in the classical theory. Self psychology and relational psychoanalysis both contributed usefully to psychoanalysis by seeking to correct the loss of object relations in the narrow and exclusionary drive/defense model, a model that is also seen to be waning. But self psychology and relational psychoanalysis commit a *pars pro toto* fallacy of their own that becomes evident when we compare these new theories with the more balanced and integrated etiological model of the classical theory, which treats drive development factors and object relations as the ideal poles of an etiological complementary series with variations according to individual constitution and life history.

The fallacy of *accent* is based on an error of emphasis. By throwing the emphasis on one part of a complex theory, it can be made to appear incomplete and one-sided when it is not. For example, Freud's instinct theory may be presented as if it rendered individual development monadic and self-contained, when the theory actually includes the recognition that our instinctual life is expressed in needs that make us dependent on objects for our survival and well-being. Thus, the psychoanalytic instinct theory is coherent with the etiological model; the complementarity mentioned above is built into it. The fallacy of accent gives rise to unhelpful *straw man* arguments.

These fallacies can also have an adverse effect on clinical work. The idea of etiological complementarity requires the clinician to be steadily vigilant in estimating the relative importance in a patient's neurosis of what has been done to an analysand and what the analysand has done or, more often, wanted to do. For example, an analysand may be thrown into an obsessional anxiety compromising his ability to negotiate something he legitimately wants from a person with some authority. If the analyst's clinical orientation is based on the complementary model, he will have no theoretical basis for listening only for past painful experience at the hands of authority figures in the life of the patient or only for evidence of the handiwork of drive-motivated ambivalence causing a disturbing fantasy of retribution that nourishes anxiety in his relation to current authority figures. Theoretically, either constitutional or object-relational factors would be sufficient, along with other conditions, to cause the obsessional anxiety. The theory does not decide. The decision is left, as it should be, to the evidence of the transference and the associations of the analysand. The problem with theories that are flawed by fallacies of *pars pro toto* or of accent is that they promote exclusionary, partial, or reductive listening.

No amount of brilliantly ingenious novelty can make up, theoretically or clinically, for this partiality.

At a recent panel of the American Psychoanalytic Association, a relational psychoanalyst presented clinical material that nicely exposed the adverse effects on a boy's development caused by a perverse mother who overstimulated him by repeatedly exhibiting herself to him in the nude during his boyhood. The analyst traced the son's adult self-destructive promiscuity to the trauma of his mother's perverse seductiveness. But should we not also wonder about the son's oedipal aspirations? Are oedipal wishes always and only caused by deficits and provocations suffered by children at the hands of their parents? Or did an independently occurring incest wish in the son contribute to the traumatic impact of the mother's stimulation? The advantage of the complementarity model is that it would find acceptable whatever weight the relevant facts of this patient's life might place on the side of pathogenic parental influence, as in sexual seduction, including the finding that the child's drive-determined oedipal conflicts would probably have resolved themselves in a benign way in the absence of the parental provocations and with the assistance of adequate parenting. The disadvantage of the relational theory as a clinical orientation is that it turns a blind eye to neuroses occurring in the absence of parental provocations and to the drive components of neuroses when motivations arising from parenting and development are intertwined and mutually reinforcing. Yet apart from these problems, the exploration of alternative and counter-hypotheses can be not only beneficial for but also necessary to the growth of psychoanalysis, just as it is useful, at the clinical level, for the analyst to be able to entertain a number of possible interpretative hypotheses until the indications of the associative process and the transference provide a basis for a choice.

The problem is that theorizing and interpreting according to differing, even inconsistent, points of view has tended recently to take the place of the testing of theories against ongoing clinical observations. Unfortunately, the avoidance of this challenge has been rationalized by subjectivist epistemology. Although some versions of subjectivism can allow for and justify clinical testing within a theory, subjectivist epistemology cuts the feet out from under the possibility of clinically testing differing theories. On the basis of a subjectivist epistemology, the answer to the question, "Is the classical theory of the genesis of the Oedipus complex true, or is the self-psychological theory true?" is that both are true and can be observed to be true within the observational constraints of each theory even though the two theories are incompatible. Logically, if two propositions are contraries, they cannot both be true. Here the propositions in question are, "The Oedipus complex owes its origins to drive development," and "The Oedipus complex does not owe its origins to drive development but to inadequate parenting." Logically, these are contraries. Consequently, psychoanalysis has to adopt one and reject the other, or show that both are false, if it is to be a logically rational body of knowledge. Logic alone requires an end to the theoretical permissiveness that has tended to characterize contemporary psychoanalysis. Such permissiveness may be a political solution to theoretical differences, but it is not a scientific solution.

On the surface of it, one might want to claim that intellectual history presents us with examples of different theories about the same thing, more than one of which is true. If so, may not intellectual history present us with traditions of differing beliefs, each of which is true to the experience of its adherents and none of which has any exclusive claim to truth? But a cursory survey of the history of ideas suggests that the opposite is more often the case. New and better ideas replace traditional ideas. Galen's idea of the discontinuity of the blood system in mammals, which persisted for centuries, did not continue side by side with Harvey's proof that it could not be true. It lived on briefly only because of having been sanctioned by the church. Lamarck's idea of the inheritance of acquired characteristics could not survive Darwin's idea of the survival of the fittest as an explanation of species change and Mendel's discovery of genetic mutation. No chemist since Boyle would dream of considering the qualitative definitions of natural elements proffered by the pre-Socratic cosmologists to be different from but still as true as the molecular theory of modern science. As noted previously, my hypothetical residents, with their preference for recentness, have it all over traditionalists with their preference for longevity, even though Archimedes' principle that a body immersed in a fluid undergoes an apparent loss in weight equal to the weight of the fluid it displaces is as true today as it was when he discovered it, and even though Plato's idea of the instinctual causes of character disorder has been shown by psychoanalysis to be as true as Plato held it to be. There is a historical reason for this state of affairs.

The most profound paradigm shift in human thought was the shift during the Renaissance from animistic thinking to scientific thinking. The psychological foundation of animism consists of a projection of the properties of the human psyche onto animate and inanimate nature. We come upon this same animism in contemporary children as a natural stage in the development of their narcissism, when it serves as a defense against helplessness. Residues of the animism that once pervaded human experience, thought, and behavior are found in the varied forms of regression to magical thinking in contemporary adults (Hanly, 1988). As recently as the nineteenth century, animistic projection could be found among scientists who could not believe that neurons house chemical and not spiritual processes (Kandel, 2006). Animism misconceives the nature of matter, motion, and force by finding in them a psychic life they do not have. It also exaggerates teleological causality, which, as (among many others) Spinoza (1677), Hobbes (1651), and Freud (1901) have shown, is an illusion of consciousness, though one no less powerful for being an illusion.

Animistic projective observing and thinking found the causality of purposes everywhere in nature, thereby subordinating material and efficient causality, which are actually determinative of events in nature, to teleology.

Although Archimedes, Euclid, and the artisans of ancient Greece were implicitly observing and thinking beyond animism, the metaphysics and cosmology of Plato and Aristotle were still invested in a rational form of animism whose religion-sanctioned influence largely pushed aside the more reality-bound atomic materialism and mechanism of Democritus and Epicurus. The scientists and some of the philosophers of the Renaissance forged the concepts and made the crucial observations that laid down the foundations of scientific knowledge and the vastly improved understanding of reality that it provides. Paradigm shifts within sciences, as from Newtonian to relativity physics or from Lamarkianism to Darwinism, are small skirmishes within a shared paradigm that is fundamentally scientific, as compared with the profound paradigm revolution that gave birth to scientific ideas and methods of thought and observation.

Consequently, although the errors of traditionalism are more conspicuous, traditionalism and modernism (postmodernism) make a fundamental and opposite error concerning the criteria for truth in psychoanalysis or any other body of knowledge. The error of traditionalism is that an idea is true because it has been held to be true for a long time. The history of ideas shows us that an idea can be reasonably held to be "tried and true" for hundreds of years because it is in agreement with the ordinary, repeated experiences of many generations and it has had reliable uses in the achievement of common human purposes such as the measurement of time. Nevertheless, the idea turns out to be untrue. This fact of intellectual history also cautions us to be careful about using criteria such as "experience-near," "consistency with experience," and "utility" without critically considering the epistemic worth and reliability of the experience and the utility. The error of modernism is that an idea is true simply because it has replaced a received idea. But Copernicus's idea of the diurnal rotation of the earth was not and is not true because of its novelty; it is true because it conceptualizes what is actually happening in nature. Neither the repetitions of longevity nor the novelty of originality have anything to do with the truth of an idea. It is neither the durability nor the modernity of an idea that makes it true; it is the evidence for its truth that makes it true, just as the absence of evidence makes its truth uncertain, and contrary evidence makes it false. As suggested above, there are but two ways to show that an idea (a proposition) is true. An idea can be deductively shown to be true by being derived from other propositions already known to be true, or it can be inductively shown to be true by means of observational evidence attesting that no other explanation or description could account for the phenomenon in question.

Thus, if it is a fact that psychoanalysts no longer consider the Oedipus complex to be universal, this does not make the generalization false any more than it would be made true by all psychoanalysts believing it to be universal. The universality of the Oedipus complex is falsified by analyses that have three characteristics: (1) the patient suffered a debilitating neurosis; (2) the patient's conflicts were ameliorated and remained ameliorated after the analysis and after the transference had dissolved; and (3) the free associations and transferences of the patient did not reveal any thoughts, memories, fantasies, or affects that could be the derivative of a repressed oedipal conflict contributing to his or her neurosis. The probable truth of the universality of the Oedipus complex requires the first two conditions above, along with different observations in the third: the free associations and the transferences of the patient revealed thoughts, memories, fantasies, and affects that could only be derivative of a repressed oedipal conflict, and their interpretation made a significant contribution to the cure or stable amelioration of the patient's neurosis.

Follow-up data are obviously hard to come by, and the analyst's intuition of what the future holds for the patient does not count. However, irrespective of these difficulties, the basic point holds that neither the reassuring longevity of an idea nor the appealing novelty of an idea can be allowed to substitute for evidence-based ideas in the construction of knowledge.

An idea is true to the extent that it corresponds to the reality of which it is an idea. This epistemological premise about the nature of truth pervades Freud and Freudian thought, and psychoanalytic thought more generally (e.g., Klein and Kleinian thought). The correspondence idea of truth assumes that the world exists and has a nature independent of our perceptions of it and our ideas about it. The task of perception is to find methods of observing it that will disclose it as it is; the task of thought is to construct ideas based on observation of the world that are adequate to its nature. This idea of truth is fundamental to all natural sciences. It is interesting to note that even Aristotle, whose ideas about physical and animate nature remained seriously inadequate to their object, nevertheless held the correspondence view of truth, as expressed in his confidence that no one could doubt the existence of nature.

A philosophical criticism (Putnam, 1981) of correspondence as a criterion of truth is that it is based on a hidden deistic assumption because it implies that some third party, some omniscient impartial being whose perspective is beyond all perspectives and is in a position to know both the experiencing observer and the experienced observed in and of themselves, and thus to know to what extent the observation of the observer agrees with the object observed. Otherwise, the observer is enclosed within the perspective governing his observation of the object, in which case the question of its correspondence with the object remains unanswerable.

The contemporary view of epistemological subjectivism, propounded by analysts who have been influenced by postmodernism, is that the observer and the observed, the analyst and the analysand, are inextricably related to the extent of being reciprocally determinative. Hence, in analysis a patient's associations and transference do not, under any conditions, convey who and what the patient is but only who and what the patient is in relation to the analyst. Subjectivists criticize psychoanalytic realists for being absolutists because they claim to be able to know who the patient really is and what motivates him, better than the patient does himself. These psychoanalytic criticisms cohere with the philosophical criticism of the critical realist's advocacy of correspondence and advance the further implication that the realist not only logically introduces a deity into epistemology but is also self-deifying with claims of omniscience.

These criticisms and the philosophical ideas on which they are based have, no doubt, a certain merit. It is possible to use a conviction of correspondence to believe that because one sees something in a certain way, it must be that way. It would be bad analytic technique to see a woman patient's recurrent complaints about male peers being privileged over her at her place of work as being necessarily complaints about not having a penis. What the motives are cannot be decided a priori; to do so would be a misuse of theory and an inadequate technique. In such a case, the analyst would be prescribing the motive rather than discovering it. Her complaints could be realistic, and the psychoanalytic question would then have to do with the motives for her passivity in the face of mistreatment. Her complaints could be unrealistic and symptomatic, yet not motivated by penis envy, or they could be realistic and also motivated by penis envy. An analyst who failed to be open to the possibilities would have failed to maintain evenly suspended attention; he would be simplistic and narrow in his grasp of psychoanalytic theory and technique, and on the assumptions we have made, probably unconsciously hostile toward the patient.

Shortcomings of this kind occur, but it would be a mistake to define an idea or to repudiate it on the basis of its misuse. The situation is more complicated. Good technique would invite the analyst to discover the motives behind his patient's complaining by facilitating and following her associations and transference, and bid the analyst not to rely on preferred ideas. The scientific, philosophical, and common-sense idea of correspondence does not include the idea that truths are easily come by or that success is guaranteed.

Psychoanalysis provides grounds for a response to the philosophical criticism of correspondence and its psychological implication of self-deification. How does the human mind acquire the capacity, without self-deification, to be appropriately and effectively skeptical of its own perceptions and ideas? How do we manage to gain a perspective on our perspectives? Psychoanalysis informs us that at first we manage this mental reflexivity by forming a dependent tie to our parents, whom we idealize and use as an auxiliary ego rendered omniscient enough that we believe that father and mother know everything of which we ourselves are ignorant. This auxiliary parental ego can be used to test the adequacy of our perceptions of things and events, and of our affective responses to them. It is, as it were, in the image of the philosopher's absolute knower whose perspective encompasses all perspectives.

With the formation of the superego, these functions that were earlier assigned to parents are internalized. Henceforth, in addition to considering what others believe to be true, we can consider what we ourselves believe to be true and evaluate the adequacy of our beliefs and the experiences that give rise to them. At first, the work of the superego is engaged in the critical surveillance of desires and aversion, but this capacity for self-criticism comes to be exercised in relation to our own perceptions and ideas as well as our motives and actions. This developmental process begins much earlier in the oral phase, with the differentiation between fantasy (the image of the satisfying object) and reality (the satisfying object). Concern about being good becomes extended to concern about whether or not our ideas are true, from which springs an ability to ask ourselves whether or not our perceptions are adequate to their various objects and to imagine that things are different from what they seem to be.

This capacity to imagine things to be different from how they appear to be, which begins in the play of children, ends in the achievements of science and literature. Copernicus must have imagined somewhat as follows:

if one were observing the earth from high above it, one might see the earth rotating on its axis, turning a part of its surface hour by hour toward the sun and then away from it, which causes day to arise and night to fall as this part turns toward and then away from the sun into its own shadow. In some such way, Copernicus, centuries ago, anticipated in imagination what astronauts are only now able to observe directly. To be sure, this "freedom" of imagination is both fallible and risky because of the interruption in the linkage of our inner cognitive processes with our perceptual contact with reality, and the greater resultant vulnerability to the influence of unconscious content and primary process thinking. Creative scientists, writers, and more ordinary mortals are able to run this risk successfully with results that often deepen or expand our education to reality. The human mind develops a capacity to take up a perspective on its own perspectives, a capacity so magnificently demonstrated by Copernicus in his revolutionary advance toward reality in astronomy.

Thus, the philosophical criticism of correspondence points in the right direction, but it misses the mark. A capacity for a perspective on perspectives is required, but this capacity does not require either a deity or self-deification. The capacity to function as a third (Hanly, 2004) is not at all divine, infallible, or absolute. It has early childhood psychological origins in the experience of being seen and of being seen in a relationship with another person (Britton 2004) or with another thing (Cavell, 1998). By means of identification, we can then take the perspective of the other on ourselves while still being ourselves. In the mature mind, an idea can be put to work as a third. For example, Locke used the idea of representation to gain such a perspective on perceptual experience (Hanly, 2004). Psychoanalysts put this capacity to work in forming impressions of how a patient is experiencing the analyst and how the analyst and analysand are interacting with each other. God need not be invoked as a third to do for us what we can do for ourselves, even if our doing of it is often imperfect, is always vulnerable to error, and may yield only perplexity and uncertainty.

Thus, our first very rudimentary acquaintance with the correspondence criterion of truth is with the origins of reality testing shortly after birth, when our experiences of pleasure and pain teach us an important difference between our image and the object of which it is an image. But here we can also detect the first glimmerings of a pragmatic criterion as well. Turning from the hallucinatory image to the object is useful in bringing about a change in the infant—the satisfaction of hunger and the reward of sensual and psychic pleasure it affords. William James (1907), the founder of pragmatism, formulated the closest possible link between correspondence and usefulness when he affirmed that to say of an idea, "It is true because it is useful," is identical with saying, "An idea works because it is true," by which he meant, "It corresponds with reality."

However, there is an ambiguity in James's use of the term "useful" that needs elucidation. For this purpose, I propose to draw a distinction between scientific and philosophical pragmatism. The term "useful" may mean, "able to be used to engineer or otherwise bring about specific changes that would not occur without the use of the idea"; or it may mean "psychologically beneficial" for the individual in the sense of having advantageous consequences for the individual who has the idea. An appreciation of this ambiguity is essential for understanding James's equation of a pragmatic criterion with a correspondence criterion. The consistency of the equation depends upon the meaning of "useful."

The problem with James's concept of pragmatism becomes clear in his application of it to religion. James claimed that if a hypothesis works satisfactorily in the broadest sense, then it is true. Therefore, if the belief that God exists works well for a believer—for example, if it enables him to respond to misfortune with beneficial fortitude—then the belief is true. But no such implication can be drawn; all that is established is that the belief in the truth of the idea is beneficial, but not that the belief is true. By parity of reasoning on the basis of James's conception of pragmatism, Agamemnon's belief in the goddess Artemis to whom he ritually sacrificed his daughter Iphigenia was true because a brisk offshore wind subsequently got up, which enabled his becalmed fleet to sail to Troy. But this reasoning no more establishes the existence of Artemis in the forests of Olympus than the utility of a belief in a Judeo-Christian god proves the existence of an infinite creator of the universe. The fact that a belief is good for one, that it is useful in the broadest sense, does not prove its truth (i.e., that there is a reality corresponding to it).

Although the link between correspondence and utility in James's definition of it is problematic, a scientific definition of "useful" is consistent with correspondence. A hypothesis is rendered pragmatically true if there can be derived from it a means of bringing about a change predicted by the hypothesis, and if it can provide an explanation, including the mechanism of its production. It is the fact that the change is predicted, explained, and brought about—and not whether the change is beneficial or adverse—that is the crucial validating element that provides pragmatic evidence of correspondence. The amelioration of the human condition is one of the great benefits of science and technology, but it is the fact that the change was predicted, and not the benefit, that confirms the hypothesis. The truth of the hypothesis that the injection of a small, controlled amount of a disease-causing virus will stimulate the production of antibodies that will then protect against future serious infections from the virus is confirmed by a change in the body—its future resistance to the disease on account of the antibodies resulting from the immunizing injection. There can be no question about the human benefits of immunization, but it is the ability to use the scientific ideas to bring about this change (granted, a highly desirable one) that provides a pragmatic confirmation of the ideas. Russell (1945) states the underlying difficulty with James's definition of pragmatism in a colorful and insightful way:

The fallacies spring from an attempt to ignore all extra-human facts. Berkeleian idealism combined with skepticism causes him to substitute belief in God for God, and to pretend that this will do just as well. But this is only a form of the subjectivistic madness which is characteristic of most modern philosophy. (pp. 772–773)

To summarize the results of our discussion thus far, the essential elements in the pragmatic criterion are: (1) a hypothesis that, if true, could explain the nature and origin of a phenomenon or some part of it; (2) the hypothesis provides a method for bringing about a specific change in the phenomenon according to a specific mechanism; (3) on the basis of the hypothesis, a prediction can be made that the change in the phenomenon will occur if the method is correctly applied; and (4) the hypothesis is confirmed if the change occurs when the method is applied and it is disconfirmed if it does not occur. The probability that a hypothesis is true is substantially increased when it works in this way.

Can the pragmatic criterion of truth be employed in the evaluation of the truth of psychoanalytic interpretations, explanations, and theories? Freud relied on a scientifically pragmatic criterion of truth in his construction of psychoanalytic knowledge. A familiar example of his use of a pragmatic criterion is his far-reaching modification of his early seduction theory when he came upon hysterical neurosis in which the stable remission of symptoms predicted by his theory was not brought about by the clinical technique that, according to the theory, should have worked. According to the principles outlined above, (1) Freud's seduction hypothesis could explain the nature and origin of these neuroses by tracing them to their causal

241

origins: repressed memories of having been sexually seduced in childhood were rendered traumatic by the onset of sexuality at puberty and caused sexuality to become symptomatic; (2) the method of cure specified by the theory would consist of a cathartic return of the affect-charged memories, by which it would disarm their interference with normal sexual development and activity; (3) the seduction hypothesis predicted that the affect-laden return of the memories of childhood seductions would cure the symptoms by allowing sexual activity to flourish; but (4) Freud discovered that, in some cases, the return to consciousness of childhood scenes of sexual seduction resulted in no symptom change or in only a temporary improvement. Freud concluded that the seduction theory, in the form in which he originally stated it, was false on the pragmatic grounds that it did not work in the way it would have to have worked if it were true.

In order to explain better the clinical phenomena he was observing, he modified the theory by introducing, in addition to the accidents of childhood object relations, the influence of an inherited sexual instinct active from birth according to a genetic program of developmental stages or infantile sexuality. He accordingly modified the cathartic method by recognizing transference and processes of repeating, remembering, and working through. The fact that these theoretical and technical changes worked better than the theory and clinical technique they replaced constituted a pragmatic confirmation of them, just as the failure of the seduction theory to work provided a pragmatic disconfirmation of it.

But is not this statement a seriously incomplete description of the use of the pragmatic criterion when it comes to psychoanalysis? Does it not suffer from a scientism that disregards the humanity of psychoanalysis and the purpose of its clinical work? There can be no doubt that the resolution by psychoanalysis of neurosis-causing conflicts is beneficial to the individual; at the very least, even if the amount of pleasure in his or her life is not significantly increased, neurotic suffering, as Freud put it, has been replaced by ordinary human unhappiness. Nor can there be any doubt that individuals seek analysis in the conscious hope of experiencing the benefits of relief from depression, inhibitions, irrational anxieties, repeated failures in relationships, and other forms of neurotic misery, even as they unconsciously seek the gratification of the very desires that cause their neuroses and resist the restorative work. But it is durable motivational and functional *maturational changes* in the inner life of the patient that are the result of the analytic work, or the failure to achieve them, that are the crucial elements of the pragmatic test of psychoanalytic therapy and theory. Science does not degrade humanity, and humanism need not quarrel with science.

The collaboration between the correspondence and pragmatic criteria of truth is evident in two respects in the example above showing Freud's pragmatic disproof of his seduction theory. First, the facts of observation used in the pragmatic test have to have been accurately ascertained in order to know that the predicted outcome has failed to occur. For example, if the clinician is intolerant of negative instances and what can be learned from them, he will have difficulty seeing that a predicted outcome is not occurring. That is to say, the correspondence criterion has to have been met in order to grasp the data on which the pragmatic test depends, that is, it has to have been correctly observed that the change predicted by the theory (in this case, an enduring amelioration of symptoms) did not occur. Here we come upon a logical and conceptual difficulty in Renik's (1998) argument that the subjectivity of the analyst can be overcome, and objectivity achieved by the use of predictions.

This argument appropriately underlines the place of prediction in critical psychoanalytic thinking, whether theoretical or clinical. But if the observations made to determine whether or not what is predicted is occurring are objective, then observations in the clinical situation cannot be irremediably subjective. Hence, the logically consistent epistemological premise of the argument is the critical realistic premise that any particular observation may be objective or subjective, depending on the analyst's capacity to perceive what is actually going on in the psyche of the patient, whether or not what is going on has to do with the analyst or someone else, and whether or not the patient is being affected by the analyst. If the analyst cannot muster enough objectivity to do so, he cannot successfully employ the pragmatic test and its requirement of predictability.

Second, in disproving the seduction theory, the pragmatic test does not by itself make evident what correction in the theory is required to enable it to correspond with reality. All that was observed was the continuation of the symptoms or their all too quick return. Freud had to rely on such observations as he had and on the logic of causal reasoning. The crucial observations were the return of memories of sexual seduction, and their affective abreaction during analysis, followed not by the release or restoration of mature sexuality but by the conservation of the neurotic symptoms. Since these memories were sexual, their sexual nature could only be explained by the hypothesis—contrary to Freud's initial, tradition-bound belief—that sexuality does not have its onset with the physical changes of puberty but is already active in childhood. If so, the analytically restored memories could be memories of wish-fulfilling fantasies rather than of real events experienced now by the patient in a distorted way as memories of the supposed real events. If so, the abreactive recall of these memories could not ameliorate the symptoms.

For example, the discharge of feelings of shame and guilt about having been seduced, complicated as they would be by feelings of angry accusation against the sexual aggressor, would not abate the real underlying guilt and anxiety caused by the sexual wish, nor would it abate the dangerous wish itself; hence the continuity or return of the neurotic symptoms. The anxiety, guilt, and shame interfering with adult sexual activities and the substitution of symptoms in their place would continue or resume unabated. This hypothesis would then provide for a different set of inferences about childhood sexuality to be explored by means of observation. These observations would have the task of testing the adequacy of the new hypotheses concerning the nature of the human sexual instinct. The hypothesis of infantile sexuality generates a series of questions concerning, for example, the existence of a period of precocious childhood genital sexuality from which the fantasied scenes of sexual seduction could arise. These questions need to be answered observationally. The correspondence and pragmatic criteria have different but conjoint tasks to perform in the work of testing psychoanalytic ideas and building the edifice of reliable psychoanalytic knowledge. In this, we find Freud struggling to free himself from an inadequate traditional idea about human sexuality, an idea that for generations was taken to be established beyond a shadow of doubt by the obvious and apparent transformations at puberty sustained by the forgetting of one's own childhood. A traditional belief built into the seduction theory doomed it to failure. But if the scandalous novelty of Freud's assertion of childhood sexuality added to its interest, it added nothing to its truth.

Freud (1916–1917) said that the patient's "conflicts will only be successfully solved, and his resistances overcome if the anticipatory ideas he is given tally with what is real in him" (p. 452). In this sentence, in a discussion of the problem of how suggestion may contaminate psychoanalytic observations with the analyst's influence, Freud implicitly states his conjoint use of correspondence and pragmatic criteria of truth. The correspondence criterion is implied by the idea that interpretations must tally with what is real in the patient. For example, the interpretation, "You are seeking to re-experience the pleasure of being comforted by your mother at the breast in your need to take in only the sound of my voice, disregarding what I say," can be effective if and only if it tallies with (i.e., corresponds with) the patient's currently operative transference wish. (Given resistance, this interpretation too will at first be experienced by the patient in terms of its sound and not its sense.) The pragmatic criterion of the effectiveness of the interpretation is linked to correspondence insofar as correspondence is the condition for effectiveness, while effectiveness is a test of correspondence.

It is to this linkage that Freud (1916–1917) attributes progress in the analytic work: "Whatever in the doctor's conjectures is inaccurate drops out in the course of the analysis; it has to be withdrawn and replaced by something more correct" (p. 452). The measure of effectiveness is twofold. It is measured by the greater correspondence of the analyst's observing of and thinking about the patient with what is real in him or her. It is also measured by predictable functional changes in the patient within and without the analysis. Thus, if we define "work" scientifically, we can agree with James that to say that an idea works because it tallies with psychic reality, and to say that an idea tallies with psychic reality because it works, amount to the same thing.

I have argued that when we adopt ideas because they are traditional and seem to be supported by the "wisdom of the ages," or when we adopt them because of their recentness, contemporaneity, or novelty, we do so in either case at our own peril. Neither the venerability nor the novelty of an idea offers us any assurance of its worth; only the evidence for an idea, such as it may be, offers any assurance of its truth. Finally, I have argued that the coherence of an idea, while necessary to its truth, is not by itself sufficient to establish its truth. What is necessary and sufficient for the truth of an idea, in addition to its coherence, is that it correspond with a reality that exists independently of our ideas about it and against which we can pragmatically test the idea's adequacy by determining whether or not it can be used to bring about predictable changes in its object.

REFERENCES

Britton, R. (2004). Subjectivity, objectivity and triangular space. *Psychoanalytic Quarterly* 73:47–61.

Cavell, M. (1998). Triangulation, one's own mind and objectivity. *International Journal of Psychoanalysis* 79:449–467.

Freud, S. (1901). *The Psychopathology of Everyday Life*. SE 6.

———— (1916–1917). *Introductory Lectures on Psycho-Analysis*. SE 15–16.

———— (1937). Analysis terminable and interminable. SE 23:216–253.

Hanly, C. (1988). From animism to rationalism. In S. Hook, W.L. O'Neill & R. O'Toole (Eds.), *Philosophy, History and Social Action: Essays in Honor of Lewis Feuer* (pp. 221–234). Boston: Kluwer.

———— (2004). The third: A brief historical analysis of an idea. *Psychoanalytic Quarterly* 73:267–290. [Chapter 7 in this volume]

Hobbes, T. (1651). *Leviathan* (Ed. M. Oakeshott). Oxford: Blackwell, 1946.

James, W. (1907). Pragmatism's conception of truth. In *Pragmatism: A New Name for Some Old Ways of Thinking* (pp. 159–176). New York: Hafner Library Classics, 1948.

Kandel, E. (2006). *In Search of Memory: The Emergence of a New Science of Mind*. New York: Norton.

Putnam, H. (1981). *Reason, Truth and History*. Cambridge: Cambridge University Press.

Renik, O. (1998). The analyst's subjectivity and the analyst's objectivity. *International Journal of Psychoanalysis.* 79:487–497.

Russell, B. (1945). *A History of Western Philosophy*. London: Routledge, 1961.

Spinoza, B. (1677). *Ethics*. In J. Wild (Ed.), *Spinoza: Selections*. New York: Scribner, 1930.

CHAPTER 12

On Truth and Clinical Psychoanalysis*

Philosophers have enumerated three criteria of truth: a coherence criterion, a correspondence one, and a pragmatic one. I shall define them and examine some of the relations among them. My overarching argument is that these three criteria, when adequately defined, can be seen not to be at odds with each other but to work together in the search for truths in clinical psychoanalysis. I write "truths" not because I think that truth is relative but because I do not subscribe to any metaphysical theory of absolute truth as in Plato, Descartes, or Hegel.

A secondary purpose is to sustain a distinction between two concepts of intersubjectivity. The first is the one that we are familiar with in common sense, scholarship, and science: an observation is intersubjective if it can be made by any competent observer of the relevant domain of fact. What is intersubjective in observation is the opposite of what is epistemologically subjective; that is, it is opposite to what, in an observation, belongs to the idiosyncrasies of the observer and not to what is being observed. The second, very different notion of intersubjectivity is that it consists of mutually inextricable transference and countertransference interactions that take place in the relation between analyst and analysand in psychoanalysis and which result in the co-creation of the analysand, whose nature and history are formed by the analytic relation. This definition of intersubjectivity

---

* Originally published in *The International Journal of Psychoanalysis* 90, no. 2 (2009):363–373.

legislates out of existence the historical being of the individual, a being that is independent of the analyst. To Aristotle's rhetorical question, "That nature exists who can doubt?" contemporary subjectivist analysts reply: "Psychoanalysts should doubt the independent existence of at least that part of nature that is psychic reality." Subjectivism repudiates the epistemic independence of the patient in his or her relation to the analyst, and consistency would require the same of the analyst in his or her relation to the patient. Of course, we analysts sometimes feel differently about different patients. The vignette below illustrates an exceptional anxiety in the analyst in response to a patient. But from these and similar facts it cannot be inferred that an analyst's capacity to know is inevitably altered by his or her responses to each patient. After all, an appropriate affective response will normally quicken the analyst's observation and thought rather than compromising it.

To be sure, our work as clinicians reminds us of the manifold ways in which our own personalities, beliefs, and affects can interfere with our clinical work. Our clinical observations and thinking are intrinsically fallible. But it does not follow that they are in principle cognitively subjective, or that we are intrinsically ensnared in intersubjectivity of the second kind, or that we can never achieve intersubjectivity of the first kind. Thomas (2007) has pointed to "a deep paradox in Freud's work" between the intersubjective and the scientific. This paradox is generated by elevating the remediable technical problems of subjectivity in the analytic situation into an intersubjectivist epistemology yielding the second meaning of the term, in which the technical problems become irremediable in principle. The paradox ceases to exist if we preserve the common-sense, scholarly, and scientific meaning of the word "intersubjectivity."

One of the problems of intersubjectivity in postmodern psychoanalytic epistemology concerns the nature of truth. The coherence criterion of truth states that a theory is true if and only if it provides a consistent explanation of the phenomena to be explained. A theory that has to rely on a hypothesis that is not consistent with the basic concepts and principles of the theory fails the test. A theory that cannot account for all of the phenomena to be explained also fails the test. Coherence requires logical consistency (non-contradiction) and explanatory completeness. The coherence theory of truth asserts that theories that meet these criteria are true. In the history of ideas, the coherence theory of truth is associated with the idealist philosophies of German Romanticism, in particular with Hegel and the neo-Hegelians (Bosanquet, 1888; Bradley, 1883; Lotze, 1888). Among contemporary English-speaking philosophers, Putnam (1981) argues that because observations are always theory-laden, they *constitute* what is observed. Reality is not given in observation, but rather is *constituted* by it. This is the basic position of postmodern subjectivist epistemology. Putnam rejects the correspondence theory of truth on the grounds that correspondence requires an idea of God, who in Cartesian fashion must be pressed into service as the infallible third who can judge whether or not a perception corresponds with the object perceived, and if so, to what extent. Epistemology should not logically require theology. Putnam also points out the *paradoxical* consequence that once coherence is adopted as a sufficient account of the nature of truth there can be more than one true theory of any phenomenon.

This philosophy of truth would be found agreeable by creationist theorists of evolution because it would make creation and natural selection equally true insofar as each is consistent with itself. It has been found agreeable by psychoanalysts (Goldberg, 1976; Spence, 1982; Wallerstein, 1988), who perhaps hoped in this way to reconcile contradictory schools of thought despite the price of having to embrace paradox, contrariety, and even contradiction in order to sustain the appearance of collegial peace by denying the reality of logical, conceptual, and factual conflicts.

A fundamental problem of the coherence theory is that it demands of logic more than it can provide. Coherence requires that all the hypotheses of a given theory be mutually consistent. But just as arguments can be valid without being sound (since the truth of the conclusions depends upon the truth of the premises), so a theory can be logically consistent without being true. Euclidean geometry is a paradigm of coherence: it is consistent, complete, and self-evident. But its coherence, completeness, and self-evidence do not make it true. From its definitions and axioms, a complete series of theorems and corollaries, among them the Pythagorean Theorem that is so useful in multiple practical applications in construction and surveying, can be deductively derived. For centuries Euclidean geometry established certainty as an ideal for knowledge. Spinoza (1677) made a valiant attempt to render a comprehensive metaphysics into a deductive system modeled on Euclid. But it turns out that, despite its coherence, comprehensiveness, and even its pragmatic utility, which are built into the definitions and axioms (e.g., the definition of a straight line and the axiom of parallel lines), there is the false assumption that space is rectilinear, when as physics has shown, space curves in the vicinity of mass. Euclidean geometry continues to be useful for surveying and for constructing buildings when lengths are short enough to make the definition of a straight line or the Pythagorean Theorem adequate approximations, but it generates errors when designing flight paths for transoceanic flights, or predicting the location of the planets of the solar system or the path of light passing through the sun's gravitational field.

During the recent debates concerning IPA training standards, it was argued that the coherence of a set of training standards is an adequate guarantee of their reliability. However, the State of New York has recently passed legislation which consistently employs the assumption that twice-weekly sessions are adequate for training psychoanalysts. This definition is then consistently applied to laying down minimum requirements for personal analysis, supervised cases, and seminars. But the coherence of these training requirements does not by itself establish the adequacy of the underlying definition of what constitutes psychoanalysis, nor does it settle the question of whether or not analysis at a greater frequency than twice weekly, other things being equal, is, for most candidates, likely to make for a significantly better personal analysis and consequently a better training. Arguments based only on a criterion of coherence overvalue logical consistency, which, while necessary, is not sufficient as a criterion.

If coherence were a sufficient and adequate criterion of truth, it would follow that the loss of reality in neurosis and psychosis would necessarily involve incoherence, but it does not. Psychotic individuals would occasionally arrive at the offices of the department of philosophy where I worked to present their metaphysical systems. The secretaries would send them to me for an evaluation of their work. It was eerie to read their sometimes beautifully articulated, coherent, comprehensive, and logically consistent worldviews. It is interesting to note that the logical functions of the mind required for coherent thinking do not seem to be damaged along with the severe hallucinatory impairment of perception in psychosis. One of these individuals had shown that the cosmos in general required for its orderly functioning that the earth be ruled by a philosopher king. It was sad to see the dark ecstasy of this gaunt, malnourished, and unkempt street person in response to my question: "And because you understand the working of these cosmic forces, you would be best qualified to be the philosopher king of the world?" Again, we see that coherence is not a sufficient criterion of truth even though it is a necessary one. In order to be true, a theory has to be coherent, but its being coherent does not make it true.

If coherence is our sole criterion of truth, psychoanalytic theorizing is permanently relativized, according to Putnam's paradox, but in a way that renders it illogical, as the examination of competing theories in psychoanalysis will show. Freud's theory of the origins of the Oedipus complex in drive development coheres perfectly with other components of his theory (e.g., drive theory and the structural model). Similarly, Kohut's theory of the genesis of the Oedipus complex in narcissistically inadequate parenting coheres well with other tenets of self psychology (e.g., the primacy of narcissistic libido and of object relations). But the two theories are mutually opposed and incompatible: Freud's theory of the Oedipus complex asserts that all instances of the Oedipus complex result from drive development, whereas self psychology asserts that no instance of the Oedipus complex results from drive development. In other words, they *cannot* both be true, although they may both be false. Consequently, contrary to Putnam (1981), their truth cannot simply depend on their coherence. Coherence is a *necessary* condition for the truth of any theory, but it is not a *sufficient* condition.

Finally, if all we have to go on in psychoanalysis when assessing the truth of a theory is coherence, then truth will depend on consensus, that is, on the theoretical preferences of analysts. This view takes us dangerously close to the edge of Schopenhauer's world as will and idea, if it does not plunge us into the abyss of wishful thinking. On this view, a theory is true because analysts subjectively will it to be true, or equivalently, objectivity derives from a subjective but coherent will. Two paradoxical corollaries follow: whenever there is no consensus in psychoanalysis, there is no truth in psychoanalysis; and its contrary, whenever there is no consensus in psychoanalysis, all theories are true or there are as many true theories as there are analysts who advocate them.

The concept of correspondence with an independently existing reality offers a way out of this dilemma. The correspondence theory of truth states that a belief, hypothesis, or idea is true to the extent that it corresponds to reality. The correspondence criterion of truth is a basic premise of common sense as well as of scientific and philosophical empiricism. Throughout his work, Freud (1915, 1933) stated his adherence to correspondence, for which the word "tally" in the tally argument (Freud, 1916–1917, p. 452) is a synonym. Kleinian psychoanalysts share Freud's view of the primacy of correspondence in the evaluation of truth. It is taken for granted by science (Dawkins, 2003; Guth, 1997; Hawking, 1988; Sokal & Bricmont, 1998; Weinberg, 1992).

Advocates of the coherence criterion criticize those who advocate correspondence for being absolutistic, uncritically naive, and authoritarian. These criticisms are supported by Putnam's (1981) argument that a correspondence criterion relies upon an omniscient "third" for the verification of the correspondence between an independently existing object with a nature of its own, and its perceptual, imaginary, and ideational human representations. But the estimation of correspondence does not require the assumption of omniscience with an absolute standard of truth at its disposal. The charge of absolutism does, I think, apply to the idealizing realism of Plato, Descartes, and Hegel, but it does not apply to empiricist, scientific, or as I have called it, *critical* realism (Hanly, 1999, 2001; Hanly & Nichols, 2001). Correspondence can be evaluated without omniscience, without absolute knowledge, and without certainty. This is illustrated by the astronomical observations that showed that predictions, based on Einstein's theory of gravitation, of the deflection of light from a star passing through the sun's gravitational field corresponded more closely to the actual deflection of light than the Newtonian predictions (Isaacson, 2007). Here, the third is the object in nature, which is allowed to reveal itself in part by the internal third, which is the capacity for doubt and criticism of what we think we know linked to curiosity and respect for nature.

Similarly, in psychoanalysis, clinical observations can show that Bowlby's (1973) ethological theory of anxiety is not sufficient to explain the phenomena of phobia and neurotic anxiety generally. Contrary to Bowlby, his enumerated ethological factors require Freud's developmental sexual and aggressive factors to adequately account for phobia, and thus meet both the coherence and correspondence requirements of completeness (Hanly, 1978). The psychological source of a third perspective on our observations and our ideas about what we observe in psychoanalysis (and in science generally) is the superego, with its ideal of veracity not only adding motivational heft to the reality principle, but also adding the capacity for self-awareness and self-criticism to the ego functions of perception, imagination, and thought that serve the reality principle (Hanly, 2001; Hanly & Nichols, 2001). It is this capacity that allows us to question the reliability of what we see and what we think about what we see.

This is not the place to consider the developmental stages of the reality principle first undertaken by Freud ([1895]1950) and subsequently developed by Ferenczi (1913). Suffice it to say that there is good reason to think that the first stage of a complex development occurs when the neonate driven by hunger differentiates the object that satisfies from the image of the satisfying object, which does not (Freud, [1895]1950). Here correspondence makes its first appearance in the differentiation between image and object, however inchoate the memories that form the image and however partial and incomplete the experience of the object. The infant needs the object that corresponds to the image. Thus, correspondence finds its way into the first, most elementary experience of satisfaction and hunger. The need for correspondence has its onset long before language and thought, let alone speculations about truth. It is present in the need to satisfy hunger, which will eventually become the scientific or critical realism of mature thought. It is from this psychological ground that questions about what is true arise (Hanly, 1990).

The intrinsic relativity of the coherence thesis *can* account for empirical certainties within ideologies and theories (Goldberg, 1976), but it *cannot* account for empirical certainties that transcend ideologies and theories. Correspondence is not a question of absolute, automatic, intuitive certainty; it is a matter of accumulated evidence. Accumulated evidence gives us reason to think that heavenly bodies are composed of chemical matter, that the blood in mammals circulates, that space curves in the vicinity of matter, that species have evolved, and that unconscious psychic processes occur. These descriptions state empirical certainties. Whatever the future developments in science may be, it is highly unlikely that new discoveries will falsify these truths.

Pragmatism is the third criterion of truth. Philosophical pragmatism was developed by Peirce, James, and Dewey. James's philosophical concept of pragmatism, which *could* offer support to postmodern epistemological relativism, has been subjected to devastating criticism by Russell (1946). Consequently, I prefer what I shall call scientific or critical pragmatism. An idea or theory is true if, by means of a technology specified by it and coherent with it, the theory can be used to change the course of nature. It is this concept of pragmatism that we find at work in Freud's development of psychoanalytic theory and technique. In psychoanalysis, the change in the course of nature we look for is the amelioration of neurotic disorders; the technique is the interpretation of free associations and transferences in the analytic setup; and the theories are about the causes of neuroses. Freud's first etiological theory, the seduction theory, provided for an abreactive technique. The technique was specified by the theory and was coherent with it, as were the predictions about the conditions under which recovery and a maturation of sexual life would occur. However, the coherence among the theory, the technique, and the predictions did not establish the truth of the seduction theory. The theory was pragmatically falsified and had to be substantially revised because the predicted amelioration of symptoms did not occur. As James pointed out, pragmatic falsification is the failure of a theory to correspond to what actually happened in the psychic life of the patient. Hence, the pragmatic criterion rests conceptually on correspondence.

I shall conclude by exploring the use of coherence, correspondence, and pragmatic criteria of truth in clinical psychoanalysis. As we have seen, coherence is a *necessary* but not a *sufficient* condition of the truth of a theory, whereas correspondence is a necessary *and* sufficient condition of truth. I propose to illustrate this relation in clinical psychoanalysis by considering a situation in which the analyst's need to know was urgently intensified by an unusual circumstance. A borderline patient (Hanly, 1998) in his second year of analysis, a young professional man who had lost his first job on account of a pretentious insubordination motivated by envy, and was now a student in his professional field, came to his session beside himself with rage and threatening to kill an external examiner who, he believed, had failed him. I quickly became aware of how badly I needed to be able to estimate, by the end of the session, his capacity to contain the rage that drove his wish to avenge the insult to his grandiosity, and how much I needed to help him with this task during the session. The patient had, during periods of severe depression, told me of wanting to let the world know that he was "somebody" by committing a mass murder; he owned a substantial arsenal of guns and ammunition. I was painfully aware of how much I needed to know whether or not he was likely to carry out his threats and how difficult it would be to know. There were no self-evident certainties on which to rely, nor anything either absolutist or naive about my urgent search for understanding. I was alone with his urgent need for my help without having any clear idea of what might emerge that would make it possible for me to help him. I did not for a moment think that his enraged murderous threat was a co-creation of his analysis or that I had any interpretive access to it for that reason; and I was aware that I would not be able to know with the confidence I wanted to have how well my thinking about him corresponded with his reality, and what confidence I could place in whatever interventions I could make before the end of the session. The crucial observation would be what would happen to his murderous rage, and for that observation I had no alternative but to wait for what would unfold in the session. I had no acceptable choice but to give myself up to the task.

I concluded from his account of the damaging interview with the examining professor, punctuated and disorganized as it was by outpourings of vengeful rage and death threats, that there was some possibility that he had been neither passed nor failed, but would be required to resubmit his work after dealing with criticisms. I was confident enough of this construction, despite the fear that it might be the product of my own wishful thinking, that I communicated it to him as something he might want to explore further. I was concerned about the risk, should it turn out not to be true, but at least it might buy time for further analytic work. I offered this reality testing in the context of interpreting to him the intensity of his rage in words that implicitly pointed to but did not explicitly mention the work of a phantasy of having been castrated. I had learned to link interpretations with tentative alternatives to his view of the reality of situations in which he found himself because of his difficulties with reality testing. Instead of interpreting his grandiosity or his castration anxiety directly, I interpreted his hurt pride (Ferenczi, 1913). These interpretations facilitated an encouraging sequence of associations toward the end of the session about his immigrant father, often the object of his derogating criticism, who he now acknowledged had had the "balls" to leave his homeland and try to make a go of it in a new country, even though it did not work out very well for him. I hoped that he was letting me know that he too might have the balls to go back to his faculty and find out what really confronted him instead of carrying out his death threats.

By the end of the session, I observed a diminution in the frequency of his outbursts of indignant rage and sensed some reduction in their intensity. But he was by no means either calm or appeased. I was left with the anxiety-provoking question as to whether or not he could sustain this fragile improvement in self-mastery after the session. I was confident enough of what I had seen and understood not to warn my colleague or inform the police because of my impression that my interpretations corresponded well enough to be heard and because they appeared to have had at least some temporary beneficial effect. I was not confident enough to sleep that night. Without more evidence than I had, I was taking a risk. I believed that any other action on my part would very likely be ruinous to the analysis. He had previously gone through a period in which he believed that I was taping his sessions in order to inform the police. All these perceptions, estimations, hopes, fears, and judgments were fallibly based on the evidence that became available during the session.

I was relieved and grateful for the efficacy of psychoanalytic interpretation, when my patient arrived the next morning and kept subsequent appointments, with only rumblings of his rage and humiliation audible in his complaints of unfairness, in a mood that was by no means calm but was sufficiently reconciled to his situation to abandon his threats of revenge and to get on with the tasks at hand. I was lucky that, as I had surmised, he had not been failed: there were simply some inadequacies in his work that required improvement for the examination to qualify him for his graduate degree. I could now be reasonably satisfied that the observations and the ideas that guided my actions corresponded well enough with the reality of my patient's psychic life. They had survived a pragmatic test.

I conclude with some reflections on the place of truth in the analytic situation. Correspondence is at the heart of the matter. In my view, the analyst has no alternative during a session to seeking to be as receptive as possible to what is really going on in the motivational life of the analysand. Fortunately, the stakes are not usually as high as they were in the session I have described, but the issue of how well our interpretations tally with the inner life, character, and circumstances of the analysand is always unavoidably present. We are able to test the ideas we form as the session unfolds by looking for changes in the associations, the affects, and the transference.

In this session, there were changes in the content of my patient's associations and in his affects. I infer that a regressed positive transference, which had eclipsed his earlier paranoid transference fear that I would report him to the police, enabled him to bring his destructive rage into the session in a desperate hope for help with it—a hope compromised, but in the circumstances beneficially compromised, by an aggrandizing family romance projection of an omnipotence that I would exercise by intervening on his behalf with his examiners, without him having to make further effort on his own behalf. This transference was only implicitly interpreted by not being enacted in interpretations that left him with his own problem. If he needed this transference phantasy, I was not about to deprive him of it and force him back into raging helplessness. Besides, it might help him take confidence from my tentative holding out to him the *possibility* (which was the best that I could offer) that his plight was not quite as bad as he believed it to be. The shifts in associative content, the memories of his father's struggles to achieve a modest success, and the diminution of the intensity of his vengeful rage provided evidence that the interpretations were having a beneficial effect.

Here we come upon the joint work of pragmatic and correspondence criteria. It is this joint work of pragmatic and correspondence criteria that James (1907) captured when he said that it is the same to say that an idea works because it true (the correspondence criterion) and that it is true because it works (the pragmatic criterion). A beneficial change in the patient's psychic functioning was occurring. The implied prediction that this would happen was shown to be probably correct. But notice that this use of the pragmatic criterion itself relies on the correspondence criterion. The two criteria work hand in hand. The observations that indicate functional improvement must themselves tally with what is actually going on in the patient. And it is the realization of one's irremediable fallibility that appropriately and beneficially kept signal anxiety alive in me in the aftermath of such a session. This anxiety underlines the potential for the subjectivity that can be caused by wishful thinking and other biases and the need to make further as yet unobtainable observations to gain a more satisfactory degree of probability. It was the rigorous demands of correspondence combined with the highly unusual circumstances that gave the analyst a sleepless night.

The pragmatic criteria at work in clinical psychoanalysis are not satisfied by subjective or personal utility or with experiential coherence according to James's (1907) formulation of pragmatism. They are satisfied by seeing real change, for better or for worse, in the patient's functioning. Since the reliability and durability of a beneficial change cannot be evaluated by the limited evidence available from one session, we are obliged to live with uncertainty. But clinical uncertainty can be reduced with further evidence. Uncertainty need not be chronic. This observational evidence is not theory-relative, as subjectivists claim, although it is also true that one needs to be able to entertain a theory in order to make observations. Evidence is in principle available to any competent observer in the appropriate circumstances (i.e., for analysts in the analytic setup). Although we need ideas in order to observe, our observations can be epistemically independent of our theories in the sense that the observations can either falsify or confirm the ideas (Hanly, 1994).

And it would surely be grandiose and magical to suppose that in some hidden way my subjectivity led my patient into the postgraduate course only to fail it and bring his vengeful rage into the session. Another analyst may have responded similarly (but in his or her own way), or differently and with a different outcome, but the desperate struggle with rage caused by potentially disastrous, overwhelmingly painful feelings of helplessness and humiliation belonged to the patient's life independently of who his analyst was. And whatever help I was able to offer, his eventual success in overcoming these liabilities also belonged to him as *his* achievement.

Although subjectivists, to be consistent, have to repudiate the correspondence criterion in their advocacy of coherence, it would be an equal and opposite error to repudiate the usefulness of coherence in clinical thinking. In the opening phase of a session, we largely rely on coherence in forming our first thoughts and in making a choice of interpretation. In my case, the observation of my patient's chaotic and violently angry state stimulated a preconscious recollection of similar rage reactions earlier in his analysis (e.g., being dismissed for insubordination, a car splashing him with muddy water). A coherence criterion is at work in reviving the memory of previous clinical events on the basis of similarity, consistency, and the common affect that links them, in this case the patient's rage reactions to insult. These recollections bring past experience to bear on the choice of an interpretation. The recollections are coherent, and an interpretation guided by them will be coherent with what the analyst has already learned about the patient's anger, but in the end it is left to the correspondence and pragmatic criteria to decide the adequacy of an interpretation; otherwise, changes in the patient can leave the analyst out of touch with the patient's reality. Therefore, in my view, each of the three criteria of truth makes its specific contributions to sound clinical observing and thinking in psychoanalysis.

As I see it, the fundamental philosophical problem for postmodern intersubjectivity in all of its variations (narratology, irreducible subjectivity, dialectical and relational thirds, relational unconscious, dyadic intersubjective fields, etc.) is that it is conceptually limited to coherence and philosophical pragmatism for its criteria of truth. Postmodern intersubjectivity can find no adequate place for correspondence and scientifically pragmatic criteria. For this reason, in subjectivist epistemologies, truth is relative in principle, and theory-independent facts against which theories could be tested do not exist.

At the heart of the issue between subjectivism and critical realism, there is also a question of being. For psychoanalysis, it is a question of the being of the patient. Is the patient the bearer of his or her own life—an individual life that is intelligible in its own right, knowable in itself, and existing independently of our experiences of it and our ideas about it? It is not possible to doubt the importance of relations between persons. In the clinical excerpt above, I have reason to believe that a positive transference involving trust, but also entwined with expectations of my grandiose beneficence and complicated by a regression to a preoedipal use of me as a surrogate ego, usefully sustained a working relation in this moment of crisis, even while requiring further work in the future. But neither is it possible to doubt the patient's independent reality. As I see it, the autonomous independence of the patient's being is evident in his turning inward—rather than persisting in his grandiose demands upon me—in his own search for the strength to do for himself what I could not do for him. He found confidence, however precarious it was at the time, in revived memories of his father. These memories released a sufficient measure of pride in him to abandon enough of both his grandiosity and his helplessness to tackle the difficult task before him, at which in due course he succeeded.

REFERENCES

Bosanquet, B. (1888). *Logic*. Oxford: Clarendon Press.

Bradley, F.H. (1883). *The Principles of Logic*. London: Kegan Paul, Trench, Trubner.

Bowlby, J. (1973). *Attachment and Loss*. Vol. 2: *Separation: Anxiety and Anger*. New York: Basic Books.

Dawkins, R. (2003). *A Devil's Chaplain*. New York: Houghton Mifflin.

Ferenczi, S. (1913). Stages in the development of the sense of reality. In *First Contributions to Psycho-Analysis* (pp. 213–239). London: Hogarth Press, 1952.

Freud, S. ([1895]1950). Project for a scientific psychology. SE 1:292–343.

———— (1915). Instincts and their vicissitudes. SE 14:117–140.

———— (1916–1917). *Introductory Lectures on Psycho-Analysis*. SE 15–16.

———— (1933). New introductory lectures on psycho-analysis. SE 22:7–182.

Goldberg, A. (1976). A discussion of the paper by C. Hanly and J. Masson on "A critical examination of the new narcissism." *International Journal of Psychoanalysis* 57:67–87.

Guth. A. (1997). *The Inflationary Universe*. New York: Helix Books.

Hanly, C. (1978). A critical consideration of Bowlby's ethological theory of anxiety. *Psychoanalytic Quarterly* 47:364–380.

———— (1990). The concept of truth in psychoanalysis. In *The Problem of Truth in Applied Psychoanalysis* (pp. 1–24). New York: Guilford. [Chapter 10 in this volume]

———— (1994). Reflections on the place of the therapeutic alliance in psychoanalysis. *International Journal of Psychoanalysis* 75:457–467.

———— (1998). Reflections on the analyst's self-disclosure. *Psychoanalytic Inquiry* 18:550–565.

———— (1999). Subjectivity and objectivity in psychoanalysis. *Journal of the American Psychoanalytic Association* 47:427–444.

———— (2001). Oedipus and the search for reality. In P. Hartocollis (Ed.), *Mankind's Oedipal Destiny* (pp. 187–207). Madison, CT: International Universities Press.

Hanly, C., & Nichols C. (2001). A disturbance of psychoanalytic memory. *Philosophy of the Social Sciences* 31: 279–301.

Hawking, S. (1988). *A Brief History of Time*. Toronto: Bantam Books.

Isaacson, W. (2007). *Einstein*. New York: Simon & Schuster.

James, W. (1907). *Pragmatism*. New York: Longmans.

Lotze, H. (1888). *Logic* (Trans. B. Bosanquet). Oxford: Clarendon Press.

Putnam, H. (1981). *Reason, Truth and History*. Cambridge: Cambridge University Press.

Russell, B. (1946). *A History of Western Philosophy*. London: George Allan & Unwin. 1961.

Sokal, A., & Bricmont, J. (1998). *Intellectual Impostures*. London: Profile Books.

Spence, D.P. (1982). *Narrative Truth and Historical Truth*. New York: Norton.

Spinoza, B. (1677). *Ethics*. In *Spinoza: Selections* (Ed. J. Wild). New York: Scribner, 1930.

Thomas, H. (2007). Contemporary controversial discussions, intersubjectivity and the future of psychoanalysis. Unpublished panel presentation, International Psychoanalytical Association, Berlin Congress.

Weinberg, S. (1992). *Dreams of a Final Theory*. New York: Random House.

Wallerstein R.S. (1988). One psychoanalysis or many? *International Journal of Psychoanalysis* 69:5–21.

III

On Relational Psychoanalysis: A Critique

CHAPTER 13

The Unconscious and Relational Psychoanalysis*

The dynamic unconscious is the creation of repressions and other defensive processes mobilized by anxiety against instinctual demands and their impulse, affect, and ideational (memory and phantasy) derivatives. Repression may be caused either by the instinctual demands themselves or by object-relational trauma, or frequently by both working in concert, entwined and mutually reinforcing. This chapter is an exploration of the impact on our understanding of unconscious processes of what has come to be known as relational psychoanalysis. The relational view is based on two cardinal premises: (1) object relations are the fundamental causal factors in psychic life in general and in neurosis, taking precedence over drives and drive development; (2) the object relation that exists between analyst and analysand is one of reciprocating transference (countertransference enactment). The expression "relational psychoanalysis" does not include Kleinian thought, since Kleinian theory is Freudian in its recognition of the importance of both drives and object relations in psychic development and pathogenesis.

---

* Originally published in J.C. Calich & H. Hinz (Eds.), *The Unconscious: Further Reflections* (London: The International Psychoanalytical Society, 2007), pp. 47–62.

The "relational turn" in psychoanalytic thinking had its origins in Fairbairn's (1946) opposition to Freud's hypothesis of libido as an instinct that exerts its own decisive influence upon psychic development. This opposition has been kept alive partly by analysts who have wanted to detach the mind from its biological and physical origins. The "relational turn" is often associated with certain other philosophical ideas such as Kohut's (1959) repudiation of psychic determinism, the denial of the scientific nature of psychoanalytic knowledge as in Spence (1994), and epistemological subjectivism as described by Ornstein and Ornstein (1994). Kohut (1977) also gave exclusive priority to object relations in his claim that the Oedipus complex derives from inadequate parenting. These ideas form a cluster, although they do not cohere logically, since some of them can occur without the others. Together, they tend to have the character of a secularized religious humanism of the kind that one finds in the existentialism of Sartre (1943), Merleau-Ponty (1945), and Heidegger (1927), despite their avowed atheism.

Epistemologically and methodologically, the "relational turn" assumes that knowledge of persons, whether of self or of others, is grounded in the relations between persons. Relations are treated as synthetic a priori conditions in the Kantian sense, that is, as grounds of clinical knowledge. Kant's (1781) forms of experience and categories of understanding are replaced by person-to-person relations, to be sure, but, like their Kantian predecessors, person-to-person relations are treated as universal and necessary conditions for any possible experience or understanding of self or other. Of course, no one would agree with Kant that Euclidean geometry is universally and necessarily true, or deny that space is relative to mass, as general relativity theory assumes, rather than relative to the human observer, as Kant's (1781) epistemology attempts (but fails) to prove. The epistemology of the "relational turn" shares only one point with Kant's epistemology. It is, however, the crucial point that knowledge of persons is universally and necessarily grounded in relations. Relation is prior to and constitutive of the knowledge of self and other. The consequence for psychoanalysis is the following: such knowledge as an analyst is able to gain of the motives, character, and conflicts of a patient in analysis is inevitably conditioned by and the product of the interaction between the analyst and the patient. It is this idea that gives to transference and countertransference their importance in the epistemology of the "relational turn."

It is, of course, an inescapable truism that direct knowledge of another person—for example, knowledge by acquaintance—requires a relation with the person to be known. He must be perceived, experienced in his various capacities, habits, and ways. And if the knowledge is to be of the kind required for a psychoanalytic understanding of him, a relationship will have to be established with him that will activate attitudes and elicit feelings towards him in the observing analyst. Psychoanalytic observation is not encumbered by the physical visual illusions that long deceived mankind about the nature, organization, and dynamics of heavenly bodies and man's place in nature.

However, does not psychoanalytic clinical observation have the dual disadvantage of being qualitative rather than quantitative, and inevitably subject to the subversive influence of unconsciously aroused affects, memories, and ideas? Scientific and philosophical rationalism—for example, that of Descartes (1649) or Spinoza (1677)—has from the beginning distrusted emotions and feared their influence on rational observation and thought. This critical attitude is amply justified by the havoc wrought by anxiety and hostile affects that have twisted and distorted the perceptions of other individuals and groups and have thus provided provocations and excuses for manifold private and public violence. It is little wonder that Freud (1933) encouraged analysts to cultivate a clinical attitude of benign dispassionate curiosity.

But could it be that such an attitude is psychologically unattainable, that it is no less based on an illusion of the invulnerability of detached intellect? The rationalist attitude, however sound it is in general, is itself flawed or at least limited when it comes to knowing others and ourselves. Cartesian intellectual clarity and distinctness is not a litmus test of truth. To be sure, in psychoanalysis we should be able to state what we claim to know with a clarity and distinctness that leaves no room for misunderstanding and provides for evidential testing. But traditional rationalism has failed to appreciate the contribution that affects can make to the motivation of enquiry, to the organization of perception, and to the clarity of judgment. Envy, cruelty, hatred, violence, and perverse love need to be combated by moral reason (Kant, 1788), to be sure, but moral reason is ineffective and exhausting unless it is guided and informed by the countervailing affects of pity, love, and respect for the welfare of others as advocated by utilitarianism. Duty enlivened and humanized by social feelings (Mill, 1863)—or failing these, fear of exposure and punishment—is essential to sound moral thought. It is true of humane moral thought, and it is also true of humane psychological knowledge. Rationalism represented a noble hope, but it was a hope that unrealistically denied the unavoidable dependency of human character on genetic endowment, instinct life, family relations, and identifications.

Proust has brilliantly illustrated the notion that ideas enable us to perceive things as they are (Hanly, 1995). But cultivated feeling also enables us to perceive things as they are. Love helps us to discern and to discriminate. The animal lover notices in the forest the tracks of diverse wild species, which others would fail to perceive, let alone accurately identify by spoor and footprint. Adequate psychoanalytic work requires a discernment and discrimination that only affective attunement and responsiveness to another can provide. However, although the love of animals may be enough for the cognitive purposes and tasks of the game warden, the love of analysands is not enough for the analyst. The analyst's affective attunement must be more variegated, more vulgar, ribald, ironic, iconoclastic, impious, scandalous, suspicious, rueful, and whimsical, more Chaucerian and Shakespearean in order to be accurately and sympathetically discerning and discriminating of the vagaries and vicissitudes of psychic life. Without affective discrimination, the derivatives of the unconscious phantasies of the patient, and therefore unconscious aggression and libido, the defenses against them, and their investment in the transference and other object relations of the patient, will continue to be unacknowledged, unseen, and misunderstood by the analyst.

Psychoanalysts who have taken the "relational turn" convey the impression that they are the advocates of a new idea and that classical analysis (i.e., psychoanalysis before the "relational turn" of intersubjectivity) does not acknowledge object relations. Freud's psychology is supposed to be a one-person psychology. Fairbairn (1946, 1963) initiated this critique somewhat earlier than those who have recently taken the "relational turn," with his repudiation of Freud's concept of libido as an instinct. Fairbairn's critique was a way of drawing the sting from the primacy and instinctuality of libido—its capacity to generate powerful needs independently and spontaneously. Fairbairn's critique seemed to imply that the primacy of libido, as Freud (1915) defined it, was at odds with or expressed a failure to appreciate the importance of object relations.

I believe that this implication is unjustified. Freud (1915) makes this clear when he affirms that "a better term for an instinctual stimulus is a 'need'" (pp. 118–119). A need depends on an object for its satisfaction; it motivates a search for a satisfying object; it forms an object relation of a specific kind. The first insult to infantile primary narcissism, an insult that sets the reality principle to work (S. Freud, [1895]1950), is the anxious feeling of helplessness aroused by hunger. In this struggle, if the infant is to survive, narcissism must lose and yield some libido to object love. This is so even if narcissism has to try to repair the rent in its omnipotence with the illusion of an undifferentiated breast. Freud (1914) had already described narcissistic object relations and differentiated them from dependent libidinal ties to objects. Accordingly, Freud (1915) proceeds to include in his schematic definition of an instinct the object and a relation to it. Even the formation of the agency within the ego that enables it to form a relationship with itself—the superego—is originally and prototypically an internalized object relation brought about by the strengthened identification with the same-sex parent (S. Freud, 1923b). The relation is modeled on the oedipal boy's experience of his father's relation to him or the oedipal girl's experience of her mother's relation to her.

Object relations enter into the very fabric of the tripartite organization of the psyche. Although Freud (1923b) mistakenly speculated about the origin of the superego as an archaic residue, his theory does not require this hypothesis because his developmental account provides a sufficient explanation of its psychogenesis in these primary object relations. And Freud's clinical thinking from beginning ([1895]1950) to end (1937) is rooted in the object relation of analyst to patient and patient to analyst, yielding along the way the identification and eventual understanding of transference and countertransference. We are not surprised, therefore, that Freud placed equal importance on subjective developmental and object relational factors (what one has suffered on account of one's own being and what one has suffered on account of others) in the causation of neuroses. In Freud's (1915) view, it makes no more sense to insert an exclusive alternative between internal developments and object relations in the causation of neurosis than to opt for either the female's ovum or the male's sperm in conception but not both. This general etiological schema is rooted in Freud's case histories. Object relations and instinctual vicissitudes are reciprocally enmeshed codeterminants of the lives of persons. No theory will serve our understanding of psychic reality that does not keep both endogenous and exogenous causal factors in view. Although, in pursuit of their claims to originality, the "relational turn" psychoanalysts sometimes attribute to classical psychoanalysis a disregard of object relations in favor of instinctual determinants, a fair-minded reading of Freud will find the attribution to be erroneous.

What, then, is the "relational turn," and what does it achieve? If object relations have never been abandoned, what is being accomplished by the relational turn? It can be argued that there was a tendency in Freudian American ego psychology during the period after World War II to emphasize libidinal and aggressive developmental factors at the expense of object relations. This tendency was to be found in an exclusionary and oversimplified reliance on the "drive-defense model," as if the psychic reality of individual lives needed no other categories of understanding. It was found in the idea that a person who survived the traumatic depredations of the Holocaust could become neurotic only as a consequence of an infantile developmental precondition. This attitude failed to recognize that trauma caused by being brutally treated can severely damage healthy psychic structures and functions. But if some ego psychologists exaggerated drives at the expense of object relations, Freud never wavered from his repeated repudiation of any such idea (Hanly, 1986).

Klein's theory has sometimes been thought to have granted more to object relations than did Freud's because of its elaboration of internal object relations. However, by taking over and working out the implications of Freud's death instinct theory for very early development, Klein's theory has also increased the extent to which ego development is instinct-driven and determined. Specifically, the very early paranoid-schizoid and depressive positions are postulated to unfold under the influence of the infant's struggle with the death instinct independently of object-relational contributions. The infant ego's primary objects—first the mother's breast and then the mother herself—owe their primary experiential meanings and ego-forming influence to the work of the death instinct and libido. The foundational Kleinian drama of the oral phase is played out in a way that overrides and preempts the nature of the object relations offered to the infant by the mother and her breast. Indeed, because of Klein's adherence to the death instinct, her theorizing is more Freudian than is the theorizing of many Freudians (Hanly, 1978). Klein's theory of the general relation between instinctual determinants and object-relational determinants in psychic development is Freudian not only in its adherence to the death instinct but also in the emphasis it places on the contribution of instincts to psychic development, relations, and the experience of objects.

If object relations have been neglected by some American Freudian ego psychologists, they have not been neglected by others. The work of Abrams (1986), Chused (1986), Loewald (1951), Neubauer (1987), Novick and Novick (1987), Shengold (1989), and many others makes this clear. In the controversies between Melanie Klein and Anna Freud, American ego psychologists were aligned with Anna Freud. Anna Freud's psychology of early development was not as invested in Freud's death instinct as was Klein's psychology of early development; consequently, the mother and her mothering of the infant and the needs of the infant are more clearly codeterminants of early development in the work of Anna Freud (1946, 1949), although they are not neglected by Klein either. The repressions and other defensive processes that supply and bring the psychic unconscious alive may be caused by indigenously generated anxiety or by the traumatic force of failed object relations. The most realistic assumption seems to be that both factors are always at work, at least to some degree. However, in my opinion this local disagreement about the oral stage can easily be exaggerated. Fundamentally, Klein agreed with Freud that object relations are motivated and informed by the needs of the individual, whether infant or adult. This deeper agreement comes clearly into focus when one considers the premises of relational psychoanalysis.

There is a fundamental respect in which the account given thus far altogether misses the point of the idea of object relations in contemporary psychoanalytic subjectivism. This theorizing pretty much begins and ends with one object relation, although there is an important exception: the relation between the patient and the analyst. It draws upon the recent discussions of one- and two-person psychologies in which classical psychoanalysis is treated as though it were a one-person psychology when it is not (Hanly & Nichols, 2001). It lays claim to being more respectful of the analysand by treating her or him as an equal partner in the work. It avoids the authoritarianism of classical analysts. It is democratic and egalitarian. It is custom-fitted to the patient. It avoids the subjugation and humiliation of the analysand. Its aim is to overthrow the antiquated orthodoxy of unilateral action on the analysand's encapsulated mind by the analyst's encapsulated mind. To achieve all of this, some more radical ideas than we have yet considered must be at work.

Relational psychoanalysis takes the transference-countertransference matrix as given and provides a rationalization for a radical form of it that could more properly be described, from my perspective, as *transference-transference*. Indeed, this use of terms would better bring out the equality of the partners in the relational dyad. The classical notion that transference can occur without the analyst necessarily responding with a countertransference is repudiated. This repudiation radically calls into question the obligation it implies on the part of the analyst to see to it that countertransferences not disturb his analytic capacity. If countertransferences really are inevitable, to resolve them would be impossible, and analysts can hardly be expected to do the impossible. Such attempts would be Sisyphean and illusory if countertransference really is unavoidable. Neither does relational psychoanalysis allow the analyst to use countertransference to better understand the patient's transference. If there is no identifiable transference that belongs to the patient independently of the analyst's transference to the patient, the analyst is deprived of any position from which he could get at a view of the patient or the patient's transference that is not compromised by his own subjective unconscious primary thought activity. Since unconscious thought activity is driven by the analyst's unconscious unsatisfied childhood satisfaction-seeking needs, the transference-countertransference nexus becomes a transference-transference tangle.

Relational theory also makes an ontological claim about what is fundamental and what is derivative. Relation is taken to be the ground of the being of persons. This assumption contradicts the view that relations deeply influence personality and character because of their impact on the needs of the individual, just as the individual's needs exert a profound influence on his/her relationships. This view is implicit, for example, in Freud's (1915) hypothesis that our personality is formed in part by identifications with lost love objects in an attempt to preserve a relation to the object. In this view, relations, needs, and, we might add, genetic endowment, are equally fundamental.

The transference-countertransference nexus is taken one step further by the idea of co-creation. Who the analysand is and has been is a co-creation of the relation between the analyst and the analysand. By parity of reasoning from the co-creation postulate, who the analyst is and has been is a co-creation of the interactions governed by the same relation. A consequence of this theory is that the analyst, unlike the analysand, will have to be capable of undergoing as many co-creations as he/she has patients—a vertiginous prospect, at least superficially. But let us take leave of the relational dyad for a moment. If an analyst's family members and friends are as important to him as are his patients, and if we take the premise of the primacy of relation seriously and not just as an experimental idea with which to attack classical analysis and scientific realism, would the analyst not also have some further co-creations to perform and undergo after his co-creations at work? If relation precedes and conditions being (nature) in the analytic dyad, would not the same precedence and conditions apply quite generally? What delicate balance of being for oneself and being for others—to borrow Sartre's (1943) terminology—allows the relational analyst consistency or coherence of being? Would he not suffer a Kohutian fractured self? Can the personal identity of the analyst and analysand be sustained on the basis of these assumptions if a relation always alters, constricts, or facilitates what one remembers of one's past, insofar as personal identity depends on remembering one's past? If relation is prior to being, can we even appropriately use the expression "one's past" to refer to a reality the whole of which we may not be able to remember, but which nonetheless has happened whether we can remember it or not? Does not the relational premise when linked to co-creationism imply that our past is merely the sum of the pasts yielded by the co-creations in which we have engaged?

The relation between analyst and analysand is prior (in the sense of being fundamental and determinative) to such analytic procedures as trial identifications. On the relational premise, trial identification in analysis is not with the analysand: it is with the co-created analysand. It is with the image of the analysand created by the analyst. I use "image" here in the sense of perceptual image, memory image, and synthetic idea. Can the relational analyst escape a vertiginous identity because he only has to deal with his own image of the patient, an image that will be informed by his theory, character, moods, feelings, and needs, and for the most part unconsciously? But it is the analyst's image of the analysand that changes from relation to relation, not the analyst; the analyst is saved from vertiginous mutability. But the question now arises as to what influence the analysand has on the analyst's image of the analysand. What has been gained for the analyst has been lost to the analysand. And there is a further question: Are we to think of the empathy in a trial identification with the analyst's image of the analysand rather than with the analysand himself/herself?

The problem is further complicated by the idea of the analyst's irremediable subjectivity (Renik, 1993). This idea has gained some merited acceptance among analysts who espouse relational theory. If analysts' observations and ideas about their analysands are indeed epistemologically incorrigible, then whatever influence the analysand has on the image of him co-created with the analyst, the analyst's personality, theory, and so on, will override that influence sufficiently to make it irremediably subjective. It will be primarily an image of the analyst rather than an image of the analysand. It will irremediably lack objectivity.

This implication follows from the premise of the analyst's irremediable subjectivity when subjectivity is given an epistemological interpretation. This implication has not been well understood. It has been supposed that analytic objectivity can be achieved, despite irremediable subjectivity, by making predictions about the course of the analysis and observing whether the predictions are in fact borne out. But this statement implies that the analyst's subjectivity is remediable after all. A hypothesis can be entertained by the analyst that (1) does not influence the course of the analysis in such a way as to make it a self-fulfilling prophecy or the result of suggestion, and (2) can be empirically tested as the process unfolds by observations that are not compromised by the analyst's biases and wishful thinking, in other words, by observations that are objective. But if this can be done, the irremediably subjective thesis has been falsified. Consequently, the irremediable subjectivity thesis is either solipsistic or contradictory.

The conceptual innovations of relational theory are no doubt well-intentioned. Moreover, these ideas have useful purposes to serve. Once the implication of the analyst's objectivity (Renik, 1998) is taken into account and the epistemological idea of the irreducibly subjective analyst is modified by being made consistent with it, the idea provides a salutary caution to analysts to treat our observations, feelings, and ideas about our patients with an informed skepticism and never to take them for granted in the way that a generation of American ego psychologists apparently did. This modified position is critical realism (Hanly, 1999; Hanly & Hanly, 2001).

An Oxford analytic philosopher would say that the epistemological rendering of "irremediable subjectivity" is a category mistake arising out of expressing an idea that makes an urgent recommendation—a wake-up call—in the logical grammar of a description of fact, leaving the impression of a deep insight into the nature of psychoanalytic knowledge. That is to say, the proposition "The analyst's interpretations are irremediably subjective" has the logical grammatical form of a description of an unexpected cognitive state of affairs, but its correct, logically consistent form, while it implies a description, or more precisely a large class of descriptions, is optative or imperative, as in the proposition, "I wish analysts were always aware of their subjectivity, but they often are not," or "Analysts should always be aware of the risk that their interpretations are subjective." The idea, thus stated, serves as a valuable cautionary summary of all the ways in which our observations and ideas about our patients—and, indeed, about our therapy and science—can go wrong. There is a rich array in the literature of specific contributions to the ways in which the analyst's affective responses and interpretations can go wrong as a result of suggestion, countertransference, projective identification, and so forth. These indispensable contributions do not imply the epistemological idea that our perceptual, memory, and thought processes are incorrigible, but they do imply the cautionary idea of how vulnerable we analysts are to subjectivity in our impressions of patients even while diligently practicing free-floating attention.

However, the idea of the irreducible subjectivity of the analyst taken as an epistemological description implies that the patient and the unconscious of the patient are unknowable because they can never be extricated from the analyst's subjectively saturated and compromised impressions and ideas, even though these ideas may even have the appearance of being empirical, inductive, and scientific. But taken as a recommendation, the idea functions as a useful psychoanalytic third—a position from which analysts are able to use to the greatest advantage for patient and science the finite and fallible cognitive capacities for objectivity provided to us by evolution and our individual efforts at self-mastery, method, and eventual understanding.

However, it must be acknowledged that co-creation is an unavoidable fact of the analytic situation. The relationists and solipsists among us make an important point. The question we need to ask about the analytic situation is: What in the analytic process is co-created, and what is not?

Some years ago, analyst A referred a female patient, a gifted artist who could afford psychotherapy only once a week at a reduced fee, to a medical colleague whose services were completely covered by the provincial insurance scheme. The patient had developed a positive oedipal transference to analyst A after having been able to use the therapy to work through a severe depression. In my opinion, however, she needed more sessions per week to work through her intense idealizing/denigrating oedipal attachment, but the analyst felt that to offer her four hours per week for the same weekly payment would have been, for her, a gratification that would have immunized her to further interpretations of her libidinal transference attachment and the resistance that it fostered. As an artist, she was particularly sensitive to her surroundings. Her sessions took place in an office on the first floor of the analyst's home in a large, well-appointed room with book-covered walls and a large antique walnut desk at one end. Her perception of this piece of furniture became the kernel around which developed a transference phantasy and a resistance. She imagined that her analyst had been born into great wealth, that he had inherited the large house in a prestigious neighborhood, and that he had never had to work for a living but could devote himself to a life of culture, science, psychoanalysis, and luxury; he therefore could never understand her, for she had been born to a poor rural farm family without culture. She had had to work and suffer delays in her struggle to become a painter, her talent for which had only recently made it possible for her to rent a small flat and to begin to have a better life. The desk became a nodal associative link to her reiterated complaint that the analyst could never understand her. He would never share her left-wing political views or be able to appreciate her life or her art. These and other complaints warded off feelings of envious possessiveness, which occasionally peaked through her associations. She seemed to be unconsciously protesting that she appeared too pathetic to her analyst for him to ever want to marry her, but if he would only share his wealth and house with her, she would know how to make him happy. An unconscious family romance phantasy was mobilizing a resistance.

She had selected (female) analyst B from among three analysts with whom she had extensively consulted before her decision. The office of the analyst she eventually chose was commodious enough, but it was in a hospital with institutional appointments illuminated by ceiling lights rather than by floor and desk lamps. At first, the patient engaged in a disparagement of the analyst, her office, and its furnishings. The disparagement suggested hurt, angry feelings at being jilted by analyst A, who, she felt, could have afforded to treat her for a nominal fee. But then she began to settle into the analysis with analyst B by forming what appeared to be a homosexual transference. This interpretation of her transference was suggested by her beginning to remove her sweater, which she regularly wore, in an exaggerated slow motion after lying on the couch and commenting about "undressing," when she actually remained well enough covered by the shirt or blouse she was wearing. Having settled into the analysis, she now formed a new resistance. The light in the office was wrong, and she was required to lie on the couch looking up at the ceiling into lights that hurt her eyes; she would accept it, but she would have to keep her eyes closed all the time. To this the analyst gently responded, "So you won't be able to look at anything about you or me when you are with me." The patient's further associations suggested that she wanted to ask her analyst to have the room rewired so that she could see. Thus, just as her first analyst was too rich to analyze her, her second analyst was too poor.

Obviously, there is plenty of co-creation going on in this vignette made visible by a change of analyst. I shall briefly consider three elements: the choice of a focus and rationale for resistance, the phantasy mobilizing the resistance, and the transference. In all three there is a co-creation at work. The nodal points of resistance differ: the desk in the office of analyst A, the ceiling lights in the office of analyst B. The office of each analyst and its location and furnishings contributed in a material way to the different choices of a focus for resistance by the patient. These same influences of the two analysts also entered into the formation of the patient's phantasy of a wealthy, haut-bourgeois analyst A born with a silver spoon in his mouth and a rather poor, hard-working, hospital-doctor analyst B. The masculinity of analyst A invited a positive oedipal transference; the femininity of analyst B facilitated a negative oedipal transference. But how deep does this co-creation go? Are there some constants in the change of analyst despite these real differences? How Heraclitean is the patient?

I think that the co-creation can best be characterized by means of an analogy with the structure of dreams. For the most part, the co-creation is limited to the manifest content of the patient's neurosis; it does not reach into the latent content except for the transference. Very well—but surely the transference expresses what is fundamental in the latent content, which was heterosexual with analyst A and homosexual with analyst B. Does not the evidence suggest that the change of analyst has brought about a major shift in the unconscious libidinal organization at work in the patient's neurosis, a co-creation at a deep level of the latent content? The available evidence did not indicate the co-creation of an unconscious homosexual organization by analyst B and the patient. This organization had been there in the associations of the patient with analyst A. Freud (1908a) described the bisexual nature of some hysterical phantasies. The transference phantasy of the somewhat pathetic, impoverished analyst with the punishing lights included a heterosexual as well as a homosexual component yoked together in the image, behind which was the unconscious image of a defeated (castrated) mother no longer dangerous and needing to be looked after, linked to a powerful castrating, damaging, and abandoning father. The change in the transference did not involve the creation of a new unconscious organization; it only involved a gender shift in its expression in the transference. Now the influence of the dangerous, exciting father is expressed in the choice of focus for the resistance and its meaning: the light that blinds. Co-creation occurs, but it is limited to manifest associations, resistances, and transferences. The underlying unconscious psychic reality is not vulnerable to co-creation.

The relationalist thesis encounters similar problems. It is not that relations are unimportant: in Freudian theory, object relations share center stage with drive development in health and neurosis, as I have sought to show. It is therefore the case that object relations play an equal part with drive vicissitudes in the formation of the individual unconscious psychic reality. This psychic reality exists and has a nature that is also relatively independent of current relationships—independent of the analyst, that is, or in the case above, the analysts: independent in being portable from one relation to another. The residues of unconscious infantile and childhood wishes and the defensive formations against them, aided and abetted as they are by identifications, do not exactly have a life of their own, although they are inexorable. After all, these wishes also seek objects for their satisfaction. Anyone who has doubts about this fact can reflect on the transferences of their patients, even the most subtle and unobtrusive of which, such as the positive idealizing transference, garner a yield of narcissistic gratification from the resultant feeling of being special, not to mention the even less conspicuous embedded oedipal possibilities and the vague elational aggressive pleasure of having deceived and disarmed a hated rival or a traumatically disappointing object. It is the defenses that impose substitute solipsistic satisfactions on these fixated infantile and childhood wishes. One of the difficult but necessary preconditions of analytic work is that analysts allow themselves to be an object for these unconscious strivings—a necessary first step in the therapeutic reduction in the influence of their demands in the psychic life of the patient. These transferences require analysts to let themselves be for their analysands in the analytic relation what they are not for themselves. If in the end the essential content of the relational thesis asserts nothing more than this, then it is only recommending a change in terminology which does not seem to be particularly helpful.

Relational theorists tend to first make a straw man of classical theory and attack it with statements with which classical analysts might not disagree in substance, although they might well disagree with a certain sentimentality of the kind found in Buber's (1923) I-Thou relation or with the recourse to anti-scientific social constructionist ideas or vague, untestable assertions about some heretofore unrecognized bond that unites the analyst and analysand in which all specific transferences and countertransferences are embedded. However, if this submerged bond actually determines what transferences and countertransferences occur in an analysis, it is surely a very powerful force that is greater than the unconscious forces otherwise at work in the lives of the analysand and analyst. This force is prior to the psychic reality of the analysand and analyst, as a condition of their developing a transference-countertransference relation, for it determines the shape that the transference and countertransference will take, the enactments that will occur, the defenses that will be modified, the libidinal and aggressive demands that come into play in the associations, and the range of the analyst's interpretations of them.

The claim of relational theorists, however much they may otherwise differ, seems to be that a relation between analysand and analyst overrides the forces at work in the analysand causing his/her transferences and the forces at work in the analyst causing his/her countertransferences. Whether the analytic relation is conceived of as an intersubjective field (Stolorow & Atwood, 1997), a relational unconscious (Gerson, 1996), or an intersubjective third (Ogden, 1999), this shared relational premise is implied. If not, what could the concept refer to but what we know as the working alliance or analytic alliance? If so, are not these concepts of relation so many ways to "soften" with words the power of the unconscious ego and drive forces in our analysands and in ourselves, with which we have no choice but to contend in our therapeutic work? Who would not be greatly relieved, who would not applaud, if this could be done? But illusions or wishful thinking do not change either material or psychic reality. They only obscure the real difficulties with which we are called upon to contend. In the end, relational psychoanalysis may turn out to be more of an escape from the unconscious rather than a deeper insight into its nature and its ways of working.

REFERENCES

Abrams, S. (1986). Disposition and the environment. *Psychoanalytic Study of the Child* 42:41–60.

Buber, M. (1923). *I and Thou* (Trans. W. Kaufmann). New York: Scribner's, 1970.

Chused, J. (1986). Consequences of parental nurturing. *Psychoanalytic Study of the Child* 41:419–438.

Descartes, R. (1649). *The Passions of the Soul* (Trans. E.S. Haldane & G.R.T. Ross). In *The Philosophical Works of Descartes*. vol. 1 (pp. 329–427), New York: Dover, 1955.

Fairbairn, W.R.D. (1946). Object-relationships and dynamic structure. *International Journal of Psychoanalysis* 27:30–37.

——— (1963). Synopsis of an object-relations theory of personality. *International Journal of Psychoanalysis* 44:224–225.

Freud, A. (1946). The psychoanalytic study of infantile feeding disturbances. In *The Writings of Anna Freud*, vol. 4 (pp. 39–59). New York: International Universities Press, 1968.

———— (1949). Notes on aggression. In *The Writings of Anna Freud*, vol. 4 (pp. 60–74). New York: International Universities Press, 1968.

Freud, S. ([1895]1950). Project for a scientific psychology. SE 1:295–343.

———— (1908). Hysterical phantasies and their relation to bisexuality. SE 9: 159–166.

———— (1914). On narcissism, an introduction. SE 14:73–104.

———— (1915). Instincts and their vicissitudes. SE 14:117–140.

———— (1917). Mourning and melancholia. SE 14:239–258.

———— (1923). The ego and the id. SE 19:12–68.

———— (1933). New introductory lectures on psycho-analysis. SE 22:1–182.

———— (1937). Analysis terminable and interminable. SE 23:216–254.

Gerson, S. (1996). Neutrality, resistance and self-disclosure in an intersubjective psychoanalysis. *Psychoanalytic Dialogues* 6:623–647.

Hanly, C. (1978). Instincts and hostile affects. *International Journal of Psychoanalysis* 59:149–156. [Chapter 17 in this volume]

———— (1986). Review of *The Assault of Truth: Freud's Suppression of the Seduction Theory*, by Jeffrey Moussaieff Masson. *International Journal of Psychoanalysis* 67:517–519.

———— (1995). On facts and ideas in psychoanalysis. *International Journal of Psychoanalysis*, 76:901–908. [Chapter 4 in this volume]

———— (1999). Subjectivity and objectivity in analysis. *Journal of the American Psychoanalytic Association* 47:427–444.

Hanly, C., & Hanly, M.A.F. (2001). Critical realism: Distinguishing the psychological subjectivity of the analyst from epistemological subjectivism. *Journal of the American Psychoanalytic Association* 49:515–532.

Hanly, C., & Nichols, C. (2001). A disturbance of psychoanalytic memory. *Philosophy of the Social Sciences* 31:279–301.

Heidegger, M. (1927). *Being and Time* (Trans. J. Macquarrie & E. Robinson). London: SCM Press, 1962.

Kant, I. (1781). *Critique of Pure Reason* (Trans. N.K. Smith). London: Macmillan, 1950.

———— (1788). *Critique of Practical Reason* (Trans. T.K. Abbott). Toronto: Longmans, Green, 1909.

Kohut, H. (1959). Introspection, empathy and psychoanalysis. In *The Search for the Self* (pp. 3–23). New York: International Universities Press, 1975.

———— (1977). *The Restoration of the Self.* New York: International Universities Press.

Loewald, H. (1951). Ego and reality. *International Journal of Psychoanalysis* 32:10–18.

Merleau-Ponty, M. (1945). *Phenomenology of Perception* (Trans. C. Smith). London: Routledge & Kegan Paul, 1962.

Mill, J.S. (1863). *Utilitarianism.* London: Longmans, Green, 1907.

Neubauer, P. (1987). Disturbances in object representation. *Psychoanalytic Study of the Child* 42:335–351.

Novick, K., & Novick, J. (1987). The essence of masochism. *Psychoanalytic Study of the Child* 42:353–384.

Ogden, T. (1999). The analytic third: An overview. In S. Mitchell & L. Aron (Eds.), *Relational Perspectives in Psychoanalysis: The Emergence of a Tradition* (pp. 487–492). Hillside, NJ: Analytic Press.

Ornstein, A., & Ornstein, P. (1994). On the conceptualization of clinical facts. *International Journal of Psychoanalysis* 75:977–994.

Renik, O. (1993). Analytic interaction: Conceptualizing technique in light of the analyst's irreducible subjectivity. *Psychoanalytic Quarterly* 62:553–571.

———— (1998). The analyst's subjectivity and the analyst's objectivity. *International Journal of Psychoanalysis* 79:487–497.

Sartre, J.-P. (1943). *Being and Nothingness* (Trans. H.E. Barnes). New York: Philosophical Library, 1956.

Segal, H. (1979). *Melanie Klein.* New York: Viking.

Shengold, L. (1989). *Soul Murder: The Effects of Childhood Abuse and Deprivation.* New Haven: Yale University Press.

Spence, D. (1994). The special nature of psychoanalytic facts. *International Journal of Psychoanalysis* 75:915–925.

Spinoza, B. (1677). *Ethics.* In J. Wild (Ed.), *Spinoza: Selections* (pp. 94–400). New York: Scribner's. 1939.

Stolorow, R., & Atwood, G. (1997). Deconstructing the myth of the neutral analyst: An alternative from intersubjective systems theory. *Psychoanalytic Quarterly* 66:431–449.

CHAPTER 14

Response to Rachel B. Blass, "On Winnicott's Clinical Innovations in the Analysis of Adults"*

The recent series of papers on Winnicott's technical innovations (Abram, 2012; Blass, 2012; Bonaminio, 2012; Eigen, 2012) provides us with interesting reflections on Winnicott's contribution to adult analysis. It raises the question of whether the importance Winnicott attaches to the analyst's role of providing good enough parenting is consistent with a traditional or classical view of psychoanalysis. If Freud and Klein affirm the primacy of interpretation of the dynamic psychic unconscious in the analytic cure, as I believe they do (Hanly, 1994), then the answer would have to be that Winnicott's view is not consistent with a traditional view of psychoanalysis. In what follows I will explain my reasoning.

Although Grunbaum (1984) exaggerated Freud's reliance on the tally argument, there is no question that Freud considered sound interpretations of what is actively unconscious in the patient in the analysis as the primary and indispensable instruments of therapeutic efficacy. Freud (1914, 1916–1917, 1937a, 1940) did not disregard the fact that psychoanalysis is a human relation, but he was primarily concerned with considerations about the possibility of analytic collaboration, rather than with advocating building a relationship in which the analyst is able, by means of empathy

---

* Originally published in *The International Journal of Psychoanalysis* 94, no. 1 (2013):128–130.

or emotional responsiveness, to provide the patient with that of which life has deprived him/her (except insofar as the analysis can enable him/her to mourn its loss and to find substitute satisfactions in his/her present life). Similarly, Freud (1914) realized that the therapeutic results he sought could not be achieved simply by the analyst putting conflicts, unconscious wishes, and symptoms into words. If the necessary maturation of instinctual organizations were to take place, then these words had to be found or accepted by the patient in bringing about the transforming therapeutic effect of the work of associating and forming transferences during analysis. In this painful struggle, Freud consistently sees the analyst's role as attending to the patient's process of repetition and working through, as the patient is in search of instinct maturation while resisting the work required by it. Accordingly, Freud would have thought that the gratifications provided by role responsiveness, by empathy, or by corrective emotional experience in the absence of interpretation, run the risk of causing a transference repetition that diminishes the prospect of it being worked through, a process which lies at the heart of psychoanalysis. Role responsiveness (or empathy), in the absence of interpretation, might also have the effect of increasing the anxiety caused by the patient's regression to an infantile state and mode of functioning (formal regression). I would add to this that without the vehicle and context provided by interpretation, there would seem to be at least two more problems: (1) Given the analytic setup, how is the adult patient to take in and experience therapeutic benefit without verbal communication? (2) What better verbal communication could there be than interpretations that tally with the patient's inner struggle as the therapeutic work proceeds? Gratifying the instinctual need of very regressed patients, in the absence of interpretations that touch upon the conflicts, risks consolidating the need rather than working it through and opening up paths to maturation.

It should be noted that to kindly acknowledge, accept, and interpret a demand for maternal transference love is not to gratify it, but neither is it to repudiate the transference love, or criticize it, or deny the patient whatever she/he needs in the regressed transference in order to become more fully engaged in the work of her analysis. The analyst's interpreting activity could have the effect of allowing the patient to satisfy her longing for maternal loving care in the transference relationship, a love that she was deprived of in her childhood, while maintaining the position of the transference love as play—as something that is neither real nor refused, but contained and available for working through. Of course, without any effort on the part of the analyst to supply, by emulation, a good mother-child relation, a patient may provide him/herself with this experience by means of unconscious fantasy in the analysis; the patient may find a location for the longed-for satisfaction in an idealizing transference attachment to the analyst. In this light, Michael Eigen's description of transferences as "joyful" strikes me as a denial of the totality of the memories involved in the transference, which may include rage aroused by the privation and the excruciating pain of utter helplessness. Nor, in my view, would an analyst's presence, witnessing, or just being there for a patient be sufficient. And is there not a risk that if an analyst believes that it is sufficient for him to be a good enough restorative mother, then he would not be motivated to search for interpretations that might enable the patient to work through her regressed, idealizing maternal transference with, in all likelihood, concomitant repressed destructive rage? In colluding with the patient's regressed oral elation, being a good enough mother could, in my view, make it difficult for the analyst to be a good enough analyst.

Some of Winnicott's innovations may be regarded as enriching Freudian technique by conceptualizing and elaborating ways in which the analyst's relation to the patient facilitates the associations and transferences that make sound interpretations evident and effective, especially when preoedipal traumata are important causal factors in the neurosis. In this sense, Winnicott's interpretations would have a special importance in what I have called (Hanly, 1994) the "implicit meaning of interpretations"—the analyst's emotional responsiveness to the patient's transferences and associations. Such emotional responsiveness is meaningful to patients. For example, the quality of the analyst's voice may reassure a patient that she is safe, and that the analyst will not repeat the traumatic privations she has suffered in a way that explicit reassurances could not. Appropriate affective responsiveness works best implicitly.

However, if Winnicott's technical innovations are taken to mean that the analyst's emotional or affective responsiveness (to the patient's associations, memories, and the transference experiences that accompany them) or transference gratification (as in the attempt to be the good enough mother) can take the place of interpretation, then they surely go beyond Freudian technique, in which interpretation, with its explicit and implicit meanings, carries the burden of the therapeutic work (Hanly, 1994).

In treating affect responsiveness, corrective emotional experience, empathy, and the like as curative of neurosis, independent of accompanying interpretations, it is my impression that the "Winnicottian turn," like the Alexandrian, Kohutian, and relational turns, pushes psychoanalysis in the direction of supportive psychotherapy. In this way, the Winnicottian turn has turned away from Freud's understanding of the nature of the dynamic psychic unconscious.

REFERENCES

Abram, J. (2012). On Winnicott's clinical innovations in the analysis of adults. *International Journal of Psychoanalysis* 93:1461–1473.

Blass, R.B. (2012). "On Winnicott's clinical innovations in the analysis of adults": Introduction to a controversy. *International Journal of Psychoanalysis* 93:1439–1448.

Bonaminio, V. (2012). On Winnicott's clinical innovations in the analysis of adults. *International Journal of Psychoanalysis* 93:1475–1485.

Eigen, M. (2012). On Winnicott's clinical innovations in the analysis of adults. *International Journal of Psychoanalysis* 93:1449–1459.

Freud, S. (1900). *The Interpretation of Dreams*. SE 4–5.

——— (1914). Remembering, repeating and working through. SE 12:145–156.

——— (1916–1917). *Introductory Lectures on Psycho-Analysis*. SE 15–16.

——— (1937a). Analysis terminable and interminable. SE 23:216–254.

——— (1937b). Constructions in analysis. SE 23:255–270.

——— (1940). An outline of psycho-analysis. SE 144–208.

Grunbaum, A. (1984). *The Foundations of Psychoanalysis*. Berkeley: University of California Press.

Hanly, C. (1994). Reflections of the place of the therapeutic alliance in psychoanalysis. *International Journal of Psychoanalysis* 75:457–468.

Nagel, E. (1959). Methodological issues in psychoanalytic theory. In S. Hook (Ed.), *Psychoanalysis, Scientific Method and Philosophy* (pp. 38–56). New York: Grove Press.

Poland, W. (2000). The analyst's witnessing and otherness. *Journal of the American Psychoanalytic Association* 48:17–34.

Zetzel, E. (1966). The analytic situation. In R.E. Litman (Ed.), *Psychoanalysis in the Americas* (pp. 86–106). New York: International Universities Press.

IV

On Psychoanalysis and Philosophy

CHAPTER 15

Phenomenology, Consciousness, and Freedom*

The phenomenological theory of motivation was first developed extensively by Sartre in his early *Sketch of a Theory of Emotions* and then in *The Transcendence of the Ego, Being and Nothingness,* and the *Critique of Dialectical Reason.* Sartre's theory presents three difficulties which were recognized by Merleau-Ponty, whose position, as formulated in the *Phenomenology of Perception,* is in part an attempt to resolve them. The point of view of this paper is that Merleau-Ponty has not satisfactorily resolved these difficulties and that, moreover, no adaptations of the theory could resolve them, short of abandoning Merleau-Ponty's concept of freedom.

THREE FLAWS IN THE EXISTENTIALIST THEORY OF MOTIVATION

Sartre bases his theory on the idea that consciousness is pure spontaneity. This means that all forms of mental energy are, in their initial phase of formation, pure, psychically unqualified intentions toward the world. The initial upsurges of consciousness (pre-reflective consciousness) that originate

---

* Originally published in *Dialogue: Canadian Philosophical Review* 5 (1966):323–345.

projects and situations exist first without as yet having a nature. Viewed from the perspective of human behavior, objects and artifacts, customs, institutions, and legal and moral laws, as well as instincts, desires, and aversions, are only so many abstract schemata representing possibilities for action until they are freely endowed by pre-reflective consciousness with motive force. Therefore, consciousness cannot stand in a passive relation to anything else which might determine its nature and manner of acting. To be sure, impure reflective consciousness fabricates a phantom self which *appears* to be subject to causal influences. But such a self is a flight from the anxiety associated with the spontaneity of unreflective consciousness. It is, for Sartre, a form of inauthentic existence, or bad faith.

This conception of consciousness is at odds with traditional thought, which appears to be unanimously opposed to it. The plight of Leontius, which Plato uses to demonstrate the existence of the spirit function in the soul (*Republic* IV.439–440), implies a concept of a consciousness which passively attests to the triumph of a perverse appetitive lust of his eyes. Plato describes Leontius wanting to take pleasure in looking at the dead bodies of recently executed criminals. Leontius curses his eyes for what they want him to do, but his voyeuristic appetite overwhelms his moral scruples: his spirit (his moral will) fails to master his sensual appetites. According to Plato's description, Leontius's self-awareness attests to his moral defeat but does not contrive it. The Hobbesian conception of volition as the last desire or aversion in a sequence of desires and aversions implies that consciousness is simply a witness of the internal process that precedes behavior (Hobbes, 1651, Part 1, chap. 6). Correspondingly, the common assumption of both the Platonic and Hobbesian conceptions is that emotional life moves forward under its own steam rather than on a spontaneity "borrowed" from consciousness. The same assumptions about consciousness and emotions are adopted by Kant, despite obvious differences between his concept of volition and that of Hobbes.

Secondly, Sartre's (1943) theory logically requires an unconscious. For he takes the following view:

> Psychological determinism, before being a theoretical conception, is... the basis of all attitudes of excuse. It is reflective conduct with respect to anguish; it asserts that there are within us antagonistic forces whose type of existence is comparable to that of things.... It provides us with a *nature* productive of our acts.... Psychological determinism denies that transcendence of human reality which makes it emerge in anguish beyond its own essence. (p. 40)

Let us suppose that what Sartre says about psychological determinism is in fact true. Sartre must then build into the logic of his theory some way of explaining how it is that persons using normal self-awareness, philosophers and psychoanalytic psychologists can be so mistaken about human reality, especially when they are themselves examples of that reality, and in the latter case, trained observers of it. After all, what is at issue is not some accidental characteristic that varies from individual to individual.

Sartre's difficulty is not diminished by his adoption of the assumption that consciousness is the existence of the self. He writes: "Self-consciousness... [is] *the only mode of existence which is possible for a consciousness of something. Just as an extended object is compelled to exist according to three dimensions, so an intention, a pleasure, a grief can exist only as immediate self-consciousness*" (1943, p. liv). How then can Sartre account for being in bad faith? What his theory requires is more than the "knowing without knowing that one knows" of, for example, Plato's *Meno*. In the *Meno*, Plato has Socrates "prove" that a slave boy knows the Pythagorean theorem that the square of the hypotenuse equals the sum of the squares of the other two sides of all right triangles, despite the boy believing that he has no such knowledge. Although Plato's belief that knowledge is based on memory depends on mythological assumptions, self-ignorance is compatible with a simple absence of knowing, whereas Sartre's bad faith requires a positive state of self-deception.

Psychoanalytic theory would appear to provide just the explanation Sartre's theory requires. But following Stekel, Sartre rejects the psychoanalytic concept of the unconscious which, according to Sartre, establishes bad faith in bad faith because it explains self-deception as the product of an involuntary and unconscious mental process. Sartre also found the psychoanalytic theory of the instincts untenable: a position logically required by his concept of consciousness as pure spontaneity. In effect, the drive of the instincts of libido and aggression are withdrawn by Sartre from the instincts and attributed to the spontaneity of consciousness:

> Shall I uncover in myself "drives," even though it be to affirm them in shame? But is this not deliberately to forget that these drives are realized with my consent, that they are not forces of nature but that I lend them their efficacy by a perpetually renewed decision concerning their value. (1943, p. 63)

The resulting logical predicament is crucial. If deterministic thinking is a flight from the anguish of freedom, it must be conscious of being so. But how then can it fail to acknowledge its own falsification of human reality? As Sartre (1943) says, "I flee in order not to know, but I cannot avoid knowing that I am fleeing.... Thus, anguish can be neither hidden nor avoided" (p. 43). Therefore, in order to provide an account of the *Meno*'s "river of Lethe effect" (the trauma of the incarnation of the soul by being born) on which bad faith is based, Sartre is obliged to attribute to consciousness a nihilating power by means of which it can be anguish in the form of not being it.

Superficially, existential nihilation is similar to what psychodynamic psychiatry and psychoanalysis refer to as the mechanisms of denial (Frank,

1960) and repression (Freud, 1900). The effect of inner deception is the same, but otherwise they are completely different conceptions. Sartre (1943) does not explain how the individual's ability to "decenter himself" in relation to what he is and his ability to "dispose of a nihilating power at the heart of anguish itself" (p. 44) can actually create all the effects he attributes to it. Elsewhere Sartre likens putting oneself in bad faith to going to sleep, but the point of the metaphor would appear to be to suggest a similarity between segments of waking life and the state of unconsciousness induced in us by alterations in levels of brain activity when sensory activity is extensively reduced. Sartre's sense of reality appears to be sounder than his conceptual formulations, and he found a way to smuggle unconscious psychic activity back into his theory. But the core problem remains: we are confronted either by a major inconsistency or by an ontological category of nothingness, which, if it is meaningful at all, has no more than a contextual meaning within existentialist philosophy itself—and we are probably confronted by both.

It is ironic that although the word "existential" in Sartre's philosophy is given a coherent contextual meaning in his philosophy, this meaning is absent from its frequent current popular use. For example, it is often used to describe various crises, as in "Putin is causing an existential crisis on the Ukrainian border." The philosophical meaning of "existential" is that Putin will not be caused to attack or refrain from attacking Ukraine by what he has done in the past, which has already been nihilated, or by deliberations about current circumstances or future considerations because their weight will have already been decided by an uncaused, spontaneous choice of a way of being by a spontaneous consciousness. This choice, if it is made authentically, will be an anguished acknowledgement of its uncaused arbitrariness. The popular use of the term only asserts what the sentence "Putin is causing a crisis on the Ukrainian border" asserts. The use of the word "existential" says nothing about the nature of the crisis, its causes, or how it could be resolved. This use of "existential" could be intended to mean that the existence of Ukraine is at stake, based on Putin's assertion that the Ukraine does not deserve to be a nation, and if it is now a state it is a Nazi state. But existentialism is not about the fate of nations; it is about the fate of the individual, given the "existential" meaning of the philosophical use of the term when used as a predicate.

Finally, once consciousness has been defined as pure spontaneity and endowed with a nihilating power which it cannot but use, selfhood must be understood as perpetual disengagement. This disengagement has several forms, but a consideration of one will suffice. Insofar as a self is related to his/her past, that relation must take the form of a consciousness of being what he/she was in the past. But the consciousness which remembers the past is already not the past which it remembers. Nihilation effects the conversion of present into past, and in so doing liberates a new unqualified consciousness in the present. This means for Sartre that what one has done, and consequently has been, cannot causally influence the new formation of consciousness that arises out of the disengagement of the self from its last project. There is no way in which being a loyal husband or wife for many years can absolve one of the need to re-establish that commitment each morning and throughout the day when differences with one's spouse occur. This does not mean that Sartre denies that people preserve the natures they have gradually accumulated or claims that they do not find motives in their past for present undertakings, but rather that past motives must be incorporated into the present by a free, uncaused act of renewal. Therefore, past experiences cannot in and by themselves determine behavior. Longstanding habits have to be renewed daily. Consequently, the facticity of the past, combined with fresh possibilities for action in the present, defines the total range of possibilities from which consciousness can choose. But these possibilities *and* their negations are *equipossible*. The extent to which Sartre generalizes this concept is shown by the statement that consciousness "can be limited only by itself." The metaphysical ancestor of Sartrean consciousness is Spinoza's God.

The result is a harvest of paradoxes. The schizophrenic woman who pushed a stranger into the path of a subway train in response to "voices" must have elected to credit them and adopt them as the motive for a gratuitous homicide. The discipline of the ascetic by which he seeks mastery over his animal nature is repeatedly undone, unknown to him, from within himself. Or, looking at the ascetic's life from another perspective, the mastery he seeks now over his instincts is already vouchsafed him because they too are no more than permanent possibilities for action. A man or woman is homosexual because they choose to take pleasure in performing homosexual acts, just as heterosexuals choose to take pleasure in heterosexual acts. Homosexuality and heterosexuality are equally the result of equally possible choices by a spontaneous, unmotivated consciousness.

These difficulties in the existentialist theory have long been recognized. I state them here because they provide a useful perspective on Merleau-Ponty's thought, which can be construed as an attempt to modify the phenomenological theory of motivation with a view to resolving them. But before examining some of these modifications, it should be made clear that Merleau-Ponty shares Sartre's philosophical purposes, as the following quotation makes clear:

Whether we are concerned with my body, the natural world, the past, birth or death, the question is always how I can be open to phenomena which transcend me, and which nevertheless exist only to the extent that I take them up and live them; *how the presence to myself which establishes my own limits and conditions every alien presence is at the same time de-presentation and throws me outside myself.* Both idealism and realism, the former by making the external world immanent in me, the latter by subjecting me to a causal action,

305

falsify the motivational relations existing between the external and internal worlds, and make this relationship unintelligible. (1945, pp. 363–364)

MERLEAU-PONTY'S ATTEMPT TO REMEDY THE FLAWS

In *Phenomenology of Perception,* Merleau-Ponty replaces the concept of pre-reflective consciousness with the idea of a pre-personal self. The pre-personal self is a project toward the world "in which there are so far no 'states of consciousness,' nor, a *fortiori,* qualifications of any sort." Consequently, Merleau-Ponty shares with Sartre (and Russell) the view that the veridical content of the Cartesian *cogito* is not "I think," which presupposes an ego, but "There is thinking." Pre-personal thinking does not have the character, qualities, or affects of the person whose project it will become.

In other respects, however, his conception is different. Merleau-Ponty's anonymous self is not pure consciousness as in Sartre. It can be metaphorically described as a mute conversation of a person's living body with the world. But a more precise conceptual clarification is possible by means of a phenomenological description of a psychological error that involves spatial orientation. An example of an error of spatial orientation follows. (If the appropriateness of this selection of an explanatory example is not apparent, it should be remembered that Merleau-Ponty considered Freud to be one of the great phenomenologists, who sadly lost his way philosophically in scientific naturalism. Merleau-Ponty admired Freud's case descriptions but repudiated his explanations of them.) A woman was driving north on an expressway deep in conversation with a new acquaintance about a matter of great personal importance to the driver. Her intention was to drive home, which involved making an exit from the expressway via a cloverleaf interchange, which would take her under the expressway and so toward her home. What she in fact did was drive the car back onto the expressway by proceeding under the bridge, then up the ramp, and so back onto the expressway from which she had just come, but now in the opposite direction leading away from her home. She drove almost a mile back along it before she discovered her predicament: for a dizzy moment, the "world" seemed to revolve through a ninety-degree arc around the axis of her body and come to rest again in reality. She expressed astonishment at her mistake and began looking for a route that would take her to where she intended to go and had thought she was going.

The psychological error reveals and is made possible by an existential structure that permits a discontinuity and ambiguity in spatial orientation. The spatial orientation of the situation formed by the driver's intention to drive home came to be out of phase with the spatial orientation established by her body and which enabled her, *in fact* and *in reality*, to execute safely the erroneous driving maneuver, despite her belief that nothing was amiss and that she was heading home. Furthermore, it was this spatial orientation of her impersonal pre-personal self that also provided the polarities for her reorientation.

If so, the anonymous self cannot be understood as a pure upsurge of consciousness as Sartre supposes. For the life of the pre-personal self preserves in existence, among other things, a projection of spatial directions onto the world. It also establishes pre-personal evaluations of things, actions, and persons. In this case, informed by the wish to continue the conversation, the importance to her of which she did not want to acknowledge to herself. Similarly, a person who is "wrapped up" in grief and withdrawn from society into himself or herself as a result of the death of a loved one, will nevertheless begin to experience a disintegration of the grief to which his or her personal life is committed, through the reabsorption of the person's life back into the world of objects and persons that can again engage the person's interest and desire. It is a pre-personal self that performs the work of reabsorption and establishes the absolute impersonal value of life and the world. Consequently, personal existence does not rest, as Sartre assumes, upon a pure spontaneous upsurge of consciousness, but rather upon a preconscious foundation of relatively stable and reliable acquired experience. Merleau-Ponty's theory could account for the driver's ability to safely and competently drive her car in the direction that was opposite to the direction she believed herself to be driving.

The concept of the pre-personal self provides phenomenology with two important theoretical assets. First, it can provide an object for a witnessing and attesting self-awareness which is not itself the originator of what it witnesses, like a playwright at the performance of his own play (Sartre's pure reflection), nor committed necessarily to a falsifying gestalt of the self (Sartre's impure reflection). Second, it provides for a concept of the unconscious and an account of self-deception that is consistent with the philosophical goals and commitments of phenomenology, that is, to give an account of human experience independently of causal and "objective" (scientific) categories of thought and to preserve for consciousness a nuclear role in mental life—something that the phenomenological method itself requires.

Merleau-Ponty (1945) rejects both Sartre's concept of a pure spontaneous consciousness that is transparent to itself and the psychoanalytic concept of the unconscious, for essentially the same reason: they both involve the same "retrospective illusion" (p. 381). For they locate as an explicit object in the person everything that is slowly going to dawn upon that person about himself/herself. Thus, if being in love or being a political activist is the consequence of a constantly renewed self-transparent choice, how can it come about that the awareness of being in love or being keenly committed to political goals occurs only at the end of a period in which that awareness has been in a process of formation? And according to Merleau-Ponty, neither can the love or the political investment be already constituted in my unconscious to be gradually converted into consciousness. For Merleau-Ponty, these Sartrean and Freudian conceptions, each in its own way, diminish the reality of becoming. Accordingly, Merleau-Ponty recognizes both a passive, attesting self-awareness and a self-ignorance that is not a form of deliberate dissimulation: "We are not perpetually in possession of ourselves in our whole reality, and we are justified in speaking of an inner perception... working from us to ourselves which ceaselessly goes some, but not all, the way in providing knowledge of our life and our being" (1945, p. 380).

Merleau-Ponty's phenomenological account of self-ignorance constitutes a non-mechanistic theory of the unconscious. One of the most striking forms of self-ignorance is the dream experience—an experience sufficiently impenetrable to consciousness that ancient peoples, for example, experienced dreaming as a form of perception revealing a world unavailable to the waking senses but forming part of a complete system of reality. Freud conceptualized this fact about dreaming by distinguishing the *manifest* content of a dream from its *latent* content. The manifest content is the distorted conscious surface of the dream, of which the dreamer is aware; the latent content is constituted by the memories from which the manifest dream images are drawn, as well as the desires and emotions which animate them, of which the dreamer is not aware. The manifest dream images stand for, or symbolize, the unconscious memories and wishes. Phenomenology can accept (given the modifications involved in the concepts of pre-personal self and passive consciousness) the fact about dreaming indicated by the psychoanalytic distinction between manifest and latent content. What it cannot accept is the psychoanalytic *causal explanation* of this fact.

Merleau-Ponty's account turns on (1) the differentiation he finds within the human being between the personal self and the pre-personal self, and (2) his view that the correlate of this differentiation in a field of awareness is its organization into a figure on a background. Thus, the

309

formation of an explicit perception of an object takes place on the basis of a pre-perceptual detachment of an object from its background (1945, pp. 3–12, 52–53). To take a specific case, the bricklayer who inspects a batch of mortar for consistency is exploiting an organization of his field of awareness into an object for inspection, with everything else held in suspense. His inspection of the mortar, which is an expression of his personal life as a worker, is able to cooperate with a pre-personal life to call into existence a "workman's world." By contrast, an inexperienced person who visits a construction site will often find that objects in his perceptual field will undergo a minor spatial distortion, in that they appear "flattened" into a single plane or in a weird disarray; he will find the experience itself mildly upsetting and will feel relieved to return to a work environment in which he can "feel at home." This is because such a person cannot manipulate any of the machinery, tools, or materials on the site. His body is "closed" to them, and consequently their links with the masses of earth, concrete, steel, and wire that form the unfinished building are not exhibited in his concious visual field. The result is a "collapse" within the visual field. The significance of that "collapse" is that objects acquire an unreality and begin to look like one-dimensional cardboard figures; it is in the visual field of the tradesman that their materiality and their utility for construction is revealed.

By employing these ideas, phenomenology is able to render an account of the self-ignorance peculiar to dream experience. In sleep, the personal self is absent through a retreat into the anonymity of the pre-personal self. Consequently, cooperation in the formation of a field of awareness cannot occur between the personal self and the pre-personal self. Merleau-Ponty concludes that, for this reason, when one dreams in sleep, the entire field of awareness is uniformly dominated by sexuality. This saturation of the images of the manifest dream content terminates in a dream world in which sexual meanings cannot stand out because there are no non-sexual elements to form a background against which they can emerge (Merleau-Ponty, 1945, pp. 154ff., 381). Accordingly, the pre-personal spatializing function organizes a world in which experiences like falling through the air, scaling a ladder, or ascending a stair acquire a sexual significance. But this meaning, even while being lived by the dreamer, cannot be recognized by him because within "the dream world" there can occur no falling, climbing, or ascending actions that is asexual and merely mechanical—hence the inability of the dreamer to be conscious of the sexual nature of his dream or to comprehend its meaning, and hence the presence within the person of an unacknowledged life.

Merleau-Ponty's account of the self-ignorance involved in dreaming is a specific application of a more generic concept. It is not because of the specific and forbidding nature of the wishes that produce a dream that the dreamer remains unaware of its meaning; he remains unaware of the meaning of the dream because of the uniformity with which sexuality pervades it. (This notion is similar to the ancient Pythagorean idea that the motions of astronomical bodies produce a music that we cannot hear because it always and everywhere uniformly permeates our hearing.) Similarly, a person cannot form an explicit thought about his own death as he can about the deaths of others. What we can explicitly conceptualize is rather the negation of our own death, as when we form the thought that we are the creatures through whom creation becomes known, and who should for that reason outlast nature. But one's own death has an existential significance that pervades the horizon of one's fields of awareness. It is neither an explicit object of consciousness nor a fear bound to an explicit representation of "my" death which has been repressed. My own death, in Merleau-Ponty's phenomenology, is the lived personal sense that contingency has for me.

As a result, Merleau-Ponty's phenomenology can account for an opacity within consciousness that lays down the theoretical foundation necessary for understanding how the intellectual errors involved in a mechanistic psychology (psychoanalysis) could arise. Illusion is possible because consciousness can cease to know what it is doing; otherwise, it would be conscious of having formed the illusion and could not treat it as anything other than what it is, in which case it would not be an illusion. Thus, the coincidence of oneself with oneself through self-awareness is never a real coincidence, "but merely an intentional and presumptive one" (p. 344). The phenomenological interpretation of the unconscious, combined with the concept of the anonymity of the pre-personal self, provides the logical basis needed for understanding psychoanalysis as intellectual error rather than intellectual perversity. Merleau-Ponty has been able to disengage the phenomenological critique of the empirical sciences of man from the moral connotations implicit in Sartre's categories of authentic and inauthentic existence, and at the same time to avoid the inconsistency implicit in existentialism.

But has Merleau-Ponty been as successful in dealing with the problems involved in the concepts of disengagement, transcendence, nihilation, and choice in Sartre's existentialism? Has he discovered a way of avoiding the paradoxes of the equipossibility of motives and actions with the unwanted consequence of appearing to reduce the human lot to the dilemma that defeated Buridan's ass? Would not motivational helplessness arise whenever hunger and thirst are equal and the distances to a bale of hay and a pale of water are equidistant, if needs are only "intentional and presumptive" and not determinative? Sartre's theory is committed to the existence of nothingness as the real separation between past and present, instinct and instinctive behavior. At the same time, the direction of force is always from a spontaneous consciousness which readopts past motives and aims or chooses new ones. Consequently, for existentialism the individual's latitude of decision is infinite.

Merleau-Ponty has introduced an important clarification and modification in the phenomenological categories of disengagement and transcendence. It is agreed that the person can at any time interrupt his own projects: having given one's support to one political party, it is always possible to withdraw that support and give it to another. But the disengagement involved has an inevitable structure such that: (1) one cannot choose oneself continually from "a starting point of nothing at all"; (2) one can disengage oneself from one project only by becoming engaged in another: "I may defy all accepted form, and spurn everything, for there is no case in which I am utterly committed: but, in this case, I do not withdraw into my freedom, I commit myself elsewhere" (Merleau-Ponty, 1945, p. 452); and (3) the self is dependent on a social and natural environment that offers "invitations" to act, and these invitations enter into the formation of the behavior that takes them up: if men were able to choose themselves as workers or capitalists with an absolute initiative, neither personal history nor national history could have the stable structure or direction over time which it does in fact have. Furthermore, persons are always located in a specific social environment, are endowed with the powers of a specific body, and have already lived a certain kind of life. Therefore, even though one can commit oneself elsewhere, one cannot transform oneself instantaneously into what one decides to be: a teacher can go into business, but it takes time to become a businessman, that is, to assume the style of life that makes the difference between being a teacher and a businessman. The result is a concept of disengagement that provides the theoretical basis for a rejection of determinism without a logical commitment to the existence of nothingness. Merleau-Ponty has freed phenomenology from the necessity of treating nothingness as itself a kind of existent. For him, the concept of nothingness or non-existence is limited to two meanings: (1) as a description of the ontological status of things and states of affairs which once were or which are yet to be; and (2) as a reference to the absence of any causal mechanisms that fix a person's actions and motives, causing them to become repetitive.

By extending this "naturalization" of existential categories to time, Merleau-Ponty is able both to provide a diagnosis of a major source of Sartre's philosophical difficulties and to lay the groundwork for a more plausible phenomenology of motivational stability and uniformity in human beings. Time cannot be deduced as Sartre attempts to deduce it from the spontaneity of consciousness: to be sure, it is through subjectivity that time appears, but the time through which we unfold our personal lives is itself grounded in the natural time of our bodies. The anonymous organic rhythms of the bodily functions—respiration, pulse, and the cyclical fluctuations of the appetites—adumbrate a continuous passage from cessation or quiescence to action in a process of development, fulfillment, a return to quiescence, and so on, as the pattern repeats itself. Hence there is a natural ground in the living body itself for a *subjectivity that is constantly in a process of making itself without ever having to be fixed once and for all in what it has already made of itself.* This ground does not depend on consciousness for its being. Like the other functions of the pre-personal self, it rests upon itself. It incorporates man's life in the passage of time of the natural world.

If, on the other hand, as Sartre supposed, temporality is originated by the spontaneity of consciousness; the movement which carries existence into the future and transfers the present into the past must then be sustained by an act. Consequently, not only must conscious acts move our personal lives forward, they must also generate such things as the respiratory reflex. Thus, Sartre's understanding of humanity involves the notion that the decision to go to work in the morning, which organizes and dedicates our personal life for the day, also brings in train with it all the vital functions of our bodies. One motivates oneself to breathe just as one motivates oneself to go to work. It is this conception of temporality that gives Sartre's notion of anxiety its pathological dimensions. For if the existential concept of temporality were sound, then every act of authentic awareness would reveal that the choice to go on living could just as easily be reversed at any time. But human existence is not, in fact, intrinsically that precarious. Suicide, either physical or moral, is not an option for most people most of the time.

Merleau-Ponty (1945) is able to derive the more plausible conclusion that "a consciousness for which the world 'can be taken for granted,' which finds it 'already constituted' and present even in consciousness itself, does not *absolutely* choose either its being or its manner of being" (p. 453). Persons do not choose to be alive; nor do we choose to want to be alive. A pre-personal yearning after life may be either taken up and confirmed in the style of our personal lives or neglected, but it is there in the way in which our bodies are there.

Merleau-Ponty's phenomenology of human temporality has a specific theoretical utility denied to both existentialism and its theoretical antithesis, physiological determinism. His conception allows for a dissonance between the pre-personal temporality of the body and the temporality of personal life that parallels the possibility of ambiguity in spatial organization described above. The phenomena of arrestment and regression uncovered by psychoanalysis imply just such a dissonance in human temporality. The personal life of the individual, as defined by the experiences of satisfaction that he seeks, can either take up and put to use the matured sexual powers of the body or adopt a form of refusal, such as a perversion or a character formation that combines public moral fastidiousness with political or religious fanaticism.

Binswanger, who has contributed much to the creation of existential psychiatry, has made his contribution in part by importing these phenomenological concepts of spatiality and temporality into psychiatry, where he has put them to work providing new explanations of the formation of neurosis. Binswanger (1958a, 1958b) is in agreement with Merleau-Ponty concerning psychic temporality, although he borrowed more explicitly from Heidegger. In his case study of his severely depressed patient Ellen West, Binswanger understands the disturbances of the subject's adult life terminating in suicide in terms of an extreme case of dissonance in the temporal structure of her existence, resulting from her having lived out her entire personal history, including her adulthood, in her childhood through a fantasy adult bodily life, leaving her adult bodily life without a subjectivity to live it. Suicide was the only way she had of reuniting the psychic meaning of her bodily life with her personal life and thus unifying the temporal structures of her existence. To quote Binswanger (1958a):

The life-meaning of this *Dasein* had already been fulfilled "in early years," in accordance with the stormy life-tempo and the circular life-movement of this existence, in which the *Dasein* had soon "run idle." (*Dasein* is Heidegger's basic term for the human psyche.) Existential aging had hurried ahead of biological aging, just as existential death, the "being-a-corpse among people" had hurried ahead of the biological end of life. (p. 295)

The suicide is the necessary-voluntary consequence of this existential state of affairs. It is true that children fantasize about being adult. Much of the play of children is organized and motivated by these fantasies. But adulthood arrives in due course with its expectable natural time unaltered unless by illness or accident, even though neurosis or psychoses may make it difficult for it to be lived in a satisfying way. The problem is not with time; the problem is with fixations from childhood caused by trauma, or in cases of schizophrenia, by neurological liabilities. Binswanger's account has the appearance of an intellectualizing rationalization of a clinical failure in the treatment of a very severe neurosis.

Minkowski (1958) assumes more generally that the way in which an individual temporalizes his/her existence is a fundamental determinant of his/her entire mental life. Existential psychiatry precisely reverses the classical picture of the relationship between a person's affectivity and his/her sense of time. Classical psychiatry would explain a disorder in a subject's sense of the future, such as the depressed paranoid feeling that the future exists for others but not for the subject, as the effect of, say, a delusional belief that he is to be executed for an uncommitted crime. Existential psychiatry assumes on the contrary that the primary disorder is the distorted attitude toward the future, a delusion of execution being only a manifestation of the distorted attitude toward the future.

Merleau-Ponty uses these modified existential categories to formulate a theory of motivation that is rather closer to traditional conceptions than to Sartre's, except for one crucial agreement with Sartre: freedom cannot be located in an act of will. An individual who has already elected to guarantee his own safety by not attempting a rescue when confronted with a situation in which someone is drowning may have recourse to an act of will to force himself into the water, or again, an individual who is bent on adultery may impose a joyless fidelity on himself, but the real decision is to secure one's own life or to enjoy a mistress. These determining decisions are not made by the will. The more fundamental decisions to which the will has no access can undermine willed behavior from within, leaving it hollow and ineffective. All that willed behavior can do is to demonstrate our powerlessness rather than to express our autonomy. Kant and Descartes would have claimed that willed choices demonstrate the autonomy of will. Consequently, it is an error to interpret the meaning of transcendence in phenomenology in terms of the power of the will to impose duties on amoral affects and motivations. Merleau-Ponty (1945) agrees with Sartre in rejecting the classical conception of freedom as a deliberately willed act: "The classical conception of deliberation is relevant only to a freedom 'in bad faith' which secretly harbours antagonistic motives without being prepared to act on them, and so itself manufactures the alleged proofs of its impotence" (p. 438). But if Merleau-Ponty rejects the view that human freedom can be understood in terms of a self-determining will (as Descartes and Kant held), he also refuses to understand it in terms of Sartre's nihilating power of consciousness.

Freedom can never be understood simply as an attitude of intellectual reserve expressed by the words, "I could always do and be otherwise." Freedom is the activity of bringing things about; consequently, social, economic, political, and natural realities can reduce or increase its scope and to facilitate or frustrate its realization. More importantly, freedom is always engaged in a situation. This means that freedom must find its motives in things; it cannot find a motivational self-sufficiency in itself. The politician who is fed up with injustices and is getting ready to launch an attack on government policies will ground his discontent and his attack in the facts of the situation as he sees them; similarly, the individual who engages in an act of personal heroism will enlist as a motive for his act his friendship for the endangered person, a hatred of suffering, or an identification with the victim. Freedom must find a bulwark for its existence and stabilize itself in things, circumstances, conditions, and motives. Consequently, psychological and environmental determinism are not understood adequately by Sartre's existential category "attitudes of excuse," for their explanations contain a truth—the dependency relations our egos have with our own instinct life and with our environments in satisfying our needs.

Nevertheless, for Merleau-Ponty, events, desires, states of affairs, and things cannot in and by *themselves* act as causes of human choices. There is no way in which the events of a war, their description in the media, or their domestic consequences could of themselves bring it about that this or that politician will become a government critic. Events can make the time ripe for an action, but they cannot of themselves determine the agent or produce his action. Events and their consequences need the compliance of persons in order to be converted into human actions of political protest. Consequently, as Merleau-Ponty (1945) puts it in a crucial statement, "Our freedom does not destroy our situation, but gears itself to it: as long as we are alive, our situation is open, which implies both that it calls up specially favoured modes of resolution, and also that it is powerless to bring one into being by itself" (p. 442). Merleau-Ponty thus is able to assign sense and significance to probable predictions about human behavior and events. Freedom is dependent in its existence on situations; situations, in turn, make their own demands for modes of resolution, yielding success to some actions and dooming others to futility. Similarly, there is a "sedimentation" of repeated personal decisions and undertakings into the general forms of existence of the prepersonal self. Consequently, it makes sense to say of the banker who has taken satisfaction in the confidence placed in him by the clients of his bank over the years that it is most unlikely that he would commit larceny. With this conception, the existential paradoxes would appear to have been removed from phenomenology. Merleau-Ponty has found a phenomenological basis for probabilistic and statistical thinking about human behavior.

Merleau-Ponty's work, having abandoned the intuitionism of existentialism, appears to amply justify Binswanger's (1958b) distinction between two types of empirical scientific knowledge: *discursive inductive* knowledge, in the sense of describing, explaining, and controlling natural events; and *phenomenological empirical* knowledge, in the sense of a methodical and critical interpretation of the phenomenal contents of experience. Phenomenology, then, has yielded up to philosophical thought a domain of fresh philosophical data which can claim to have provided a basis in fact for bypassing the old dichotomies of subject and object, freedom and determinism, mind and matter, and to have restored philosophy to the status of a substantive enquiry.

THE INHERENT LIMITATIONS OF PHENOMENOLOGY

But the problem is with the dynamic nature of psychic life in itself and in its relations. To be sure, Merleau-Ponty has managed to conceptualize the significance of Sartre's phenomenological descriptions more adequately and realistically than Sartre himself did, but difficulties remain. I shall argue that these difficulties are intrinsic to *any* consistent phenomenology. Methodologically, they stem from the abandonment of *explanation* in favor of *description*. Philosophically, they stem from an overestimation of consciousness, an underestimation of causality, and a misunderstanding of the nature of freedom. These inadequacies intersect at a number of points, one of which I shall now examine: the phenomenological account of self-ignorance in dreaming.

Analysis shows that the phenomenological account of dreaming cannot be true. For if the sexual nature of dream experience cannot be recognized because of the uniform saturation of dream images with sexual affect, then how can the sexual nature of dream experience ever be known? *Ex hypothesi*, the sleeping dreamer cannot recognize it; it is the awakened dreamer who must do the recognizing. Now, according to phenomenology, the waking state is the return of the activities of personal life out of the pre-personal anonymity of the sleeper. This change brings in train a re-engagement of life with the spatiality, temporality, and objectivity of the world. Waking experience thus acts immediately as a background against which the sexual significance of the dream experience can stand out and thereby attain the clarity of an explicit consciousness. Therefore, the integration of the remembered dream experience with renewed waking experience should bring its meaning to light. Yet what actually happens runs counter to Merleau-Ponty's claim. It typically happens that people who recall their dreams and recount them, recognize their disparity with reality but remain ignorant of their meaning.

Phenomenology can adopt either of two strategies to meet this difficulty: (1) it can assign additional weight to the openness of the future to undetermined possibility and less weight to the presumptive nature of a person's self-awareness; or (2) it can invoke the principle of gestalt indeterminacy that characterizes our perceptions of intrinsically ambiguous images. The first strategy works altogether too well, for it would make it impossible to explain how phenomenology got to know that dreams have a sexual meaning and are not visions of what the future holds for the dreamer, or that dreams are not just senseless and random combinations of images as pre-psychoanalytic medical theory and common experience suppose. People have difficulty understanding what they were dreaming about. Further, we know that the wishes that cause us to dream may be sexual, but they also may be caused by non-sexual wishes. Merleau-Ponty is mistaken in this. The second strategy, by contrast, does not work well enough. Though it might account for the fact that some persons (those who do not use their waking experience as a ground against which to put their dream experience into perspective) do not become aware of the meaning of their dreams, it cannot account at all for those who do discover the strangeness of the dream experience by setting it over against waking experience but who nevertheless remain entirely unable to grasp the significance of this strangeness. Thus, a logical analysis of the phenomenological account of dreaming shows that it cannot do the work of describing the phenomena it was designed to explain.

The phenomenological hypothesis is not helped by the fact that not all dreams have a sexual significance. Dreams are caused by wishes that have been aroused by the experiences of the previous day but which were left unsatisfied either because of the lack of opportunity externally or because their satisfaction is internally prohibited by anxiety and guilt. When these unsatisfied wishes are of the first sort, they may cause dreams that Freud described as naively wish-fulfilling. The distortion in these dreams is that the unsatisfied wishes are being satisfied when in reality they are not. An example is the three-year-old child who, having been greatly stimulated by a visit to Santa Claus in a shopping mall, dreamt that she had opened her gifts and played with her toys; upon waking, she hurried downstairs to the family tree to continue her play, only to discover that her opened presents were not there, and wanted to know where they were and who had taken them. Adults have fewer naive dreams, but they occur. Scott, the British Antarctic explorer who with his companions died of hunger and exposure to cold during their return from the pole, reported in his diary that they frequently had dreams of feasting in rooms heated by roaring fires. These dreams are not primarily caused by frustrated sexual wishes—the Christmas dream was caused by the wish to play with longed for toys, while Scott and his companions wished for the means of survival—although naive dreams may be caused by sexual wishes when the wishes are not repressed. It is when sexual wishes have been repressed that the dream work uses displacements, condensations, and symbolism to gratify them in a latent dream that makes no sense to self-awareness.

But the phenomenological account cannot accommodate these facts. For if some of the images of a dream are sexual in meaning and some non-sexual, then the conditions are present within the manifest content of the dream itself to provide the ground against which the meaning of the images could be apprised, in which case the dream has lost its opacity and strangeness. This argument suggests that Merleau-Ponty has not found a way to avoid the transparency of consciousness as defined by Sartre's existentialism.

What is required to understand the phenomena is just what phenomenology rejects: memory experiences strongly charged with emotion and need for satisfaction, from which the dream images are detached and reassembled by the distorting processes of the dream work (displacement, condensation, and symbolism), and a force (repression) within the psyche that frustrates a person's efforts to decipher the dream (i.e., to become aware of the memories that have been repressed). That is to say, what is required is (1) an unconscious, in the sense of memories that cannot be voluntarily recovered and cannot become preconscious memory associations reactivated by perceptions, but can nevertheless decisively influence the formation of conscious experience and behavior; and (2) the operation of involuntary causal forces within the personality that are unconscious and which produce their effects independently of the conscious wishes of the individual modified by anxiety and without conscious ego wishes being able to intervene. Without these psychic causalities it is impossible to account for the way in which circuits of attitude, affect, and behavior that are potentially open and available to individuals remain closed off and unavailable to consciousness and reality testing. Moreover, we need these causalities to understand the way in which individuals become fixed in circuits of behavior from which they cannot detach themselves despite severe maladaptation to others and the world and despite personal suffering. But it is precisely these factors that phenomenology systematically rejects along with its rejection of inferential thinking and scientific techniques of observation (in psychoanalysis, the observation of the free association of patients) resulting in an overestimation of the epistemic value and practical efficacy of consciousness in the pursuit of the self-knowledge needed for authentic living.

The flaws uncovered in the modified phenomenological concept of the unconscious in connection with dream experience lead directly to similar difficulties in the phenomenological understanding of subjective temporality. Merleau-Ponty's descriptions of subjective temporality represent a substantial improvement on existentialism, but they are still not adequate to the phenomena. When the concept of pre-personal temporality is defined precisely, an ambiguity emerges at a crucial point. This point is not merely a matter of words, or of whether we are referring to a quiescent phase of a continuing appetite or to an actual interval of cessation in which the continuity of the individual's existence is sustained, not by the appetite itself but by the synthesis of consciousness. If the latter is true, then phenomenology has a sound footing; but if the former is the true description of the phenomena, then phenomenology remains inadequate to the task of understanding human nature as it is.

Crucial situations indicate that there is continuity of the appetites. Crucial situations, in this context, are those in which a transformation of behavior patterns sustained by an appetite is needed and sought; Merleau-Ponty (1945, pp. 438–439) would agree that such situations are crucial for understanding the nature of freedom. For example, a child may remain fixated in the pursuit of oral satisfaction as a source of inner comfort (e.g., thumb sucking) even after hunger and thirst have abandoned the sucking reflex to find satisfaction, with the arrival of teeth and solid food and liquids from a cup. The child may want to abandon sucking his/her thumb when frustrated or anxious, out of wanting to be as his parents wish him/her to be, and internally out of shame caused by not wanting to be a baby and wanting to be like an older sibling who does not suck his thumb. The underlying causality will not change if the child finds a less apparent symptom substitute (e.g., tongue sucking or nose picking). But nothing will change in reality until the child realizes within himself/herself that whatever has happened in the past—the birth of a sibling or oral libidinal trauma, or most likely both—his/her parents or substitutes do love and take pleasure, pride, and time in caring for him/her—what he/she feared had been lost forever. Problematic psychic organizations of need and the means of satisfying them have resilience and continuity that are no less inconsistent with the phenomenological freedom espoused by Merleau-Ponty than with the more radical form of freedom in Sartre's existentialism.

Similarly, an adult who is homosexual will experience the same periodicity of sexuality as heterosexual adults. But this does not mean that a person who experiences the periodicity is offered a periodic opportunity either to cooperate with the demands of his desires or to gradually deflect them into heterosexuality. The tragic histories of men and women who have actively committed themselves to finding grounds for heterosexuality "in the world" through allegiance to a church and dedication to its moral ideals, and by even attempting to incarnate heterosexuality by marrying and having children on the mistaken assumption that engagement of their lives and bodies in the personal and social forms of heterosexuality would induce in them the passion itself, present phenomena that demand causal interpretation. These histories refer us to instinctual forces at work in psychophysical structures that have their influence on conscious life and behavior, independently of our conscious preferences, causing physical genital excitement and psychic sexual desire opposed by anxiety or facilitated by pleasure and its promise. These psychophysical processes are causal, as are the psychic processes involved which shed an especially clear light on the inadequacies of the phenomenological theory of motivation. And it would be a serious error to suppose that heterosexual appetites function any differently. Hospers (1950) makes a similar point. His position is in agreement with the conclusions advanced here. Only the impact of powerful frustrations can produce a regression in sexual libido that will break down the behavior patterns it had previously stabilized and cause it to reactivate psychophysical formations that had been largely abandoned since puberty. One of the cruelties of the punishment of imprisonment of heterosexual criminals is the regression it can cause in them to the homosexuality of latency in these men and women.

Thus, despite Merleau-Ponty's modifications in existentialist categories and principles, phenomenology still subscribes to two ideas that are inconsistent with the facts. In relation to what we are by reason of our genetic endowment, our acquisitions from experience and the world in which we find ourselves, we have a power of placing motives in abeyance, and this suffices to ensure our freedom from determinism (p. 395). The corollary of this principle is that neither relations, bodily states, a neurosis, character, instincts, ego ideals, anxiety, desire, nor aversion is sufficient in itself to move a person to act in a determinate way without a free act of compliance. Consequently, Merleau-Ponty can affirm: "Since freedom does not tolerate any motive in its path, my habitual being in the world is at each moment equally precarious, and the complexes which I have allowed to develop over the years always remain equally soothing, and the free act can with no difficulty blow them sky-high." (1945, p. 441). But it is a serious distortion of the facts of individual psychic life to say that an individual allows an inferiority complex to develop by taking a pleasure in feelings of inadequacy and submission, although it is perfectly true that he does in fact receive a kind of pleasure from so acting.

Consider a specific case. A university student suffers from a pervasive feeling of futility and worthlessness. He feels that he is an incompetent impostor, and suffers profound fits of depression lasting for days at a time, during which he cannot work. Nevertheless, he applies himself with great success to his studies and achieves high standing in them, demonstrating genuine abilities and promise in his field. His abilities are acknowledged by peers and teachers, in some cases enthusiastically and encouragingly. If freedom, as phenomenology claims, can find a bulwark for itself in things, without bondage to the past, then there could hardly be a better motivational foundation on which to base a gradual self-transformation into a happy, confident person than real achievement that is actually recognized. But, in fact, the student cannot take satisfaction in his work. His achievements do not "rub off" on his sense of self, despite the fact that he is perfectly conscious of them, and try as he might, he is unable to take courage from them. Thus, we encounter in the phenomena of human life the work of causal forces producing unwanted and even frightening effects in consciousness and behavior. With or without an invitation, they act to produce a range of involuntary effects, the existence of which phenomenology cannot in principle comprehend because doing them justice requires causal explanation and not merely phenomenological description.

Alternative concepts of consciousness and freedom emerge from this examination of phenomenology. Consciousness is a quality of some (but not all) mental activities, structures, and processes. It is a category mistake to treat consciousness as substantive, and ultimately as a *causa sui*, as phenomenology is logically committed to doing. Similarly, freedom is a quality of some (but not all) human actions. Motives are those causes determining us to act of which we are aware; however, the fact that we are aware of them does not alter their causal nature. Moreover, the question of human freedom or enslavement is decided not by the presence or absence of causes motivating us to act, but by the *nature* of the causes that are at work motivating us. Freud (1901) pointed out that we do not claim that the important decisions of life are volitionally optional, citing Luther's statement at the Diet of Worms: "Here I stand; I can do no other" (pp. 253–254). However, we tend to claim arbitrary volition with respect to unimportant decisions, like the choice of ice cream for dessert, but these decisions are motivated without our knowing how, and for the most part not much caring to know. It is for these reasons that neither existentialism nor phenomenology can provide useful basic concepts about the nature of motivation for psychoanalysis. The character that we inherit and acquire by experience is our *daimon*.

REFERENCES

Binswanger, L. (1958a). The case of Ellen West: An anthropological-clinical study. In R. May, E. Angel & H.F. Ellenberger (Eds.), *Existence: A New Dimension in Psychiatry and Psychology* (pp. 237–364). New York: Basic Books.

——— (1958b). The existential analysis school of thought. In: R. May, E. Angel & H.F. Ellenberger (Eds.), *Existence: A New Dimension in Psychiatry and Psychology* (pp. 191–213). New York: Basic Books.

Frank. J.D. (1960). Breaking the thought barrier: Psychological challenges of the nuclear age. *Psychiatry: Journal for the Study of Interpersonal Processes* 23:245–266.

Freud, S. (1900). *The Interpretation of Dreams*. SE 4–5.

——— (1901). *Psychopathology of Everyday Life*. SE 6.

Hobbes, T. (1651). *Leviathan* (Ed. M. Oakshott). Oxford: Blackwell, 1946.

Hospers, J. (1950). Meaning and free will. *Philosophy and Phenomenological Research* 10:316–330.

Merleau-Ponty, M. (1945). *Phenomenology of Perception* (Trans. C. Smith). London: Routledge & Kegan Paul, 1962.

Minkowski, E. (1958). Findings in a case of schizophrenic depression. In R. May, E. Angel & H.F. Ellenberger (Eds.), *Existence: A New Dimension in Psychiatry and Psychology* (pp. 127–138). New York: Basic Books.

Plato. *The Republic* (Trans. B. Jowett). New York: Liberal Arts Press, 1948.

Sartre, J.-P. (1943). *Being and Nothingness: An Essay on Phenomenological Ontology* (Trans. H.E. Barnes). New York: Philosophical Library, 1956.

CHAPTER 16

Emotion, Anatomy, and the Synthetic A Priori*

Modern philosophy, if it has not settled any other of the chronic disputes that have troubled the history of the subject, appears to have decided once and for all the question of synthetic a priori principles. Logical analysis has demonstrated that synthetic propositions are empirical while a priori propositions are analytical and notational. Nevertheless, a broader survey of the contemporary philosophical scene reveals that the strict meaning of the expression "modern philosophy" above should be rendered as "philosophers of one of the current schools of philosophy." For contemporary European philosophers have not abandoned the notion of synthetic a priori principles altogether. They have modified Kant's (1781) "Copernican" discovery of the laws of nature in the human mind without abandoning it. There are, to be sure, two ways of viewing the situation. Either logical analysis has overlooked certain unique phenomena and thus has failed to comprehend the arguments which take their description as premises, or existentialism has persisted in the use of an inadequate logic. The purpose of this paper is to test this issue, and in so doing to explore the psychological roots of the idea of synthetic a priori principles. The means adopted is a critical study of the existentialist theory of emotion which claims to have discovered a previously

---

* Originally published in *Dialogue: Canadian Philosophical Review* 14 (1975):101–118.

unrecognized basis for synthetic a priori principles in the phenomenology of human existence.

EXISTENCE AS GROUND FOR SYNTHETIC A PRIORI PRINCIPLES

The form of the Kantian critical question and the phenomenological question concerning existence are the same; only the content is different. A comparison makes this clear:

How is knowledge of causal relations possible? (Kant, 1781)

How is an emotional experience possible? (Sartre, 1939)

Of course, the Kantian question leads to an epistemological theory, whereas the existentialist question leads to an anthropological theory, but the logical form of both questions is the same and the logical form of the answers to both is also the same. A closer comparison will clarify the point. Kant began from the realistic position that nature is known, insofar as it is known, by means of scientific knowledge. Scientific knowledge is a fact. But then philosophy must investigate the meaning of this fact by examining the grounds in the formation of experience that makes scientific knowledge possible. In this undertaking, Kant (1781) makes the assumption that the "manifold of intuition (sense experience)" is not in itself sufficiently organized for the acquisition of scientific knowledge. Accordingly, the result of this investigation is the "discovery" of the two forms of sensibility and the twelve categories of the understanding which govern the integration of our perceptions of nature into cognitions in the form of descriptive and explanatory statements about things and their interrelationships. The essence of Kant's (1781) "discovery" is the idea that the forms and the twelve categories, which are integral to the functioning of the human mind, are laws which prescribe to nature the properties that objects must have in order to be known. But since the mind therefore cannot know the nature of things apart from the conditions imposed by itself, it cannot know what things really are. Man can know nature scientifically only as a system of appearances.

Now, if we replace the term "knowledge" in the Kantian argument with "emotion," we get the existentialist argument. Emotions exist. Yet empirical investigations of the emotions have failed to grasp the meaning of this fact because they have been oriented only toward studying the origin of specific emotions and their influence on personality and behavior. Philosophy sets in with a critical reflection on how emotional experience as such is possible. This reflection, it is claimed, uncovers a hidden existential structure which is the ground in the human being for the formation of emotional experience. The categories of the understanding are to knowledge in the Kantian system what the existential structures of consciousness are to experience in phenomenology. Just as the categories are pre-experiential conditions for knowing, so the existential structures are pre-experiential conditions for human experiences. The existential structure is a kind of schematic formula for any and every emotional experience. This basic structuring of emotional experiences is therefore to be considered historically and culturally invariant and independent of the nature of the emotion at work in the experience. If there are such existential structures governing the formation of experience, then it is most important that we understand them. For psychological and psychiatric theories would have to take them into account and philosophy would have to come to terms with the restoration of the synthetic a priori in a new domain, that of philosophical anthropology. Rapaport (1966) has made these connections between philosophy and psychoanalysis.

Two further points of clarification are important. First, the meaning of "pre-experiential" as a qualifying adjective for "structure" can be analyzed into three logically interdependent components. The adjective indicates (1) that the structure in question is intrinsic to human existence, (2) that it governs the formation of experience, and (3) that it is invariant irrespective of the quality and content of experience. Consequently, if any such structures exist, they are not subject to modification by external influence or internal mutation. Therefore, they can function as grounds for *a priori* principles. Similarly, the philosophical knowledge of these structures can be intuitive and certain, whereas the empirical knowledge of the behavior of specific emotions can be known only with varying degrees of probability. This conception of philosophical knowledge has determined the organization of Sartre's (1936, 1940) major treatises on imagination, *The Imaginary*, which is divided into two parts: a phenomenological description of the existential structure in which imaginative consciousness is grounded, on behalf of which Sartre (1936) claims *certainty*, and an empirical description of the style and matter of contemporary imaginative life, which contains only probable knowledge. The organization of *The Psychology of the Imagination* (1940) established a pattern for the line of argument in *Being and Nothingness* (1943) and the *Critique of Dialectical Reason* (1960).

Second, existential structures cannot be analyzed in terms of anatomical structures. One might suppose that an answer to the question, "How are emotional experiences possible?" would best be made by reference to the chemical substances and the anatomical systems involved in the production of emotions. Existentialism claims, however, that there is a distinctly philosophical answer to this question which is not psychological or physiological, but ontological. The claim is based on the argument that the original body is the living body, from which the anatomical body is constructed by abstraction. The living body is the physical instrument of our project and the plastic medium through which the meaning of our living is symbolically expressed.

The existentialist distinction between the living and the anatomical body is supported in part by psychiatric evidence, since it is exhibited by hysterical symptoms. For example, the objective anatomical visage of a female hysteric may remain to the external observer both graceful and attractive, if somewhat strained, while to the hysteric herself it is marred by unsightly scars. There is a discrepancy between the face of the woman as observed externally and as lived expressively by the woman herself. It appears that the anatomical body does not exercise an absolute influence over the formation of the person's vital sense of his or her own body. It is this vital, corporeal experience that defines "my body" for each individual as a system of realized capacities and incapacities for living. The anatomical body exists as a system of potentialities to be lived, without being able to determine by itself the realization of its own potentialities. On the contrary, the anatomically defined potentialities may be negated and subverted as in the case of the hysteric. Consequently, the living body is an ambiguous medium, the vital significance of which is only partly determined by anatomical structures, the remainder being available for psychic determination. It is upon the base provided by this "residual domain" that the existential structures form themselves. Merleau-Ponty (1945) has conceptualized the distinction using the term "corporeal schema"; psychoanalysis has adopted a similar term, "body image," to mark a similar ambiguity in human nature.

Originally, Freud conceived of the eroticization of various organs in terms of the distribution of sexual substances to that part of the body. However, this conception was gradually replaced by the notion of body image, which is a synthetic representation of the anatomical body and may be more or less adequate to it. It is the body image that is thought to be cathected with libidinous or aggressive affect. Jacobsen (1954) has elaborated the psychoanalytic conception as follows:

By a realistic concept of the self we mean one that mirrors correctly the state and characteristics, the potentialities, and abilities, the assets and limits of our bodily and mental ego: on the one hand of our physical appearance, our anatomy and physiology: on the other hand, of our conscious and pre-conscious feelings and thoughts, wishes, impulses and attitudes, of our physical and mental activities. Whereas all these single specific features will have corresponding psychic representations, a concept of their sum total, i.e., of the self as a differentiated but organized entity, will simultaneously develop. (p. 87)

However, she also points out that "the universal persistence in women of the unconscious fantasy that their genital is a castrated organ, frequently with simultaneous denial and development of illusory fantasies, is the best example of how far the impact of infantile emotional experiences prevents us from forming even correct body images" (p. 87). Thus, the distinction in question is general for phenomenology, psychiatry, and psychoanalysis. Unfortunately, it is not possible to leave the matter at that, since they differ sharply concerning the significance of the distinction and the theoretical use to which it is put. But this is not an opportune place to take up the issues involved.

THE EXISTENTIALIST THEORY OF EMOTION

The essence of the existentialist theory of emotion can be stated in the formula: Emotion is a transformation of our perceptions of the world. The non-emotional consciousness of the world is formed of perceptions that expose the mechanical organization of the world, thus providing the ground in experience for the realization of projects through the ordering of the environment into objects to be attained and means to attain them; thus, the guiding principle of the non-emotional consciousness is rational and realistic. This situation is upset when the individual is confronted by impassable barriers to the realization of his projects, so that the realistic manipulation and exploitation of objects is frustrated. If, under such circumstances, the project is still urgently motivated, the individual undertakes a global modification of his perceptions of the world in order to achieve a fantasied realization of his project or to fabricate a motivation in things to abandon it (Jacobsen, 1954). For example, the hiker who has spent an exhausting day climbing toward a glacier, only to find the afternoon closing in with the glacier still two hours away, may undertake a modification of his perceptions of the glacier: by fixing on the muddy gravel at its base and the wreckage of the moraine, he is able to debase the glacier and justify its abandonment in the conviction that it probably was not worth exploring anyway. The introspectable psychic event, the feeling of disgust aroused by the "discovery" of the glacier's ugliness, arises on the foundation of this modulation of perception which is its pre-experiential ground. The concrete feeling of disgust can then be linked with the state of fatigue in a falsifying ego image in which the disgust is apprehended as an effect, of which the exhaustion is the cause. This ego image effectively negates the consciousness of having chosen to be disgusted by the glacier in the act whereby the perception of it was transformed. Sartre's theory entails that the formula for the origin of this specific emotion should be: "The choice to perceive the glacier as dirty motivates the emotion of disgust with it, which motivates the abandonment of the project to explore it." The choice exploits an intrinsic gestalt ambiguity in perception to fabricate a debased object to turn away from in disgust. However, the falsifying ego image, which synthesizes feelings of physical fatigue with the changed perceptions and the disgust into a causal relationship, masks the reality of the choice to abandon the project behind the impression of having been forced to give it up. The unconscious motive here, which Sartre does not acknowledge, is the need to preserve a sense of mastery over the world.

A number of important theoretical implications follow from Sartre's analysis:

1. Perception is more fundamental than emotion.
2. An alteration in the perception of objects precedes the formation of an emotional response to objects.
3. The altered perception of the object is the motive for the emotion which is pre-reflectively intended by the altered perception.
4. Objects do not cause emotions.
5. Emotions do not cause behavior.
6. A falsified ego image is formed by "normal" reflective introspection, which yields a sequence in which fatigue precedes both the altered perception and the emotion of disgust, the sequence itself being causal; that is, the altered perception and the emotion of disgust are effects of, or symptoms of, the fatigue.
7. Common sense and psychology have been hoodwinked into crediting the causal efficacy of emotions and causal explanations of behavior by the falsified ego image.
8. The real source of behavior is an uncaused choice of a way of being in the world. When the choice is to-be-disgusted, it can use an intrinsic ambivalence in perception to conjure up a perceptual field at the nucleus of which there is a disgusting object.
9. The same analysis applies to all emotional experiences, whatever their specific nature: love, hate, disappointment, hope, joy, despondency, etc.

The properties described in 1–9 are universal and necessary structural and dynamic features of human emotional experience.

In turn this summary of Sartre's analysis of the dynamics of emotion brings into focus two closely connected problems. The first problem has a logical solution, at least within Sartre's theory; the second does not, and constitutes an irremediable logical flaw in his theory. Sartre specifies three conditions which motivate the transition from a rational experience of the world to an emotional experience. One of these conditions is objective and two are subjective. These are (1) the presence of an impassable natural barrier to the realization of a project, (2) the presence of a continuing urgent need or wish to realize it, and (3) frustration. The problem then arises of giving accounts of positive emotions such as joy, pride, satisfaction, and contentment, which appear to be stimulated by situations in which just the opposite of conditions 2 and 3 obtain. If the problem cannot find a solution within Sartre's theory, then his theory is at best a universal theory of negative emotions such as chagrin, disenchantment, dejection, disappointment, and despair, but it is not a theory of emotion *per se* or a definition of the essence of emotion.

Sartre's thought is nothing if not ingenious. His existential analysis of joy provides the pattern for the generalization of the theory to include positive emotions. His definition of joy is as follows: "Joy is that magical behavior which attempts to achieve by means of incantation the possession of a desired object as an instantaneous totality" (Sartre, 1948, p. 38). Sartre is envisaging as typical the following kind of situation. Having lived a life of penny-pinching poverty for many years, an individual has made his existence tolerable by dreaming of all the things he could buy and do if only he could win a lottery. From time to time, he buys lottery tickets. One day he receives a letter informing him that he has won $200,000, and is overcome by joy. How are we to understand this joy? According to existentialism, the joy is not the effect of the sudden release of his desires from inhibiting penury. Rather, it is a response to his magically overcoming the limits of time which are imposed on his acquisition and use of his newfound wealth by a perceptual transformation of the letter into the money which it has only announced, and the money into the sum of all the pleasures he will acquire with it over a considerable period of time. There is an inevitable barrier irrevocably established by time to the simultaneous fulfillment of all one's wants. Joy then is the magical revocation of time as a barrier to the instantaneous satisfaction of wants grounded in a perceptual transformation of an object. By supplementing Sartre's theory with the idea developed by Plato in the *Symposium* that desire is not only for the possession of an object, but for the secure and continuing enjoyment of it, one can build into Sartre's theory the logical basis that is required to account for positive emotions such as joy in terms of magical perceptual behavior in response to frustration. The feeling of complacent contentment experienced after a fine dinner can now be interpreted as the emotion liberated by the intention which envisions this meal magically as the gratification offered by all future meals.

The philosophical point of Sartre's analysis is to disqualify emotions as causes of behavior by showing them to be subject to—because intended by and derivative from—a choice of being-in-the-world. Sartre's analysis does achieve this result, but at what cost? One forms the impression that Sartre's analysis of positive emotions is not only ingenious but artificial as well: that Sartre's philosophical goal—the formulation and defense of a radical concept of human freedom—has unduly influenced his argument. Is it even plausible to assume that emotions of excitement and pleasure are universally and necessarily preceded by a chosen reorientation toward objects as a result of frustration? Is it not more plausible to think that we often do manage to abandon a preoccupation with the future, leaving it to take whatever shape the combination of our past efforts and chance will give to it, and settle into the enjoyment of what the present has to offer? Is not this abandonment of our preoccupation with the future made possible precisely by our having landed ourselves in a situation in which our hopes and wishes are being fulfilled now with reasonable assurances about the future? Sartre's theory seems to betray the influence of an Atlas complex in that each present situation must have within it certain reference points that are foredoomed to bear the burden of all future situations. These reference points are magically transformed objects which then can liberate positive emotions. Thus, in Sartre's *The Emotions* (1939) there is to be found the tragic sense of the human condition that is later explicitly formulated throughout *Being and Nothingness* (1943). Even positive emotions, such as joy, pride, and contentment, and the engagement that they provide for living, exist on a more fundamental orientation of consciousness toward baleful contingency. For Sartre, the most valid symbolic expression of human gaiety is Pierrot.

However, the artificiality of Sartre's account of positive emotions leads to a more basic artificiality in the logical syntax of his theory. The theory cannot be consistently stated without adopting an artificial notation which will guarantee consistency. According to Sartre's theory, as has been noted above, three conditions characterize any situation that undergoes a conversion to the emotional: the individual encounters a barrier to the fulfillment of a project in which he is engaged, the project nevertheless retains its urgency, and there is frustration; the analysis of emotion in terms of a magical transformation of the object in perception follows. But what is it that gives such urgency to a project that it cannot be abandoned without the formation of a misperception of reality? What is it that produces the misperception? The answer must be, in a word, emotions. Is not frustration itself a negative emotional state that acts as the cause of behavior? In defining the conditions that must obtain in order for a human situation to become emotional, Sartre has introduced emotions which, at first glance at least, appear to function as causes. They not only act independently of perceptions, they also influence the formation of perceptions. Sartre's existential theory of emotions as the psychic expressions of intentions is logically based on an unacknowledged causal theory of emotions. But it is not merely that Sartre's theory depends on an unacknowledged supplementary concept of emotion; the unacknowledged concept is inconsistent with the acknowledged one.

One way to defend Sartre's thesis against the charge of inconsistency would be to adopt two denials: (1) that the urgency of a project (its being difficult to abandon) is contributed to it by an emotion; (2) that frustration is an emotion. One would have to deny two assertions that are usually thought to be true. Sartre had never made an explicit statement concerning this logical difficulty in his theory. However, the formulation of his concept of psychic energy in *The Transcendence of the Ego* (1936) indicates an implicit awareness of the problem, and perhaps the conviction that it had already been satisfactorily solved. Sartre adopts the first denial, by implication, when he postulates a pure spontaneity of consciousness. This spontaneity could account for the tenacity with which an individual holds to a project without reference to emotions. But is the pure spontaneity of consciousness anything more substantial than a logical device for avoiding the difficulty? The urgency of projects refers, surely, to such things as the discomfort of an overloaded bladder, an empty stomach, sexual desire, curiosity, craving after power or esteem, and so on. If Sartre's intention is to represent these things by the expression "pure spontaneity of consciousness," then his notation is surely misleading. And his solution is at best only verbal anyway. For if his intention is to claim that all mental energy is initially undifferentiated, conscious, and spontaneous (uncaused), then his claim is falsified by such facts as the motivational primacy of the discomfort caused by a painfully distended bladder. Such discomfort is highly differentiated and specific, and while it is either conscious or preconscious, it is certainly not uncaused. In either case, the problem remains unsolved. The first denial is untenable. The second denial is also untenable. The use of emotional words in ordinary language does not sanction the removal of frustration from the domain of emotions. In the verbal form "I feel x," x can be filled in as "disgust," "hope," "disappointment," "pleasure," and so on, and also as "frustration."

A second strategy would be to accept that emotions motivate projects and that frustration is an emotion, and then to integrate the statement of the conditions into the theory of emotion which is based on a phenomenological analysis of situations specified by the three conditions. But this strategy will not work. If frustration is an emotion, then it must be generated on the basis of the same existential structure as any other emotion, namely, the perception of the world as other than it is, or at least as other than it is thought to be by the individual. Hence, frustration must be the psychic expression of the intention to perceive the world as containing barriers to the successful realization of projects. There is, of course, a form of masochism which "makes mountains out of molehills," so that such a definition can be phenomenologically exemplified. But it is inconsistent with the definition of frustration given by Sartre when he specifies the conditions that lead to emotional experience. In that definition, frustration arises as the response to a real impasse presented by the world. Consequently, the concept of emotion is assigned two logically inconsistent uses in Sartre's theory of emotion. Sartre's existentialist theory of emotion cannot function as a unified theory of emotion per se. If existential structures provide a basis for synthetic a priori principles, Sartre's theory of emotion has failed to uncover such a structure.

This critique of Sartre's theory of emotions has wider implications for existentialism because the logic of his analysis of emotion is replicated in other existentialist theories. For example, Sartre's theory of the nature of the ego as developed in *The Transcendence of the Ego* (1936) is built upon the same basic philosophical principles as is the theory of emotion outlined in *The Emotions* (1939) and follows the theoretical guidelines established in it. It would take too long to state the details of the argument here; but the essence of the position is as follows:

1. Beginning with the Cartesian cogito, Sartre denies along with Russell that its veridical content is "I think," since all that can be affirmed is "There is thinking." The *cogito* takes its origin from a pre-egotistical consciousness which Sartre calls prereflective consciousness.

2. Pre-reflective consciousness performs a choice of being-in-the-world which takes the form of an investment of objects with instrumental

values: The alarm clock having to be obeyed, the job requiring one to be at the office by nine o'clock, etc.

3. The ego is the ideal transcendent pole of the actions and states implicit in these instrumental values. As such it is an object of consciousness which is aimed at by intentional acts. It derives its existence from them.

4. The ego cannot influence choices of being-in-the-world.

According to this analysis, Descartes's *res cogitans* is a fabricated self—the ego correlate of the "world" that emerged from Descartes's choice of being-in-the-world. As a theoretical concept in Descartes' philosophy, it is his means of ignoring his own origins in the spontaneity of pre-reflective consciousness. The two aspects of Sartre' s theory that are important for this paper are (1) his logical claim that he has uncovered the universal and necessary law of the origin and nature of the ego, and (2) his substantive claims that (a) the ego is intrinsically a passive, inert object of consciousness and that (b) the sequence of its formation follows the pattern: uncaused choice of being-in-the-world, appearance of objects with instrumental values, action and reaction, ego formation. Sartre's ego theory is formally and materially of a piece with his theory of emotion. For this reason, the difficulty located in the theory of emotion will have its counterpart in the existentialist theory of the ego.

Sartre's theory of the ego needs revisions for it cannot accommodate the real distinction that exists in nature between a developing and a developed ego. Sartre's theory has an applicability to the former that it does not have to the latter. It is a fact of the early phases of ego formation that the child envisages his own being in the persons of others, discovers his own rage in his frighteningly distorted perceptions of the features of others, and so on. Sartre's concept of the ego does have application to this stage of development. His account of the sequence of events out of which it is formed is phenomenologically correct for the early stages of ego development and it applies as well to episodes of crises which precipitate regressions to it, although it leaves out of the picture the initiatives of others such as parents and teachers and the powerfully influential identifications formed by the child with the mature egos of these persons. But from the latency period on, the ego has normally acquired a developed nature which reverses the sequence specified by the existential theory in the following way: initially there is a coexistence of the self—qualified by wants and capabilities—with objects having a variety of intrinsic properties, then reaction to perceptions of the objects stimulates action designed to satisfy wants according to the ego's needs and the capacity of the object to satisfy them. The ego, far from being the end product of the process, has a crucial influence on the wants themselves and on the reactions to objects that precede behavior. Therefore, Sartre's (1936) conclusion that the ego cannot influence choices of being does not apply to the developed ego, but only to the developing ego. Sartre has based his theory on an intuition of the dynamics of one phase of ego development. The generalization of the dynamics of that phase to all phases generated the notion of a perpetual self-recreation, which forms the radical content of Sartre's concept of freedom.

One can find a related inadequacy in Sartre's (1948) theory of emotion. A phenomenological investigation of emotional experiences discloses experiences that have a formation that is inconsistent with Sartre's theory. For example, frustration can take the form of a perceptual alteration of objects, but it need not do so. Frustration may be tolerated without any change in one's perception of reality through the acceptance of disappointment and loss. Or it may, also without change in one's perception of reality, energize renewed attempts at realistic problem-solving. Again, Sartre has taken special cases, generalized from them, and has implicitly claimed that counterexamples are covert examples of his special cases.

It will assist our understanding of existentialism if we can find a consistent error that explains the theoretical difficulties in which existentialism finds itself, especially if it will also explain how the difficulties arose. There follows such an explanatory hypothesis. Sartre's theory of emotion is a description of emotions that have been subjected to a distortion by the work of one or both of two ego defenses: projection and denial (Brenner, 1957, pp. 100–103). Projection and denial are the ego functioning so as to ward off various painful emotions, of which frustration is one. Projection functions in the following way: an object is badly wanted but cannot be had; the impact of the resulting frustration can arouse a sense of helplessness and self-devaluation; and projection defends against the formation of this depressing sense of self by transferring the devaluation to the object, which is then "seen" to be not really worth the trouble and hence can be abandoned with the "appropriate" emotion felt toward it. ("Seen" and "appropriate" are placed in scare quotes because they displace in experience objective observation and emotional response.) Denial is the process whereby frustration-arousing perceptions are warded off by the fixation of perception on the pleasant and manageable objects in our environment.

In both cases, a twofold distortion of reality is introduced: secondary disguising emotional responses are set up, and the world is seen to be other than it actually is. In cases of projection, objects are underestimated as their perceived nature is forced to undergo a debasement; in cases of denial, objects are overestimated as they are required to provide substitutive utilities and satisfactions for other desired but unyielding objects. The motive force behind the defenses is the same: the need to maintain ego narcissism and omnipotence against experiences that confirm the indifference of the world to our needs and our inability to do anything about it. Of course, these experiences are themselves generated by the desire for unattainable objects.

Sartre's theory of emotion is based on a generalization from phenomenological descriptions of projective and denial experiences made from inside these experiences. This hypothesis explains the inconsistent concepts of emotion in the statement of Sartre's theory. The theory is based on a description of the formation of the secondary emotions set in motion by projection and denial. From the interior of the experiences, it *does* appear that the emotions originate in "perceiving the world differently"; however, in order to specify the conditions under which "perceiving the world differently" occurs, Sartre had to employ a concept of emotion that was inconsistent with his existential definition. The statements of the three conditions in Sartre's theory refer to the wants and emotions that precipitate the projective and denial experiences themselves. Hence, Sartre's theory of emotion is based on an interior description of the precipitated experience. His phenomenology of emotional experience is thus rooted in a distorted ego image which attributes to perception the power to reconstruct and reassemble the world. Hence, it is to be expected that it is both partial and inconsistent.

The hypothesis that Sartre's theory of emotion was derived from interior descriptions of projective and denial experiences can be extended to his theory of the ego. This theory is a consistent account of what the ego would appear to be from the interior of experiences organized by projection and denial. The self appears on things as their instrumental values. If an urgent wish to catch a bus is subjected to projection, the conscious sense of the experience is rendered better by the expression "The bus having to be caught" than "I want desperately to catch the bus, but I may not make it." The ego has not as yet made its appearance in the former structuring of the experience, or to put it differently, it makes its appearance before consciousness as the goal of consciousness's activity. Therefore, the formation of the experience can appear to precede the formation of the ego and provide the phenomenological data required by the theory that the ego is a constantly renewed creation. In the initial stages of every projective experience, the ego appears to be absent. Similarly, the ego can appear as

345

the ideal unity of an identify aimed at, but never achieved. Finally, the ego can appear to be just as Sartre (1936) described it to be "neither formally nor materially *in* consciousness" but "outside, *in the world*... being of the world, like the ego of another" (p. 31).

Our hypothesis is confirmed by Sartre's statement of one of his most important philosophical conclusions: each person is responsible for his own being. The philosophical point of the existentialist theories of emotion and the ego is to provide a systematic refutation of any claims of the type, "I couldn't help myself: I was carried away by my feelings," or "I ran away because I am a cowardly person." Existentialism requires the classification of all statements such as "I was roused to anger by his outrageous behavior" as evasive rationalizing substitutes for the authentic or true avowals, "I was roused to anger because I chose to find his behavior outrageous." Thus, the quality of "outrageousness" is referred back to the subject. In general, all instrumental values in things and situations such as their being demanding, urgent, alluring, unpleasant, provocative, enraging, etc., are treated as so many inscriptions of spontaneous subjectivity upon things.

Now, the psychological utility of projection and denial is, precisely, the reduction of anxiety that they bring about, as a result of their ability to create the inner illusion that something in the world is bad while the self is good. This characteristic of experiences transformed by projection is particularly well illustrated in the social phenomenon of racial prejudice. As a result of projection, the racist who suffers from an unconscious fixation of sexual interest upon incestuous objects can "find" in Black men a dangerous desire to seduce the pure women of the racist's kith and kin. He can then experience the secondary emotion of righteous indignation against the "dangerously promiscuous Black" who must be kept in his place in order to be made chaste. Sartre's claim that existentialism has achieved a clarifying intuition of these situations when it insists upon relocating the motive for the reaction of righteous indignation in the subject who chooses to perceive Black persons as dangerous is certainly justified. The intuition of self that reveals that it has contrived the racist response is clearly a correction of the self-perception that a committed racist would have.

However, it is also just at this point that Sartre's thought fails, for three principal reasons. (1) Sartre could not find an orientation point from which he could gain an objective perspective on projective and denial experiences themselves; iIndeed, existential epistemology, unfortunately, systematically denies the validity of such a perspective. (2) He could not get beyond the idea that choosing is a necessary as well as a sufficient condition of responsibility. (3) He could not get beyond the Cartesian *cogito*, despite his reformulation of it, which identifies consciousness with the being of mental activities and contents. Consequently, Sartre could not make the discovery that projection and denial are not the essence of emotion and that his definition of emotion in terms of them is not a synthetic a priori truth in the sense of a universal and necessary law for the formation of any emotional experience.

Nevertheless, existentialism, when interpreted in terms of projection and denial defenses, paves the way for the restoration of a modified notion of the synthetic a priori. A statement of this modified notion will conclude this study. Kant found the essence of the synthetic a priori to be constituted by three factors: (1) a mental organization that functions as a law for the organization of experience, (2) the subordination of perceptions of things to the requirements of this law, and (3) the reduction of objects so subordinated to the status of appearances. These three factors describe in the most precise way the phenomenology of projective and denial experiences.

It plays out in detail, as follows, for racial prejudice as a form of social experience. Factor 1 becomes, in this specific context, the unconscious sexual interest in incestuous objects that are taboo. These sexual feelings cannot be tolerated, and so they are transferred by projection onto a race which has been subjected to a pre-established social debasement, which then facilitates the projection. Factor 2 is that Black people are perceived as sexually dangerous, threatening objects. Factor 3 is that Black people, so perceived, are reduced to mere appearances, beyond which their human reality lies obscure. In this way an experiential structure is set up in which socially and subjectively preferred beliefs appear to be confirmed by perceptions, and what is most important, the subjects involved (racists) cannot recognize that the objects of their perception (Black people) do not confirm their expectations. "What Black people really are," and "the appearance they must necessarily have" are subject to a "transcendental derivation." This derivation is automatically performed by all racists. Consequently, synthetic a priori organizations of experience do occur. They are not, however, what Kant assumed them to be (i.e., necessary conditions of knowledge), nor what Sartre assumed them to be (i.e., existential structures of consciousness); they are either psychological systems of defense against aggressive and libidinal impulses, or the expression of the anatomical organization of the human body and its physical relations with its environment.

Nevertheless, such synthetic a priori organizations of experience, once formed, have a durability and resistance to modification that gives them the appearance of eternal truths for those who are subject to them. Thus, it is important to differentiate carefully between the internal and external perspectives on what may be called synthetic a priori experiential complexes. The psychological organization that governs the formation of the racist's beliefs, perceptions, and actions has from the inside all the appearance of an eternal law of nature that can all too easily be referred to a god who established it and created man according to it. It is only by means of an external viewpoint that its contingency becomes apparent to the observer who as a result is able (1) to establish an independent basis for comparing the perceptions of objects influenced and uninfluenced by an a priori experiential complex and (2) to bring the conditions that cause the formation of the complex under observation.

This point is illustrated by the history of Kant's idea that the axioms of Euclidean geometry are synthetic a priori principles that *must* describe the properties of physical space. With the invention of non-Euclidean geometries and relativity physics, a basis was provided for discovering that the inevitably Euclidean appearance of physical space in human perceptions derives from the contingent facts of the mechanics of the human sensory apparatus. It is true that Euclidean geometry will always be an accurate description of space insofar as we are able to experience it directly; however, Euclidean geometry does not define, as Kant believed it did, the necessary conditions of our knowledge of space, since physicists have been able to design experiments that provide special indirect observations showing that physical space is non-Euclidean.

There are, perhaps, three types of synthetic a priori experiential complexes: of the individual, of the group, and of the species. Sartre's philosophical theories of emotion and the ego are examples of the individual type. In order to demonstrate this point, the argument of this paper can be simplified into the following categorical syllogism: all philosophical theories based on the phenomenology of ego defenses are based on synthetic a priori experiential complexes; Sartre's theories of emotion and the ego are philosophical theories based on the phenomenology of ego defenses, and are therefore based on synthetic a priori experiential complexes. On the same argument, racism is an example of a synthetic apriority of the group, just as the invariably Euclidean nature of our lived experience of space is an example of an experiential a priori of the species.

The concept of a synthetic a priori experiential complex provides the basis for a new understanding of the logical nature of propositions. Logical positivism has been too simple-minded in its rejection of the synthetic a priori. The classification into analytic and synthetic is intrinsically correct for all propositions except those that have their function and reference within experiential complexes as the expression of the law of their formation. Such propositions do not express objective truths; they do, however, formulate crucial subjective certitudes upon which individuals and groups of individuals have based their dignity and their folly.

REFERENCES

Brenner, C. (1957). *An Elementary Textbook of Psychoanalysis.* New York: International Universities Press.

Jacobsen, E. (1954). The self and the object world—vicissitudes of their infantile cathexes and their influence on ideational and affective development. *Psychoanalytic Study of the Child* 9:75–127.

Kant I. (1781). *Critique of Pure Reason* (Trans. N.K. Smith). London: Macmillan, 1952.

Merleau-Ponty, M. (1945). *Phenomenology of Perception* (Trans. C. Smith). London: Routledge & Kegan Paul, 1962.

Rapaport, D. (1966). Dynamic psychology and Kantian epistemology. In M.M. Gill (Ed.) *The Collected Papers of David Rapaport* (pp. 289–298). New York: Basic Books, 1967.

Sartre, J.-P. (1936). *The Transcendence of the Ego* (Trans. F. Williams & R. Kirkpatrick). New York: Farrar, Straus & Giroux,1957.

—— (1939). *The Emotions: Outline of a Theory* (Trans. B. Frechtman). New York: Philosophical Library, 1948.

—— (1940). *The Psychology of Imagination* (Trans. H.E. Barnes). New York: Philosophical Library, 1948.

—— (1943). *Being and Nothingness: An Essay on Phenomenological Ontology* (Trans. H.E. Barnes). New York: Philosophical Library, 1956.

—— (1960). *Critique of Dialectical Reason* (Trans. A. Sheridan-Smith). London: Verso, 2004.

CHAPTER 17

Instincts and Hostile Affects*

Considering the question of the truth or falsity of an alternative hypothesis enables one to examine the relevant facts afresh and from a different angle. Freud (1915, 1920, 1933) always treated his instinct theory with skepticism, as the following statement indicates: "The theory of the instincts is, so to say, our mythology. Instincts are mythical entities, magnificent in their indefiniteness. In our work we cannot for a moment disregard them, yet we are never sure that we are seeing them clearly" (1933, p. 95). It is in the same spirit that this alternative to Freud's theory is advanced.

Although Freudians such as Rosenberg (1991) and Eissler (1971) have defended and used Freud's death instinct theory, many others, including A. Freud (1949, 1972) and Denis (2002), consider the theory to be more metaphysical than metapsychological, despite Freud's (1920) effort to ground it clinically and biologically. Philosophical views have also been divided on the nature of aggression. The argument of this paper is that, although there is an aggressive instinct which is not simply a property of libido as Freud's early theory posited, contrary to his death instinct theory, aggression is considered to be neither primarily masochistic nor primarily destructive because, unlike libido which works spontaneously, it is a reactive instinct.

---

* Originally published in *The International Journal of Psychoanalysis* 59 (1978):149–156.

Therefore, the question posed by this paper is whether or not the aggressive instinct acts in the same way as the sexual instinct. I propose to consider this question by advancing the hypothesis that, whereas the sexual instinct is a spontaneous demand instinct, the aggressive instinct is a reflex instinct. Stated differently, the aggressive instinct is a readiness to respond with a demand for action upon the psychic apparatus, but the occurrence of a demand must be released by a stimulus that is extrinsic to the instinct itself, such as anxiety, physical pain, or danger, either real or imagined. If so, the aggressive instinct does not on its own and by itself initiate a "demand for work" within the psychic apparatus.

This hypothesis also places the psychic role of affects in a somewhat different light. Anxiety not only activates defenses, but may also release aggression. Frustration of libidinal and egoistical needs also activates aggression. Affects such as rage, hatred, resentment—indeed, the whole range of hostile affects which are the psychic manifestations of aggression—develop under specific conditions to be considered later. Other affects, such as disappointment, sadness, despair, chagrin, ruefulness, and resignation, appear to partially discharge the excitation of an instinctual demand in the absence of gratification. These affects do not express the instinctual want, but rather the barrier to its gratification (Freud, [1895]1950; Sartre, 1939; Hanly, 1966, 1975). Accordingly, there are three vantage points from which the psychodynamics of affects can be studied: as expressions of instinct, as reactions to barriers to gratification, and as activators of instincts. My emphasis will be on the last, but all three need to be kept in mind.

The hypothesis of a reactive-aggressive instinct differs from Freud's final instinct theory in two fundamental respects. Freud (1920, 1930, 1933) considered that the first phase of the development of the aggressive instinct is one of primary destructiveness (Bibring, 1941)—a condition which is analogous to the primary narcissism of the libidinal instinct. This description can be deduced from a theoretical premise, the spontaneity of the aggressive instinct, and the fact that infant consciousness is unable to differentiate self and object, and consequently lives in a solipsistic world. However, once the intrinsic masochism of aggression is questioned, a different understanding of the initial psychological situation results. Although the rage reactions of the neonate are ambiguous with respect to their object, this state of affairs should persist only until subject–object differentiation has been achieved. Primary destructiveness would not constitute an intrinsic aim of the aggressive instinct; it would only be an accident of the structural inability of the infant psyche to differentiate itself from others during the phase of primary narcissism. Subsequently, on the hypothesis proposed, since the aggressive instinct would be assigned its object by the nature of the stimulus that released it, it could sustain an introverted death wish only if some pathological process involving regression to narcissistic organizations selected the ego as its target as a means of defying object dependency. On this hypothesis, masochism would always involve some recurrence of a disturbance in subject-object differentiation. Psychoanalysis is already familiar with various mechanisms that bring about this condition, for example, identification with the disappointing object in melancholia (Freud, 1917), identification with the aggressor (A. Freud, 1936). These processes can be seen as the attempt of the ego to preserve the illusion of its strength and worth, or, alternatively and equivalently, as the demand of the pleasure principle for tension reduction under grossly provocative circumstances which have precipitated a libidinal regression to narcissism (Hanly & Masson, 1976). Thus, on this hypothesis, masochistic phenomena would be seen as owing their origin initially to the absence of psychic organization in the infant and, subsequently, to libidinal disturbances of identity. Thus, while the aggressive instinct can sustain destructive impulses towards the self, it can more easily sustain them towards other objects. Masochism is contrary to nature but sometimes necessary for psychic existence, although such an

353

adjustment is intrinsically precarious; sadism is according to nature, but is contrary to the conditions for existence (Hobbes, 1651).

One further implication requires elaboration. If the aggressive instinct has an intrinsically masochistic aim, it can only receive an extroverted orientation as a consequence of fusion with the libidinal instinct. During the phase of primary narcissism this orientation cannot be accomplished for the reasons already stated. This circumstance, particularly on the assumption of a spontaneous action of the instinct, would place the infant organism in a peculiarly precarious situation which would appear to be inconsistent with normal development. This implication is avoided by the assumption of a fusion with the narcissistically organized libidinal instinct. In *Three Essays on the Theory of Sexuality* (Freud, 1905), in a footnote added in 1924 (p. 158), Freud refers to an *erotogenic* primary masochism, which is presumably brought about by such a fusion. However, the question remains as to how effective this fusion can be in binding a spontaneously acting destructive instinct during early infancy, or if it is effective, how it comes about that in subsequent stages of development, narcissism does not protect against psychopathology but rather contributes to it (Hanly & Masson, 1976).

The second respect in which this hypothesis differs from the classical theory is its rejection of the spontaneity of the aggressive instinct. The classical theory assumes (1) that the aggressive instinct has a periodicity of its own, (2) that it produces an accumulation of excitation within the psychic apparatus even without provocation, and (3) that it demands periodic gratification through release in some appropriate tension-reducing action. The present hypothesis differs from Freud's theory by postulating the necessity of a provoking stimulus to call the instinct into play. It also implies a dual function for at least certain affects. An affect need not only be the discharge of an instinct, but may also act as the trigger of an instinctive reaction, just as it may act as the trigger for a defense (Brenner, 1974, 1975). This concept brings the aggressive instinct under the rule of the pleasure principle and into connection with the libidinal instinct. Obstacles which inhibit the discharge function of an affect will produce pain (the affect of frustration), which in turn will release an aggressive impulse aimed at removing the obstacles, whether real or imaginary.

It must be admitted that from a theoretical point of view there is much that counts against this hypothesis. Psychoanalysis is deprived of a convenient explanation of masochism, of the unpleasure principle of repression, of the compulsion to repeat, and of the necessity of death. Schur (1966, pp. 146–149) established the equation of the unpleasure principle (now separated from the pleasure principle) with the constancy principle and the death instinct in Freud's late theoretical work. Freud (1924) stated: "The *Nirvana* principle [the constancy principle] expresses the trend of the death instinct; the *pleasure* principle represents the demands of the libido" (p. 160). It is the death instinct that is set in motion to institute repression when a reaction of anxiety is made to an internal or external danger. The consequence of repression is a "mortification" of a segment of memory. The compulsion to repeat a painful experience, which Freud took to be an abrogation of the pleasure principle, could be explained by the "epicyclical" nature of the action of the death instinct, that is, its tendency to return by a circuitous route to an earlier state of affairs. Finally, there is the cycle of conception, life, and death, with its origin out of the inorganic and its return to the inorganic. Freud believed that the death instinct enabled psychoanalytic theory to establish further points of contact with biology. When a hypothesis offers such impressive advantages, is it not foolhardy to call it in question?

Freud's death instinct and the compulsion to repeat have already been subjected to criticism. Schur (1960, 1966, 1972) has pointed to inadequacies in the empirical evidence (post-traumatic anxiety dreams, certain games of children, the fate neurosis, and the transference neurosis) that Freud relied upon to substantiate a death instinct. Schur (1972) is less convincing when he accuses Freud of circularity of reasoning in his arguments on behalf of the death instinct: "The constancy-Nirvana-pleasure and repetition-compulsion principles are... taken as proof of the death-instinct concept, which in turn is used as an explanation for these same principles—a classical example of circular reasoning" (p. 323; cf. p. 325). But Freud's reasoning is not an instance of the material fallacy of *petitio principii*, of which circular reasoning is one type. Freud's reasoning is "circular" only in the sense in which all causal reasoning in science is circular. A causal law is introduced to explain a group of phenomena, and the phenomena thus explained serve as evidence for the truth of the causal law. Perhaps Schur overlooked this fact because of his wish to prepare the ground for a psychological explanation of the genesis of Freud's final instinct theory.

Whatever one may think of Schur's psychological explanation of Freud's commitment to his theory of aggression as a death instinct or of Schur's critique of that theory—I find both to be plausible—Schur stops short of the hypothesis I am considering here. The same can be said of others who have criticized the hypothesis of a compulsion to repeat which abrogates the pleasure principle and thus implies the operation of a death instinct (Symons, 1927; Fenichel, 1935; Wälder, 1936; Kubie, 1939, 1941; Bibring, 1943; Gifford, 1964; Loewald, 1971). The predominant concept of the aggressive instinct in current psychoanalytic theory combines skepticism about its inherently masochistic organization with acceptance of its spontaneity (Brenner, 1973). I propose to question its spontaneity as well.

There are a number of general reasons for doubting the spontaneity of aggression. Equivalents of the sexual instinct's erogenous zones have not been found for the aggressive instinct; no equivalents of the biochemistry of the hormones have been found for an aggressive instinct; and among healthy people there is no aggressive equivalent for the characteristic periodicity of the sexual instinct. Yet if there were a spontaneous aggressive instinct, one would expect to find clear evidence of these anatomical, biochemical, and life phenomena. If the aggressive instinct is independent and spontaneous in its action, it should produce periodic demands for pleasure through discharge by means of appropriate action. It would appear that divine Thanatos is a *deus absconditus*.

But this statement cannot be altogether true either. Philosophers from Empedocles (see Kirk & Raven, 1930, pp. 320–361) and Plato (*Republic*) to Hobbes (1651) and recently Sartre (1943) have conceived of destructive aggression as a fundamental and spontaneous force in human nature. Lorenz (1955, 1963) has inferred from his ethological investigations the existence of a surplus of aggressive energy. However, there is a second tradition, represented by Aristotle (*Politics*), Rousseau in his idea of a noble savage, and Marx in his utopianism which conceives of aggression as a reaction to frustration and privation. If we assume that there is some measure of truth in both of these apparently contradictory conceptions of the nature of aggression, the question arises as to whether or not psychoanalytic instinct theory can be stated in such a way as to uncover these partial truths and integrate them into a unified and consistent conception. Stated differently, if the aggressive instinct acts reactively rather than spontaneously, how can we account for the manifold manifestations of a destructiveness that has all the appearance of an unprovoked will to overpower, to rob, to enslave, and if need be, to destroy? How can a biologically endowed reflex instinct come to act in the manner of a spontaneous demand instinct? It can, if as a consequence of a psychological development it comes to be connected with a motivational system that triggers it into action, in the absence of a stimulus appropriate to the ego (namely, reality) but in the presence of one appropriate to the id (fantasy). In this case, the aggression will appear to be gratuitous (spontaneously motivated), but will in fact be released by an intrapsychically predetermined preparation for arousal by stimuli of a particular kind.

Let us now turn from these abstract considerations to some clinical observations. A male patient in his mid-twenties, manifested the following sadomasochistic symptom. While "taking care to walk across the street in a safe and considerate manner," he would "accidentally" locate himself so that a passing car would splash him with water outside my office. His timing on these occasions was faultless. He would then appear, dripping wet and in a state of rage at the driver who had thus mistreated him and who did not even have the decency to stop and offer to pay for the cleaning bill. In such instances, one certainly has the impression of an aggressive impulse in search of an opportunity for release. Other similar instances of the patient's behavior and his precarious obsessional defenses only served to confirm the impression of a spontaneously acting aggression inadequately mitigated by suitable neutralizing sublimations.

However, one wants to know about the genetic origin of this formation, which one might call, employing a term from the literary criticism of T.S. Eliot (1919), the affect of rage in search of an "objective correlative," that is, an object or circumstance which could serve as a sufficient reason for its existence. It turned out that the rage was by no means the product of a "surplus of aggression"; it was a displacement from another situation that had left him impotent, helpless, and enraged. The patient had formed the fantasy that the firm for which he worked was on the verge of disaster as a consequence of mismanagement by his superior. Acting on this fantasy, he had written to the owner accusing his superior of incompetence, outlining a plan of his own to save the company and offering his services to implement it; his pains were rewarded with dismissal. His rage was precipitated by the frustration of his wish to take over the firm; it also acted as an affective defense against (denial of) his humiliation.

Is not this evidence precisely of a spontaneous aggressive instinct? Although it appears to be, I think that it is not. The patient's dismissal from work was another in a series of similar experiences in his life; in every instance, his hopes and ambitions were dealt shattering blows, but no amount of suffering was sufficient to discourage him from a repetition later on. In the light of the two episodes already presented, it will surprise no one that these and other failures in the patient's life traced themselves back in his analysis to his Oedipus complex. It is the implication of this perfectly ordinary clinical finding that is of interest.

The patient suffered from a fate neurosis and its characteristic compulsion to repeat. Consequently, the case falls into a major class of evidence that has been cited on behalf of the death instinct, or at least in favor of a spontaneous aggressive instinct. If the aggressive instinct acts spontaneously, we can assume that it must activate the negative ambivalent affects towards the father in the Oedipus complex. A further implication is that these negative affects may occur even in the absence of incest wishes toward the mother. For if the instinct acts spontaneously and independently, any relationship could become the site of hostile feelings. A relationship as fundamental as the relation to the father would inevitably be selected as the site for the liberation of such affects. Since sons do regularly experience hostile feelings toward their fathers, the hypothesis would appear to be confirmed. Freud's death instinct theory does not have this implication, since if aggression is directed toward an object other than the self, it is as a result of a fusion with libido. Consequently, an aggressive impulse must always be part of a motivational structure that also involves a libidinal impulse.

However, there is an alternative. If the aggressive instinct is reactive rather than spontaneous, we can assume that it will be activated when there is a perceived or fantasied threat to a strongly charged wish. The aggressive instinct, *ex hypothesi*, will not on its own produce wishes that could act as triggers, since if it did, it would in effect be acting spontaneously. The wishes in question would have to be libidinal ones. Therefore, the alternative theory is as follows: hostile affects toward the father are caused by his being an obstacle to a libidinal wish for the mother. The little boy has a *reason* for hating his father, but he is *caused* to love his mother. This hypothesis has two advantages. It makes possible a clear formulation of the dynamic and structural relationships between these two instincts, one aspect of which can be stated as follows: the action of the aggressive instinct is released by the frustration of a libidinal want. It also provides an explanation of the choice of aggressive behavior as to mode, aim, and object, for it would be determined by the libidinal organization specific to the stage of development of the libidinal wish that is being frustrated.

But before being carried away by the prospect of theoretical gains, let us remind ourselves that theories are necessary, but they do not determine what there is and how it works. They have to be tested against facts. The fate neurosis under consideration does appear to be an instance of straightforward aggression connected with career ambitions as a consequence of displacement from the infantile aggression against the father. However, the patient did not have libidinal fantasies about the wife of his superior whom he wanted to replace; accordingly, it would seem that my hypothesis must be rejected. Since the evidence of the case indicates the formation of aggressive wishes independently of sexual ones, it appears to support the hypothesis of an independent spontaneous instinct.

However, the facts are not so simple. Although the libidinal component of the Oedipus complex was not integrated into these symptomatic manifestations, this was because there had occurred a separation of the conscious ideational and behavioral derivatives of the incest wish from the derivatives of the parricidal wish. The patient did not develop fantasies about his superior's wife, although he had displaced his oedipal aggression onto his person, because he had established a displacement elsewhere for the incest wish. The essence of this defensive structure was contained in a fantasy that had acquired the status of a personal myth (Kris, 1956; Hanly, 1970, 1977). The patient had identified with an enemy hero of World War I, a war ace who had kept his beloved, unspoiled by sex, in a convent during the war. One is reminded of the hallucinatory appearance to Achilles of Hera, mother of the gods, and her fateful promise that if he abandoned his determination to kill Agamemnon she would vouchsafe to him his choice of an immortality of fame or a fulfilled life. But my patient's mother did not stand on the side of either deferred narcissistic gratification or maturity (Achilles' two choices), but rather on the side of a promised gratification if the son would prove himself in battle for her. The patient's personal myth expressed the unconscious idea that the patient had been promised special libidinal rewards once he had vanquished the father. A derivative of the fantasy of the waiting cloistered virgin was a fantasy of being an immensely rich and powerful head of a community and of being loved by all the women, from among whom he could choose at will. These fantasies were concurrently at work in attachments to women, where they received partial gratification. It was for this reason that they did not make their appearance in the patient's work situation. Only after the abandonment of these relationships, and after the establishment of a transference neurosis was the patient able to make progress towards the resolution of his aggressive conflicts.

Consequently, we may infer that it was the continued action of an arrested libido that caused two things. First, the fantasies of triumph which were only the representations in the ego of an unconscious, libidinally sponsored aggressive demand which subverted the patient's efforts to advance his career. It was this unconscious demand which made it appear to his ego that he was called upon to take over from his superior—that the situation and his destiny demanded it. Second, it was the libidinal demand and the expectation of at last being able to fulfill it that readied him for an act of aggression against his superior. One of the striking features of the patient's reaction to his dismissal was his sense of its injustice—he felt that something that had been promised to him had been denied.

The patient's reaction of rage had more than one significance. He had suffered a severe narcissistic blow because unconsciously he had disappointed the expectations of his ego ideal. The rage aroused by his dismissal was denied in a counterphobic manner by his rage at inconsiderate drivers; it also denied the castration anxiety aroused by his defeat. Accordingly, he was prepared to humiliate himself by means of the parapraxes (allowing himself to be splashed with muddy water) in order to create a situation in which he could appeal for justice and flaunt his masculine willingness to secure his just deserts by recourse to physical violence. This parapraxis was only one of a series of transference symptoms which sought to declare to the analyst: "Now you must see how badly I am being treated. If you do not, you can expect to bear the brunt of my anger." The entire sequence of my patient's hostile, aggressive affects was stimulated by the continued action of a fixated libidinal wish.

If this conclusion is correct, it follows that sexuality, because of its spontaneity, has a preeminent and preemptive role in psychic life. Nevertheless, aggressive impulses, once released, do not take second place to libidinal ones. The aggression against the father in the positive Oedipus complex is motivated by a libidinal wish for the mother and by a wish to get rid of the father, to triumph over him and to take his place with the mother. From an economic point of view, it obviously need not be assumed that the aggressive instinct is energized by libido, but only that aggression is released by it under conditions of frustration or threat. Also, aggression may be released by factors other than threats to libidinal wants, if we assume the existence of, for example, an independent ego instinct for survival. If, on the other hand, the instinct for self-preservation is a derivative of secondary narcissism, the simple formula need not be complicated, at least not on that account.

However, the problem that concerns us here is the definition of the conditions under which aggression acts in the fashion of a spontaneous instinct. The sequence of development envisaged by this hypothesis is the following: the spontaneous occurrence of the incest wish causes the father to be perceived as an obstacle to its satisfaction; this perception arouses envy and frustration; these affects release aggression towards the father and another group of affects made up of angry hostility and hatred set in, bringing about the characteristic painful ambivalence of feeling; the aggression soon finds for itself suitable fantasies to represent what it would be like to realize its demands; these fantasies then come into conflict with the child's perception of his father's superior strength, yielding the realization that his father can do to him what he would see done to his father; the component of phallic envy (the wish to rob the father of his superior phallic power) joins the results of the boy's sexual researches to release castration anxiety; the castration anxiety now brings about the repression of the total constellation of aggression against the father and the libidinal wishes which stimulated its release. Since repression does not in itself nullify or neutralize the libidinal wishes, insofar as they remain active they continue to excite the release of aggression, which, through displacement and acting out, or through sublimation and neutralization, continues to make its contribution to psychopathology or maturation.

In this description I have sought to do two things both of which are consistent with the psychoanalytic understanding of the Oedipus complex. I have emphasized the role of affects acting as triggers for the release of aggression, just as the affects of depression and anxiety set ego defenses in motion (Brenner, 1974, 1975). I have attempted to show that it is possible to conceive of the aggressive instinct as a reactive instinct, insofar as all the phenomena of the Oedipus complex and its subsequent history in development can be accounted for on the basis of this hypothesis.

We are now in a position to explain the *appearance* of spontaneity in the aggressive instinct. Spontaneous libidinal developments create conditions for the mobilization of a powerful aggressive impulse (the patricidal wish). The libidinal demand and the aggressive demand it motivates must together undergo repression. Insofar as the repression results in a fixation of a sum of libido at the phallic stage, there will continue to be a proportional excitation of the aggressive instinct within the id. Consequently, the ego will have imposed upon it the task of gratifying or defending against hostile affects, which, as a consequence of the repression, are no longer directed towards their original object. The introspective awareness of this state of affairs, as well as the observation of its behavioral manifestations, suggests the activity of a spontaneous instinct. This impression is not altogether wrong; for according to this argument, in the aftermath of the repression of the Oedipus complex the aggressive instinct has acquired a *psychological* spontaneity because of the connection established between repressed libido and aggression. The sexual instinct is *biologically* spontaneous; the aggressive instinct is psychologically spontaneous. The impulses to rival, rob, and destroy, the need to hate, and the more diffuse "irritable" states and hostile affects are released into the ego in the absence of suitable, provoking objective correlatives because of the continued action of infantile sexual wants that are deprived of gratification by reality or are prohibited by the superego.

We can now see how the various philosophical concepts of aggression each contained a partial truth. Plato, Hobbes, Sartre, and Lorenz correctly perceived the psychological formation that is established after the formation of the Oedipus complex, but their concept of aggression is unnecessarily pessimistic and fails to grasp the psychogenesis of spontaneous aggression. Aristotle, Rousseau, and Marx, who conceived of aggression as a reaction to frustration, privation, and anxiety, are so far correct, but they erroneously draw the unjustifiably utopian conclusion that if all environmental frustration were removed, individuals would be pacific, cooperative, and sociable. Their understanding of aggression is correct so far as it goes, but it fails to take into account the developmental vicissitudes of sexuality and its impact on aggressiveness. Libidinal frustration is inevitable and necessary, and no amount of improvement in social justice will reduce that fateful necessity out of which civilized, yet conflicted, human personality is born. Consequently, Freud's (1930) criticism of Marxist utopianism is equally deducible from our hypothesis as from the premise of a death instinct. With the repression and fixation of the maternal complex there is established a permanent endogenous source of arousal for the aggressive instinct, which then impels the psychic apparatus to provide its characteristic gratification, subject to the displacements, sublimations, and other defenses that the ego is able to institute. In the adult, the instinct of aggression is pacified to the extent that the sexual instinct has matured, while it continues to be stimulated into activity by the frustration of and threats (imagined as well as real) to other ego needs (e.g., threats to survival, food, and safety).

It should be admitted that the argument of this paper has at least one glaring deficiency. It does not consider the organization of aggression during the prephallic phases, and merely assumes that it follows the dictates of the libidinal and ego organizations of these periods and is activated by frustrations to them. Whether or not this is so is a question that requires a factual answer from clinical evidence. However, the hypothesis advanced has several merits. Theoretically, it re-establishes the primacy of pleasure/unpleasure as the regulatory principle of the id. It does not require the introduction of a compulsion to repeat as an independent regulatory principle. It reasserts the nuclear role of the Oedipus complex and its derivatives within the id (Calef, 1969). Although it does not imply a monistic instinct theory, it does assign to the libidinal instinct a motivating and directing role in the activation of aggression. The object-relatedness of aggression no longer requires a primary fusion of libido with aggression; consequently, masochism and sadism can be conceived of as unequivocally pathological forms of aggression. Therapeutically, the hypothesis implies that the successful treatment of neurotic aggression depends upon the resolution of the libidinal drives of the Oedipus complex. Philosophically, this hypothesis explains the origin of the antithetical views found in the history of ideas concerning the nature of aggression, and provides a theoretical basis for integrating the partial insights of the philosophers into a unified theory. Nevertheless, it must be acknowledged that this hypothesis is not well-established and must be treated with skepticism. All this paper attempts to do is to explain some of its implications and consider a single instance of supporting clinical evidence. Of course, one clinical example cannot establish a general hypothesis. However, on behalf of the example, two things may be legitimately claimed: first, it is not an untypical clinical case; second, it is an example of a fate neurosis, which has been taken to be decisive evidence in support of a death instinct. Moreover, the hypothesis merely spells out a relationship between the instincts of sexuality and aggression that is consistent with Freud's earlier instinct theory, except that it assumes that there is an instinct of aggression that is not merely a potentiality of libido. Psychoanalysis is familiar with the idea that it is sometimes necessary to return to an earlier state of affairs in order to make further progress.

REFERENCES

Aristotle. *Politics.* In R. McKeon (Ed.), *Introduction to Aristotle* (pp. 549–617). New York: Random House, 1947.

Bibring, E. (1941). The development and problems of the theory of the instincts. *International Journal of Psychoanalysis* 22:102–131.

——— (1943). The conception of the repetition compulsion. *Psychoanalytic Quarterly* 12:486–519.

Brenner, C. (1973). *An Elementary Textbook of Psychoanalysis.* New York: International Universities Press.

——— (1974). On the nature and development of affects: A unified theory. *Psychoanalytic Quarterly* 43:532–556.

—— (1975). Affects and psychic conflict. *Psychoanalytic Quarterly* 44:5–28.

Calef, V. (1969). Lady Macbeth and infanticide: Or "How many children had Lady Macbeth murdered?" *Journal of the American Psychoanalytic Association* 17:528–548.

Denis, P. (2002). *Emprise et satisfaction*. Paris: Presses Universitaires de France.

Eissler, K.R. (1971). Death drive, ambivalence, and narcissism. *Psychoanalytic Studies of the Child* 26:25–78.

Eliot, T.S. (1919). Hamlet. In *The Sacred Wood: Essays on Poetry and Criticism* (pp. 95–111). London: Methuen, 1920.

Fenichel, O. (1935). A critique of the death instinct. In *Collected Papers of Otto Fenichel: 1st Series* (pp. 363–372). New York: Norton, 1953.

Freud, A. (1936). *The Ego and the Mechanisms of Defence*. London: Hogarth Press, 1973.

—— (1949). Aggression in relation to emotional development: Normal and pathological. *Psychoanalytic Studies of the Child* 3:37–42.

—— (1972). Comments on aggression. *International Journal of Psychoanalysis* 53:163–171.

Freud, S. ([1895] 1950). Project for a scientific psychology. SE 1:281–391.

—— (1905). Three essays on the theory of sexuality. SE 7:123–246.

—— (1915). Instincts and their vicissitudes. SE 14:109–140.

—— (1917). Mourning and melancholia. SE 14:237–258.

—— (1920). Beyond the pleasure principle. SE 18:1–64.

—— (1924). The economic problem of masochism. SE 19:155–170.

—— (1930). Civilization and its discontents. SE 21:57–146.

—— (1933). New introductory lectures on psycho-analysis. SE 22.

Gifford, S. (1964). Repetition compulsion. *Journal of the American Psychoanalytic Association* 12:632–649.

Hanly, C. (1966). Phenomenology, consciousness and freedom. *Dialogue: Journal of the Canadian Philosophical Association* 5:323–345. [Chapter 15 in this volume]

——— (1970). On being and dreaming. In C.M. Hanly & M. Lazerowitz (Eds.), *Psychoanalysis and Philosophy* (pp. 155–187). New York: International Universities Press.

——— (1975). Emotion, anatomy and the synthetic a priori. *Dialogue: Journal of the Canadian Philosophical Association* 14:101–118. [Chapter 16 in this volume]

——— (1977). An unconscious irony in Plato's *Republic*. *Psychoanalytic Quarterly* 46:116–147.

Hanly, C., & Masson, J. (1976). A critical examination of the new narcissism. *International Journal of Psychoanalysis* 57:49–66.

Hobbes, T. (1651). *Leviathan* (Ed. M. Oakeshott). Oxford: Blackwell, 1946.

Kirk, G.S., & Raven, J.E. (1930). *The Pre-Socratic Philosophers*. Cambridge: Cambridge University Press.

Kris, E. (1956). The personal myth: A problem in psychoanalytic technique. *Journal of the American Psychoanalytic Association* 4:653–681.

Kubie, L. (1939). A critical analysis of the concept of the repetition compulsion. *International Journal of Psychoanalysis* 20:390–402.

———. (1941). The repetitive core of neurosis. *Psychoanalytic Quarterly* 10:23–43.

Loewald, H.W. (1971). Some considerations of repetition and repetition compulsion. *International Journal of Psychoanalysis* 52:59–66.

Lorenz, K. (1963). *On Aggression*. London: Methuen, 1967.

Plato. *Republic* (Trans. B. Jowett). New York: Liberal Arts Press, 1948.

Rosenberg, B. (1991). *Masochisme mortifère et masochisme gardien de la vie*. Paris: Presses Universitaires de France.

Sartre, J.-P. (1936). *The Emotions: Outline of a Theory* (Trans. B. Frechtman). New York: Philosophical Library, 1948.

———— (1943). *Being and Nothingness* (Trans. H.E. Barnes). New York: Philosophical Library, 1956.

Schur, M. (1960). Phylogenesis and ontogenesis of affect- and structure-formation and the phenomenon of repetition compulsion. *International Journal of Psychoanalysis* 41:275–287.

————. (1966). *The Id and the Regulatory Principles of Mental Functioning.* New York: International Universities Press.

———— (1972). *Freud: Living and Dying.* New York: International Universities Press.

Symons, N.J. (1927). Does masochism necessarily imply the existence of a death-instinct? *International Journal of Psychoanalysis* 8:38–46.

Wälder, R. (1937). The problem of the genesis of psychical conflict in earliest infancy—Remarks on a paper by Joan Riviere. *International Journal of Psychoanalysis* 18:406–473.

CHAPTER 18

Logical and Conceptual Problems of Existential Psychiatry*

A study of the logical and conceptual problems of existential psychiatry encounters difficulty at the very outset. Existential psychiatry draws upon existential philosophy for its guiding premises. But existential philosophy is not itself a unified body of thought. There is no generalized statement of existentialist ideas. Existentialism is not a coherent evolving body of doctrines to which different thinkers have made contributions after the fashion of a natural science, or even a theological doctrine such as Catholicism.

The diversity of thought that falls under the general title "existential" can be easily illustrated. Kierkegaard (1844, 1846), a religious thinker, opposed Hegel's systematization of theology in favor of the primacy of immediate experience and faith. Husserl (1913), starting from phenomenal experience, constructed a systematic philosophy aimed at solving epistemological problems. Buber (1922) was an unsystematic and mystical religious thinker whose ideas have some of the characteristics of animism. Sartre (1943, 1946), an avowed atheist, built an ontology, epistemology, and psychology upon the phenomenology of immediate experience. His existentialism led him to Marxism and the advocacy of urban terrorism.

---

* Originally published in *The Journal of Nervous and Mental Disease* 5 (1985):263–275.

Merleau-Ponty (1945) offered a series of critiques of scientific theories of the human being (mechanistic causal thinking) and of empiricism and rationalism, drawing in part upon gestalt psychology and on Sartre's (1943) phenomenological descriptions; he did not construct an explicit substantive doctrine of his own. Heidegger (1927) undertook the task of guiding thought back to an authentic (anxious) encounter with being, as against an escape into an inauthentic preoccupation with the mundane. He explicitly rejected the application of the term "existentialist" to his thought. His own authentic being-in-the-world did not deter him from collaborating with the Nazis, who made him rector of Heidelberg University. Kierkegaard's thought was throughout anti-Hegelian; Merleau-Ponty's thought is sympathetic to Hegelian notions.

The problem which thus confronts this paper confronts existential psychiatry no less. When psychodynamic psychiatry is based on existentialist premises, we need to know whether these are Kierkegaardian, Husserlian, Sartrean, Heideggerian, or what have you. I know of no attempt by any psychiatrist committed to the enterprise of constructing an existential psychiatry, to sift through the diverse ideas within existentialism in order to collect a consistent group of concepts for this purpose. For example, Binswanger (1942) takes over Heidegger's (1927) notion of *mit-sein* (being-with-others) without considering the fact that Sartre, using the same method—the description of phenomenological contents of experience—deliberately rejected Heidegger's notion and proposed one diametrically opposed to it. No doubt there has been an implicit, eclectic sifting of existential ideas by psychotherapists such as Laing (1960), May (1960, 1983) and Yalom (1980), but the work is not done explicitly, nor are the problems of contradictory ideas derived from the same method of thought—namely, phenomenology—anywhere explicitly addressed. This paper may act as a stimulus to such inquiries.

I shall adopt the following strategy for dealing with the problem within the confines of a single paper. Sartre (1943) most unequivocally unfurled the banner of existentialism over the battlement of his philosophy, and is the only major member of this school of philosophy who used the term to describe his own thought. He gave one form of existentialism a clear definition, which he consistently followed in both his philosophical and his literary works, where its ramifications are explored extensively. Moreover, in his major work, Sartre (1943) himself undertook the construction of an existentialist psychoanalysis, the precepts of which inform his novels and plays. He is the most psychologically-minded of this group of philosophers, and the most fascinated by the intricacies of human relations and the range and meaning of individual experience. For these reasons, Sartre's ideas have to be taken into account by anyone seriously involved in the construction of existential psychiatry, whether or not one considers him to be the greatest of these philosophers, and whether or not his ideas are ultimately accepted or rejected for this purpose. Indeed, existential psychologists such as Laing (1960), May (1960, 1983) and Yalom (1980) have drawn upon Sartre's ideas. Accordingly, I shall emphasize Sartre in what follows, although I shall also extend the discussion to Merleau-Ponty, Kierkegaard, and Heidegger.

Despite the doctrinal differences among these philosophers, they hold certain ideas in common. They are phenomenologists in the sense that they treat the description of the structure, content, and meaning of immediate experience as an epistemological, if not an ontological, absolute. With the exception of Husserl, and to a lesser extent Merleau-Ponty, they emphasize the epistemic importance of certain emotional experiences which are supposed to uniquely reveal the meaning of human existence. One of the things supposed to be thus revealed is freedom in acts of self-creation; one of the things thus denied is the reality of psychic determinism. Something else denied is the reality of a dynamic unconscious with a "savoir faire" of its own. About as close as phenomenology can come to such a concept is a version of the economic preconscious, which Merleau-Ponty analyzed in terms of the gestalt psychology of foreground and background of the experiential field. Finally, while asserting the corporeal worldly nature of human existence, existentialists deny biological causality as expressed in drives that impose demands for work on the psychic apparatus; instead, they insist on the primacy of relationships of meaning between the subject and his or her body. As existentialists would say, a person may have a deformed body, but that person's consciousness will create the significance of the deformity in his or her choice of a way of living with its inescapability. The body can make instinctual demands for gratification, but the nature and quality of the gratification will be freely chosen by the subject. In what follows, I shall select issues involving tenets which have some commonality among existentialists. Therefore, although for the sake of simplicity and for the reasons already given, it is Sartre's ideas that will be emphasized, where they are not reasonably representative of the more commonly held ideas of existential philosophers the differences will be identified.

Given these few common tenets, a problem for existential psychiatry emerges at once. Existential thought is incompatible with Freudian psychoanalysis. For example, phenomenological description (in the form of case histories) in psychoanalysis is only a first step in an enquiry leading to causal explanations. For an existentialist, Freud's account of the history of Little Hans's childhood neurosis is true, but his explanation of it is a falsification. Psychoanalytic metapsychology and clinical causal hypotheses must be abandoned. (In this respect, Schafer [1978] is an existentialist.)

But this state of affairs is most agreeable to existential psychology. No small part of the appeal of existentialism is that it is a cudgel with which to beat metapsychology to the ground, and along with it the instinctual unconscious. At the same time, a window is opened onto new horizons—actually very old ones—such as religion, freedom, self-creativity, and the meaning and purpose of life. As Freud (1936) once wrote to his friend

Binswanger, "I have always confined myself to the ground floor and basement of the edifice—you maintain that by changing one's point of view, one can also see an upper storey, in which dwell such distinguished guests as religion, art, etc." (pp. 211–212). Freud goes on, in a friendly way, to chide Binswanger for being a traditionalist and leaving it to future enquiries to determine the outcome of their differences. In this respect, existential psychology is part of a broad movement away from metapsychology and the instinctual unconscious, a movement which includes Schafer (1978), Gill (1976), and Kohut (1959, 1965). Whether this movement is an advance or a retreat is not a question to be considered here. The argument of this paper is that, in the case of existential psychology, certain difficulties arise when existentialist philosophical ideas are used to replace psychoanalytic metapsychology as a frame of reference for psychodynamic theorizing.

THE PROBLEM OF ONTOLOGY

Existentialism, as Sartre formulated it, is an ontology. It is logically possible to derive the whole of Sartre's thought from a number of basic premises which claim to describe the nature and meaning of human existence as such. These premises and their logical derivatives can be phenomenologically exemplified; Sartre equates such exemplification with demonstration (Sartre, 1936, p. 126; Hanly, 1979, pp. 16–18). Merleau-Ponty (1945) develops a critique of empiricist and rationalist constructions of reality without advancing a substantive ontology. For Wittgenstein (1918), as for Merleau-Ponty, philosophy is a method of reflection by means of which one gains a view of reality without being able to characterize that reality philosophically. Nevertheless, if one can know that empiricism is a false construction of reality, in the end it must be because some other description of reality is true. And indeed, Merleau-Ponty claims to know that psychic determinism is false; and if he is right, something like Sartre's ontology of the self must be true. In any case, Sartre's basic propositions concerning the existence of the self are not intended to describe psychological states or even general patterns of psychological processes; they are intended to describe invariant structural characteristics of consciousness and all of its modalities: perception, feeling, thought, imagination, behavior.

Sartre thought that nothingness is intrinsic to the being of consciousness. Thus, consciousness is always and necessarily both what it is and not what it is. This apriority of self-existence gives rise to or is expressed in a group of anxieties which reflect to consciousness its omnipotent yet permanently precarious existence. Nausea is disgust aroused by the contingency of things, among which most prominently is the contingency of consciousness itself. The contingency of the self shares the contingency of all natural things, but added to it in the case of the self is the more disquieting contingency which derives from the "fact" that consciousness must both freely create a self and then negate (transcend) the self thus created, in an unrelenting series of nihilations terminated only by death. Anguish and vertigo .are so many forms of anxiety released by the awareness that one's actions are not the product of stable character, attachments, and needs, but a spontaneous creation of consciousness. They are the affective realizations of the nothingness that separates us from our past, our present investments, our bodies, and ourselves.

Laing (1960), one of the first writers in English to attempt to derive a psychodynamic psychiatry from Sartre's ideas, makes the deliberate error of treating Sartre's existential categories as though they were psychological rather than ontological concepts. Laing acknowledges that he is employing these concepts as though they were empirical, but does not consider the radical alteration in their use and meaning that follows when this step is taken. Laing treats these affects under the category of "primary ontological insecurity," as though they were merely painful psychopathological states and not the invariant structural characteristics of consciousness that Sartre meant them to be. The purpose of drawing upon the term "existential" is to deny that debilitating anxiety states are caused (rejection of psychic and organic determinism) and to assert that they are not caused by psychic conflicts in which the sexual instinct plays a predominant part (rejection of libido). Sartre does in fact repudiate psychic determinism and the economic drive theory of psychoanalysis. These anxiety states are treated within existentialism as universal and necessary qualities of a consciousness which must continually recreate itself because it must also always "nihilate" itself. Laing contrasts "primary ontological insecurity" with "primary ontological security." The latter has no place in existential thought. The equivalent of Laing's primary ontological security in Sartre, upon whom Laing bases his ideas, is "bad faith," which is a life based upon an inauthentic evasion of freedom and responsibility for one's own being and an evasion of the inevitable anxiety about one's being that freedom and responsibility involve. In existential philosophy, there is no passage from primary ontological insecurity to primary ontological security, as Laing supposes. For Sartre, human dignity rests irrevocably on a debility for which there is no remedy. From the point of view of Sartre's existential philosophy, existential psychiatry is an attempt, in bad faith, to cure the incurable.

CONSCIOUSNESS AND UNCONSCIOUSNESS

Because of their ethical commitment to a radical concept of freedom and their epistemological commitment to the veridicality of the immediacy of lived experience, existentialist thinkers cannot recognize the existence of unconscious mental activities. Advancing from Descartes (1641), Sartre (1943) identified consciousness as the existence of mental activities. It is consciousness that, as it were, gives existence to affects, volitions, thoughts, images, and perceptions. Existentialism has two reasons for reasserting this pre-psychoanalytic conception of the mind. First, it provides a basis for the systematic exclusion of any involuntary and impersonal processes from mental life; examples of such processes thus excluded from mental life would be reflex behavior such as the automatic fright reaction, instinctual behavior such as the sucking impulse of an infant, and psychological processes such as repression. Second, it systematically deprives everyone of any excuse for either what they do or what they are. This conclusion follows from the two premises (1) that consciousness is the existence of the mind, and (2) that consciousness nihilates itself in order to be itself. According to existentialism, the law of the existence of consciousness is that it is what it is not and is not what it is.

Sartre clarifies this obscure and contradictory formula by means of his analysis of the inevitable falsehood of sincerity. Sartre asks us to imagine a perverse homosexual man who is ashamed of his proclivities but who nevertheless, after a struggle with himself, confesses his pederasty to a friend. In doing so, he is apparently being sincere—he is refusing at last to hide any longer the fantasies, impulses, and actions of which he is ashamed. But according to existentialist principles, he is lying to himself and to his friend, not about his homosexuality, but about his "being." For in sincerely confessing that he is a homosexual, he is laying claim to being a homosexual, that is, to having a homosexual nature which causes him to perform homosexual acts. But the consciousness of his homosexuality which he forms in order to confess it must already nihilate the homosexuality of which it is a consciousness; that is, it is what it is not (the homosexuality in the form of memories of homosexual activities, etc.) and it is not what it is (the consciousness of being a homosexual is not in itself homosexual). The lie of the sincere self-confessed homosexual is constituted by his attempt, in all sincerity, to pass himself off as nothing but a pedophilic homosexual—of being a pedophilic homosexual by nature or by upbringing. He thus claims that his homosexual acts are the products of a homosexual nature that he is at the mercy of. In reality, existentialism claims, that the homosexual constitutes himself as a homosexual pedophile by choosing to take pleasure in these homosexual acts. In this way, sincerity is a falsification of the reality of human existence. It is motivated by ontological anxiety—the dread of realizing that one is the sole and perpetual creator of one's own being. Thus, sincerity is a form of bad faith.

Similar ideas are to be found in Kierkegaard's notions of dread, freedom, and the vacillation between the subjective and objective attitudes (1844, pp. 38–40, 55, 99–100; 1846, p. 84). Furthermore, bad faith is conscious of itself. When we seek to escape from the inevitable anxiety of human existence by adopting an attitude of sincerity, we are conscious of choosing to do so. We do not discover ourselves to be in bad faith (except by a self-deception that is itself in bad faith); rather, we consciously put ourselves in bad faith in order to avoid ontological anxiety, even though that attempt must fail.

The idea of a psychic unconscious is, according to existentialism, among the highest intellectual achievements of bad faith. Both Merleau-Ponty in *Phenomenology of Perception* (1945, p. 184) and Sartre in *Being and Nothingness* (1943, pp. 47ff.) refer favorably to Stekel's (1920) assertion that frigidity in women is rooted in a conscious and deliberate refusal to participate in the sex act, and proceed to differentiate between intentions (motives) and causes in a way that Freud would not have found acceptable. Freud recognized the existence of bad faith (the self falsifying itself to itself), but he went on to offer an explanation of it which an existentialist would consider to be in bad faith. According to psychoanalysis, a wish that arouses anxiety is warded off by means of a defense which acts unconsciously (at the behest of the superego) to render the anxiety-provoking wish unconscious and to block it, at least in its original form, from behavior. We come upon the substitute formation in ourselves without knowing how or from what sources it arose. The instinctual demand, and the defense against it, occur unconsciously as a result of a psychological causal mechanism about which we know no more than we know, by means of unaided sense perception, about the rotation of the earth or about the molecular structure of material objects. Hence, psychoanalysis posits a human nature in each individual made up of instinctual and ego endowments—a nature which combines with that individual's environment to form his or her individuality. It is this individual nature reacting to the demands, restrictions, and opportunities for gratification present in the environment that causes a person to carry out particular actions in particular ways. Thus, psychoanalysis is in contradiction with existentialism on these four crucial points: (1) it posits a psychic unconscious; (2) it introduces an individual human nature productive of that person's actions; (3) it assumes that human actions are subject to causality; and (4) it seeks to causally understand the motives for self-justifying excuses, whereas existentialism does not, insisting that such an inquiry is already in bad faith.

Sartre's major argument against the existence of a psychic unconscious is that, while it explains the self-falsification of experience, it implies a lie without a liar. Inanimate nature does not lie; it merely is what it is. If we are deceived about it, it is we who deceive ourselves. Psychoanalysis, according to Sartre, cannot offer a coherent account of self-deception in terms of repression. In order for the repressing activity to carry out its activity, it must know what its target is; otherwise, it would produce random results. *Ex hypothesi*, however, it represses just those wishes that are unacceptable to the ego. But any knowing activity must be conscious; hence, psychoanalysis has in effect reified a segment of mental life by means of its twin concepts of psychic determinism and psychic unconscious. Merleau-Ponty (1945), proceeding by a somewhat different route, reached the same conclusion (p. 19).

Sartre's argument against this essential proposition of psychoanalytic theory turns out not to be an argument at all, but simply a derivation from the first principle of his philosophy, namely, that consciousness is the existence of the mind. From this premise follows the proposition that any cognitive activity must be conscious, and Sartre's counterargument depends logically upon the truth of this proposition. If, however, there is a psychic unconscious, then there may also be unconscious thought activities, for example, primary process thought activity as well as unconscious thought activity within the ego (superego). These thought activities would be both cognitive and unconscious. The question cannot be decided on the basis of definition, as existentialism attempts to do. It can only be answered on the basis of the facts.

Despite these inescapable contradictions between psychoanalysis and existentialism, existential psychologists have attempted to combine them in their psychodynamic theories. May (1983), for example, asserts that "without some concepts of 'being' and 'non-being' we cannot even understand our most commonly used psychological mechanisms" (p. 21). He then goes on to consider repression as one of these mechanisms, describing it as "a phenomenon we observe all the time" (p. 22). Repression is an involuntary and unconscious process that, in the absence of sublimation and neutralization, subjects thoughts, impulses, and memories to amnesia, and thereby blocks them from expression in behavior but without removing their causal influence from psychic life, where they continue to appear and seek a disguised gratification. No existentialist philosopher could logically admit that such a process could occur, but according to existential psychologists its occurrence is routine. Moreover, the regular occurrence of repression can only be properly understood by means of two philosophical categories, being and non-being. If these terms are to be given an existential definition, then "non-being" must refer to the nothingness that consciousness is, as expressed by Sartre (1943), or to a primacy of existence over essence in humanity, as expressed by Heidegger (1927, p. 43), or to the dreaded openness to the possibilities of an intrinsically undetermined future, as expressed by

Kierkegaard (1844). These concepts have a basic affinity, for an essential logical implication of each is that "our most commonly used psychological mechanisms" apply only to a humanity degraded by inauthenticity and not to authentic human existence—to the appearance of humanity and not to its reality.

Given these contradictions, it is not surprising that both the psycho-analytic conception of human nature and the existentialist conception of human nature should be subjected to distortions of definition in existential psychology. May (1961) claims that psychoanalysis attributes repression to the patient's fear of parental (societal) disapproval, whereas in May's view it is actually motivated by a fear of the patient's own powers—the unlived potentialities which remain unconscious within. In May's theory, castration anxiety has been banished in favor of the need for security and approval from parents. Repression has been redefined as conscious self-control or risk avoidance. Unfortunately, the observed facts are different. Repression occurs unconsciously and involuntarily; even in the case of a simple, temporary amnesia, as in the parapraxis of being unable to recall a person's name when one is attempting an introduction at a party, one is not aware of having repressed the name or why, and is taken by embarrassed surprise when it happens. The understanding of psychic defense in psychoanalysis can no longer be recognized in May's redefinition of it.

The unconscious seems in fact to be quite mischievous. A prominent American existential psychologist once gave a public address in Toronto during which he traced the history of existentialism from Kierkegaard to contemporary authors (disregarding, I may say, certain of their fundamental differences) in order to gather philosophical ammunition to shoot down the idea of psychic determinism and the occurrence of involuntary psychic processes such as parapraxes. Gathering momentum in this task, he drew the audience's attention to one of the great modern works in the existentialist tradition, Camus's "The Myth of Syphilis"—by which he meant, of course,

The Myth of Sisyphus (Camus, 1942)—to the amusement of the audience and to his own discomfort, a discomfort which he attempted to cover over with a rationalizing excuse. The gods of the ancient Greeks amused themselves by punishing hubris in men; the unconscious of modern human beings sometimes seems to relish tripping up those who neglect to pay it a certain homage. Perhaps the comparison owes something to the contribution that the unconscious projections of our ancestors made to Hesiod's theogony and the role of castration in the genealogy of the Olympian gods.

But existentialism fares no better than psychoanalysis in May's treatment of it. Although May uses the concept of potentiality (a term used by Sartre) and although he quotes with approval Sartre's formula for human nature, in which existence precedes essence, he does not apply the formula correctly to the concept of potentiality. Before examining how May incorporates ideas from existentialism into his psychology, I will first discuss in some detail Sartre's conception of "existential potentiality."

Sartre (1943, p. 29) analyzes existential potentiality by means of the example of a young soldier who is anxiously wakeful throughout a night of bombardment as he awaits the command, which he knows will come toward morning, to make a frontal attack on enemy positions. According to Sartre's description, he becomes anguished, not because he is afraid of the bombardment or of the attack in the morning, but because he suddenly realizes that there is nothing in himself or in his environment that can cause him to act with bravery or with cowardice. An uncaused choice, unsupported by antecedent motives and unjustified by independent standards of conduct, will decide what he will do, what he will value (duty, camaraderie, his own life, his country), and hence what he will be. No past choices, no upbringing, no military training, no affects or instincts can determine his conduct: they are all "put out of play," nihilated, by the consciousness which transcends them (i.e., detaches itself from them) by becoming aware of them. Hence, the soldier has three equal potentialities: to be brave, to be a coward, or merely to do what is required of him. But these potentialities do not exist as something in himself to be realized; they are creations of his spontaneous choice alone. It is this realization that is the meaning of existential anguish. As already indicated above, this exemplificatory account by Sartre is consistent with Kierkegaard's concept of possibility and Heidegger's *Dasein*. And though Merleau-Ponty (1945) modified Sartre's concepts of consciousness and nothingness (pp. 91–112), he is no less committed than Sartre to a radical concept of freedom which no less denies psychic determinism: "In relation to what we are by reason of our acquisitions and their preexistent world, we have a power of placing in abeyance, and that suffices to secure our freedom from determinism" (p. 395). Again, in a context in which Merleau-Ponty draws upon Sartre's account of freedom in *Being and Nothingness*, he follows Sartre in asserting that "freedom does not tolerate any motive in its path, my habitual being in the world is at each moment equally precarious, and the complexes which I have allowed to develop over the years always remain equally soothing, and the free act can with no difficulty blow them sky-high" (p. 441).

Accordingly, May distorts existentialism no less than he distorts psycho-analysis in his attempt to yoke them together. He takes the same position in his most recent work (1983), in which he states that "anxiety is the experience of the threat of imminent nonbeing" (p. 108) and uses the concept of potentiality in the sense of an unrealized capability. For May's statement of existentialism implies that potentialities are latent within the nature of the individual. He would say, for example, that a woman who is frigid may have latent within her the undeveloped capacity for sexual passion, which she represses because she is afraid of it. This view may be closer to the facts than the perspective of existentialism, despite its refusal to consider why sexual passion might be frightening, but it is not the view of existentialism. The existentialist doctrine is unequivocally clear: a woman is frigid because she refuses to take pleasure in sexual activity and distracts herself with mundane thoughts. Nothing stands between her and the choice to be sexually passionate but the choice itself, because in choosing to be frigid she has to be conscious of being frigid, and this consciousness nihilates the frigidity, sets her apart from it, and establishes the possibility of choosing to be a passionate lover. As already mentioned above, both Sartre (1943) and Merleau-Ponty (1945) refer approvingly to Stekel's (1920) assertion that the core of frigidity in a woman is always conscious. Merleau-Ponty, as noted, asserts that a choice can destroy a neurotic attitude to oneself (feelings of inferiority) even if it has existed for a long time.

This statement brings us to the second fundamental distortion of existentialism in May's use of it in existential psychology. Sartre's existentialism (and arguably Merleau-Ponty's variant of it) does not warrant the use of any concept of the psychic unconscious. One might perhaps suppose, at first glance, that the existential concept of bad faith could be equated with a psychic unconscious: after all, bad faith consists of lying about something to oneself. In effect, with his revision of the concept of repression, May has abolished the dynamic unconscious and replaced it with the preconscious of Freud's earlier topographical model. However, Sartre (1943) explicitly and unequivocally repudiates the applicability of any concept of a psychic unconscious:

Thus, on the one hand the explanation by means of the unconscious, due to the fact that it breaks the psychic unity, cannot account for the facts which at first sight it appeared to explain. And on the other hand, there exists an infinity of types of behaviour in bad faith which explicitly reject this kind of explanation because their essence implies that they can only appear in the translucency of consciousness. (p. 96)

And once one recalls that Freud's concept of the preconscious includes the functions of acting as intermediary between consciousness and the instinctual unconscious and of providing a locus for the activities of the defenses, it is difficult to see how even Merleau-Ponty's idea of the opacity of the anonymous self could be rendered consistent with it. Thus, existential psychology, as May has formulated it, would appear to be in contradiction with existential philosophy because it retains a concept of a psychic unconscious, even if only an attenuated one, and it retains a concept of a human nature with potentialities latent within it to be realized through healthy maturation. These notions may be closer to the truth than their existentialist counterparts, but they are not existentialist ideas.

HUMAN RELATIONS

Sartre (1943) concluded on the basis of both phenomenological descriptions and logical derivations from his first principles (e.g., that existence precedes essence in humans, and existential freedom) that all human relationships are intrinsically conflicted. On this point existentialist philosophers are not in agreement. Buber's (1922) idea of I-thou relations, which apply equally to humans, lower animals, and inanimate objects, is animistic, but he nevertheless, conceives of it as harmonious. Heidegger's (1927) *Mit-welt*, which was taken over by Binswanger (1942, 1944), takes cooperation to be an authentic mode of relation to others, as does Merleau-Ponty (1945). Whether Sartre's view is a more correct version of existential thought, and whether Sartre is more consistent in his development of basic existential premises, are not questions to be decided here. But independently of the outcome of this philosophical controversy, it is clear that Sartre (1943) thought that the existential idea of freedom implies that all human relations are necessarily conflicted, and that consequently respect for the freedom of another is an empty word:

> To train the child by persuasion and gentleness is no less to compel him. Thus, respect for the Other's freedom is an empty word; even if we could assume the project of respecting this freedom, each attitude which we adopt with respect to the Other would be a violation of that freedom which we claim to respect. (p. 409)

It must be clearly understood that Sartre's view of the conflictual nature of human relations is not based upon an empirical study of various forms of personal and social aggression. His view is a logical consequence of the inevitably sadomasochistic structure of all human relations. Therefore, we must briefly consider why the existential concept of freedom has this consequence.

According to existentialism, as we have seen, the human is a being without a nature, and is constantly driven by the ontological anxiety to which this condition gives rise to seek a nature. In Sartre's terminology, the human being is a for-itself (*en soi*) driven to attempt to realize the impossible project of becoming for-itself-in-itself (*en-soi-pour-soi*)—in ordinary language, becoming a person who is both self-aware and has a stable individual nature. It is for this reason that Sartre (1943) describes human reality as irremediably unhappy (p. 90) and as a "useless passion" (p. 615). This project of becoming in-itself-for-itself seeks its realization in human relations, which offer a specific temptation. Might it not be possible to acquire a definitive character either by choosing to be what another takes one to be (masochism) or by making another be the means of becoming what one has chosen to be, and thus the confirming mirror of that (sadism)? Altruism, seen from an existential perspective, is a subtle form of sadism.

For by insisting upon the autonomy of others, by treating them generously, one is attempting to subject them, as a means, to the end of making oneself a person of moral virtue, and thus one is acting in bad faith by denying that it is equally possible to choose to abuse and exploit them. Life is a psychological war of each against all, without the prospect of a Hobbesian (1651) resolution by means of a social contract.

Yalom (1980) has recently claimed that freedom is one of several "ultimate concerns" of the individual, and therefore of existential psychiatry. His concept of freedom is explicitly derived from Sartre. Freedom involves "groundlessness," that is, the responsibility for assigning meaning to things and persons by choosing projects toward them; and such responsibility involves anxiety. Individuals seek to avoid the reality of their groundless condition, which is essential to their freedom, by avoidance of responsibility. It is the task of existential psychotherapy to help them to accept responsibility for who they are and what they do.

On the face of it, this objective seems to be not only sensible but inevitable. Moreover, is not this conclusion completely in agreement with psychoanalysis? After all, when Freud (1900) considered the question of who is responsible for an individual's dreams (most poignantly, dreams of criminal violence), he answered it with the observation that only the dreamer could be responsible for them, because it was the dreamer who dreamed them, even if his or her moral conscience abhorred them and made him or her want to disown them (p. 620). Psychoanalysis is in agreement with the philosophical view that psychic determinism, freedom, and responsibility for one's motives, wishes, and actions are mutually consistent concepts.

However, the problem for existential psychoanalysis remains. Philosophical existentialism affirms that while for natural beings, including living things, their nature precedes their existence, for human beings their existence precedes their essence. Existentialist philosophy bases this fundamental difference in being on consciousness and its nihilating function.

Existential psychiatry soundly recognizes the contradiction between psychanalysis and existential philosophy. For psychoanalysis, consciousness is not the essence of the psychical. Psychoanalysis claims that unconscious psychical processes cause neuroses. It also claims that these unconscious psychic processes are causal, not simply because they are unconscious—conscious psychic processes of desire and aversion are also causal—but because they are subject to repressions that have caused the arrestment in or the regression to early forms of desires and aversion that interfere with or even deprive the person of the enjoyments and benefits of their mature forms, causing the person to become frustrated, depressed, and anxious, and to have difficulties in their relationships with others. For psychoanalysis, both compelled neurotic actions and voluntary healthy actions are causally motivated, but this does not alter the responsibility of each person for what they have done, whether or not it is beneficial or harmful to self or others. The magical, compulsive handwashing of Shakespeare's Lady Macbeth is different from a habit of washing one's hands before a meal, which is not compulsive, for the two actions serve different needs: in the one case to expunge the sin of wanting her husband to kill Duncan, in the other to be polite, and perhaps to pay respect to one's hostess and preconsciously to one's mother, and perhaps preconsciously to avoid infection. According to psychoanalysis, both the compulsive action and the voluntary action are causally motivated, and the individuals (Lady Macbeth and the hypothetical dinner guest who had been helping out with some chores) are responsible for what they do, just as the dreamer is responsible for his/her dream.

A clinical paradox comes into view once the inconsistent views of responsibility are fully elaborated and existential psychotherapy is made consistent with philosophical existentialism. The task of existential psychotherapy is to help people overcome their denial of responsibility in order to be anxiously aware of their groundlessness. But the purpose of medicine is usually to relieve suffering, whereas in following a true existentialism, the psychotherapist's purpose would be to increase suffering and make it permanent. To this suggestion it may be replied that existential self-honesty is an end in itself as well as the precondition for social and moral responsibility. Unfortunately, further consequences, contrary to common sense and ordinary human decency, follow from this defense. An Adolph Eichmann, who sends thousands of innocent victims to death because he believes himself to be merely a cog in a military administration which he must serve to the best of his ability according to his upbringing, is acting in bad faith; but so is the Roman priest who helps to save the lives of Jews because he believes that he cannot face his Maker if he has done otherwise. And the Nazi who chooses to be a Nazi and to commit atrocities in the anxious realization that he could just as well have chosen to oppose Hitler and could still so choose is living an authentic life of self-honesty.

In effect, existentialist psychiatrists and psychologists use the concept of responsibility equivocally. On the one hand, they give to it an existentialist definition; on the other hand, they import into its use the common-sense meanings which it has in ordinary discourse. To be responsible is to be mature, to be considerate of others, to consider consequences for oneself and others before acting, to refuse to blame others for one's own faults or limitations, to accept the consequences of things that have happened to one even if they are unasked for, and to deal with them to the best of one's ability. These are connotations that the term responsibility has in ordinary common-sense usage. When existential psychiatrists want concepts of freedom and responsibility with which to oppose psychic determinism, they employ the existential concept of freedom; but when they use the concept of responsibility in the context of therapy, they import the connotations of responsibility from ordinary usage and abandon the existential ideas of responsibility and freedom.

For example, Yalom (1980) states of his patient Bruce that he "realized that he was immediately and entirely the source of his own self-hatred. If he wanted to feel better about himself, or even to love himself, he had to stop doing things of which he was ashamed" (p. 282). This description presupposes that as individuals, we have a stable, organized personality including a set of ideals for our own conduct and that we cannot but feel ashamed of ourselves if we transgress these ideals. While this view of shame is, in my opinion, closer to the truth than the existential view, it is inconsistent with philosophical existentialism. If psychiatrists and psychologists wish to ground an anti-psychoanalytic psychology in a philosophical system, a more congenial setting would be Kant's (1785) moral philosophy, with its categorical imperative, autonomous will, and differentiation between autonomy and heteronomy of conduct.

The shame that Yalom describes in his patient Bruce is not existential shame as described by Sartre. Existential shame is the experience of being degraded by being seen—of becoming aware of being the object or the potential object of the look of another. To be seen is to be ashamed because it makes one aware of being embodied in postures, gestures, actions, etc., to which meaning and value are assigned by another in a way that escapes one's control. One has become included as an object in the world of another— a world that has been freely created by that other. Or, inversely, as Sartre (1943) has stated it:

Thus, the Other-as-object is an explosive instrument which I handle with care because I foresee around him the permanent possibility that they (the instrumentalities of the other's world) are going to make it explode and that with this explosion I shall suddenly experience the flight of the world away from me and the alienation of my being. Therefore, my constant concern is to contain the Other within his objectivity, and my relations with the Other-as-object are essentially made up of ruses designed to make him remain as object. But one look on the part of the Other is sufficient to make all these schemes collapse and to make me experience once more the transfiguration of the Other. (p. 297)

Existential shame is the experience of this "alienation of my being." And the "transfiguration of the Other" constitutes the Other as a free, meaning-creating subject, and the self as a mere object in his world. As Sartre (1943) dramatically states the idea, "My original fall is the existence of the Other" (p. 263). Consequently, shame and sadomasochistic conflict are necessary and irremediable qualities of every human relationship. Moreover, they are necessary and irremediable because of the existential concept of the freedom of the individual which existential psychiatry claims to espouse. Existential psychiatry cannot have Sartre's existential freedom without necessary and irremediable sadomasochistic conflict, for the elementary reason that the existential theory of interpersonal conflict is a logically valid deduction from the existential theory of freedom, at least in Sartre's version of existentialism, upon which Yalom draws.

In reply, it might be argued that this criticism is based on an abstract logical purism that is ill-suited to the opacity of human subjectivity— or more specifically, that psychoanalysis itself has uncovered a dynamic connection between looking at an object and becoming like it (identifying with it, becoming like it, being devoured by it) or making it become like oneself (projective identification with it, devouring it). Fenichel (1935), drawing largely on Freud (1905, 1917, 1923), Abraham (1924), and Strachey (1930), has demonstrated these unconscious links between looking at and devouring the object, and being devoured by it. Does not psychoanalysis actually agree with existentialism concerning this basic point? For what is devouring the object but an oral metaphor for incorporating it into one's world—swallowing it up in the meaning-creating activity of a free consciousness? And what is being devoured by the object but an oral metaphor for being incorporated into the world of another? These existentialist and psychoanalytic descriptions of relationships seem to be very close in meaning. Do they not differ only insofar as psychoanalytic metapsychology biologizes and mechanizes the psychoanalytic versions of them? From the outset, existential psychology has been determined to clear away these weedy growths of biology and determinism in order to allow the clear light of understanding to illuminate the real roots of human existence. Once psychoanalysis is "corrected" in this way, its discoveries would corroborate rather than contradict existentialism and existential psychiatry. Surely such an attitude of eclectic and dialectical tolerance, which both respects and tests differing points of view, is one that is most likely to advance knowledge.

However, when both schools of thought are closely considered, the irresolvable logical inconsistencies between existentialism and psychoanalysis reveal substantially different views of human nature and of the possibility of psychological therapy and of human happiness. In the first place, the psychoanalytic hypothesis about the relation between looking and incorporating or being incorporated depends logically and factually upon the existence of unconscious mental activities, the occurrence of a series of libidinal stages, the fixation of component libidinal instincts, the formation of unconscious fantasies, and the causal influence of these fantasies upon conscious psychic functioning. For example, early oral disappointments can form a wish in the angry and unhappy infant to swallow both the mother's milk and its source, leading by a defensive reversal to an unconscious fantasy of being devoured by others, which later finds expression in an attitude of masochistic submissiveness toward others. In existentialism, however, not only is there no place for these processes, but the very possibility of their occurring is explicitly denied.

Furthermore, psychoanalysis differentiates looking insofar as it is subject to the influence of an unconscious arrested impulse and insofar as it is not. The investment of ego functions with libido in an adult may occur normally with sexual arousal or cause an inhibition or symptom. But the investment of libido in ego functions occurs only under certain conditions and in specific ways. The repetition of the residues of infantile oral incorporative pleasures in the sexual interest of a mature individual in his or her love object during foreplay leads to neither inhibition nor symptom. But the situation is different for the looking of the voyeur. The capacity for critical self-awareness and appropriate guilt reactions of a healthy personality is in sharp contrast to the paranoid anxiety of the repressed homosexual about being watched, even when no one is there. Being seen in the first case is of no particular danger; the mere possibility of being seen in the latter case is agonizingly shameful. (It is of some interest that Sartre's account of "being for others" amounts to a description of the structure of a paranoid experience including the fact that there need not be a real person there in order to have the experience of being seen.)

The distinction between normal and pathological experiences of looking and being seen—a distinction crucial to psychoanalytic thought— has no place in the existentialist theory of the inevitable sadomasochism of looking and being looked at. Psychoanalysis and existentialism are logically incompatible systems of thought. But psychotherapy, no less than psychoanalysis, requires a distinction between normal and abnormal experiences of seeing and being seen. Consequently, the same logical incompatibility will arise between existential psychiatry and existentialism as between existentialism and psychoanalysis. Yalom has avoided this contradiction by the logically unacceptable procedure of adopting Sartre's radical concept of freedom and then suppressing the consequences that follow from this concept in the spheres of self-observation and of interpersonal relations. It is as though one were to adopt Darwin's theory of natural selection and then fit it into a teleological natural history (one employing final causes) even though Darwin's theory repudiates the idea that there are purposive forces at work in the evolution of species.

EXISTENTIALISM AND PSYCHOTHERAPY

Binswanger is perhaps the most original of the existential psychiatrists.* A Binswanger case history has been selected for this reason, and also because it exemplifies a problem of existentialist thought that is to be expected, given the implication of the arguments above. Binswanger has also been selected because the source for his existential psychiatry was not Sartre but Heidegger.

The case of Ellen West (Binswanger, 1944) is one of the classic case histories in the literature of existential psychiatry. It is a valid test of the efficacy of existential categories in psychiatry. Following Heidegger (1927), Binswanger introduced the three concepts of *Eigenwelt*, *Mitwelt*, and *Umwelt* in order to construct an understanding of the individual life history. *Eigenwelt* refers to the world of the self—of private emotions, fantasies, thoughts, etc.; *Mitwelt* refers to the domain of object relations and social involvement; and *Umwelt* refers to the life of the body and instincts. What interests us here is how Binswanger used these concepts to understand the suicide of his patient.

The life of Ellen West was suspended between an intense desire to be thin, imaginative, intellectual, poetic, and ethereal, which left her feeling empty and depressed, and suffering from a compulsion to eat in order to fill up the emptiness, which left her fat and loathsome to herself. All treatment failed. On the day of her suicide, she was able to enjoy food again, engage in lively conversations, and enjoy the society of others. Binswanger attaches his explanation of Ellen West's suicide to a remission of symptoms, which in his view was made possible by her decision to kill herself. Only by deciding to kill herself was she able to integrate and authenticate her existence: the

---

* For a complete bibliography of Binswanger's works see Sneesens (1966). English translations of some of Binswanger's publications are to be found in editions by May, Angel, and Ellenberger (1958), Ruitenbeck (1962), and Needleman (1978).

one necessary condition for an authentic existence for Ellen West was that she terminate it. He calls her suicide both necessary and free: she chose to do what she had to do. Binswanger's explanation of this state of affairs was that her *Eigenwelt* had rushed ahead, as it were, and lived out its entire time during her childhood, and so scarcely any future was left to it. The only way that her *Eigenwelt* could be integrated with her *Mitwelt* and *Umwelt*, and thus afford her an authentic existence, was to kill herself, which she realized and in due course unflinchingly carried out—hence the remission of symptoms during the time before her suicide. Binswanger's explanation of the suicide is an elaborate rationalization of the idea that her case was hopeless, and she might as well kill herself because there was no life for her anyway.

No criticism of Binswanger for failing to treat her successfully is involved here: Ellen West had already had a failed analysis. The criticism is rather that Binswanger's mode of understanding her suicide offers a romanticized rationalization for it which denies the need for clinical investigation. How can one's ego life become so detached from the passage of time that it can actually live through childhood, adolescence, maturity, and old age far in advance of one's social and bodily life? Even the most emotionally and sexually precocious of children, for all of their fantasies or seductions, cannot actually manage to live their adulthood during their childhood. By the conceptual alchemy of existential psychology, a therapeutic failure and the failure of a life have been transformed into an exalted, if tragic, destiny. In Binswanger's view, suicide was for Ellen West the one authentic act available to her by means of which she could reassert her humanity. Such a view is a poor substitute for enquiring into what caused her to kill herself; moreover, it suppresses the more humane and scientific questions about her life and death. For if Binswanger's view is true, then there was no remedy, for the simple reason that time cannot be reversed.

The notion of freedom in existential psychology involves a paradox. On the one hand, we as individuals freely create ourselves by spontaneously choosing our own way of "being-in-the-world." By this same activity, we create the meaning of our world; in the grandiose language of existentialism, "man makes the world appear." It is this idea that allows Binswanger to persuade himself that the rate of the passage of time can actually be mentally altered. We are each the master of our own fate because we ourselves create it. But now, on the other hand, just the opposite turns out to be the case. Ellen West's suicide was necessary; it was the only choice available to her, for she had already wantonly spent her *Eigenwelt*. In the end, the concept of freedom in existential psychology is no different from that of the ancient Stoics, who likened the lot of humanity to that of a captive in a victory parade bound to a war chariot by a chain around his neck: he can walk wherever he is taken with dignity, or he can be dragged, but follow he must. Having rejected natural causality and psychic determinism, existentialism and existential psychology end up with a fatalism. It is an oddly vicious fatalism from a psychological point of view, because on the one hand individuals are masters of their own fate and, on the other hand, the fundamental structures of human existence cannot be altered or modified but must be repeated. Similarly, Sartre maintains that individuals perpetually create their identity and nature by adopting an attitude to their situation and by choosing a course of action (a project) in relation to it. At the same time, he correctly draws out the implication of this "grandiose" freedom for human relations, which is that any struggle to overcome masochism must terminate in sadism, and conversely, any struggle to overcome sadism must terminate in masochism because the structure of object relations allows for no other possibility such as being kind without being either masochistic or sadistic. Individuals are fated to a fundamental sadomasochism in all of their object relations.

The error in existential philosophy that produces these paradoxes must be traced to the assumption that there are eternal laws of being human which are deeper than psychology or biology, and which must provide the frame of reference for the interpretation of all psychological, biological, and sociological facts. Although much has been learned about human animality and rationality since Aristotle, his definition of the human being as a rational animal correctly places us in nature as a proper object of scientific knowledge. It is to this reality-bound understanding of humanity and its place in nature that existentialism is opposed. Husserl (1913) rejected Aristotelian as well scientific realism as expressions of a merely "naturalistic attitude," and Merleau-Ponty (1945) passionately opposed the idea that he could be subject to causality: "I am not the outcome or the meeting-point of numerous causal agencies which determine my bodily or psychological make-up. I cannot conceive myself as nothing but a bit of the world, a mere object of biological, psychological or sociological investigation" (p. viii). Such protests on behalf of human narcissism are perhaps appropriate to philosophy, but a body of knowledge that claims to be a clinical science cannot afford this luxury.

Existential psychiatrists and psychologists tend to overlook the fact that Sartre (1943) had already worked out the implications of his philosophy of existence for psychology. His aim is to find, beneath the psychological significance of the body, its parts, and its functions, a more fundamental stratum of meaning, which one could characterize as an ontological anatomical symbolism—that is, a system of meanings that are determined by the intrinsic structure of the body. Accordingly, Sartre sets out to derive the sexual meaning of the female genitals from their forms as such rather than from the biological and psychological facts of the development of the sexual instinct and anatomy in childhood. Thus, the sexual meaning of the vagina is to be derived from the "ontology" of the hole. The hole is a cavity that offers the for-itself the possibility of realizing itself as also in-itself by pressing its body completely into its enclosure—by filling itself up with its own body:

The obscenity of the female sex is that of everything which "gapes open." It is an appeal to being as all holes are. In herself woman appeals to a strange flesh which is to transform her into fullness of being by penetration and dissolution. Conversely, woman senses her condition as an appeal precisely because she is "in the form of a hole."... Beyond any doubt her sex is a mouth and a voracious mouth which devours the penis—a fact which can easily lead to the idea of castration. The amorous act is the castration of the man; but this is above all because she is a hole. (pp. 613–614)

This remarkable derivation of the nature of female sexuality on the basis of the existential ontology of the hole is in fact a description of a pathological condition. A woman's vagina is a devouring mouth that seeks to absorb the penis—to fill itself up with it. Accordingly, intercourse is an attempt at castration. This account does describe accurately enough unconscious fantasies that certain hysterical women and obsessional men have about the vagina, but as far as existentialism is concerned, it is the invariant meaning the vagina must have because it is a hole. In its bold attempt to go beyond psychoanalysis, existential psychoanalysis has only managed to convert a psychopathological distortion of the body schema that is amenable to treatment into a universal condition of femininity that is irremediable.

One of the basic problems is that existentialism claims that its categories of understanding are necessary and universal conditions for human existence. In this respect, existentialism can be said to have ontologized psychology. But for this reason, existential categories, however intellectually intriguing they may appear to be, are not serviceable for the purposes of psychotherapy. One is reminded of Einstein's (1922) comments on the philosopher's treatment of space and time:

The only justification for our concepts and system of concepts is that they serve to represent the complex of our experience; beyond this they have no legitimacy: I am convinced that the philosophers have had a harmful effect upon the progress of scientific thinking in removing certain fundamental concepts from the domain of empiricism where they are under our control to the intangible heights of the a priori. (p. xvi)

It must be recognized that existential categories (like the Cartesian and Kantian categories of which Einstein spoke) are deemed by existentialists to be a priori in nature. Therefore, when these categories are used to formulate an understanding of a psychopathological condition, that condition itself must logically be considered to be either immutable, or if not immutable then variable in a way that makes it unavailable to therapeutic intervention. Existential anxiety is a case of the former, and existential sadomasochism is an example of the latter. The principal thrust of existentialism, when integrated authentically into psychiatry, would be to revert psychiatry to the pre-Freudian era of the *famille nevropathique* of Charcot and the inheritance of a predisposition for which therapeutic intervention can be of no avail. Existential psychiatrists and psychologists for the most part make existentialist categories appear as though they could be serviceable as a framework for therapy by modifying them so fundamentally that they cease to have their original philosophical connotations.

Johnson (1779) said that the style of the metaphysical poets resulted from the most heterogeneous ideas being yoked together by violence. When existential philosophy and psychodynamic psychiatry are "yoked together" in existential psychiatry, it is not merely a question of heterogeneous ideas, but one of inconsistent ideas and divergent aims. Such psychodynamic concepts as unconscious fantasies, defense mechanisms, and drives are logically excluded from existential philosophy. Conversely, the introduction of the existential concepts of freedom, consciousness, anxiety, ideals, and object relations must result either in their redefinition so as to remove from them their original meaning, or in the most far-reaching changes in psychodynamic psychiatry. Sadomasochistic phenomena become intractable, as do anxiety states and psychosexual pathology, and psychotherapy is limited to exhortation. For the existential idea of freedom is a radical one, even in philosophy. Consciousness, as existentialism conceives of it, places each individual beyond any influence, not only from other persons and events but even from the individual's own past. The most that any therapy could do would be to clarify what alternatives are available to a person. However, even this intervention would, according to Sartre, constitute a sadistic assault by the therapist on the patient by including the patient as an object in the therapist's world of behavioral clarity, and an attempt to deprive the patient of his or her own shadowy world of behavioral obscurity, vagueness, and uncertainty—or the patient could always reverse things by subjecting the therapist to his or her look. From this sadomasochistic trap there is no means of escape, because, according to Sartre, it is an unavoidable part of the human condition. Concepts of unconscious mental activities, defense mechanisms, and ego ideals would have to be abandoned along with psychic determinism. Either existential psychology is a logically inconsistent collection of ideas or it cannot legitimately lay claim to the term "existential." Finally, the aims of existentialist thought and psychodynamic psychology are incompatible. Despite its occasional rhetoric of violence—which in any case is Marxist—the aim of existentialist thought is to reconcile humankind to an individual human condition which is taken to be irremediable. The aim of psychodynamic psychology is to find a remedy for individual suffering, if one is to be found—or at least that is the aim of psychodynamic therapy insofar as it remains true to its origins in psychoanalysis.

At stake are two fundamental issues, one psychological, the other conceptual. The psychological issue concerns narcissism; the conceptual one concerns causality. Psychiatrists and psychologists have a special motive for turning to existentialism, if they share the existentialist sense that psychic determinism is an offense to human dignity. For some, the thought of being subject to efficient causality like any other living or inanimate thing in nature is an intolerable narcissistic blow which must be fended off. But the intolerability of the indignity is itself caused by experiences of helplessness of various kinds during childhood, which have fashioned a denying idealized ego, for which to be adult is to be the unique author of one's own fate. The psychological origins in the experience of helplessness make their appearance in existentialist philosophical thought in the nexus of the a prioris of existence, about which an individual can do nothing since they are immutable laws of one's being human. It is the awareness of this ambiguity that led Sartre (1943) to say that "one could even state that determinism—if one were careful not to confuse it with fatalism—is 'more human' than the theory of free will" (p. 453).

Of course, one should not confuse psychic determinism with fatalism, as Sartre does. If phenomena are caused, and if we can discover their causes, then we may have some chance of beneficially altering them. If cancer occurs spontaneously, or if it is a scourge imposed by an angry God upon a recalcitrant humanity—if, that is to say, it has no natural causes—then nothing can be done about the pathology that results from it; the best that could be done would be to reduce its worst effects as much as possible and as long as possible. An attitude of fatalism would be the only appropriate one. If, however, cancer does have natural causes and we can find out exactly what they are and how they work, then it may be possible to invent remedies that will attack the disease at its origins rather than merely modify its effects. The situation is no different when it comes to human behavior and psychological functioning. If individual human behavior originates in uncaused spontaneous acts, as existentialism assumes, then it cannot be subject to therapeutic influence; an attitude of fatalism toward human psychological debility is then the only justified one. Although the abandonment of narcissistic self-idealization and the acceptance of humankind's place in nature may be especially painful for some and troublesome for all, it is rewarded by a more realistic relation to human nature in oneself and others and by the prospect of being able to actually remedy some of its ills.

CONCLUSION

Existentialism is a radical school of thought which provides the conceptual basis for a far-reaching philosophical critique of psychoanalytic metapsychology and psychic determinism. I have argued that these same concepts are unsuitable as a basis for psychotherapy. The existential concepts of consciousness, nothingness, freedom, anxiety, and conflict in Sartre (and in varying degrees in other philosophers of the school) refer to invariant and unalterable structures and dynamics of human existence. For the existentialists, the plight of Sisyphus is symbolic of the human condition as such. Existential psychology, if it were a therapy that remained true to its philosophical origins, would have to accept the Sisyphean nature of the attempt to release Sisyphus from his misery. Perhaps sensing that this is so, existential psychiatrists and psychologists alter the meaning of these concepts when they use them to construct theories for psychotherapeutic purposes. In doing so, existential psychology fails to remain true to the philosophy from which it claims to have drawn its inspiration.

REFERENCES

Abraham, K.A. (1924). A short study of the development of the libido viewed in the light of mental disorders. In D. Bryan & J. Strachey (Trans.), *Selected Papers on Psycho-Analysis* (pp. 418–501). London: Hogarth Press, 1973.

Binswanger, L. (1942). *Grundformen und Erkenntnis des menschlichen Daseins* (2nd ed.). Zurich: Niehans, 1953.

———— (1944). The case of Ellen West: An anthropological-clinical study. In R. May (Ed.), *Existence: A New Dimension in Psychiatry and Psychology* (pp. 237–364). New York: Simon & Schuster, 1967.

———— (1957). *Sigmund Freud: Reminiscences of a Friendship.* New York: Grune & Stratton.

Buber, M. (1922). *I and Thou* (Trans. R.G. Smith). Edinburgh: T. & T. Clark, 1937.

Camus, A. (1942). The myth of Sisyphus. In J. O'Brien (Trans.), *The Myth of Sisyphus and Other Essays.* New York: Random House, 1955.

Descartes, R. (1641). *Meditations on First Philosophy* (Trans. E.S. Haldane & G.R.T. Ross). In *The Philosophical Works of Descartes* (pp. 131–199). New York: Omer Publications, 1955.

Einstein, A. (1922). *The Meaning of Relativity: Four Lectures Delivered at Princeton University, May, 1921* (Trans. P. Adams). London: Methuen.

Fenichel, O. (1935). The scoptophilic instinct and identification. In *Collected Papers of Otto Fenichel: First Series* (pp. 373–397). New York: Norton, 1953.

Freud, S. (1900). *The Interpretation of Dreams.* SE 4–5.

———— (1905). Three essays on the theory of sexuality. SE 7:125–245.

———— (1910). The psycho-analytic view of psychogenic disturbance of vision. SE 11:209–218.

———— (1917). Mourning and melancholia. SE 14:237–258.

———— (1923). The ego and the id. SE 19:3–66.

———— (1926). Inhibitions, symptoms and anxiety. SE 20:77–175.

———— (1936). Letter from Freud to Ludwig Binswanger, October 8, 1936. *The Sigmund Freud-Ludwig Binswanger Correspondence 1908–1938* (pp. 211–212). London: Other Press, 2003.

Gill, M.M. (1976). Metapsychology is not psychology. In M.M. Gill & P.S. Holzman (Eds.), *Psychology versus Metapsychology: Psychoanalytic Essays in Memory of George S. Klein* (pp. 71–105). New York: International Universities Press.

Hanly, C. (1966). Phenomenology, consciousness and freedom. *Dialogue* 5:323–345. [Chapter 15 in this volume]

———— (1975). Emotion, anatomy and the synthetic a priori. *Dialogue* 14:101–118. [Chapter 16 in this volume]

———— (1979). *Existentialism and Psychoanalysis*. New York: International Universities Press.

Heidegger, M. (1927). *Being and Time* (Trans. J. Macquarrie & E. Robinson). London: SCM Press, 1962.

Hobbes, T. (1651). *Leviathan* (Ed. M. Oakeshott). Oxford: Blackwell, 1946.

Husserl, E. (1913). *Ideas: General Introduction to Pure Phenomenology* (Trans. W.R. Bryce Gibson). London: Allen & Unwin, 1931.

Johnson, S. (1779). The life of Cowley. In B.H. Bronson (Ed.), *Rasselas, Poems and Selected Prose* (pp. 353–365). New York: Holt, Rinehart & Winston, 1971.

Kant, I. (1785). *Groundwork of the Metaphysics of Morals* (Trans. H.J. Paton). London: Hutchinson, 1947.

Kierkegaard S. (1844). *The Concept of Dread* (Trans. W. Lowrie). Princeton: Princeton University Press, 1957.

———— (1846). *Concluding Unscientific Postscript* (Trans. D.F. Swenson). Princeton: Princeton University Press, 1944.

Kohut, H. (1959). Introspection, empathy, and psychoanalysis: An examination of the relationship between mode of observation and theory. In *The Search for the Self* (pp. 205–232). New York: International Universities Press, 1978.

―――― (1965). *The Restoration of the Self.* New York: International Universities Press, 1977.

Laing, R.D. (1960). *The Divided Self.* Harmondsworth: Penguin.

May, R. (1961). The emergence of existential psychology. In R. May (Ed.), *Existential Psychology* (pp. 11–51). New York: Random House.

―――― (1983). *The Discovery of Being.* New York: Norton.

May, R., Angel, E., & Ellenberger, H., eds. (1958). *Existence: A New Dimension in Psychotherapy and Psychology.* New York: Basic Books.

Merleau-Ponty, M. (1945). *Phenomenology of Perception* (Trans. C. Smith). London: Routledge & Kegan Paul, 1962.

Molina, F. (1962). *Existentialism as Philosophy.* Englewood Cliffs, NJ: Prentice-Hall.

Needleman, J., ed. (1978). *Being-in-the-World: Selected Papers of Ludwig Binswanger.* New York: Harper & Row.

Ruitenbeck, N. (1962). *Psychoanalysis and Existential Philosophy,* New York: Dutton, 1968.

Rycroft, C. (1966). Introduction: Causes and meaning. In C. Rycroft (Ed.), *Psychoanalysis Observed* (pp. 7–22). London: Constable.

Sartre, J.-P. (1936). *Imagination: A Psychological Critique* (Trans. F. Williams). Ann Arbor: University of Michigan Press, 1962.

―――― (1943). *Being and Nothingness* (Trans. H.E. Barnes). New York: Philosophical Library, 1956.

―――― (1946). *Existentialism and Humanism* (Trans. P. Mairet). London: Methuen, 1948.

Schafer, R. (1978). *Language and Insight.* New Haven: Yale University Press.

Sneesens, G. (1966). Bibliographie de Ludwig Binswanger. *Revue Philosophique de Louvain* 64:594–602.

Stekel, W. (1920). *Frigidity in Woman in Relation to Her Love Life* (Trans. J.S. van Teslaar). New York: Boni & Liveright, 1926.

Strachey, J. (1930). Some unconscious factors in reading. *International Journal of Psychoanalysis* 11:322–331.

Wittgenstein, L. (1918) *Tractatus Logico-Philosophicus* (Trans. C.K. Ogden). London: Routledge & Kegan Paul, 1922.

Yalom, I. (1980). *Existential Psychiatry.* New York: Basic Books.

CHAPTER 19

Psychic Determinism Revisited: Dr. Hanly's Rejoinder to Drs. Tormey, McHugh, and Miller*

The fear which seems to lie behind all three critiques of my paper (Hanly, 1985) is the idea that psychic determinism involves the submission to blind mechanical forces, or as Ferenczi (1913) put it, we have "slavishly to obey certain irresistible instincts" (p. 216). I agree with the implicit view of my critics that being enslaved to inappropriate drive demands, demands which are abhorrent to oneself, should be viewed as a symptom of neurosis (Ferenczi's view), and not as a normative state for the human condition. My critics appear to believe that psychic determinism implies fatalism, and that the only way to avoid such a Calvinistic predestination is to postulate along with existentialism a unique capacity for self-creation inherent in human existence because of human consciousness. Only such an assumption, it seems to be supposed, can give reality to autonomy, freedom, and responsibility. Psychic determinism, they believe, must deny any reality to these human qualities. But as Wallace (1985) has shown, this view is justified neither scientifically nor philosophically. The difference between a compelled action and a free one does not lie in the fact that the compelled act is motivated (caused) and the free act is unmotivated (uncaused); it

---

* Originally published in *The Journal of Nervous and Mental Disease* 173, no. 5 (1985): 280–281.

consists rather in the nature of the motivations at work. It is according to the degree to which the motivations of an action are conflicted that the action will be compelled or free. Psychic determinism is perfectly compatible with the reality of freedom, autonomy, and responsibility (Hanly, 1979). Indeed, many philosophers, among them Ryle (1949), have pointed out that concepts of free will and existential spontaneity are incompatible with any concept of human action because their denial of motivation results in a randomness and arbitrariness of action, which is incompatible not only with character but also with freedom.

The only commentary that speaks directly to the argument of my paper is Professor Tormey's (1985). Professor Tormey agrees with the main thrust of my argument, which is that existentialist philosophy does not provide any basis for psychotherapy as it is usually understood in psychiatry, psychology, and psychoanalysis; existentialism reduces psychotherapy to a secular form of pastoral counselling. She recognizes that the basic propositions concerning the nature of human motivation according to existentialism and those concerning the nature of psychic determinism are contradictories. She then raises the issue of where the truth lies. Philosophers have always disagreed on this issue. Descartes and Kant were voluntarists, Spinoza and Mill were determinists; and the controversy continues. Professor Tormey (1985) sides with existentialism, which is a radical form of voluntarism; I have the impression that neither Dr. McHugh (1985) nor Dr. Miller (1985) is aware of the fact that existentialists such as Sartre attack traditional forms of voluntarism based on the idea of freedom of the will. After centuries of labor, philosophers have not been able to find within their own discipline any facts or principles that can settle the question. Can psychology do any better?

First, there is a pragmatic argument for postulating psychic determinism. The hypothesis of psychic determinism has provided the basis for an effective psychotherapy. To persuade a young man who is obsessed with the fear of venereal disease associated with perverse masturbatory practices, that his anxiety and masturbatory activities rest upon his choice to engage in them and that he can choose to substitute mature sexual activities for them, is in fact ineffective. The patient in question, before entering upon psychoanalysis, had already received such counsel, and thought very ill of himself for not being able to follow it. The progressive discovery by the patient of the emotion-laden memories which lay behind his disorder (its causal determinants) proved to be effective in resolving it.

Second, there is an experiential argument. In my experience, neurotic sufferers both accept and reject responsibility for their symptoms. Sometimes the repudiation of responsibility turns out to be correct insofar as their symptoms arise out of traumata that they have suffered at the hands of others. But with the uncovering of the traumatic events, patients also discover two things: first, that their own drive life has engaged them in the traumatizing situation, and they accept responsibility for that; and second, that there is no one but themselves to cope with the consequences of the trauma in themselves and in their lives, even though they have been victimized, and hence they also accept responsibility for doing what they can to ameliorate the consequences of the trauma. Sometimes the repudiation of responsibility has a defensive function; for example, an impotent male who accuses his wife of various defects which account for his sexual failures cannot tolerate the humiliation of his own failure. These repudiations of responsibility are abandoned in the course of a successful analysis, not by any uncaused choice, but by a progressive realization by the patient of the sexual anxieties in himself that have caused him to find fault with his wife. Finally, a patient may both accept responsibility for experiencing depression, for example, and yet be helpless to alter it in any useful way. Such persons accept that their lives are subject to causality, but do not see themselves as being machine-like or experience themselves as depersonalized.

Third, there is an observational argument on behalf of psychic determinism. Psychoanalysts have confirmed over and over again in their work that human actions are motivated and that these motives themselves have a history in the life of the individual leading back to the stage of their first development in childhood. It was stated by Sartre that this discovery implies a fatalism, that is, that our fate is sealed by the time we are six years old. But the opposite is the case: it is only insofar as things, including human actions, are caused, and only insofar as we are able to know what these causes are and how they work, that we have any prospect of engaging in remedial actions of any kind, including psychotherapeutic ones.

I can wholeheartedly agree with Dr. McHugh's (1985) advocacy of empirical research in his conclusion. But in order to empirically test hypotheses, it is first necessary to clarify what they assert and what their implications are. McHugh suggests that Jaspers' ideas are a viable bridge between existential philosophy and psychiatry. The fundamental problem with Jaspers' thought, from a psychological point of view, is that it does not provide a satisfactory basis for a differentiation between hallucinatory and normal perception, and from a philosophical point of view it does not provide an adequate epistemological understanding of the progressive adaptation of thought to reality.

My own estimation of Binswanger's significance as compared with Jaspers' seems to be shared by Yalom and May. Yalom, in *Existential Psychotherapy* (1980), cites Jaspers four times and Binswanger four times. In *The Discovery of Being*, May (1983) has six references of a rather cursory nature to Jaspers and thirty-five to Binswanger, most of which are substantial. May relies heavily upon Binswanger's ideas, and this preference was shared by the greatest phenomenological philosopher of recent times, Merleau-Ponty. But unfortunately, a reliance on Binswanger, despite his close relation to Freud, is unhelpful, because in the end he was more influenced by Heidegger's phenomenology than by Freud's psychic determinism. Although it is necessary for a psychotherapist to be able to describe a patient's inner world to him or her, this is only a first step toward understanding and interpreting the sources of the conflicts, inhibitions, depressions, and anxieties of the patient's inner world. Phenomenology takes us only to the level at which the real work of psychotherapy begins, by uncovering with the patients what they do not want to know but need to know about themselves and their relationships.

Without offering any reasons for his assertions, McHugh (1985) claims that there were "excesses of nihilism wrapped within" the "ideas of psychic determinism and the dynamic unconscious" and that the nihilism was "expressed in the totalitarianism of the Nazi occupation of France" (p. 278). McHugh is not the first person to advance this preposterous hypothesis, but there has never been, nor is there now, a shred of evidence for it. The Nazis who burned Freud's books, confiscated his property, drove him in his old age from his home, and murdered his aged sisters, as well as those who invaded France, were not expressing Freud's ideas, which were completely inconsistent with nihilism. Nor, for the most part, were their ideas nihilistic: they thought of themselves as idealists who had grandiose self-righteous moral duties to the Führer to carry out his racial and nationalistic programs with which they were identified and for which many of them were willing to sacrifice their lives. If nihilism is the problem, then it is existentialism that is in difficulty, because its concept of authenticity provides no basis for a differentiation between moral good and evil. The existential authenticity of a Nazi is the same as the existential authenticity of a liberal democrat, so long as the Nazi accepts responsibility for choosing to be a Nazi and the liberal democrat accepts responsibility for choosing to be a liberal democratic egalitarian.

I have the impression that Dr. Miller has not grasped the argument or the purpose of my paper. As a philosopher and a psychoanalyst, I have some concern about the indifference of Drs. Miller and McHugh to coherent theorizing, conceptual clarity, and ordinary reasoning. I am amazed by Dr. Miller's (1985) naive expectation that if we "keep mixing up our hypotheses," we will one day "get it right" (p. 279). I do not understand how such a procedure would result in any advancement of knowledge.

REFERENCES

Ferenczi, S. (1913). Stages in the development of the sense of reality. In *Contributions to Psychoanalysis* (pp. 213–239). New York: Basic Books, 1950.

Hanly, C. (1979). *Existentialism and Psychoanalysis.* New York: International Universities Press.

———— (1985). Logical and conceptual problems of existential psychiatry. *Journal of Nervous and Mental Disease* 173(5):263–275. [Chapter 18 in this volume]

May, R. (1983). *The Discovery of Being.* New York: Norton.

McHugh, P.R. (1985). Commentary on Charles Hanly's "Logical and conceptual problems of existential psychiatry." *Journal of Nervous and Mental Disease* 173(5):278.

Miller, M.H. (1985). We are good—they are bad: Commentary on "Logical and conceptual problems of existential psychiatry" by Charles Hanly. *Journal of Nervous and Mental Disease* 173(5):279.

Tormey, J.F. (1985). Commentary on Charles Hanly's "Logical and conceptual problems of existential psychiatry." *Journal of Nervous and Mental Disease* 173(5):276–277.

Ryle, G. (1949). *The Concept of Mind.* New York: Barnes & Noble, 1965.

Wallace, E.R. (1985). *Historiography and Causation in Psychoanalysis.* Hillsdale, NJ: Analytic Press.

Yalom, I. (1980). *Existential Psychotherapy.* New York: Basic Books.

CHAPTER 20

Psychoanalysis and the Foundations of Morality*

Moral philosophy, no less than any other branch of philosophy, is characterized by contradictions and dichotomies (determinism vs. freedom, naturalism vs. antinaturalism, emotion vs. reason, etc.), leading to endless debates. One gets the impression that moral experience must be influenced by individual character differences; otherwise, how can it be that philosophers who are adequately (or even exceptionally) intelligent come to such different conclusions about it? The problem is not merely an intellectual one: it is not just the value of human existence that depends on the moral values and imperatives by which human beings lead their lives, but human existence itself. A consistent and realistic understanding of morality is a perpetually pressing need that philosophy has, so far at least, not been able to meet.

I will begin by proposing that a psychoanalytic theory of morality can provide the foundation on which to construct a unified moral theory that will be able to integrate the partial insights, everywhere else mutually opposed, of the traditional moral theories—in particular, contractualism, utilitarianism, and deontological ethics. I will then argue that the discoveries of psychoanalysis about moral psychology can contribute to an exact and

---

* Originally published in French as "La psychanalyse et les fondements de la morale," *Dialogue: Canadian Philosophical Review* 26 (1987):669–682.

naturalistic understanding of the role of duty in moral conduct. Finally, I will discuss from a psychoanalytic perspective the fallibility of moral judgment—what could be called the psychopathology of conscience.

The philosophical dichotomies mentioned above become quite evident when one compares the moral philosophies of Hobbes (1651), Mill (1863), and Kant (1785). Hobbes (1651) assumed that human beings are naturally prepared to steal, enslave, and kill in order to acquire whatever they want. Morality, grounded in respect for law and order, is the result of realizing that such behavior would result in a perpetual war of each against all and that life would be "nasty, poor, brutish, and short" (Book I, chap. xiii.). Hobbes tells us in effect that man is by nature an animal that is amoral, aggressive, and egoistic. Or as Freud (1930) writes: "Men are not gentle creatures who want to be loved, and who at the most can defend themselves if they are attacked; they are, on the contrary, creatures among whose instinctual endowments is to be reckoned a powerful share of aggressiveness" (p. 58). As a result, says Freud, "their neighbour is for them not only a potential helper or sexual object, but also someone who tempts them to satisfy their aggressiveness on him, to exploit his capacity for work without compensation, to use him sexually without his consent, to seize his possessions, to humiliate him, to cause him pain, to torture and to kill him. *Homo homini lupus* [Man is a wolf to man]" (p. 111). According to Hobbes, the only way for human beings in a state of nature to control their acquisitive drives is to satisfy them. Thus, the survival of humanity depends on human reason—that is, on our capacity to assess the consequences of our actions and to react with fear when those consequences are found to be disastrous.

It is this understandably alarming apprehension of the consequences of the unrestrained pursuit of egocentric objectives that gives rise to what Hobbes articulates as his second and third laws of nature: the willingness to give up such acts against our neighbors that we would not wish to have done to ourselves, and in this way to circumscribe our own liberty as long as the others are likewise willing to limit their own (the second law of nature), and one's willingness to abide by this compromise (the third law). Morality is a compromise between what individuals want most (to be able to force others to satisfy their desires while protecting themselves) and what they want least (to be forced to satisfy the needs of others without being able to take revenge, seek compensation, or have any expectation that they will reciprocate). In this respect, Hobbes' myth of man in the state of nature is similar to Freud's (1913, chap. 4) myth of the primal horde. The brothers of the primal horde were driven to adopt the first component of totem religion—the worship of the totem as the symbol of the murdered father who became for them the father who had not been killed and still imposed the taboo rules on them. For they had become aware that the act that they had perpetrated—the murder of the father in order to take his place and seize power for themselves—they were still prepared to inflict on each other, motivated by the same goal of gaining exclusive sexual rights to the women of the horde. They also realized that the security of each depended on the willingness of all to accept a kind of equality of sexual privation among themselves—the law of exogamy.

Morality is an artifact: it arises from the sexually motivated rivalrous aggression of human nature as a problem the solution of which is psychological and culturally inheritable rather than biologically inheritable. Human beings are not naturally sociable or moral. However, morality is a fundamental artifact insofar as it makes possible all the other artifacts of society—culture, the sciences, the trades and professions—by controlling mutual aggression and the sexuality that motivates it by exchanging individual mutual rivalry for collective cooperation and thus contributing to the improvement of the human condition by means of civilization. The solution is imperfect. The eminent political commentator James Reston, when asked by a radio interviewer in a summing up during his retirement

417

whether anything in recent history troubled him, replied that old men sending young men to war disgusted him.

According to Hobbes, the existence of this indispensable artifact depends for its efficacy on the creation of a sovereign of some kind who is given the absolute right to define the content of the moral rules (as well as of other social rules) and is endowed with sufficient power to compel everyone to respect them. Hobbes has two reasons for adopting this position. First, morality has no natural foundation in man; it depends on experience and causal reasoning. Second, the fear that leads to morality does not bring about any internal changes that are sufficiently "serious" to reduce this fear to a tolerable level. Thus, the only remedy possible is an external change in society. It is necessary to create a sovereign (be it a monarch or a parliament) that will be able to intimidate everyone and thus to compel everyone to obey the moral and civil law that the sovereign establishes.

Like Hobbes, Mill (1863) has morality depend on "the pleasure (the good) or the pain (the bad) that an action produces directly or as a consequence" (p. 157). "The Greatest Happiness Principle" holds that actions are right in proportion to their tendency to promote happiness, or wrong insofar as they tend to produce the reverse of happiness" (p. 184). Mill held that moral conduct is caused by various motives, which he divided into two kinds: external and internal. External motives gain their hold on the individual by his or her desire for reward and fear of punishment (by other people or by God). The cause of internal motives to act morally is the fear of incurring discontent with oneself because of guilt (i.e., one's conscience), reinforced by compassion, love, religious feeling, childhood memories, and self-esteem, as well as egoistic motives. Thus, as regards what we are concerned with here, an important characteristic of Mill's moral thought is his conviction that there is in man a potential (though typically it is not always fully realized in the course of his development) which allows for the formation of a conscience which will motivate moral conduct independently of any external motive.

Mill (1863) declares that this is an observable fact in human nature, but offers no explanation:

> The internal sanction of duty, whatever our standard of duty may be, is one and the same—a feeling in our mind: a pain, more or less intense, attendant on violation of duty, which in properly cultivated moral nature rises, in the more serious cases into a shrinking from it as an impossibility. (p. 170)

Mill seems to be saying that the pleasure that one can take in robbing another of his property, even if one avoids getting caught, can be overpowered by the greater pain involved in committing a bad deed. He seems thus to think that the unlimited egoistic aggression posited by Hobbes can be subjugated by conscience: as Hamlet says, "Conscience doth make cowards of us all," (Act 3, scene 1) and causes us to recoil from actions that we consider morally bad. Mill's moral theory thus does not require either Hobbes's social contract or a sanction imposed by society in order for people to act morally, except in those who have failed to develop the capacity to react with pain to the thought of doing wrong. Indeed, according to Mill (1863), conscience causes us to take pleasure in actions that produce benefits and happiness for others no less than for ourselves:

> The happiness which forms the utilitarian standard of what is right in conduct, is not the agent's own happiness, but that of all concerned.... To do as one would be done by, and to love one's neighbour as oneself, constitute the ideal perfection of utilitarian morality. (p. 170)

419

Now, Freud did not have a very high opinion of the golden rule that Mill proposed as definitive of the principle of utility. Freud (1930) posed the following question: "What good is the introduction of a precept so solemn that one could not reasonably advise anyone to follow it?" (p. 110). If the term "neighbor" refers to humanity in general, says Freud, do I not have the right to keep a greater part of this love for myself, rather than the insignificant portion that millions of others might receive from me if it were equally distributed among them all? Do not my family, my friends, and my closest colleagues deserve preference in my love over some stranger, who in any case might intend me harm? Unfortunately, history suggests that Freud was right. The Christian societies of Europe, which espoused the even more radical injunction to love not just others but even one's enemies as oneself, have treated their Jewish fellow citizens (thus, their neighbors) even worse than Freud envisioned in his darkest thoughts in *Civilization and Its Discontents*.

Nevertheless, Mill's ideas are in accord with psychoanalysis. To begin with, his perspective on the individual's capacity to be motivated by considerations of the greatest good for the greatest number was realistic. Rather than humanity in general, it is for the most part those dear to oneself—one's children, one's extended family, one's closest friends—to whom the utilitarian (or golden) rule applies. There are only a few people, and those in relatively few situations, who are in a position to take actions with significant repercussions. (Mill probably had in mind as examples political and social reformers.) There is little in this position that Freud would contest. Indeed, a major component of psychoanalytic theory is its explanation of the origins of aggression and of libido that is "inhibited with regard to its goal." Through reaction formation, sadism towards others is transformed into pity for their suffering. Through repression and sublimation, perverse sexual drives are transformed into compassion, concern, affection, neighborliness, and curiosity. These sentiments are those that motivate our behavior towards others, and this meets the requirements of Mill's utilitarianism. Psychoanalysis has shown how identification with others in whom we find similarities to ourselves, or with those who have realized in themselves what we aspire to be, brings about bonds of affection that lead us to want to ensure their well-being as much as we can. Certain crucial and fundamental identifications with one's parents lead to the formation of the conscience, which induces us to taking pleasure in doing what is good and to experiencing pain, guilt, and shame when we do, or contemplate doing, what is not good. This pain was identified by Mill as the essential internal motivation of morality. Freud (1926) studied its origin and traced its various stages, beginning with the fear of losing the love object (e.g., one's mother and father, on whom a child depends), then castration anxiety, and finally the fear of the loss of the love of self (the most mature moral affect), which one experiences as guilt at the thought of acting badly (chap. 8). These stages in the development of affect constitute the transition from dependence to obedience, and then to obedience to oneself, from which arises in part one's independence during the first years of life. Psychoanalysis is in accord with Mill on two further fundamental points as well: that morality is not innate but acquired, and that pleasure and pain can work well as reliable criteria for distinguishing the good from the bad, including what is morally good or bad. (Of course, Hobbes too maintained these two basic propositions in his ethical theory.)

However, whether or not utilitarianism and contractualism can be categorized as emotivist theories—in the philosophical sense of the term—it would be a serious error to classify the moral theory found in psychoanalysis in the same way. For in addition to the role played by affects such as anxiety (which motivates action to meet the demands of immediate instinctual pleasures), and the cognitive role played by the perception of reality and the calculation of consequences, one must also consider the role played in psychoanalytic theory by the identification that establishes the strongly

421

ingrained imperatives that are both negative (prohibitive) and positive (in search of an ideal). What makes it possible for psychoanalysis to provide a naturalistic explanation of Mill's moral affects and of Kant's categorical imperative is its recognition of the process of identification in the formation of conscience. (The semantic range of the terms used to refer to different emotional states is examined by Perry, 1967, but he does not analyze them psychologically.)

Psychoanalysis recognizes three main types of affect, which follow the structural and functional differentiation of psychological processes. They are as follows:

1. Affects of the id, which are provoked by a direct discharge of drives, such as sexual pleasure and the pleasure of competition.
2. Affects of the ego such as frustration, pleasure taken in success, and anxiety as a signal of danger.
3. Affects of the superego, such as guilt and self-satisfaction.

Some of these affects, such as sexual pleasure, are usually experienced as natural. Others, such as guilt, can be experienced as counter to nature, which might lead one to think that they are therefore mistaken, or alternatively, that they have a more exalted origin; but in fact, guilt has no less natural an explanation and function than does sexual pleasure.

Though Kant preceded Mill chronologically, I have placed him after in my presentation here, since I have organized these moral theories according to the importance they attach to the internal sanctions of morality. Kant, the high priest of the autonomous conscience, completely separated an act from its consequences when it came to determining its moral worth. It is only the motivations of an act that merit our attention: an act is moral insofar as it is done for the sake of duty and only for the sake of duty. When one is judging the moral value of an act, one must entirely exclude from consideration all pleasure or pain, as well as any egoistic satisfaction. Thus, on these two points Kant's moral theory is in fundamental disagreement with those of Hobbes and Mill.

Kant recognized that one's intentions are often not entirely pure. Many who do their duty are also motivated by self-interest. But insofar as someone is motivated by intentions other than duty, his or her action does not have moral worth; one can say then that an act has moral worth *only* insofar as it is motivated by duty. It is difficult to assess the distribution of the relative strength of intentions that are not pure, but it is those acts that go against one's personal interests about which one can say unequivocally that they have true moral worth.

Kant formulated his ethical thought on the basis of a fundamental distinction he draws between the categorical imperative and the hypothetical imperative. The hypothetical imperative takes the following form (in his example of a shopkeeper): "If I want to advance in my business and prosper, I would do better by being honest in my dealings with others." What motivates honesty in the hypothetical imperative is material and egoistic ambition. The categorical imperative, on the other hand, takes the following form: "I ought to be honest because it is my duty to be honest, whether it is in my interest or not." Kant offered two basic criteria for a categorical imperative. He considered them to be general criteria for deciding what is a moral duty and what is not: first, a moral act can be universalized; and second, every moral act must consider another as an end in himself and never as a mere means. The first criterion precludes all exceptions, including oneself: morality requires renouncing, whatever the circumstances and whatever the egoistic or instinctual desires may be. The second criterion precludes manipulating or using others in any way, whatever their situation (e.g., if they are vulnerable or helpless) in order to accomplish one's own aims. Kant's moral theory exalts altruism and makes it the *sine qua non* condition of morality. His veneration of military heroism is a perfect illustration of the rigor of this ideal (this masochism, one is tempted to say). In his aesthetics, Kant (1764) considers the following question: Ought one to honour with a statue in a public square the general who leads young men to war, or the statesman who negotiates peace? The author of "Toward Perpetual Peace" (Kant, 1795) replies that it is the general who deserves this honor. Why? Because it is the general who gives young men the opportunity to risk their lives for the sake of duty. What could be more altruistic than sacrificing one's own life in the performance of one's military duty? The general is a symbol of the categorical imperative and the highest realization of the moral act, whereas the statesman, who negotiates the treaty to end the war, in the pursuit of strictly commercial and financial interests in the making of peace is being guided by hypothetical imperatives, never mind the lives of young men saved from death.

Kant thought that the sanction of moral duty is to be found in a will that is free to choose between duty and egoistic inclination whenever there might be a conflict between them. The will is a power that is sufficient in itself; it is not subject to any causality of the body or mind, of nature or society, nor does it depend on any motivation external to itself. The will produces actions which have consequences, but an act of the will is not itself a consequence of any other cause: it is totally spontaneous. Thus, according to Kant, every individual is free to choose the motive of his actions—that is, to choose duty or self-interest. Kant's moral theory postulates an absolute internal sanction that directs moral action, and this sanction is completely independent of all external authority. Kant thus situates the source of moral will in human subjectivity, conceived of as a thing in itself. Ontologically, humanity is a kingdom of ends (*Zwecke*) that is above nature and the laws of nature.

Freud claimed in *The Ego and the Id* (1923) that with his formulation of the theory of the origin and function of the superego (conscience), he had at last developed a way of understanding morality psychoanalytically. There he points out the parallel he draws between his own conception of the superego and Kant's categorical imperative. He can thus assert elsewhere that "Kant's categorical imperative is the direct descendant of the Oedipus complex" (Freud, 1924, p. 167). In fact, the superego takes its true duty to be to reject the aggressive pleasure that consists in eliminating the father so as to have the mother all to oneself. Here Freud posits a harshly imposed duty that stands over against the strongly invested, aggressive libidinal desires, and, similarly, over against aggressive egoistic ambitions.

Our goal is to use psychoanalysis to see whether there is a way to bring together different philosophical positions in order to construct an integrated and consistent moral theory. But there is an obstacle barring the way: the three moral theories under consideration are mutually exclusive. Nevertheless, we have been able to discover similarities and to identify the resemblances noted by Freud between each of these theories and the psychoanalytic ideas that bear on morality. This might lead us to think that that psychoanalysis itself, when it comes to giving an account of morality, is a jumble of inconsistent ideas, and is not a tool that can be used to construct a coherent ethical theory.

But contrary to how things might seem, perhaps we are not after all at an impasse. First, if one agrees with the psychoanalytic view that the facts of psychic life prove that the distinction of mental processes into three types (the instinctual unconscious, or id, the conscious ego, and the unconscious ego, or superego) is well-founded, then if these mental processes come into conflict, it is entirely possible that the description of how one type of process (e.g., instinctual processes) contributes will turn out to be inconsistent with the description of how another type of process (e.g., superego processes) contributes. However, these inconsistencies might disappear if we take into account the entirety of the situation. It is also possible that Freud— or I myself in the presentation I have just given—have exaggerated the similarities between psychoanalysis and one or another of these theories, while neglecting to take account of their differences.

So let us consider one last point. There are indeed differences between these moral theories and psychoanalysis, as well as similarities. Nevertheless, if it can be proven that the severity of the superego and its opposition to bodily pleasure are equivalent to Kant's deontological categorical imperative, then the following differences must also be acknowledged: (1) the severity of the superego of psychoanalysis does not require Kant's ontological hypothesis of a scientifically unknowable thing-in-itself; (2) the formation of the superego and its ability to motivate dutiful behavior is an aspect of normal human development; (3) it is not necessary to postulate an uncaused spontaneous will as the moving power that originates altruistic acts; and (4) the work of the superego is subject to psychological causality, and in a more explicit way it enforces its prohibitions and obligations by the fear of the loss of self-respect (guilt and depression—ultimately, castration anxiety) and by resort to self-approval, which substitutes for the instinctual pleasure that is lost when one requires oneself to be altruistic rather than pleasure-seeking.

Does it not then follow that the position on duty and altruism that is most consistent with the discoveries of psychoanalysis is that of Mill? At the top of Mill's hierarchy of pleasures is the capacity to take pleasure in altruistic acts when one does one's duty. What psychoanalysis would add is that this pleasure is a form of moral narcissism, that is, the pleasure one takes in one's own activities independently of the approval of others. All this is true, but between Freud's thought and Mill's there are also differences.

Freud (1930, chap. 2) recognized that our hierarchy of civilized pleasures is in some respects an artifact—a necessary one, but an artifact all the same. Human beings are civilized, but they remain, at best, rational animals. It is the direct gratification of our instinctual drives that gives us our deepest and most complete pleasures. Much of the good that we do and receive is connected with our physical life. The pleasures that have the greatest value are physical pleasures. But there is a more elementary and original unconscious hierarchy of pleasures that Mill does not recognize or understand sublimations for what they are. They are substitute editions or forms of unrequited libidinal and aggressive desires made possible by their displacement onto other objects and activities (e.g., a small boy who finds a way to satisfy his aggression against his father by playing hockey in the role of a rough defenseman who is prepared to attack other players to stop them from scoring goals). However, Mill treats the "higher" pleasures of intellect and spirit as though they were gifts of the mature mind without histories; for example, one aspect of the love of the beautiful in both nature and art derives from infantile sensual desires for the mother that have been repressed and sublimated, just as the love for the "awesome" derives from the repressed and sublimated infantile fear of the overwhelmingly greater retributive strength of the father demands respect and arouses fear.

This is not the same as saying that these experiences and the value attached to them are nothing more than the precursors in childhood of those that come later—obviously they are different. But the value that gets attached to our pleasure in the beautiful is more complex than is admitted by Mill's utilitarian idea of pleasure. This pleasure has three sources: (1) the intrinsic pleasure of sometimes elational conscious experience; (2) the pleasure that arises from the unconscious defensive function of displacement insofar as sublimation keeps unwanted wishes from childhood in an unconscious state; and (3) the disguised gratification of these same wishes in a displaced innocent form. Furthermore, Mill's account of the pleasure of sublimation avoids its link to depression. When the pleasure in the beauty of art, nature, or religion is highly elational, the pleasure can easily give way to depression, especially when some degree of ego regression occurs, involving a threat of the loss of adult ego identity and the work that went into forming it.

Consequently, Mill's moral theory, no less than Kant's, leaves out the fact that the conscience is itself corruptible, nor does either theory explain the origins of this vulnerability to corruption. During World War II, the SS were awarded medals because they had overcome their aversion to killing helpless civilians, in order to do their duty. This is an example where one follows one's will to do one's duty by overcoming a human impulse, which is thus repressed, even though this impulse is a better guide to morality than fulfilling one's duty when the duty is morally corrupt and is justified by a morally corrupt ego ideal. But pleasure and pain in themselves are not reliable guides to moral conduct. Pleasure can also be produced by the perpetration of atrocities as a result of unconscious and malicious identifications of helpless victims in the present with the objects of sadistic hostility in one's past. Nazi propaganda associated Jews with noxious insects and vermin, which forged an associative connection of Jews with unconscious memories of torturing insects to death in a childhood displacement of hatred of a sibling rival. The racist ego ideal of Aryan purity and perfection held out the tempting promise of inflicting sadistic violence on Jews with guiltless pleasure.

But a problem for the Nazis and their soldiers was that the sadism of childhood is ambivalent. The original sadism of childhood typically involves a displacement from the new sibling that the older sibling wants to remove. This sadism is caused by the older sibling's identification with the unwanted new sibling, who, like the sadistic older sibling, is helpless without the love of the mother. It is the love of the mother that the sadistic child already fears he has lost to his rival; moreover, the jealous sibling, despite his hatred, may also hope to eventually find in his rival a wanted playmate. It is this positive, loving side of the ambivalence that causes the displacement, the choice of helpless insects as a substitute object for unleashing the pleasure of sadistic torture and killing of a helpless creature, as expressed by Gloucester after being savagely blinded by Regan and Cornwall in Shakespeare's *King Lear*: "As flies to wanton boys are we to the gods" (Act 4, Scene 1) Because of the negative side of the ambivalence, Nazi soldiers were prepared to do their leader's bidding in killing Jews, whom they unconsciously associated with the childhood displacement of hostility from their sibling rivals onto insects and vermin, though they could not always do so without guilt and depression, caused by the positive affectionate and decent side of their original sadistic ambivalence toward siblings. The culture, ideology, and politics of Nazism now offered an opportunity for the guiltless murder of Jewish men, women, and children. Even so, the original ambivalence of the perpetrators obliged Nazi leaders to compromise their depraved categorical imperative with a hypothetical imperative, by rewarding those who murdered Jews with special state military honors.

Reason, by itself, is powerless before these moral dilemmas. The Nazis could have rationalized their atrocities against the Jews, the Gypsies, and the Slavs by appealing to one or another of the principles of Kant or Mill. The Nazis would not have hesitated to universalize their brutality against these peoples, whom they did not include in Kant's "Kingdom of Ends," that is, as belonging among those who should be treated as ends in themselves and never only as means: citizenship in the Kingdom of Ends was available only to members of the superior race. Similarly, a Nazi could have maintained that it was for the sake of the greatest good for the greatest number of Aryans that the inferior races had to be exterminated or reduced to slavery. Kant's universality criterion—"So act that the rule of your action can be legislated as a universal moral law"—is similarly powerless. During World War II, the Japanese military enslaved and generally ill-treated prisoners of war, contrary to the Geneva conventions; but the Japanese also generalized this ill-treatment into a rule that applied to themselves, for they expected to be treated in the same way by the Allies if they surrendered.

The possibility that moral values are corruptible leads us back to Hobbes, to find the comfort—even if a somewhat cold comfort – of a realistic judgment about the difficult moral situation of humanity. Hobbes's pessimistic cynicism perhaps captures more of the truth than the naive optimism of Mill or the grand ideas of Kant. Hobbes advanced the two following ideas, with which Freud was obliged by psychoanalytic observations to concur. First, morality is not natural to human beings: it is not part of what we are endowed with innately. Achilles was and is a hero, in part because he was a fellow human killing machine. Rather, morality is a historical phenomenon that has its own psychic and cultural evolution. To the best of my knowledge, there is no biological evidence that human beings are genetically endowed with an innate constraint on intraspecies killing. If we are not innately so endowed, the constraint on this form of aggression must be psychological. The evidence from history and what we know about individual development suggests that constraining an impulse to kill another person is left to psychic restraint because it is not available biologically. Hobbes's state-of-nature hypothesis implies this assumption: it is fear that causes the shared entering into a social contract to obey the will of a sovereign. Secondly therefore, aggression acts as a spontaneous instinctual motive force in human beings, whether it is conceived of as a death instinct (Freud, 1920), as primarily object-relational (Brenner, 1973), or as a reactive instinct triggered by frustration (Hanly, 1978). Human beings cannot rely on their aggressive instinct itself to curb intraspecies killing. Indeed, Hobbes conceived of aggression as a reactive instinct, insofar as it is activated by the need to protect the goods that one possesses and on which one has to rely, and as an instinct produced by narcissistic ambitions that cannot be satisfied—what Hobbes called the pursuit of vainglory.

It is these shared insights about the fundamental human condition that have led some commentators to note the similarities between Hobbes and Freud, especially with regard to Freud's ideas in *Civilization and Its Discontents* (1930)—similarities deeper than those that Freud himself saw between his concept of the superego and Kant's practical (moral) reason. However, the similarities cannot be pressed any further than this. Hobbes maintained that morality can be established and maintained only by an external social power—namely, the sovereign—and that the sovereign's crushing power to intimidate and constrain makes the authority and domination of the sovereign almost absolute. This power is limited, though not very realistically, only by the individual's right to use any means to defend himself should the sovereign decide to take his life, since this runs contrary to the very purpose of entering into the social contract, namely, to preserve one's life. From a psychoanalytic perspective, Hobbes views the situation of the human being as if the Oedipus complex remained always in place without any possibility of internal resolution. Consequently, humanity has to be satisfied with an essentially infantilized relation to an external sovereign: such is the price of humanity's survival.

This pessimistic view is not compatible with psychoanalysis. Freud (1923) provides us with a way of understanding the processes by which an internal resolution of the Oedipus complex is brought about—processes which are normal for individuals with normal natural abilities and living in normal conditions (see also Hanly, 1984). The cause of the resolution of the Oedipus complex need not depend on external intimidation; it will occur even when the parents are kind and do not inflict vindictive punishment. It is caused by the development of castration anxiety in boys and its equivalent in girls, as a result of which even the kindest of parents are perceived to be dangerous, whether they really are or not. Freud describes only the development of boys, but in girls the fear of the loss of the mother's love—and even worse, the fear of her revenge—is no less powerful a factor motivating the resolution of the feminine Oedipus complex. The fantasy of the sorceress who imprisons or poisons is frightening to little girls just as much as the fantasy of the werewolf that bites is to little boys. The normal resolution of the Oedipus complex imposed by the unbearable fear of the parent of the same sex consists in the withdrawal of the libido (incestuous desire) from the parent of the opposite sex, and its investment in the image of the parent of the same sex. This investment constitutes an identification with that parent, who now becomes, rather than a dangerous rival, an ego ideal (Hanly, 1984).

The ego ideal is a force in the life of the child: it is the result of the desire that is now deeply invested in being like the parent of the same sex. The prior fear of the same-sex parent has now been transformed into a fear of the disapproval of the ego ideal—that is, of the parent, who has now become a part of the child and is incorporated into his/her own identity. This fear is experienced as guilt, and it is this guilt that forbids bad actions by means of fear of punishment, and sanctions good actions by means of self-approval, self-respect, and pride. Whereas before the child depended on the approval of his or her parents for self-esteem and on their disapproval for self-criticism, he or she is now capable of carrying out independently these tasks that are so essential to morality. He or she now can and must be "well-behaved," whether under the gaze of his/her parents or not. Psychoanalysis has provided a way of understanding the grounds of the possibility of moral experience in individuals, one that Hobbes failed to take into account.

Thus, by selectively incorporating the partial insights of moral philosophy, psychoanalysis is able to furnish the basis of a unified naturalistic theory of morality. As regards Kant, psychoanalysis can explain the nature and origin of duty for the sake of duty as a moral precept. When all else has failed—when the pleasure of doing good for others has faded, and when the fear of external authority has disappeared—at that point the internally generated fear of doing wrong, the guilt that internally enforces duty for the sake of duty with the consolation of moral narcissism, is the last hope of decency. However, psychoanalysis can certainly concur with Mill that the factor that is most effective in producing altruism is a well-developed capacity for taking empathic pleasure in actions that are aimed at doing some good for another, even while accepting that the value of that good is not diminished by the hope of being paid back for it with a like good. The points of contact with Hobbes's moral theory have been identified above: the "abnormal character" of morality, the existence of an instinct for aggression that can be mastered only imperfectly at best, and the inherent vulnerability of morality to insidious corruption such that evil can take on the appearance of good.

It is this last trait that should haunt the moral thought of our era, given the regression to moral barbarism that took place in the last century. What safeguard is there to protect individuals and groups from such regression? If the psychoanalytic theory of the psychogenesis of morality is correct, then this safeguard, already weak and uncertain, must lie in the contribution made by parents to the identifications on the basis of which the individual's superego is formed. These identifications result in part from internal vicissitudes in the instinctual life of the oedipal child, but they are also formed in part by the child's experience of the personality of his or her parents, including, especially, their unconscious desires, anxieties, ideals, and attitudes, as expressed in their relation to the child. What will exercise a decisive influence on the formation of the child's ego ideal is not what the parent wants to be for his or her child, but what the parent really is without knowing it. It is this involuntary and largely unconscious transmission from one generation to the next that preserves and advances the work of civilization, or halts it, or causes it to regress.

CONCLUSION

Psychoanalysis provides us with a naturalistic explanation of the genesis of morality. This explanation is ontologically sparse: it does not require a Platonic transcendental world of Forms presided over by the Form of the Good, nor a divinely created Cartesian *res cogitans* (a thinking thing) that is a substance existing independently of the body complete with innate moral ideals that can be imposed or not by a free will, nor a Kantian division of reality into a phenomenal world of scientific knowledge and a noumenal world known only by faith and to which science has no access. In this respect, psychoanalysis is Hobbesian. It is also basically consistent with Darwinian evolution, notwithstanding Freud's Lamarckian recourse to the biological inheritance of acquired characteristics and the lingering uncertainty about which aspects (if any) of the Oedipus complex could be genetically inherited and whether or not epigenetic findings about gene expression might be relevant. In this paper, only libido, including the incest wish, is treated as being genetically inherited. No genetically acquired characteristics are required. There is an inheritance of acquired characteristics such as moral rules, but this inheritance is psychological and cultural, rather than biological as Freud (1923) had supposed.

The guiding hypothesis of this paper has been that the incest wish is a heritable (i.e., constitutional) aspect of the libidinal psychosomatic development of all humans. It arises psychologically from the stimulus of a precocious intensification of phallic (in boys) or clitoral (in girls) libidinal investment, which brings about an incestuous longing for a strongly demanding but as yet ill-defined wish for an intense sexual satisfaction with the parent (or equivalent) of the opposite sex, and a hostile ambivalence toward the parent (or equivalent) of the same sex who stands in the way of this satisfaction. The incest wish is initiated by individual physical development and retains its psychosomatic organization in latency, puberty, and adulthood, until the abatement of libido in old age. The crucial further development of the psychological capacity for moral behavior is brought about by the renunciation of the incest wish and its substitution by a strengthened identity with the same-sex parent; this identification is caused by the fear of talion punishment from the same-sex parent for the child's incest wishes. This strengthened identification then provides the basis for a homosexual attachment to the same-sex parent, whom the child no longer wishes to replace, but instead seeks to please, by accepting that the same-sex parent belongs exclusively to the opposite-sex parent, by being obedient to the same-sex parent's prohibitions, by seeking to emulate his or her ideals, and so on. It is in this renunciation of his/her incest wishes and the identificatory processes that accompany it that the five- or six-year-old boy or girl develops the capacity for obedience to moral duty within himself or herself.

It is for this reason that Freud thought of the categorical imperative as the heir to the Oedipus complex. Our moral imperatives are consciously experienced as the duty to obey ego ideals for their own sake. The unconscious experience still at work unconsciously is the fear of talion retribution by the same-sex parent if we do not. Consciously, we experience this anxiety as guilt if we act against our duty, or are even tempted to do so, but the originating anxiety remains unconscious in repressed memories. If the original anxiety is expressed behaviorally or in internal images in some way when an individual is conscious only of his/her spontaneously acting will to do one's duty, they will be experienced introspectively as inexplicable and irrelevant occurrences.

Thus, psychoanalysis does not limit morality to duty for the sake of duty as does Kant. Rather, it recognizes that much of our moral conduct is motivated by generalized attitudes of sexually aim-inhibited affection. This affection takes the form of benevolent charity toward neighbors and strangers as well as more active empathic caring for loved ones and friends. In this respect, psychoanalysis is more consistent with Mill's way of taking motivation into account, while emphasizing that the fundamental criterion of moral conduct is the beneficial or harmful consequences of our actions for others. From a psychoanalytic point of view, what is morally best is to be able to minimize duty and maximize caring and in doing things that make us cared for. This maxim includes a realistic appreciation of the fact that others may be prepared to do us harm for their own benefit; to them we owe neither empathy nor care, but only the duty of not doing to them what they would do to us and those we love, if they could. We also owe a duty to protect to the best of our ability ourselves and our loved ones from those who would do us harm.

REFERENCES

Brenner, C. (1973). *An Elementary Textbook of Psychoanalysis*. New York: International Universities Press.

Freud, S. (1913). Totem and taboo. SE 13:1–162.

—— (1920). Beyond the pleasure principle. SE 18:7–64.

—— (1923). The ego and the id. SE 19:13–66.

—— (1924). The economic problem of masochism. SE 19:159–172.

—— (1926). Inhibitions, symptoms and anxiety. SE 20:75–176.

—— (1930). Civilization and its discontents. SE 21:57–146.

Hanly, C. (1978). Instincts and hostile affects. *International Journal of Psychoanalysis* 59:149–156. [Chapter 17 in this volume]

—— (1984). Ego ideal and ideal ego. *International Review of Psycho-Analysis* 65:253–261.

Hobbes, T. (1651). *Leviathan* (Ed. M. Oakeshott). Oxford: Blackwell, 1946.

Kant, I. (1764). *Observations on the Feeling of the Beautiful and the Sublime*. In P. Frierson & P. Guyer (Eds.), *Kant: Observations on the Feeling of the Beautiful and the Sublime and Other Writings*. Cambridge: Cambridge University Press, 2011.

—— (1785). *Groundwork of the Metaphysics of Morals*. In M.J. Gregor (Ed.), *Kant: Practical Philosophy*. Cambridge: Cambridge University Press, 1996.

—— (1795). Toward perpetual peace. In M.J. Gregor (Ed.), *Kant: Practical Philosophy*. Cambridge: Cambridge University Press, 1996.

Mill, J.S. (1863). *Utilitarianism*. London: Longmans Green, 1907.

Perry, D.L. (1967). *The Concept of Pleasure*. The Hague: Mouton.

CHAPTER 21

Ideology and Psychoanalysis*

The word "ideology" has many different meanings, ranging from the philosophically neutral "science of ideas" to the value-laden "visionary theorizing." It is in this latter sense that I use it in this essay, a sense the denotations of which include Platonism, Marxism, fascism, and capitalism in some of its forms. However different these may be in some respects, they are all systems of ideas that have exerted a powerful influence upon human affairs. Without denying the multifaceted nature of ideologies, I want to focus on their psychology. Ideologies have a remarkable capacity for working powerful transformations in the lives of individuals. They can call forth heroic self-sacrifice; they can render drudgery euphoric; they can give meaning, purpose, and direction to the individual life and to an individual's experience of it. Ideologies are no less remarkable for their capacity to unite individuals into organized collectivities and to convert ordinary fellow citizens and neighbors into brothers, sisters, comrades, and especially comrades in arms. Ideologies find or create enemies. The adherents of an ideology can easily find in it justification for the destruction of others even in the absence of any real threat, or for the subjection of others to the ideology's ideals. Ideologies are characterized by a dangerous polarity—a

* Originally published in *The Canadian Journal of Psychoanalysis* 1 (1993):1–17.

polarity that can sustain a high level of beneficent mutual support among those who share the ideology's ideals and way of life, and at the same time an equal and opposite self-righteous hostility toward those who do not share it. The foundations for an understanding of the psychogenesis of this polarity were laid down by Freud in his explanation of the formation of groups in *Group Psychology and the Analysis of the Ego* (1921). There Freud defines a primary group as "a number of individuals who have put one and the same object in the place of their ego ideal and have consequently identified themselves with one another in their ego" (p. 116). The members of the group are united by identifications based on their similarity, which in turn is the result of their common identification with a leader who functions as each individual's ego ideal: each has given over an important component of his autonomous ego functioning to the group leader, who thenceforth exercises it on his behalf. The group members no longer need to discover or create purpose or meaning in their own lives but finds it in transcendent form in their dedication and service to the leader. Since the "leader" of a group may be either a person, alive or dead, or a set of abstract principles, ideologies qualify for the role of group leaders in Freud's theory. In any case, ideologies, the prophets who proclaim them, the warriors who make them historical realities, and the bureaucrats who administer them are usually bound closely together by causal and identificatory links.

Let us look more closely at the alterations in ego functioning that accompany adherence to an ideology, and contrast it with superego functioning in the absence of such adherence. But let me at the outset enter a caveat: the distinctions I shall be drawing are necessarily simplified, although I hope not oversimplified. The autonomous superego function on which the comparison is based is a fictitious ideal to which the superego life of real people only approximates to various degrees. With the formation of the superego through the resolution of the Oedipus complex, a number of ego functions acquire shape, direction, and efficacy. Central among these functions is the ability to observe oneself critically, to experience a signal of anxiety in the form of guilt in response to hostile aggressive and possessive incestuous wishes, and to exercise an instinct mastery sufficient to prohibit actions aimed at trying to satisfy such wishes. So sensitized to wrongdoing may the individual become that he feels guilty when he finds that he is better off than others for whose misfortune he has no responsibility. The omnipotence of primary process thought invests the functioning of the superego—one of the relations between the superego and the id that establishes their "deep connection."

In this there is evidence of an acceptance, brought about by the resolution of the Oedipus complex, of responsibility not only for who one is and what one does, but even for what one has not done. The formation of the superego strengthens the reality-testing capacities of the ego insofar as self-scrutiny and self-criticism also encompass cognitive activities. The critical scrutiny of one's own perceptions of persons, things, and events supplements the ordinary awareness provided by consciousness of one's perceptions. Such scrutiny demands that what is subjective in our perceptions should be owned by the self in order to allow our experience to be determined as much as possible by things as they actually are rather than by things as we believe them to be or as we would have them be. The postoedipal child can no longer runs in terror from the dark inside the closet to the safety of his parents: he must now look inside the closet to see whether the bogey is actually there. Golding's *Lord of the Flies* is a modern parable about the loss of reality and regression to group violence: a group of latency boys are guided by a totemic "choirboy" ideology, and individual autonomy, responsibility, and testing of reality lose their influence under the onslaught of regressive group identifications. Rationality depends upon a capacity for critical scanning of perceptions which enhances and consolidates subject-object differentiation. This critical scanning is aimed against the derivatives of projection and denial and thus contributes to the transition to more mature forms of ego defense which will interfere less with reality testing.

Although psychoanalysis has exercised a powerful influence upon contemporary culture, it is not in itself an ideology in the sense in which the term is being used here. Freud (1921) denied that it could even be considered to be a *Weltanschauung*. For him, the revolutionary challenge of psychoanalysis to the various forms of ideological, religious, and philosophical beliefs about human nature and destiny lies in the new scientific knowledge gained from the exploration of unconscious processes by means of free association. However revolutionary, feared, and ridiculed it may be, psychoanalysis is a body of empirical knowledge subject to continuous clinical testing by observations and interpretations based on the evenly suspended attention of analysts to the free associations of analysands. The psychological foundations of the struggle for a measure of objectivity in the observation and understanding of human nature are to be found in that part of ego psychology that I have all too schematically outlined above.

Yet psychoanalysis cannot be immunized against transformation into an ideology or against being used ideologically. Moreover, by its very nature psychoanalysis is always at risk of fostering its own deterioration into an ideology. This risk lies at the heart of psychoanalysis as a profession. The training analysis is the most essential part of psychoanalytic education. If it is to work, the candidate must develop a transference to the training analyst. Inherent in the transference is an ego regression to a repetition of the dependent tie to the oedipal and preoedipal parents. To a greater or lesser extent, in his search for self-understanding, the analysand substitutes the observing ego of the analyst for his own. This substitution enables the analysand to be affected by the analyst's interpretations of defenses and resistances, and hence facilitates their reduction and the liberation of the processes of free association that lead to the resolution of conflicts. But this identification with the observing and analyzing function of the analyst is itself problematic. Its formation is involuntary; it is bound to the transference; it involves a formal regression of the ego; it has unconscious childhood roots of dependency on parents for reality testing; it is subtle and powerful. Thus, although it facilitates reality testing and ego maturation in other respects, it can compromise the analysand's ability to be objective about his or her analyst and perpetuates a regressed dependency on him or her. The typical form of this compromise of reality testing is idealization. This idealization needs to be analyzed.

Let me illustrate. Shortly after completing his training analysis and graduating, a gifted and highly regarded university historian and psychoanalyst was asked to arrange a discussion on psychoanalysis and history for an international history conference. He invited his training analyst to take part in the main panel discussion, although he would have known that his training analyst had no expertise in any branch of history. What is even more surprising, his training analyst accepted the invitation. The training analyst gave a rambling and confused presentation, the burden of which was to cast doubt on his former analysand's historical work because of his lack of analytic experience. The junior analyst had the insight, after the event, to be astonished by the force and persistence of the idealizing transference that had caused an unconscious fantasy about his analyst's brilliance and knowledge to override his mature, critical academic judgment. He was less aware of his need to break his dependent identification with his analyst or of the hostile wish to embarrass his analyst by drawing him into a situation in which he would appear inadequate and out of his depth, and hence inferior in a field his former analysand had mastered. Evidently, a sensitivity to the narcissistic needs of his analyst had joined with his resistance to find a successful hiding place for his oedipal ambivalence in his idealizing transference and his identification with his analyst. It is equally evident that the training analyst had failed to analyze and resolve the candidate's idealizing transference to and identification with the analyst—

something that should be a continuous part of the analysis and find its resolution in the termination process.

It is the failure to work through the idealizing transference and the identification with the analyst that leaves behind in the new generation of analysts a predisposition to ideologize psychoanalysis. One needs to be able to see analytically with one's own eyes, to think analytically with one's own head, and to feel analytically with one's own heart. Otherwise, the ideas and practices of the analyst have only a specious veracity even if they happen to be correct. Theoretical ideas and technical rules that require continuous testing and re-evaluation are treated as canonical. Analysts become enthusiasts, zealots, and ciphers instead of adventurous observers and empirical thinkers. Training analysts begin to rest their authority not on a knowledge of the analytic process that works and that they are able to impart, but on their position, power, and authorization by an older generation that they themselves similarly venerated and feared. The "correct" psychoanalytic texts become quasi-sacred and are assigned an authority that only the psychological phenomena should have.

There is no theoretical position in psychoanalysis that can protect its adherents from this idolatry of ideas. Freud's epistemic legacy of a body of knowledge that he believed to be made up of empirical ideas built up from and tested by clinical observation cannot deter an adherent from treating it as an infallible system of absolute truth, or a critic from seeing in it only the imaginings of an ingenious eccentric mind. Indeed, because hostility underlies idealization, the zealous adherent easily collapses into the repudiating critic if the reaction formation that sustains the idealization should succumb to disappointment.

Of course, in this period of competing theories we like to think that the adherents of other schools of thought in psychoanalysis are invested in an ideology. How otherwise could they give credence to ideas that are so clearly and self-evidently wrong in the veridical light shed by our own?

Such an attitude is the expression of an ideologically motivated reluctance to bring our own ideas down from Olympus to be tested in the sweat and toil of the free market of ideas. The crucial test of the analyst's relation to psychoanalysis is his willingness to put his ideas to the test of reason and experience, because the only real strength an idea has lies in its usefulness in knowing life and the world, and when possible, changing them for the better.

There are various signs that psychoanalysis is being treated as an ideology. The analyst who sees a second analysis as a means of "refreshing" his identification with his training analyst has acknowledged that he survives as an analyst only through a dependent identificatory tie to his own analyst. His convictions concerning what is workable and what is not, what is true and what is false in psychoanalysis are ultimately governed by the convictions of another, his training analyst. Has not such an analyst made his training analyst into an idol, himself into a proselyte, and analysis into magic?

The answer to this question can be decided by the quality of the analyst's attitude to psychoanalytic knowledge. One suspects the worst if, mingled with the necessary and appropriate respect for privacy and confidentiality about patients, there is a hermetic secrecy, or when a legitimate insistence on high standards of training, practice, and research masks a guild possessiveness about psychoanalytic knowledge. The training analyst who sees no difficulty in undertaking the supervision of a candidate who has recently terminated a training analysis with him is a promising psychoanalytic ideologue; so is the analyst who claims that the theoretical innovation he has espoused can be understood and observationally confirmed only by those who are convinced of its truth. The Augustinian *credo ut intelligam* (I believe in order to understand) is fitting for religious philosophy based on infallible faith, but it is not tenable for psychoanalysis, which is based on hard-won, fallible observation. The analyst who defends a theoretical innovation against falsifying clinical evidence by claiming that the falsifying observations are artifacts of his critic's theory is manifesting the same ideological attitude toward psychoanalytic knowledge of which he accuses his critic.

If psychoanalysis is not intrinsically and in principle an ideology, does it provide a basis for a critique of ideology? Is it compatible with some ideologies and incompatible with others? If it does not entail an ideology, does it entail a way of life? Does it have implications for the conduct of social, political, and economic life beyond the sphere of intimate personal relations? Freud's few remarks on communism indicate a sympathetic interest in it as a social experiment aimed at trying to find a more equitable distribution of goods and services, tempered by a critique of Marx's failure to take into account the role of sexuality in the motivation of conflict in individuals and among individuals and groups. This denial could be said to be the source of Marx's dangerously naive utopianism. Many of the communist governments of Eastern Europe prohibited psychoanalysis because they believed that it fostered an egotistical individualism incompatible with communist utopian fraternity. Not a few of the democratic governments that have replaced them wish to foster psychoanalysis because they believe that it fosters the kind of individual initiative and responsibility for oneself that is needed by democratic institutions and a market economy. If these perceptions are correct, it would appear that psychoanalysis does have social, political, and economic implications insofar as different social, political, and economic organizations require different attitudes, expectations, and motives in the people whose lives they organize.

But are these perceptions correct? Is not psychoanalysis a body of knowledge and a method of psychological investigation that seeks to examine the unconscious psychological roots of ideological beliefs and investments in the absence of any ideological commitments or investments of its own? If conflicts due to ambivalence are at work in the political life of a patient, the analysis must seek to resolve this ambivalence, but without trying to make the patient into a conservative, a liberal, or a socialist. If a female patient's dedication to feminism is rooted in a denial and repression of some sexual aspects of her femininity, the analyst must help her work through these conflicts without needing to abate her advocacy of rights and opportunities for women. Still, if we press too far in trying to make psychoanalysis into a value-free, value-neutral science and therapy, we soon lose touch with reality. The clinical and theoretical reflections that follow are aimed at redressing the balance.

Without trying to, our psychoanalytic work does in fact alter the values of our patients. A severely hysterical woman patient held extraordinarily redneck views about the punishment of offenders. She was a staunch advocate of capital punishment. Reports of crimes aroused in her fantasies of cruel public punishments that she believed the miscreants deserved. Among the unconscious factors contributing to this attitude toward criminals were feelings of revenge toward her father and men generally, castration wishes, sadistic voyeuristic impulses, and envious hatred of disordered and unruly boy cousins whose misdemeanors had been indulged by her mother, from whom she herself received reliably swift punishment. Her memories of these cousins did not change in the course of the analysis, but as she recounted that one had died behind the wheel of his car which he had crashed while driving drunk, and that another was in prison for fraud, she was able to experience waves of pity for them, along with remorse for having wished them so much ill. Her analysis had altered her conscious attitude to crime and punishment from retribution to prevention, with all the modifications in her political, social, and economic ideas that such a change entailed.

A male professor being treated for a debilitating depression was a convinced socialist in the Swedish or British sense. His sense of social justice made him an advocate of the welfare state: the state, with all its seemingly limitless powers of taxation, should protect all citizens as far as possible from the helplessness that can result from unemployment, illness, accident, and injury. Motivating his political beliefs there was an oedipal rebellion:

his father was a prominent local Conservative, and the patient's wish, if not to slay the dragons of free enterprise and corporate profits, then at least to imprison them in the chains of taxation for income redistribution and social services, owed a debt to an unconscious and unresolved oedipal rivalry. A more significant determinant was a severe oral trauma that was exacerbated by inadequate parenting during the birth of a sibling. His depressive anxiety about abandonment, about being unloved and helpless, caused by unsatisfied needs for parental attention and love, made itself felt in a dependent oral transference. He developed an intense need to have the analyst protect him from the ordinary hazards of life. If he missed a session because his bus was delayed, he felt rejected and mortified by being required to pay for the missed session, at once frightened and unbelieving that his analyst could neither protect him from such an occurrence nor avoid charging him on account of his own need. He believed that the analyst had unlimited resources of wealth and power. As the transference and the traumas that gave rise to it were worked through, the patient did not abandon his concerns about social justice, but became realistic about his adult responsibility for his own welfare and about the capacity of governments to provide social services. He could consider political, social, and economic alternatives, and he could acknowledge that government social programs could be costly and had to be paid for by taxation. Thus, social and political beliefs are sometimes altered by indirection, as religious beliefs often are, in the course of an analysis that does not seek these results but occupies itself only with the resolution of neurotic conflicts.

Theoretically, the psychoanalytic understanding of group formation and dynamics and the suppression of individuality by social collectivities runs counter to that espoused by many ideologies in the explanation it provides for the psychogenesis of this suppression. For example, so completely did Plato (*Republic*) seek the destruction of individuality in his ideal republic, that he recommended abolishing family life, making it impossible for men and women to form permanent ties, for mothers and fathers to know their own children, or for children to know who their mother and father are. Children were to know only collective parents—all the men and women of the older generation—so that they would become in themselves collective beings who would rejoice and grieve for the same things, in the same way, and at the same time. The two great modern forms of ideological totalitarianism, National Socialism and Communism, sought to invade family life, weaken family ties, and terrorize family members with the threat of betrayal by exploiting the inevitable ambivalences of parents and children toward each other and by forging, especially in the children, such powerful identificatory ties with the state, its leaders, and their doctrines that for many children, hostile betrayal of parents in thought and affect became a possibility in reality. Political betrayal became a permanent possibility, and its socially rewarded enactment became a more frequent occurrence than one would like to think. The difficulties of practicing analysis in such a society—even if it were not forbidden by the state—are not hard to imagine. One of the first tasks of the analysis would have to be the resolution of the defensive libidinal identification tie in fantasy to the state and this work would inevitably be experienced by the analysand as a treasonous attempt to subvert and degrade him. In such social and political environments, psychoanalysis would be correctly perceived by state officials as subversive.

Platonic, Nazi, and Marxist ideologues consider political and social collectivities superordinate to the individuals who make them up. Their ideologies include the assumption that the state (or "the people," "the nation," etc.) has an existence of its own that transcends the individual. One finds the same assumption underlying Hegel's philosophy of history and his political philosophy. The psychoanalytic understanding of the origin and dynamics of groups suggests that this view of the state is an illusion—an illusion that political ideologues need if they are to realize their visions for the transformation of the human condition, an illusion that under particular historical circumstances can be made to appear all too real in the guise of a secret police and other instruments of suppression, but an illusion nonetheless.

Freud hypothesized that a group is formed out of two identifications: an idealizing identification with a leader, and an identification, based on similarity, with others who have adopted the same leader as their ego ideal. This dynamic is currently at work in the followers of Trump in their belief that the last US presidential election was fraudulently stolen from him and that Trump would have made America "great" again. An ideologue invites just such an identification with himself and his ideology, his doctrine of salvation. These identifications give the leader the authority that enables him to exercise power over his followers and, under the right historical conditions, gives him the means to take over government, impose his ideology on everyone, and thus make it into a social reality. Of course, political, judicial, and social institutions have an existence of their own and yield power to those who control them, but they do not have a life of their own. Who gives life to them, who controls them, by what means and to what ends, is ultimately determined by the dominant mass of idealizing identifications formed by individual citizens. The road to power of the few— of ideologies and their prophets—is paved with the need of the many to submit to idealized objects.

Ideologues do not like this understanding of the origins of power. They need people to deny to themselves that they have made sacrifices of individual autonomy and reality testing in order to believe instead that freedom for the individual can be realized only through the group in a feeling of being exalted by the leader and the group. At the level of explicit statement and doctrine, ideologies are at odds with psychoanalysis concerning the primacy of individuals or groups. At the level of action, ideologues reveal an extraordinary practical knowledge of the dynamics of idealizing identifications and how to exploit them. In totalitarian regimes, hostility and abuse is directed at culturally selected minorities who dare to be different in some way that is felt by the regime to be threatening. The leader of the regime can rely upon the need of the majority to form idealizing identifications with him to escape from individual responsibility, which provides the leader with the passive collusion of unconscious approval that he needs for the persecution, even genocide, of the minority.

Psychoanalysis does have an affinity with ideals of liberal democracy: freedom of thought and speech, the freedom to pursue one's own welfare so long as this pursuit does not damage the welfare of others, the right to contribute directly or by representatives to the making of the laws that define the general good of the community, the right and the ability to elect to office and remove from office those who govern. Psychoanalysis shares this affinity to the principles of liberal democracy with other natural sciences, with literature, the arts, scholarship, and critical thought generally. Psychoanalysts as citizens have a responsibility to support these principles, just as psychoanalysts as members of an organized profession have the same responsibility to establish and maintain these principles in the conduct of their societal and institutional affairs, and especially in their training programs. It is for this reason that the International Psychoanalytical Association insists that the constitutions of member societies embody these principles and that their members respect them in both their letter and their spirit.

But psychoanalysis has a special affinity for these principles. Free association is a radical form of freedom of thought: it is the freedom to put into words the thoughts and affects that are forbidden by one's own ideals and anxieties, and by the prohibitions of others. In a modern totalitarian state, a mathematician, a physicist, a neuroanatomist, or an organic psychiatrist can pursue their enquiries, make original discoveries, and publish them, provided the dictatorship is sensible enough not to force scientists to employ the dialectical logic of Hegel or Marx (for example). Life is often less easy for creative writers, musicians, and artists, although restricted fields of creative activity may remain; for psychoanalysis it is impossible. Psychoanalysis can survive these conditions only in secrecy, as an underground movement, or by means of self-falsifying and self-destructive dissimulation, like what was left of psychoanalysis in Germany during the Nazi regime.

At the heart of psychoanalysis is the ideal of an open and unconstrained search by individuals to know the truth of their own lives. Psychoanalysis can make Socrates' injunction to know oneself practical. Reality testing must be allowed the freest possible range, no less over one's ideals, morals, religious beliefs, and political convictions than over one's drive life, one's motivations and wishes, one's objects, and one's world. Psychoanalysis therefore finds itself at odds with ideologies, for they demand that observation and thought be governed by ideas and values that are exempted from critical investigation. And it is precisely this ideal that requires candidate analysands and training analysts to bring transference into the analysis and work it through before termination. No matter how genuinely distinguished, how justifiably venerable, how worthy of idealization the training analyst may be, an unresolved idealizing transference leads to the cult of personality, which is no more desirable in psychoanalysis (and this includes the cult of Freud) than it is in politics or anywhere else in human affairs.

There is also in psychoanalysis the ideal of the primacy of the individual life and the individual's responsibility for it. Freud concluded *The Interpretation of Dreams* (1900) with the assertion that "there seems to be no justification for people's reluctance in accepting responsibility for the immorality of their dreams" (p. 620). Where else could responsibility lie, no matter how thoroughly involuntary dreaming is? The individual is thus responsible for his own drive life and its derivatives, just as he is for his own well-being. But these are hard responsibilities to bear, and individual responsibility is at best an only partially attainable ideal. The libidinal identificatory bonds that form groups and give ideologies their power over individual thought, feeling, judgment, and action offer paths of escape which all of us to some extent follow. The ubiquity and tenacity of these identifications are well illustrated by Paul Coulson, a former aide to US president Richard Nixon who was imprisoned for criminal activities on Nixon's behalf, who had declared that for Nixon he would kill his own grandmother. Coulson "saw the light" of fundamentalist Christianity while in prison and recently received a handsome award for charitable work among prisoners. No doubt his "grandmother" is now safer than she was, but we can be sure that his hostility is still available for use against targets selected by his new ideals. There is no need to doubt the genuineness of Coulson's transformation in order to doubt its efficacy: for the substitution of one ideology for another is not the same as reducing one's dependency on ideology and gaining a measure of freedom. And by the same token, shifting allegiance from one school of psychoanalytic thought to another is nothing more than abandoning one ideology for another, unless the change is conditional on the critical and reasoned consideration of unmistakable clinical evidence.

Wise people who have cared about individual freedom have long been aware of this vulnerability in men and women to alienating their own freedom. The citizens of the ancient Athenian democracy sought some protection from this predisposition by banishing those they found to have become too powerful or too charismatic. The American constitution, following Montesquieu, separated the three powers of government, and when it appeared that a popular president like FDR could become too powerful despite the separation of powers, they limited future presidents to two terms of office. The British parliamentary system provides for the removal of a government by majority vote of a House of Commons consisting of the people's elected representatives. Thus it is that the IPA requires the constitutions of its Component Societies to specify fixed terms for their officers, who must be democratically elected by their members. It must never be forgotten, however, that Hitler came to power in a democratic election, and it is far from obvious that he would have been defeated in any later election. A state's democratic institutions can no more protect its citizens from extremes of political folly than psychoanalysis as a body of knowledge can protect itself from analysts who would make it, in whole or in part, into an ideology.

It is therefore important to emphasize that we have been talking throughout about ideals, to which human beings, including analysts, can only approximate. Idealizing identifications with Freud or Klein, or with lesser figures like Kohut, Winnicott, Fairbairn, or Lacan, or their representatives among our training analysts, may cause any of us to become more zealous in the defense of the ideas of the "master" than in the testing of the "master" ideas—the only valid way of defending those ideas, but one which always risks falsifying them. Sometimes the best that an idea can achieve is to have been the stimulus for its replacement by a better idea. Similarly, while we may be more or less united in our identification with psychoanalysis, we are also differentiated by our national, political, linguistic, and cultural identifications and investments, and what differentiates us in these ways can easily divide us.

Freud wrote of being swept away by patriotic excitement during the early part of World War I, even though the army with whose valor, strength, and victory he identified was pitting him against his British, French, and Russian colleagues. In the end, his patriotism was no match for his attachment to these "enemies" and his disillusionment with the war and its senseless suffering of young men. Freud's self-analysis also contributed to his return to reality about the war. He gives eloquent testimony to his struggle with his own nationalist feelings in his letter to members of the B'nai B'rith Lodge (1926).

The primitive power of nationalist ideology has demonstrated its strength with the fall of Communist ideology in Eastern Europe. Communism, with its ideal of a fraternal utopia, had seven decades in the Soviet Union and four decades elsewhere in Eastern Europe to establish its ascendency over national identities, but it proved to have had no lasting success whatsoever. The current centripetal forces of Western Europe are matched by the centrifugal forces of Eastern Europe. One reading of this situation is that communism, despite its internationalist utopianism, actually inhibited the development of a stable basis for cooperation among national, ethnic, and cultural groups in the search for solutions to common economic, social, and political problems. Nationalist and ethnocentric goals, for the time being at least, seem to have acquired in some regions a greater importance than economic, social, and political well-being.

Nationalism everywhere poses a problem for psychoanalysis. No science can be confined to national boundaries; and, unlike other sciences, psychoanalysis as a profession was from early in its history and still remains primarily an international organization. Yet psychoanalysts are also citizens, which means that they are identified in themselves with their national communities. How is an analyst to solve a conflict between an obligation he feels to his country and one he feels to psychoanalysis, especially under conditions of political violence or war? How is organized psychoanalysis, the EPF or IPA, to best proceed when its members or prospective members are divided by national conflicts? These problems do not have solutions in the way problems in Euclidean geometry have solutions. Solutions are often in the nature of compromises: they require tolerance for disagreement, and need the participation of persons with differing views and commitments, because often, however sympathetic to other viewpoints we may be, we may not have all the relevant information and we may not be able with any accuracy to grasp in imagination the predicaments in which others find themselves. However, what we analysts can do, or should be able to do if we cannot abandon our own identificatory idealizations, is to be aware of other viewpoints and not allow them to compromise our acceptance and search for understanding of our patient's associations, transferences, and identificatory idealizations. We ought not to expect of psychoanalysis more than it can offer us, but at least this much we should be able to provide.

SUMMARY

Although psychoanalysis is not in itself an ideology, it always runs the risk of being "ideologized." This risk is created by an unanalyzed idealization of the training analyst which compromises the analytic reality testing of the graduate analyst. Repetition is substituted for exploration, and theories become self-evident truths rather than hypotheses to be tested. Psychoanalysis offers a way of understanding and correcting the need to ideologize by providing a psychological critique of ideologies. Psychoanalysis has an affinity for the basic principles of liberal democracy, upon which it depends if it is to flourish as a science and as a practice.

REFERENCES

Freud, S. (1900). *The Interpretation of Dreams*. SE 4–5.

———— (1921). Group psychology and the analysis of the ego. SE 18:69–143.

———— (1926). To members of the B'nai B'rith Lodge. In E.L. Freud (Ed.), *Letters of Sigmund Freud* (p. 366). London: Hogarth Press, 1970.

———— (1933). New introductory lectures on psycho-analysis. SE 22:1–182.

Plato. *Republic* (Trans. B. Jowett). New York: Liberal Arts Press, 1948.

CHAPTER 22

Reflections on Feminine and Masculine Authority: A Developmental Perspective*

Is there a difference between feminine and masculine authority? If so, does affiliation to authority figures in psychoanalysis make a difference according to the gender of the authority? Is there a difference in the thinking of Kleinian analysts as compared with Freudian analysts that in some way underlies their theoretical and technical differences and arises out of the relation each has to the authoritative figure who founded the school of thought? Could a male analyst have established Kleinian thought? Could a female analyst have established Freudian thought? Does the choice by an analyst to be a Kleinian or a Freudian involve a choice of authority based on gender?

Immediately, doubts crowd in. Are these questions not foolish? Is it not obvious that we analysts adopt theoretical ideas according to the evidence for them that emerges from our personal analysis, our studies, and our clinical observations in our analyses of others? What does the fact that Klein was a woman and Freud a man have to do with finding the theories of one more plausible than the theories of the other? I shall argue later that these are foolish questions in certain respects. But fools and their foolish questions may be worth thinking about. Shakespeare made the fool the

---

* Originally published in *Psychoanalytic Quarterly* 65 (1996):84–101.

bearer of truths denied by others, as, for example, in *King Lear* (Act 2, scene 2). So I shall dare to play the fool, though without any claim to the wisdom of Shakespeare's fools.

If the authority of the father is based upon law, the authority of the mother is based upon desire. This formulation suggests a gender difference in the way in which we experience the authoritative object. It might be thought that in this differentiation there is a debasement of the mother and of women. The mother (the woman) is able to command because she is the object of the desire of her child or her lover. The father (the man) is able to command because he is the source of the law—of prohibitions and permissions. But now we must ask how the father becomes the source of law. Part of the answer must be that he is the object of fear, just as the mother is the object of desire. Both are idealized or demonized by the child but the idealizations are differentiated by the principle affects that cause them.

The mother's capacity to satisfy needs gives her authority over those whose needs she satisfies. She bears in her own person the power to give life, to sustain life during its most helpless state, and to give the first and—because all of instinctual life is simultaneously involved—the most unitary and intense of life's pleasures. To the extent that infants are able to experience the mother only as a part object scarcely differentiated from themselves, their experience of the mother as a breast is symbiotically invested with omnipotent bountifulness. This symbiotic investment is the precursor of the projection of omnipotence that the mother receives as infants slowly begin to come to terms with their own precarious and helpless finitude (Hanly, 1992). The symbiosis and projection are the source of an aura that unifies and eventually envelops the infant's experience of the good mother, whom the child protects from the bad mother by splitting.

Grunberger (1971) has traced narcissism to a prenatal elational state generated by the illusion of uterine self-sufficiency. The belief in immortality, the feeling of infinity, ideas of a blissful disembodied state, beliefs in nirvana, utopian ideals, pantheism, nature mysticism, and so on are, on Grunberger's hypothesis, adult elaborations of the memory of this primordial biological tie to the mother and derive from a longing to return to it. If there is such a retained memory, its first elaborations are the infant's symbiosis with the mother, followed by the projection of his or her narcissism onto the mother. If the infant does not retain intrauterine sensations, it is my view that the phenomena that Grunberger explains by means of them can be just as well explained by the elational aura with which symbiosis and narcissistic projection envelop first the mother's breast and then the mother herself. The nature and timing of the neurological startup of memory is still imperfectly known. In either case, in these beliefs, psychic states, intimations, and experiences of adult life, there is an implicit evocation of the benign presence of the mother at the beginning of life. These beliefs, states, intimations, and experiences are the soil from which spring up law and morality of various kinds with various contents. An unconscious longing for reunification with a perfect being or for the attainment of an ideal state are powerful motivating forces for a morality and a way of life that promises their fulfillment. The melodies, tonalities, and rhythms of great religious music express these motivational sources of moral striving.

It turns out then that there was a false dichotomy in our first formulation, which based the authority of the mother on desire and the authority of the father on fear. Desire, specifically desire for the mother, is no less important than fear as a source of law. Hence, there is an elemental feminine contribution to the authority that gives rise to law; or to put it differently, we unconsciously experience the mother's authority as that of a lawgiver.

But there is yet another falsification in our initial formulation. The mother, like the father, is an object of fear. Klein (1946) saw that if the ego life of the infant were more organized at birth than Freud had thought it to be, the infant would be assailed by nameless fears of disintegration and annihilation by the death instinct, and would be forced to project its aggression upon its first, only, and most loved object—the scarcely differentiated mother's breast. As a result, the infant would begin to feel endangered by the breast. This intolerable state of affairs would trigger a splitting of the object, giving rise to the paranoid-schizoid organization of infantile experience. The nameless anxieties would now have become a nameless dread and would be attached to the steadily differentiating breast of the mother. Thus, an alien, dangerous presence, identified with the mother, would be introduced into the child's world.

Even if one is skeptical about Freud's death instinct (which I am) or finds Klein's hypothesis of infantile ego functioning implausible (which I do not), it is necessary to acknowledge the infant's fear of the mother. Klein describes what happens phenomenologically and developmentally under conditions that are not good enough—for example, conditions of oral deprivation. The differences are two: (1) the cause of the phenomena of projection and splitting is a trauma from without rather than a drive; and (2) with good enough care, the paranoid-schizoid position does not occur until later. In good enough circumstances, growing infants are progressively thrust forward into self-object differentiation and into awareness of their own helplessness in a strange, alien, massive world that escapes their understanding and defies their control. Their anxiety causes them to project their narcissism onto their mothers, who thus become their omnipotent caretakers—their sun by day, their moon by night. This projection of narcissism does not exactly correspond with, but it is at least to some extent functionally equivalent to, the same processes Klein (1946) described as the idealization of the object by the projection of the loving ego, which Segal (1979) identifies as the source of narcissistic object relations. From this situation, a new anxiety arises as the child becomes aware of the mother's moods and learns that her care depends on her love. The loss of the mother's love is dangerous, and the child must struggle to preserve it. The struggle is motivated from within by signal anxiety in the form of shame. The child's retained narcissism makes him or her believe that if the mother is angry, it is because the child has made her so. At the very least, the child feels her withdrawal and feels life to be out of joint, helpless, and worthless.

The child's vulnerability to the loss of love gives the mother an extraordinary power over the child. By withholding her love, she can cause him or her to experience a fall in her eyes and hence in the child's own eyes. The first internal sanction for obedience—the first experience of authority, and therefore the first experience of the law—arises out of the relation with the mother. The incipient rebellions, the hitting and biting, the various robust defiances of the small child toward the mother, do not contradict this view; rather, they are made possible by the child's confidence in the mother's love, a confidence that he or she does not always enjoy.

But what of the father? Is his contribution to the developing child's sense of authority also caricatured by his identification as lawgiver? Because he cannot exercise the authority of the breast, the father's contribution during the oral phase is only accidentally connected with the drives, the events that they cause, and the structures that begin to develop as the ego acquires and strengthens its defensive capacities. Under the ordinary circumstances of good enough mothering, the father's presence and his care for the infant are less fateful, less inexorable in their influence. Probably, the father is at first an acceptable, only partially differentiated substitute for the mother, to the extent that he is significantly involved in the care of the infant.

Through his caring activities he may find his way into the mother-infant monad. Grunberger (1989) introduced the idea of the monad as a virtual space that includes the mother and protects the infant from the world and from the infant's own instinctuality. It is the developmental precursor of what I have called narcissistic projection (Hanly, 1992). But unless the infant is being bottle-fed, the father is barred from entering into the central nursing ceremony of the monad or from becoming the object of the intense attachment that it forms. If nature takes its course during the first months of life, the father is an ambiguous presence who is both included in the infant's maternal world and left out of it. It is this ambiguity, which is based on biological differentiation, that allows the father to function for the infant as a referent to, representative of, and intruder from the world beyond the monad. Physical and biological differences come specifically into their own with particular clarity if the father is called upon to comfort and help a child who is experiencing difficulty in giving up the breast—an instinctual resignation which forms the portal through which the child can enter into a world that is shared with mother and father.

Chasseguet-Smirgel (1984) has illuminated the importance of the boy's idealizing identification with the father by showing that the consequences of the failure to do so rest upon a denial of the father's "prerogatives and capacities" in order to maintain the illusion that his own "little pregenital penis is as valid as his father's" (p. 70). The boy's primary identification with the father (Freud, 1923) comes to have the part Freud attributed to it in the formation and resolution of the Oedipus complex, for it gradually leads the child out of the mother's world, where the oral and anal stages are for the most part lived out, and into the parental world, where the Oedipus complex has to take place. This idea assumes that triangulation and a rudimentary superego development take place before the onset and resolution of the Oedipus complex, as Klein (1945, 1957) affirmed. However, I am inclined to think that while aggressive rivalry and jealousy, along with sporadic phallic/clitoral interests, are involved, the triangulations of the oral and anal phases are not strictly oedipal, for two reasons: (1) the phallic/clitoral interests are secondary to and derive from the oral and anal drive organizations and their leading erotogenic zones; and (2) for the most part, the rivalry for both boys and girls is primarily with the father for the mother. For this reason, the mother's pride of place as the source of self-authorization diminishes only gradually, until it gives way to the reorganizations of the oedipal stage.

Despite the importance of the drive determinants, however, one must not lose sight of the role in this transition of the relation to the father and of the father himself. Various authors from various points of view, including Lacan's (1955–1956) "name-of-the-father" and "law of the father" and Grunberger's (1989) "father principle," have focused on the role of the father in leading the child out of the maternal world. This office is performed by the father for the boy through the child's identification with him and for the girl through her object love for him. This identification and love have very important oedipal precursors, but they are brought to fruition developmentally by the Oedipus complex, the resolution of which further completes and lays down crucial templates for maturation.

If the father is enlisted in this way by the burgeoning developmental needs of children, what are we to infer concerning the paternal contribution to the definition of authority? Where is the maternal contribution left? Is it simply left behind? Is it assigned a permanently secondary place? One thing is clear: the dichotomy between maternal authority/desire and paternal authority/law is as inadequate to the role of the father as it is to the role of the mother. No doubt, the child may fill his or her maternal world with polymorphous perverse delights; and no doubt, adult men and women may have a potent unconscious fantasy of the enjoyment of the blissful, unconstrained, sensual, gratifying plenitude of the mother's body, a fantasy that is threatening because of its regressive pull toward an earlier infantile solipsistic, monadic bond to the mother.

Evidence of the generality of such fantasies can be found in the trials of heroes and knights, as in Homer's *Odyssey* or in Spenser's *The Faerie Queene*, in which "The Bower of Bliss" is a powerful evocation of dangerous beauty and pleasure. The maternal authority that desire assigns is nowhere more powerfully evoked than in Hesiod's cosmological-genealogical poem, the *Theogony*. During the work of creation, Ouranos, the sky god, became jealous of his progeny and would not let them be born to Gaea, who became

461

overburdened, "and she contrived a crafty evil device…. She sent [her son Kronos] into a hidden place of ambush, placed in his hands a jagged-toothed sickle, and enjoined on him the whole deceit" (Kirk & Raven, 1957, p. 35). A variation on a grand sociopolitical yet human scale is the power of women to corrupt their sons, and thus the state, accorded to them by Plato (*Republic*, Book VIII, 549–550). In the ruling families of the timocracy (the rule of the military elite), there are mothers who complain to their sons that their soldier fathers are unmanly, neglectful of them, and indifferent to the good things of life that wealth could provide, leading the sons to be ruled by the pursuit of material goods and causing them to bring about a degeneration of the state into oligarchy (the rule of the wealthy few). This constitutional descent, according to Plato, passes via democratic anarchy into the sensual, appetite-driven tyranny symbolized by Spenser's Bower of Bliss. One is reminded of the mother in Chasseguet-Smirgel's example, who encourages her son to believe that, indeed, his little penis is better than his father's. These are mothers from whom children need to be rescued by fathers strong enough in their masculinity to sustain some of the maternal functions needed by the child.

But however important these fantasies are, they are not a reliable basis for understanding the role of the mother in the creation and definition of authority. It can hardly escape our attention that the fantasy of the all-satisfying mother is more likely to be a fantasy that denies memories of painful disappointments in her as much as it secures solace from memories of fulfilling happiness with her. Similarly, there is surely a measure of projection of male aggression in Hesiod's and Plato's mythic portrayals of the malignant power of mothers over their rivalrous and patricidal sons. This projection denies that sons, quite on their own initiative and without the encouragement of mothers, will be caused by their incest wishes to want to get rid of their fathers and take his place with the mother. The fact that maternal encouragement does not help the son with his patricidal wish does not imply that it is the cause of the patricidal wish. But the cause does involve the mother: the cause of the patricidal wish is the son's incest wish to take the place of the father with his mother with or without her seductive encouragement. May we not hypothesize then that these fantasies of the aggressively powerful, dominating mother, who imposes patricidal motives on her son, evade and deny the maternal authority created by the child's fear of the loss of her love, by which mothers discipline rather than gratify their sons and daughters? They also deny the biological and psychological forces within women that move them—fatigue, and the wish to repossess their own bodies, their adult sexuality, and their own identities—to encourage the disruption of the mother-child monad and to lead their offspring roughly or gently out of the maternal world. These are the motives in healthy mothers that facilitate the process of gradual education to reality that Ferenczi (1913) brilliantly described.

But these motives, when supported by a sadistic-narcissistic need for the reflected glory of perfect children, can cause mothers to risk traumatizing their children by pushing them beyond their tolerance for instinctual and ego maturation. When the sadism is not mitigated by narcissism, the use of authority by the mother turns into psychopathogenic violence. The images of this sort of violently punishing mother, as seen in works on object relations and in the subjectively originated persecutory figures explored by Klein (1957), are also found in legend, myth, and literature: the awesome beauty of Helen of Troy, the destroyer of ships, of men, and of cities; the ruinous Erinyes of ancient Greek mythology; and the envious and murderous Lady Macbeth, in whose domicile kings are unsafe.

If the virtues of women are not always soft, neither are the virtues of men always hard. The boy's identification with his father is from the beginning a form of love. Anaclitic love for the mother on account of her nourishing would be no less than the love for the father as protector. But these paternal attributes are somewhat but not altogether gender-specific, since fathers can

463

be nourishing and mothers can be protective. Freud's (1914) account, correct as it may be in its fundamentals, is too simplified. Moreover, a good enough father, who has no reason within himself to be afraid of his identification with his mother, knows how to soften with mercy the anger of his wife's exercise of maternal authority when it is unnecessarily severe and possessive. Even the mother who in anger warns her wayward child of the punishment he or she can expect when father arrives, while restraining her wish to punish the child physically, has already punished him or her with the withdrawal of her love, intensified all the more by the treachery of her alliance with the father. However, a father can serve well as a substitute mother in this way only if he is secure enough in his own male identity to be able to act maternally toward his children without compromising their sense of his masculinity. Successful parents are able to share parental authority in this fashion without contributing to gender confusion in their children.

This issue brings us to the question of the Oedipus complex and its contribution to the formation of a viable and valid recognition of paternal and maternal authority in the parent-child relation. Such a relation is essential to the formation of a conscience that is sufficient for the degree of internal instinct mastery required by civilized life and for the internal sustenance of a legitimate self-esteem. It is for this reason that I attach as much importance as did Freud (1923) to the place of the resolution of the Oedipus complex in psychic development generally and to the development of a valid internal and external relation to authority in particular, while acknowledging the importance of oedipal precursors of the kind recently described by Britton, Feldman, and O'Shaughnessy (1989). The essential point is that the resolution of the Oedipus complex requires an intensification of the identification with both the mother and the father as a consequence of the urgency of the child's need to modify her or his relationship to them. The girl must moderate her hatred for her mother and her too dangerous rebellious rivalry with her by an intensification of her identification with the mother, as must the boy in his identification with his father. The aggression that had been invested in the relationship is now directed against the self and becomes a major factor in self-restraint and aim inhibition. The girl is also driven to modify her love for her father, without which the necessary alteration in the relation to the mother could not take place, since it is the love of the father that converts tolerable jealousy of the mother into dangerously envious hatred; in this there is a loss, which is repaired by an intensification of the identification with the father. The same transformation is required of the boy in relation to his mother. The authority of conscience is based on these dual identifications.

This description of oedipal identifications differs from Freud's (1923) account in two respects. First, it avoids the paradox involved in attributing an intensifying identification with the same-sex parent directly to the loss of the incestuous love relation with the opposite-sex parent and that concept's inconsistency with Freud's (1917) formula for the genesis of melancholia. And second, it does not imply that the male superego is more effective than its female equivalent, even though they are qualitatively different. This approach avoids both the invidiousness of Freud's (1923) comparison between male and female superegos, and its inconsistency with his death instinct theory. Freud's death instinct theory postulates that aggression has an intrinsically masochistic organization in men and women, which accounts for the inevitability of death, the motivating force of oedipal repression, and the restraining guilt of the superego, which is presumably no less effective in women than in men: death, after all, is just as common among women as among men.

The problem for this rather different account is to explain gender difference insofar as it depends upon the greater strength of the identification with the same-sex parent. Let us try. The positive Oedipus complex is itself a heterosexual organization. The transformation of the child's relation with each parent, brought about through their internalization by means of strengthened primary identifications with the same-sex parent and a strengthened secondary identification with the opposite-sex parent, in order to be effective needs only to be invested by the child's oedipal libidinal and aggressive investments, now turned inward by the strengthened identifications. In place of the wish to replace his father, the boy now substitutes the wish to become like him; in place of the wish to have his mother, he now substitutes the wish to have someone like her in the future. Gratification is deferred and can be realized later when the boy has become a man like his father. The idealizations that motivate the preparations for deferred pleasures are themselves grounded in anxiety. The prohibitive efficacy of these idealizations will be proportional to the anxiety, which will in turn be proportional to the strength of his incestuous and aggressive envious wishes.

Since I see no reason why such wishes should be less demanding in girls than they are in boys, I do not see either why the boy's castration anxiety should be a more effective source of moral guilt than the girl's fear of being poisoned, of being imprisoned for life, of becoming the victim of a witch's spell, or of having deformed, ill, or dead babies. What is lost in specificity, immediacy, and the dreaded irreversibility of the physical injury of castration in the girl's fantasies of punishment is at least made up for by the fact that for her, the mother who has loved and cared for her from birth is now her most dangerous enemy. The mother, whose cunning is powerful enough to cast a spell upon the father, which the small oedipal girl can see with her own eyes, is certainly able to cast a mortifying evil spell on her. It is perhaps for this reason that it is primarily the fear of the loss of love that gives the girl's conscience the authority to exact obedience from her, leaving guilt in a secondary place— whereas guilt is primary in the boy, with fear of the loss of love secondary.

Thus, if moral authority is more impersonal and severe in men, as Freud (1925) claimed, but more object-related and compassionate in women, it is equally effective in both. Moral authority in women is not an Adam's rib. If, on the whole, it is true that in their relations to authority women place a higher value on love, relationships, seduction, and manipulation, while men place a higher value on justice, obligation, cheating, and law-breaking, it is also true that women suffer guilty prohibitions of pleasure on account of duty, and men can learn to temper justice with compassion. The ideal appears to be an integration of the maternal and the paternal identifications, with primacy going to the parent of the same sex; this is made possible by the resolution of the Oedipus complex. Britton, Feldman, and O'Shaughnessy (1989) have described the pathological consequences of failures to carry out this integration.

But the conclusion of this argument raises a question: If authority is more or less equivalently masculine and feminine, are there psychological as well as cultural and physical reasons why Judeo-Christian women and men have worshipped a male deity for so many centuries? I have argued elsewhere (Hanly, 1988) that the difference has to do with the differences in the Oedipus complex in boys and girls. The fundamental attitude toward deity on the part of men is one of supplication on account of awe (sublimated castration anxiety) and sublimated homosexual submission; on the part of women, it is because of sublimated love for the father and the longing to be loved by him.

* * *

I have thus far failed to attempt an answer to the fool's question that introduced this paper. Does the gender of analysts influence their theorizing? This is a question for which this paper provides at best a background for the search for an answer, but here are some preliminary reflections.

Is it accidental that a group of brilliant women analysts pioneered the exploration of the dynamics of the mother-child dyad? Melanie Klein

(1946) worked out the implications of the death instinct for the earliest phases of the infant's relation to the mother; Annie Reich (1940) traced the sources of flaws in women's self-evaluation to the preoedipal relation to the mother; and Elizabeth Zetzel (1970), in the area of technique, attributed the importance of her concept of the working alliance to the influence of early maternal attachment. Women have contributed much else to psychoanalytic theory and practice, and one wonders whether gender has played a part in these contributions. It is easy enough to suppose that gender is a factor in the motivation to explore the psychology of infant and mother.

But however interesting and important the question of motivation may be, it pales before the question of whether gender is an important factor in the creation of ideas for understanding and of perceptions for testing them. But before attempting even a tentative suggestion about gender and insight, we must remind ourselves that men have also made important contributions to the most womanly of terrains. Abraham (1924) first systematically elaborated the preoedipal stages; Grunberger's (1971) understanding of narcissism begins in reflections upon the psychological derivatives of intrauterine existence and the mother-baby monad; and Winnicott's concepts of transitional object, false self, and facilitating environment are deeply rooted in the mother-infant dyad. Is there then no basis for a psychological epistemology that would recognize a cognitive differentiation based on gender?

Psychoanalytic perception and understanding depends in an important way on memory. Is there anything in the girl baby's experience of her very early childhood that is gender-specific, the memory of which would give her a distinct advantage as an adult woman analyst in understanding the psychology of the mother-child dyad? Does a baby girl experience her mother differently than a baby boy does? It seems reasonable to suppose that the infant's experience will be different according to the mother's unconscious feelings about the infant's gender. These feelings will influence the care the mother gives, and hence the infant's experience of her. But may we not assume that the contributions of the infant to the shaping and content of the earliest experience of the mother will be essentially the same for boys and girls? The mother as object of infantile experience will be the same for boys and girls, except insofar as the mother is affected unconsciously by the gender of the infant. If this is so, there seems to be no gender advantage in the search for knowledge of early infancy. However, women analysts may have one cognitive advantage that is gender-dependent: for while the experience of the dependent tie to a mother may be no different for girls and boys, only women can experience being the object of this tie as mothers. The tie to the father in early infancy is a derivative one as a partial substitute. The subject needs further study and reflection.

Thus far, I have pursued an understanding of masculine and feminine authority by means of a somewhat dialectical method. To be sure, it is not a dialectical method after the fashion of Plato's pursuit of knowledge of the divine, nor does it suppress the principle of noncontradiction, as did the dialectic of Hegel and Marx. It seeks only to gain a view of the complexities of the authority inevitably exercised by men and by women in relation to their children. It does so by means of a series of affirmations and negations, assertions and qualifications, in the perhaps fond hope of doing some kind of rough justice to the contending contributions of drive development and object relations, as well as of being at least open to social and cultural determinants. It is, in a certain sense, a dialectic born of the limitations of our observations, of our categories of thought, and of propositional language.

In this spirit, I wish to conclude, as I promised at the beginning, with a brief exploration of two qualifications of what I have thus far said. There is a recognition of authority by both men and women that transcends male and female differences. This authority lies within the sphere of knowledge rather than that of morality, which has largely been my focus above. Access to authoritative knowledge is a great and convenient asset: small children are obliged to rely on their parents for authoritative knowledge about what is safe and beneficial and what is dangerous and hurtful; children have to trust their parents to carry out on their behalf the work of reality testing which they cannot yet perform themselves; and even as adults, we are not infrequently thrust into the situation of being unable to verify some idea of importance to us, so that we are obliged to consult experts and take their word for it. We have to rely for much of our knowledge on the authority of the expert.

But to argue from authority is to commit a material fallacy. Children who claim that something is true because father told them so are committing a material fallacy called *argumentum ad verecundiam*, or argument from authority. The truth of a statement depends not on its source, no matter how worthy of respect that source may be, but on the evidence for it. The strength of the wish to submit to authority in order to be relieved of the burden of responsibility for even remarkably creative discoveries that challenge established ideas is illustrated by Harvey's assertion that he had come upon the idea of the circulation of the blood in the works of the venerable Galen (where it is not to be found), when in reality he had discovered it himself. He dressed up a beautiful truth in the tatters of a fallacy (though given the reverential attitude toward authority among his contemporaries, it would not have appeared so at the time). Freud and Klein seem to have been little troubled by this need: both seem to have taken pride in and courage from the originality of their ideas.

However, even if we cannot avoid reliance on authorities for many of our beliefs, since we do not have the means to test them for ourselves, we analysts have no such excuse where psychoanalytic knowledge is concerned. Analysts are the experts and the authorities in the field of depth psychology. We have confidence in the authorities in other fields because we think that they have reliable facts from which to infer the knowledge claims they make. We must demand no less of the knowledge claims that make up psychoanalysis.

Here we come upon a different type of authority: that of fact and logic. This gives us access to the impersonal authority of reality—not what we believe there is or what we wish there to be, but what there is. This is an impersonal domain of observation and thought. A fact about male narcissism is not itself male any more than a fact about female narcissism is female. Men and women have to bow equally before the impersonal authority of the facts of observation, out of which our theories have to be built if they are to survive as contributions to scientific knowledge. To be sure, it may well be that men and women have specialized aptitudes for observation based on sexual and gender differences: differing interests, life experiences, and orientations to life may guide observations differently in the two sexes. However, when the work of observation is carried out successfully, it will issue in an observation that owes its content and meaning not to the subjectivity or the gender of the observer, but to the object observed. It is out of such observations that knowledge in any field is constructed. It is our ability to submit our perceptions and thoughts to the authority of fact that enables us to move beyond Tiresias.

The psychological development that makes objectivity possible involves two aspects of the resolution of the Oedipus complex: the formation of the superego, which makes self-criticism possible, and the supply of neutralized drive energy to the ego functions through sublimation (Wälder, 1934). Neutralization is currently neglected or repudiated in psychoanalytic theorizing, being suspect for some on account of its relation to the idea of energy. Neutrality as the desired attitude of the analyst is sometimes repudiated on the grounds that it is an ideal rendered unattainable by the ubiquity of countertransference. I agree that our understanding of neutralization is problematic. Yet surely we can trace with Freud ([1895]1950) the first fragile beginnings of the reality principle in the differentiation of the image of the satisfying object from the object that satisfies; this is followed by the release of interest in things and curiosity about them for their own sake, which, in the aftermath of the resolution of the Oedipus complex, eventually finds its highest expression in the observing and thinking of adults that is open to the world. It was to this last stage of neutralized object hunger that Aristotle was pointing in the opening sentences of the *Metaphysics*: "All men by nature desire to know. An indication of this is the delight we take in our senses; for even apart from their usefulness they are loved for themselves." The recognition of the authority of experience liberates in us the capacity to test the beliefs that we have adopted on the authority of persons.

In my view, it is essential that analysts develop in themselves and through their training a good measure of this impersonal desire to know the lives of others and that they be able to use it in their analytic work. It is essential if psychoanalysis is to be a body of knowledge as well as a healing art. It is essential because whether we like it or not, the transferences of our patients inevitably invest us with the struggles they have had with parental authority along with the authority of the experts they expect us to be, for which they pay us a fee to help in ways that they themselves have been unable to do on their own. Whenever we exploit our vicarious, transferential, parental authority as a substitute for the quest for the authority of fact, for observing and understanding the patient, we betray the patient's trust. It has been the purpose of this paper to attempt to clarify some of the developmental commonalities and variations in parental authority that are likely to appear in transferences.

We are left with a dialectic that is different from the dialectic of exposition that I have sought to use in this paper. It is a deeper dialectic that is alive in each of us in our struggle to harmonize the authority of persons to whom we owe much with the authority of the facts onto which we have the good fortune to stumble.

REFERENCES

Abraham, K. (1924). A short study of the development of the libido, viewed in the light of mental disorders. In *Selected Papers*, vol. 1 (pp. 418–501). New York: Basic Books, 1953.

Aristotle. *Metaphysics*. In R. McKeon (Ed.), *Introduction to Aristotle* (pp. 238–297). New York: Modern Library, 1947.

Britton, R., Feldman, M., & O'Shaughnessy, E. (1989). *The Oedipus Complex Today: Clinical Implications*. London: Karnac.

Chasseguet-Smirgel, J. (1984). *Creativity and Perversion*. London: Free Association Press.

Ferenczi, S. (1913). Stages in the development of the sense of reality. In *First Contributions to Psycho-Analysis* (pp. 213–239). New York: Brunner/ Mazel, 1980.

Freud, S. ([1895]1950). Project for a scientific psychology. SE 1:281–391.

——— (1914). On narcissism: An introduction. SE 14:67–102.

——— (1917). Mourning and melancholia. SE 14:237–258.

———. (1923). The ego and the id. SE 19:1–66.

——— (1925). Some psychical consequences of the anatomical distinction between the sexes. SE 19: 241–258.

Grunberger, B. (1971). *Le narcissisme: Essais de psychanalyse*. Paris: Payot.

——— (1989). *New Essays on Narcissism* (Ed. and trans. D. Macey). London: Free Association Press.

Hanly, C. (1988). Metaphysics and innateness. In *The Problem of Truth in Applied Psychoanalysis* (pp. 50–70). New York and London: Guilford, 1991.

——— (1992). On narcissistic defenses. *Psychoanalytic Study of the Child* 47:139–157.

Kirk, G.S., & Raven, J.E. (1957). *The Presocratic Philosophers*. Cambridge: Cambridge University Press.

Klein, M. (1945). The Oedipus complex in the light of early anxieties. In *Love, Guilt and Reparation and Other Works, 1921–1945* (pp. 370–419). New York: Delacorte, 1975.

——— (1946). Notes on some schizoid mechanisms. In *Envy and Gratitude and Other Works, 1946–1963* (pp. 1–24). New York: Delacorte, 1975.

——— (1957). Envy and gratitude. In *Envy and Gratitude and Other Works, 1946–1963* (pp. 176–235). New York: Delacorte, 1975.

Lacan, J. (1955–1956). *The Seminar of Jacques Lacan, Book III: The Psychoses, 1955–1956* (Trans. R. Grigg). New York: Norton, 1997.

Plato. *Republic* (Trans. B. Jowett). New York: Liberal Arts Press, 1948.

Reich, A. (1940). Contributions to the psychoanalysis of extreme submissiveness in women. *Psychoanalytic Quarterly* 9:470–480.

Segal, H. (1979). *Melanie Klein*. New York: Viking.

Wälder, R. (1934). The problem of freedom in psychoanalysis and the problem of reality testing. In *Psychoanalysis: Observation, Theory, Applications* (pp. 101–120). New York: International University Press, 1976.

Zetzel, E. (1970). *The Capacity for Emotional Growth*. New York: International Universities Press.